BIRTH TO BUYOUT

LAW FOR THE LIFE CYCLE OF YOUR BUSINESS

author	**COCO SOODEK**
book design	**ROXANNE SAYLOR**
character illustrations	**TOM PIETRI,** www.BYBASAN.COM

PROFIT AND LAWS
press.

BIRTH TO BUYOUT, SECOND EDITION

Published by Profit and Laws Press
Profit and Laws, Inc.
Chicago, Illinois
www.profitandlaws.com

DISCLAIMER

The information provided in this book, BIRTH TO BUYOUT, is not legal advice, but general information on legal issues commonly encountered. **The information only relates to general law in the United States of America.** Profit and Laws, Inc. is not a law firm and is not a substitute for an attorney or law firm. Profit and Laws, Inc. cannot provide legal advice and can only provide information. We strongly recommend that you engage a lawyer to advise you specifically. We also strongly urge you not to rely on BIRTH TO BUYOUT when making decisions or acting or omitting to act. We disclaim all warranties, express or implied, related to BIRTH TO BUYOUT, including without limitation, accuracy, merchantability or fitness for a particular purpose. Seriously, once again: please get a lawyer. Profit and Laws, Inc. is an Illinois corporation headquartered in Chicago, Illinois 60625.

ISBN 13: 978-0-9834258-2-3
ISBN 10: 0-9834-2582-5

ABOUT THE AUTHOR

COCO SOODEK

Coco Soodek has worked in "Big Law" for 16 years, helping businesses navigate legal risks, obligations and opportunities. With broad experience as outside general counsel to a wide variety of companies, Coco helps craft and complete business deals in art, advertising, stage, trade and rock shows, and digital media, as well as steel, manufacturing, trucking, warehousing and consumer electronics. In 2007, Coco established the Bryan Cave Art Law Team, and Bryan Cave's first blog at www.artlawteam.com, which she continues to lead. She serves as Chair Emeritus for the Midwest Board of the American Committee for the Weizmann Institute, a prominent scientific research institute in Israel. In 2009, Coco was honored to make "40 Under 40" in *Crain's Chicago Business* – an annual list naming outstanding young professionals to watch. She has also been admitted as a Fellow to the American Bar Association. Coco frequently speaks about art law and not-for-profit legal issues, teaches a business law boot camp based on *Birth to Buyout*, and currently hosts *The Profit and Laws Radio Hour* – a show dedicated to helping entrepreneurs navigate business – on the national Lifestyle Talk Radio Network. Additionally, she operates www.profitandlaws.com, a blog on legal and business issues. Coco has been admitted to practice law in Illinois since 1997, immediately following graduation from Northwestern University School of Law. Please contact her with questions at coco@profitandlaws.com or follow her on Twitter @profitandlaws.

for the American entrepreneur

INTRO

A LIFE IN THE LAW

I've helped businesses of all kinds navigate legal problems. I've incorporated dozens of companies, crafted agreements among founders, negotiated employment contracts and leases, written fundraising circulars and set up nearly every kind of click-through contract. I've played business marriage counselor to help save or euthanize the business.

I've cleared copyrights, registered trademarks and gotten the bad guys to cease and desist. I've written hundreds of license agreements and helped billionaires buy multimillion dollar works of art (some horrid, some glorious). I helped two artists – both studies in persistence and genius – win a thirty-year fight to mount one of the greatest works of public art this century.

I've helped clients hire manufacturers and fire them. I've written warehousing and trucking contracts for sculpture, canned goods and beer. I've discovered serious mismatches between a company's sales policies and its sales practices. I've done the legal work to help people make award winning ads (boom de yada, boom de yada) as well as infomercials.

I've played Chicken Little with my clients' risks and chicken with opposing counsel. I've caffeinated through insurance policy endorsements and battled against sneaky exclusions. I've implemented risk management policies and gone toe to toe on indemnity obligations. I've helped clients cash out of a business they started and watched them deal with the joy, relief and bewilderment that comes from being suddenly rich and suddenly free.

I've helped people in restaurants, guns, art, trucking, warehousing, advertising, digital media, ecommerce, retail, manufacturing, green technology, renewable energy, consumer electronics, food production, fast food restaurants, consulting, video production, video editing, rock and roll, music publishing, film distribution, theatrical production, medical devices, mapping, roofing materials and financial services. I've represented world class scoundrels, most of whom I found frustrating but delightful.

I've picked up, studied, used, ignored and discarded an enormous amount of knowledge about law, business and people. The law is fascinating and fun and humbling. Just when you think you know it all, you make a mistake you didn't know you were making and the blood drains from your brain and your tongue goes numb. But you suck it up, clean it up and learn, learn, learn.

The best part of these 16 years has been working with business people, helping them understand, employ and prosper. Make no mistake: everything I've done has been in service to someone else's vision – that's enriching, but it is also disappointing.

After I made Partner, I decided to write this book – to package what I know, to put all this law in one place – where it is accessible and usable for much less than $500 an hour. And, to help people set themselves free and enrich their communities and create jobs.

WHAT IS BIRTH TO BUYOUT?

Birth to Buyout is a big cheat sheet on American business law, in order and in context.

This book is not a substitute for a lawyer. Experience matters. Objectivity matters. Even a seasoned lawyer needs a lawyer.   A surgeon wouldn't remove his own appendix.

Only the experience and trial and error of law practice can teach you to know what you don't know. Once you understand there is an issue, figuring out the strategy and evaluating the risks are easy; asking the right questions is hard.

With each success and each mistake, the same phrase has played in my head for the last 14 years, written and sung by Paul David Hewson, when he was still a boy:

"We thought we had the answers, it was the questions we had wrong."

This book is my attempt to help us ask the right questions, even if it won't supply the entirety of the answers. (If it gave all the answers, it would be 20 volumes and cost $5,000.)

Midway through writing, I noticed the book was boring. So, I created some characters and a story about two guys named Hap and Hazard who strike out to make something new with the help of their corporate lawyer, Gravity, and an engineer named Seymour. Having spent a year with these four, I love them all.

USING BIRTH TO BUYOUT

Birth to Buyout is organized into natural milestones in the lifecycle of a business. In the beginning, *Birth to Buyout* was merely my notes and personal law wikis sewn together. As it grew, I wanted to put it together in a way that would make sense and be correct, all at the same time. This is a relatively new way of organizing legal questions, so I am eager to hear your thoughts and criticisms.

Here is a diagram of the organization of *Birth to Buyout*:

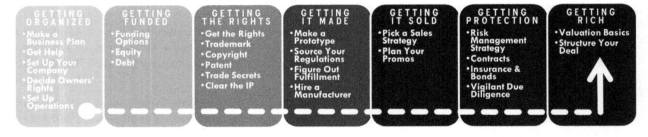

You should use *Birth to Buyout* in any way that makes sense to you. Some people may want to start on page 1 and work their way through towards the end (personally, I'd give up around SOURCE YOUR REGS, but you may have more stamina). Some people may put it in their bathroom and read a little bit as part of their morning ablutions. Some people may want to use it as a crib sheet that they hide in their desk drawer. Some people may just read it to see what happens to the heroes, Hap, Hazard, Seymour and Gravity. A couple other things to help guide you: 1) endnotes appear at the end of each Section; and 2) if you would find it helpful to have a digital version of the book, so that you can pull it up on your computer (which will make clicking on all the links throughout the book much easier, for instance), you can visit www.profitandlaws.com, go to "Contact Us" at the top of the page, and request your free copy. We hope you'll also share any comments or questions while you're at it, and visit our website often for a host of other useful information.

Here is how I use *Birth to Buyout*. I use *Birth to Buyout* as a big crib note. I keep a hard copy on my desk and a digital copy in my Dropbox folder. When I approach a particular issue, I: (a) search electronically; (b) use the index or table of contents; or (c) thumb through the book until I get to the area I need. Then, I usually pull the text out, drop the text into a new Word document and either make a to-do list out of it, or I use it as source material for a client or another lawyer.

The odd thing is that even though I wrote every word, I still need the book. I have a limited capacity to pull information into my consciousness. There have been dozens of times over the years when particular words or concepts escape me and I have used *Birth to Buyout* as a memory tool.

Let me give you an example. When you put out an ad, your ad will make certain arguments about your product – in advertising law, those arguments are called "**claims**" (See Chapter 20: Plan Your Promos). Under law, every claim must be verifiably truthful – it must be *substantiated* with actual facts or reliable evidence. But, that word – *substantiated* – will Not Stay In My Head. So, I am always grasping for it, not remembering it and quickly thumbing through old versions of *Birth to Buyout* to seize the word – *substantiate*. I also can never remember the difference between a **Rule 505** exemption from registration under Reg D and a **Rule 506** exemption (See Chapter 7: Equity).

Birth to Buyout is a work in progress. I intend to grow it, finesse it, make it prettier and more accessible, and continue to explore the lives of Hap, Hazard, Seymour and Gravity.

Regardless of how you use *Birth to Buyout*, I hope it helps you. I hope it helps you live an entrepreneurial life or help others live an entrepreneurial life. I hope it helps you create jobs and wealth for people. I hope it helps you make things in America. And, I hope you let me know your thoughts and your progress and criticisms, so I can continue to make it better, more useful, and business law more clear.

Coco Soodek
Chicago, 2013

ACKNOWLEDGEMENTS

I've been lucky to have been well trained, well mentored and well friended by a variety of lawyers over the years. Scott Hodes showed me the world. David Guin taught me the law. Brian Sher taught me friendship and grace. All three showed me tough love (sometimes more tough than love), and I am eternally grateful. Monroe Freedman taught me to love the contract and to honor the profession. Dozens and dozens of lawyers have demonstrated their professionalism and dedication. And a few schmucks showed me how not to act. JP Benitez remains the finest protégé around. And several young lawyers helped me with research, including Adam Kirgis, Matt Robinson and, of course, Mr. Benitez. Others who gave me invaluable input: Hope Goldstein read an early draft of the employment section (Chapter 2 – Get Help) and critiqued mercilessly; Dave Slavkin, one of the most honorable lawyers I know, read the risk management parts (Section 6 – Getting Protection); Karen Lennon actually read the whole thing and gave great comments. Thank you also to Bryan Cave LLP, because the Firm has always supported me and encouraged me to do exactly what I want, and for that I am very fortunate.

The look, feel, graphics, fonts, layout and, in many cases, organization, were all done by Roxanne Saylor, the most talented artist, and best person, I know.

TABLE OF CONTENTS

TABLE OF CONTENTS

prologue

MEET HAP & HAZ

IN THIS SECTION:
- ⇨ Meet Hap & Haz
- ⇨ Meet Gravity

This is the story of Hap and Hazard, two cube dwellers in the cubicle farm of the soap maker, McDouchey Suds. Hap was paid to create new ways to get other cube dwellers to buy his boss's soap. His advertisements sparkled and he earned very big bonuses. Hazard was an accountant — he spent his days counting things in rows and columns. Hazard loved numbers and equations. Sometimes, he got a special warm feeling from tying off a particularly tricky expense. Hap and Hazard had worked for the soap maker for 7 years alongside thousands of strangers, mostly communications majors from land grant colleges. At first, they were accustomed to the job; sometimes, they even enjoyed it. They liked when something was hard and then they figured it out. They liked working together. They liked Saturdays.

The soap maker liked to shift his cube dwellers around different offices and cubes, and Hap and Hazard never knew where they were going to sit. They may work at Cubes 137 and 139 for a week. Then suddenly the soap maker may change his mind and move them to Cubes 452 and 454, sometimes just for one day. This was a very popular thing to do with cube dwellers in many big companies in the early 21st Century.

Hap and Hazard, like all cube dwellers, carried office belongings in a knapsack and devoted the first and last 45 minutes of each day to packing and unpacking its contents. With so many moves, many cube dwellers misplaced their tools.

The most commonly lost items were:

- ✓ Laptop cords
- ✓ Cell phone cords
- ✓ Successories®

Not only did Hap and Hazard duck many requests to borrow their power cords, they also had to keep an eye on them, taking them along to meetings, to lunch and to the men's room. Occasionally, they forgot and would return to their desks, their computer or a cell phone untethered, just a few hours of power left. The soap maker charged employees $75.00 for each replacement cord. Selling power cords to employees had become such an important part of the soap maker's business that the soap maker talked about it in a special box on his tax return and reports to the Securities Exchange Commission.

After years of work for the soap maker, Hap and Hazard grew bored and bewildered – every week seemed the same. One day, their moods brightened when they got My Space pages – but after a few weeks, their moods darkened. Then, they joined Facebook and their world changed - then it changed back. Then, they watched the Superbowl and ate spicy chicken wings.

One day, Hap and Hazard were walking back to their office carrying long sacks from Subway ($5.00 for a foot long, $.75 extra meat).

Hap said, "Hazard, do you ever want something more than just a cube and a salary?"

Hazard answered, "Yes. Hap, of course I do. But, I'm realistic. This is not the time to be taking risks."

And, they went back to work.

A week later, Hap and Hazard were walking back to their office carrying cardboard Sbarro triangles. While they waited for the light, a dented Ford Gran Torino station wagon with wooden trim drove by them, belching black smoke out of its back end. Behind the wagon, a gigantic Hummer honked his horn. The Hummer had a "Support the Troops" bumper sticker and a license plate that said "13MPG HA."

Hazard said, "Hap, I sure wish someone would do something about the old cars and the mean cars. Maybe if someone could make a new car that was beautiful and affordable and clean, more people would buy it."

Hap replied, "Why don't we do it, Hazard? We're smart. We are determined. Why not us?"

"Hap, we're just cube dwellers in the soap maker's work room. Who are we? Sometimes, Hap, I think you are a dreamer."

Hap muttered, "Sometimes, Hazard, I think you refuse to dream. I don't want to work for the soap maker forever. I would like to do bigger things."

When Hap and Hazard got back to the office, Hap saw that his laptop cord was gone and his battery half full. Hazard also lost his laptop cord and his battery was half empty.

"I wish our computer got power like our calculator," said Hap.

"Wouldn't that be great," agreed Hazard.

Turning to their computers, they each opened this email:

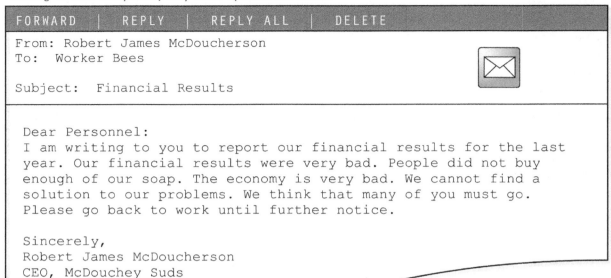

FORWARD | REPLY | REPLY ALL | DELETE

From: Robert James McDoucherson
To: Worker Bees

Subject: Financial Results

Dear Personnel:
I am writing to you to report our financial results for the last
year. Our financial results were very bad. People did not buy
enough of our soap. The economy is very bad. We cannot find a
solution to our problems. We think that many of you must go.
Please go back to work until further notice.

Sincerely,
Robert James McDoucherson
CEO, McDouchey Suds

After that email, they each opened this email:

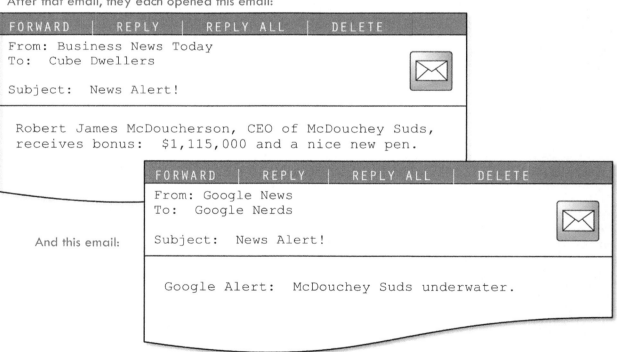

FORWARD | REPLY | REPLY ALL | DELETE

From: Business News Today
To: Cube Dwellers

Subject: News Alert!

Robert James McDoucherson, CEO of McDouchey Suds,
receives bonus: $1,115,000 and a nice new pen.

FORWARD | REPLY | REPLY ALL | DELETE

From: Google News
To: Google Nerds

Subject: News Alert!

And this email:

Google Alert: McDouchey Suds underwater.

Hap grunted. Hazard shook. They both went back to work.

For many days afterwards, the soap maker's work room, usually still with boredom and piped in white noise, fluttered. Monster.com pages, whispered conversations, pleas to sick children to get back in bed because mommy can't be away from work right now, and resumes. Lots of resumes. Everything but typing and talking about how to make and sell more soap.

Hap peered over his cube wall.

"What are you doing, Haz?"

"I'm reading a blog."

"What is the blog about?"

"Solar power."

"What about solar power?"

"Some guy just found a way to make solar panels cheap and thin."

"Wow. I didn't even know solar panels were thick and pricey. Gosh, Haz. You must be the smartest guy I know. You are always finding different stuff and reading about it."

Just then, Douchey McDoucherson, the chief marketing officer (and the nephew of the CEO), appeared.

"Hap!"

"Hello Douchey, how are you?"

"I'm very busy. I've just a second to tell you we read your proposal."

Hap was very proud of his latest proposal for an ad campaign.

"And?"

"Absolutely ridiculous. Why would we want children around the world carving sculptures out of our bars of soap? Do you have any idea how much money it would cost to supply children with free soap – for arts and crafts?"

"But, Sir, all of the newspapers and blogs would talk about us. And the children would get to make things with their own two hands."

"Rubbish. It's a waste of money and time. Hap, management is beginning to doubt you are Douchey material."

After he left, Hazard looked at his friend.

"I thought it was a brilliant idea, Hap. I don't know why they don't get it."

Hap did not respond. He erased his proposal from his computer. He returned to work.

In the meantime, Hazard focused on his most wonderful time of the year: 10-K Spring. During 10-K Spring, all of the publicly traded boys and girls place the answers to the question "How did you do last year?" into a very pretty package called a Form 10-K and set it under a tree called EDGAR (or the "Electronic Data-Gathering, Analysis and Retrieval system" for short) for a big and open unwrapping. Hazard was proceeding joyfully with his work, when he came across a row that said, "10,000,000 units, Parked Dollar Stores, 9/30." He knew he had seen a similar row before. So, he peered and peered and peered and, Eureka! There it was. 10,000,000 units of Douchey Soap shipped on September 30 to a warehouse in Grand Rapids. And, there, on his desk, was a bill that had just arrived from a warehouse in Grand Rapids for storage of 10,000,000 units. Hazard could not find a purchase order from any customer called "Parked Dollar Stores." And Hazard became very afraid.

That day, Hap and Hazard stayed with their lunch where they bought it.

"What do I do, Hap? I don't want to get anyone in trouble and I don't want to get fired. But, I also don't want to help people think we sold more soap than we did."

"Haz, you know what we need?"

"What's that, Hap?"

"A lawyer!"

"But, Hap, lawyers are so expensive. I don't think I can afford a lawyer."

"I used to date a girl who became a lawyer. Maybe she can help us."

"What's her name?"

"Gravity."

Gravity had short spiky hair, a firm, solid grip and a deep voice pitched from the back of her throat. Gravity beckoned Hap and Hazard into her office while she finished up a call.

When Hap saw her, he was quite surprised. The last time he had seen Gravity, she had long blond hair and high heels.

"Gravity, thank you for seeing us."

Gravity smiled warmly. "I'm glad you called. What can I do to help?"

Hazard told Gravity his predicament. Gravity listened carefully until the end of the story.

"Hazard, you are a good and noble person. I know this is difficult for you. But, you are doing the right thing."

"But, I haven't done anything yet. I don't know what to do."

"You have promised people you would help them by giving them true information so that they can decide whether to buy, sell or hold the soap maker's stock. That tells you what you must do. You feel you need to keep your job. That tells you that you must be careful. This will not be easy. You must prepare yourself for the possibility that you will do the right thing and the wrong will be done to you."

"So, I should…?"

"You should decide whether you want to do the right but risky thing or the safe thing."

Haz thought for a few minutes.

"I want to do the safe thing. But, I think it will only be safe in the short term. If it is being done in secret, it probably shouldn't be done and it will probably come to light eventually. I am going to come forward. But, carefully."

With Gravity's guidance, Hazard mapped out a plan.

They returned to the office and Hazard asked to speak with his supervisor, Mr. Catatonic. But, Mr. Catatonic told him to pipe down. So, he went to Mr. Catatonic's boss, Mr. Corporatool.

"Mr. Corporatool, I have identified a delivery of 10,000,000 units that was booked as a sale, but was really stored in a warehouse by the soap maker." Hazard presented the storage receipt and income statement.

Mr. Corporatool said, "Well, Hazard. That's excellent work. Excellent. I'll take care of it from here."

One week later, McDouchey Suds presented the world with its 10-K. Inside the 10-K was a surprise: a footnote that read, "due to the error of a former employee in our accounting department, we mischaracterized a sale of certain inventory during Q3, and, accordingly, we have restated our revenues for the period."

Hazard read this note and looked up to see Mr. Catatonic and Mr. Corporatool standing there with Gruffy, the soap maker's security officer. Haz gave them his badge and Blackberry and left the building.

Hap watched and then made a call. Ten minutes later, Gravity was on the phone with the McDouchey General Counsel, telling him a thing or two about a thing or two. One week later, Hazard sat in his cube, now equipped with a printer and a new name plate: Supervisor. Sadly, Mr. Catatonic and Mr. Corporatool were not able to stay with the soap maker.

At first, Haz was excited about his new job. But, then he discovered that it was just like his old job plus meetings on Saturday. Haz spent more and more of his time reading blogs about business and green energy. He began to dream about doing things during the day he liked.

Meanwhile, Hap had figured out that the soap maker liked just one kind of advertisement. To please the soap maker, Hap made a mold and then cast each advertisement from it. Now, instead of weeks, he could make advertisements in a few minutes — he had lots and lots and lots of free time. Hap spent that time reading about different ways to tell people about something you want to sell to them. Blogs, Tweets, dynamic sites, eBooks, old - school books, podcasts and webinars. So many people saying so many things about so many ways to talk to people who may be interested in your business. Hap began to dream about making something completely new that would bring people very much happiness — and freedom.

One day, Haz and Hap returned to work after chicken nuggets and fries. Half of their neighboring cube dwellers had disappeared.

"What happened?" Hap asked.

"RIF," whispered a fellow cube dweller, not lifting his hands or eyes from his computer.

"Haz, I think the soap maker spared us."

"For now."

Hap and Haz sat for a moment.

"Hap, I'm tired of the soap maker. I'm tired of being afraid. I'm tired of problems that can't be fixed. I'm tired of the big work room and the white noise and this cube. I'm tired of lunch."

"Me too, Haz. What should we do about it?"

"Let's go out on our own."

"But, Haz. You're afraid of everything. What changed now?"

"I'm more afraid of staying than I am of leaving."

Hap and Hazard spent the next three months exploring and mulling, debating and swaying. They wanted to make something totally new that would solve a problem.

One day, Douchey McDoucherson shouted,

"Hap. Hazard. Conference Room K. Now. Leave your stuff."

In the conference room, Hap and Hazard learned that their health insurance coverage would be cut to critical care only with a $7,500 deductible and 62% copay. They returned to their desks to discover their power cords (and Hap's breakfast bar) gone.

"Doggone it."

"Haz, wouldn't it be great if we could power our computer like our calculator?"

"You said that before, Hap."

"I did, didn't I?"

"Yes."

"Maybe that's what we should do."

"What?"

"Make a battery that takes energy from light and converts it to power for a laptop."

"C'mon, Hap, we can't do that."

"Why not?"

"Because if it could have been done, then it would have been done."

"So, you don't know if it can be done."

"No, I don't know. But, I'll bet you it can't."

"But, what if it can?"

"Even if it can be done, we can't do it."

"Why?"

"Because we are just." Haz paused. "Us."

"So? Most inventors were just like us before they were like them."

"C'mon Hap."

"It's a good idea, though, isn't it?"

"Yes, it's a good idea."

"So, let's at least look into it. C'mon, I spent 3 days trying to see if people would buy a doggy litter box. "

"Who knew it was already for sale in Sky Mall?"

"So you owe me."

 "Okay. Fine. We'll look into it."

Hazard spent a couple of weeks reading everything about solar power technology and batteries. He discovered that scientists and engineers had created hybrid batteries that collect and store energy and transform that energy into power in a variety of ways.

"It's possible," he told Hap.

"I knew it, Haz. While you were studying technology, I was studying the market. Do you know that batteries – scalable, mobile and efficient batteries – are the single greatest consumer request and that a lack of them are the single greatest consumer complaint?"

"Maybe we have our product. But Hap, we still don't know anything about how to actually do it. You know how to make things buyable."

"And you know numbers and limits."

 "But not much else."

"Haz, you know who we need?"

"Who?"

"Gravity. She helps people start businesses all the time."

"You are right, Hap. Gravity knows everything. What are we waiting for?"

Gravity showed Hap and Hazard into her office.

 "How can I help you?"

"Gravity, we would like to go into business. We want to make a small solar battery for laptops embedded in a computer mouse."

"Hap, Hazard, that is a great idea. How can I help?"

"We don't know how to start."

Gravity nodded and asked, "Do you know how to make it?

"No."

"Do you know where you want to sell it?"

"No."

"Do you know how you are going to pay for it?"

Hap and Hazard looked at each other and then back at her.

"No."

"Do you know what it's called?"

Hazard looked at Hap. Hap looked scared, then happy.

"The MouseTrap!"

"The MouseTrap. I love it. Have you started on a business plan?"

"Not yet. We don't know if we need a business plan or how we would make one. Can you help us?"

"I CAN TRY," Gravity answered.

GETTING ORGANIZED

section one

MAKE A BUSINESS PLAN

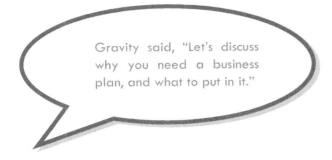

Gravity said, "Let's discuss why you need a business plan, and what to put in it."

CHAPTER 01

WHY YOU NEED A BUSINESS PLAN

A business plan is a written report on how your business will act, produce and be. You need a business plan to work through business issues and questions; to have something tangible for potential stake holders; and to give yourself a living roadmap.

To work through business issues and questions. The process of putting together your business plan — asking yourself tough questions and researching and writing down the answers — is the exercise that will make your business, and your command of it, stronger.

To have something tangible. The business plan gives you something concrete for potential lenders, investors, employees, advisors, future customers and your skeptical relatives.

To give yourself a living roadmap. Your business plan is your recording of how you plan to execute your vision — it ought to keep you organized and focused. However don't be afraid to change or refine it as you learn and grow.

WHAT TO PUT IN YOUR BUSINESS PLAN

Most business plans are broken into sections, such as: (1) Executive Summary, (2) The Business; (3) Industry & Competition, (4) Sales & Marketing; (5) Company; and (6) Finance & Accounting.

1. EXECUTIVE SUMMARY

The Executive Summary is the nice, neat nutshell of the rest of your plan — it ought to be compelling, persuasive and short. This is the most important part of your business plan, because it is the part that people may actually read. The Executive Summary should have general information, including the date your business began, the founders and management and what they do, the number of employees, the locations and general descriptions of offices, debt and amounts invested, highlights of company growth and highlights of future plans. In addition, Executive Summaries often include shorter subsections like (a) Mission; (b) Product & Service; (c) Revenue & Pricing; and (d) Customers.

MISSION

The mission statement contains your broad goals for your business. There are two kinds of businesses: those that exist merely to enrich their owners and those that exist to solve problems, profitably. Whatever your big goals are, try and describe them in 10 words or less (with active verbs).[1]

PRODUCTS & SERVICES

In this subsection, describe what you are offering to provide—and what human problem it solves. Some businesses start by picking a product or service, some start by picking a type of customer. Wherever you start, eventually you have to decide what product or service you will deliver for money.

REVENUE & PRICING

The business plan ought to contain an explanation about how you will earn money. So, summarize your revenue sources and your plans for pricing.

CUSTOMERS

You should have some expectation of who your customers could be. Briefly describe who they are, their problem you will solve and approximately how many of them there are.

2. THE BUSINESS

The body of the business plan should, of course, lead with a description of the business, including (a) your service or product line; (b) your target markets; (c) your supply chain; and (d) your business risks.

SERVICE OR PRODUCT LINE

Every business plan should begin with the products and services that will be the focus of the company.

- ✓ Describe your service or product
- ✓ Discuss the benefits to potential and current customers, and how it will address a human need
- ✓ Give the reader evidence that people are, or will be, willing to pay for your solution
- ✓ Provide details regarding suppliers, availability of products/services, and service or product costs
- ✓ Give a roadmap of future products or features

TARGET MARKETS

The Target Market section usually defines the specific customer segments or niches you intend to pursue. You may need to do research on these questions. Resources might include directories, trade association publications, and government documents. Like a math test, show your work and describe your research method and results. Niche down as far as possible. Below are some questions you could answer to help you fill it out:

- ✓ Who is your target market? Who are the people who have the problem you are trying to solve?
- ✓ What are the characteristics of your target markets - geography, generation, ethnicity, income bracket, ideology, family status, gender,

sexual orientation, religion, cultural heritage, etc.?
- ✓ Why are their needs not being met currently?
- ✓ Are there any seasons or cycles that impact when and how much you can expect your target market to need you?
- ✓ How big is your target market?
- ✓ Why will they love you more than competitors? How much of that market do you think you'll get, why, how and when?
- ✓ How will you price your products?
- ✓ Define the levels of your pricing, your gross margin levels, and any discount structures that you plan to set up for your business, such as volume/bulk discounts or prompt payment discounts.
- ✓ How will you talk to your target market and tell them about you? Website, social networks, loyalty programs, newspaper, radio, television, other mass market advertising?
- ✓ Who are your secondary markets? What are their needs, demographics and trends?

SUPPLY CHAIN AND LEAD TIMES

Supply chain is the process and players involved in getting your product from raw material to your customer. Lead time is the amount of time between when a customer places an order and when the product or service is actually delivered. When you are researching this information, determine what your lead time will be for the initial order, reorders, and volume purchases.

RISKS

Business plans (and all fundraising offerings) typically include a marginally embarrassing list of risks that could befall your business. Those risks include everything that could possibly go wrong.

3. INDUSTRY AND COMPETITION

You should (a) describe your industry; (b) identify the competition; and (c) barriers to entering the industry.

INDUSTRY DESCRIPTION AND OUTLOOK

Most business plans have some definition of the industry, and its size, idiosyncrasies and trends.

If you have no idea, look at how other companies in the same area describe their industry by looking at competitor "About Us" webpages or SEC filings at www.sec.gov/edgar.shtml. But, don't just lift the text and use it as your own.

Below are some questions you could answer to help you fill it out:

- ✓ What is the life cycle of your industry? (e.g. introduction, growth, maturity, decline, or dead)?
- ✓ What is the growth trajectory of your industry?
- ✓ Who are the major customer groups in your industry? (e.g. Business, Government, Consumers?)

COMPETITION

Business plans often include a discussion on existing competitors. Below are some questions you could answer to help you fill it out:

- ✓ Who are the companies already doing what you want to do? Do they already target the same markets you intend to pursue?
- ✓ What product lines or services do your competitors offer?
- ✓ How will you crush them? What barriers are there that could keep you from crushing them?
- ✓ What is their market share?
- ✓ Who are secondary or indirect competitors?
- ✓ Why and when do you think other competitors will jump in the market?
- ✓ What are their strengths and weaknesses? Such as:
  - o Size of market share or market dominance
  - o Customer service
  - o Reputation
  - o Track record
  - o Amount of cash or credit to fund expansion
  - o Management talent
  - o Depth of market penetration
  - o Identification with product or service or
  - o Ability to satisfy customer needs

BARRIERS TO ENTRY

You will probably need to plan around any barriers to enter your target markets and/or the market for your products and services. These barriers may include:

- ✓ Big upfront costs
- ✓ Set up time
- ✓ Evolving technology
- ✓ Scarcity of qualified people
- ✓ Customer conversion due to existing relationships and brand loyalty
- ✓ Intellectual property protected by patents

4. SALES AND MARKETING

Sales and marketing is the process of creating and understanding customers, which never ends. Your description may include (a) your growth strategy; (b) your communication strategy; and (c) your sales strategy.

GROWTH STRATEGY

Identify your strategy for market penetration and sales:

- ✓ Horizontal strategy where you would provide the same type of products to different users
- ✓ Vertical strategy where you would continue providing the same products but would offer them at different levels of the distribution chain. This could include original equipment manufacturers (OEMs), an internal sales force, distributors, or retailers
- ✓ Franchise strategy for branching out
- ✓ An acquisition strategy

COMMUNICATION STRATEGY

Discuss how you will reach your customers. Below are the types of strategies usually used in combination:

- ✓ Promotions
- ✓ Advertising
- ✓ Public relations
- ✓ Personal selling
- ✓ Printed materials such as brochures, catalogs, flyers, etc.
- ✓ Web content

Once you have defined your marketing strategy, you can then define your sales strategy.

Internet Strategy. An online sales strategy is becoming increasingly prevalent. Some companies find that they can adopt a sales strategy that uses existing sales arms without incurring the substantial cost or commitment that comes with sales people. Your own website, 3rd party auction and sales sites, affiliate programs and partnering arrangements may be a good start.

A Sales Force Strategy. Most companies use a sales force to move some or all of their products and services. Building a sales force, even if small, takes resources.

- ✓ If you do plan to hire salespeople, do you plan to use internal or independent representatives? How many salespeople will you recruit for your sales force?
- ✓ What type of recruitment strategies will you use?
- ✓ How will you train your sales force?
- ✓ How will you compensate your sales force?

Your Sales Activities. When you are defining your sales strategy, it is important that you break it down into activities. For instance, you could:

- ✓ Identify and prioritize your prospects
- ✓ Estimate and discuss the number of sales calls you will make over a certain period of time and the average number of sales calls you will need to make per sale, the average dollar size per sale, and the average dollar size per vendor

5. COMPANY

The Company Description section is the place where you provide an overview of your company, identify all the parts of your business and how it all fits together, as well as the factors that will make you a success. This section should include descriptions of (a) your organization; (b) ownership; (c) management; (d) board of directors; and (e) regulations and legal restrictions.

This section should discuss your company's management and structure, ownership, bios of management and your Board of Directors. Identify who's in charge and management's duties and responsibilities. You should also discuss compensation and how you incentivize people to stay engaged. You may also want to include an organizational chart.

The ownership section should identify all of the equity owners of the company. Include:

- ✓ Names of owners
- ✓ Percentage ownership
- ✓ Their involvement with the company
- ✓ Class or series of shares they own
- ✓ Any warrants or options
- ✓ Compensation
- ✓ Investment amount

Make sure you provide meaningful information about your leaders and managers. You can attach their resumes to the appendix, but you should also provide some prose in the body of the business plan, describing:

- ✓ Name
- ✓ Position
- ✓ Duties and authority
- ✓ Education
- ✓ Unique experience and skills
- ✓ Prior employment
- ✓ Past track record and recognition; better if you can provide quantitative past accomplishments
- ✓ Community involvement
- ✓ Number of years with company
- ✓ Compensation basis and levels
- ✓ Why each person's experience and talents will make your business a success

BOARD OF DIRECTORS

Identify the members of your Board of Directors, including:

- ✓ Names
- ✓ Positions on the board
- ✓ Involvement with company
- ✓ Background
- ✓ Past/future contribution to the company's success
- ✓ Compensation (if any)

REGULATIONS AND LEGAL RESTRICTIONS

You may want to include a discussion on the regulations and legal restrictions that impact your business. Figure out whether your product and service or market is regulated by the government. Below are some questions you could answer to help you fill it out:

- ✓ What are the regulations that affect your business?
- ✓ What will you have to do to comply with them?
- ✓ What is the impact on your business?
- ✓ Do you know any changes on the horizon?

6. FINANCE AND ACCOUNTING

The finance and accounting section covers information about the money into and out of your company, including (a) funding requirements; and (b) financials.

FUNDING REQUIREMENTS

In this section, give a reasonable explanation of how much investment you will need to accomplish your business plan. Include:

- ✓ Different levels of funding to achieve different levels of your business plan
- ✓ Your expectations for how much funding you need in the short term and in the long term
- ✓ How these funds will be put to use
- ✓ Any strategic information related to your business that may have an impact on your financial situation in the future, such as:
  - ○ going public with your company
  - ○ having a leveraged buyout
  - ○ being acquired by another company
  - ○ the method with which you will service your debt
  - ○ whether or not you plan to sell your business in the future

Each of these is extremely important to a future creditor or investor

FINANCIALS

The financials should be developed after you've analyzed the market and set clear objectives. Make sure to include the following:

Projections. All businesses must provide financial projections over the following 3-5 years. You should provide:

- ✓ Forecasted income statements
- ✓ Balance sheets
- ✓ Cash flow statements
- ✓ Capital expenditure budgets

For the first year, you should supply monthly or quarterly projections. Your projections must match your funding needs. These are by definition just guesses, but don't make them worse by exaggerating them, because you'll look goofy.

Pretty Pictures. Pictures speak louder than words. If it sheds light on your financial position, then include a graphic showing a ratio and trend analysis for all of your financial statements (both historical and prospective) and any other depictions of your financial position.

The Appendix. The appendix section should be provided to readers on an as-needed basis. The appendix would include:

- ✓ Credit history (personal & business)
- ✓ Resumes of key managers
- ✓ Product pictures
- ✓ Letters of reference
- ✓ Details of market studies
- ✓ Relevant magazine articles or book references
- ✓ Licenses, permits, or patents
- ✓ Legal documents
- ✓ Copies of leases

- ✓ Building permits
- ✓ Contracts
- ✓ List of business consultants, including attorney and accountant

Historical Financial Data. For established businesses, the standard is to provide data for the last three to five years. You should provide income statements, balance sheets, and cash flow statements for each year you have been in business (up to 3 to 5 years).

7. WRITING & USING THE BUSINESS PLAN

There are few rules in business plans, but here is some guidance about (a) length and depth; and (b) safety and security.

LENGTH AND DEPTH

How long should your business plan be? As short as possible. The best business plans are clear, instructive, reasonable and changeable. Be careful about hyperbole – you want to make the case for how and why your business will succeed without exaggerating your assumptions, predictions or reality.

SAFETY & SECURITY

When you are ready to distribute your business plan, keep track of copies of your business plan and a record of its distribution. Make sure you get the recipient to sign a confidentiality agreement prior to getting your business plan. And, ask a lawyer about the myriad disclaimers you should stick on the thing to alert readers to the limits of the information.

HAP AND HAZ WRITE A BUSINESS PLAN – WITH SOME STRUGGLE

By day, Hap and Hazard toiled for the soap maker. At night and on weekends, they worked to make the MouseTrap a reality.

Okay, that's a lie - by day, they also worked to make the MouseTrap a reality. Hap and Hazard found that, even with many less people working for the soap maker, they could still finish their work by 2:00 in the afternoon. By bringing their lunch and cutting out gossip, sometimes they could even finish their work for the soap maker by noon,

leaving their afternoons free. Hap and Hazard felt very guilty.

Hap and Hazard divided the business plan in half. Hap became responsible for the sections on products, target markets, and sales and marketing. Of course, Hazard outlined the finance and accounting sections. Hazard loved science and innovation nearly as much as he loved equations, so Hazard also studied everything about the competition.

But, they had one huge problem: they still didn't know how to make the MouseTrap, so they couldn't make a plan to make it.

Hap tried to help by making this initial plan:

> "Take one mouse. Yank out the solar cell from Hazard's 1989 Texas Instruments calculator. Paste the solar cell onto the mouse. Take a wire. Connect one end of the wire to the solar panels. Connect the other end of the wire to the internal engine of the mouse."

> "Hap, that won't work."

> "Why not, Haz?"

> "So many reasons. Let's go ask Gravity. Maybe she'll have some ideas."

GRAVITY'S ADVICE

Gravity listened and then replied,

> "Boys, what you need is someone who can help you figure this out."

> "But, we need to figure this out for ourselves."

> "No," Gravity explained. "You need help now and you will need it in the future.

> "We don't know how to get help. Can you tell us how?"

> "I CAN TRY."

GET HELP

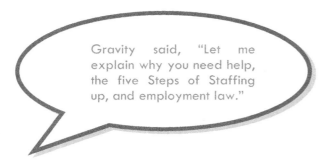

Gravity said, "Let me explain why you need help, the five Steps of Staffing up, and employment law."

CHAPTER 02

WHY YOU NEED HELP

You can't expect to have every skill you need for something so complex. It is better to expect that you won't know everything than to pretend that you do. You need to find someone with the expertise, skills or time you lack. That person can be a partner, but it is more likely that the person will be someone you pay for his expertise and time.

5 S'S OF STAFFING UP

There are five steps to finding help: (1) Search; (2) Specify; (3) Screen; (4) Solidify; and (5) Start. Let's go over these in more detail.

1. SPECIFY

The first thing to do is to specify the job. Write down what you need done, what the end result should be and what skills someone needs to get you that result. Then, consider how and where they will work and how they will communicate with you. Finally, set a range of compensation for the position.

2. SEARCH

Once you know what you need someone to do, the next step is to search for candidates. There are several ways to find people to work for you.

YOUR CONTACTS

The first and best way is to get referrals from your networks of people. Dig into your contacts and ask people for recommendations. Consider asking other companies with similar products for recommendations.

ADVERTISE

You could also place an ad for applicants. There are a variety of ways to place the ads:

- ⇨ www.craigslist.org
- ⇨ any of the job placement sites like www.monster.com
- ⇨ local newspapers
- ⇨ university job boards and placement offices
- ⇨ posting a notice on your Facebook page or other social media outlets

You can do your own searches online to find websites of people or companies that may fit your bill. For instance, searching relevant trade associations may reveal members who claim the experience you need.

RECRUITERS

Finally, you could hire a professional recruiter who specializes in finding the types of people you need. However, recruiters charge anywhere from 10-33% of your hire's first year compensation.

3. SCREEN

Once you identify where you will search, the next step is to collect and contact applicants. If you intend to give them confidential information during the selection process, then you may want to have them sign a confidentiality agreement.

4. SOLIDIFY

After you have narrowed your list to just one or a couple of candidates, it is time to start negotiating terms. No matter how much you liked the person during the screening phase, they still may blow the job during negotiation. You will have completed this phase when you both have a mutual understanding of the job duties and compensation, as well as the consequences if things go awry. **If you put terms in writing, clearly state whether the position is for a guaranteed amount of time or if it is "at will" and can be terminated at any time.** And, always make it clear that job duties may change and the worker is required to complete all assigned tasks.

5. START

Once you have solidified your deal, you can schedule the start date of their work for you and their deadlines and milestones.

TYPES OF HELP

The relationship created between your business and its helpers will be governed by some tricky rules. First, let's define your possible relationships to your helpers. There are basically 4 types of relationships you create when an individual helps you:

- ✓ Employment
- ✓ Independent Contractor
- ✓ Partnership/Joint Venture
- ✓ Licensing

A person you hire to work for you is either an "employee" or an "independent contractor." Trying to tell employees from independent contractors can be surprisingly difficult. The IRS used to have a 20-Factor Test that you would use to figure out the difference. But, recently they killed the 20 Factor Test and came up with the 3 Part Test, each with 6 subparts. So, it's much clearer now.

EMPLOYEE V. INDEPENDENT CONTRACTOR

A worker is an **employee**[2] if you have the right to control the end result of the person's efforts plus how, where and when they work to get that end result. A worker is an **independent contractor** if you have the right to control or direct the end result of the person's efforts, but not the efforts or the how, where and when they work to get that end result.

Statutory Employees. There are also workers that are "statutory employees." Statutory employees are employees for FICA and federal tax purposes – this is a creature of the federal tax code.[3] No matter what, if a worker falls into this category, that worker is an employee for tax purposes. Some work at home workers, drivers and sales people are statutory employees. But, talk to an employment lawyer for more.

WHY IT MATTERS

Whether someone is an employee or independent contractor is a surprisingly knotty question, with different rules for tax and employment law. Be aware: just because you say someone is an independent contractor does not mean that the IRS or a court is going to agree. There are two big reasons why it matters: (1) you have different rights and responsibilities for employees and independent contractors; and (2) you could be liable for cash money if you call someone an independent contractor that you should have called an employee.

1. YOUR RIGHTS AND RESPONSIBILITIES SHIFT

FOR YOU, THE BOSS

IF SHE IS AN EMPLOYEE	IF SHE IS AN INDEPENDENT CONTRACTOR
✓ You have to deduct payroll taxes and withholding.	✓ She pays her own payroll tax and Social Security and Medicare withholding.
✓ You have to get worker's compensation insurance.	✓ You may not have to get her workers' compensation insurance. But, without worker's compensation, she could sue you for damages she suffers without the liability limitations built into worker's compensation insurance.
✓ You can't discriminate against them on the basis of sex, race, national origin, religion, sexual orientation, disability or veteran's status.	
✓ You are liable for the acts of your employees.	✓ Discrimination laws may not apply to her.
✓ You have to withhold income tax from the employee on payday.	✓ She may be excluded from your obligation to provide health insurance in 2014 under Health Care Reform. She also won't count under the 50-employee threshold for employers who have to provide health insurance.
✓ You may have to provide health insurance under health care reform.	
✓ Communications with her about inventions do not start the clock running on the maximum to file a patent application.	✓ Disclosures about inventions probably need a special confidentiality agreement to not start the patent application filing.
✓ Every copyrightable work she makes connected to her job belongs to you.	✓ Nothing she makes connected to her job belongs to you, unless you get it in writing.

FOR THE WORKER

IF SHE IS AN EMPLOYEE	IF SHE IS AN INDEPENDENT CONTRACTOR
✓ Withholding taken care of; she also only pays half of payroll tax that she would pay as an independent contractor.	✓ She can deduct business expenses directly.
	✓ No unemployment benefits.
✓ Gets unemployment benefits.	✓ Maybe no Worker's Compensation (but if so, fewer limits on the boss's potential liability).
✓ Gets worker's compensation.	
✓ Ability to deduct business expenses very limited.	✓ Pays self-employment tax (which includes full amount of Social Security and Medicare.
✓ Protected by lots of laws, like wage and hour, antidiscrimination and laws about indemnification by employer.	✓ Must sue to collect any unpaid wages/compensation.
✓ Probably not liable for stupid things you do while at work. But, could be liable for intentionally stupid things she does while at work.	✓ Can be sued by third parties for harm caused while working for the boss.
	✓ Can set up self-employed retirement plans.

2. YOU OWE MONEY TO THE IRS IF YOU SHOULD HAVE TREATED THE WORKER AS YOUR EMPLOYEE

If you treat an employee as an independent contractor, you are liable for FICA if the employee doesn't pay it himself[4] and the amount you should have withheld for income taxes if he doesn't pay.[5] Be aware: the person who had control over the decision about whether to treat the worker as an employee or independent contractor is on the hook <u>personally</u> for this money. (But, there may be ways to reduce or erase your tax liability. Talk to your employment lawyer or accountant.)

IS SHE AN EMPLOYEE OR AN INDEPENDENT CONTRACTOR? THE IRS' NEW 3 PART TEST

An employee is someone exclusive to you who does the work the way you say it should be done. An independent contractor is someone who works for you and other people and does your work the way she wants to do it. The IRS says you can tell the difference between an employee and independent contractor by looking at (1) behavioral control; (2) financial control; and (3) the factual clues that reveal the real relationship.

Behavioral Control. If you have behavioral control over the worker, then the IRS thinks you are the employer. Behavioral control means the right to control the moment to moment and day to day work performed to get the job done. So, these questions are designed to tease out who gets to pick the process, time and location of work. There are two parts: (a) Instructions; and (b) Training.

(a) **Instructions**. If you provide instructions on the actual how-to over the job, then you look like an employer. Ask yourself if you kept control over:

- ✓ When to work
- ✓ Where to work
- ✓ What tools or equipment to use
- ✓ What sub-workers to hire to assist
- ✓ Where to get supplies or services

- ✓ Work that must be done by certain people
- ✓ What order or sequence of action steps to follow

(b) **Training**. If you train a worker on how to do something, the IRS thinks you look like an employer. After all, independent contractors ought to have their own methods. Ask yourself if you provide training on how to get the job done.

Financial Control. If you have control over financial decisions, then the IRS thinks you look like an employer. Financial control is about who bears the financial burdens and possible benefits and thus calls the shots.

- ✓ Significant investment. Significant investment in a venture is evidence that the independent contractor is a stand-alone business.

- ✓ Unreimbursed business expenses. Stand-alone businesses bear their own expenses. Fixed ongoing costs incurred whether work done is not are a sign that the worker is an independent contractor. But, if you reimburse the worker for all incurred expenses, you look like an employer.

- ✓ On the market. Independent contractors work for many clients; employees work for just one company. If the worker markets his services to others, he is free to seek out other opportunities, he advertises and has a visible business, he looks like an independent contractor.

- ✓ Compensation Structure. The IRS thinks that independent contractors get paid on a project or flat fee basis and employees get guaranteed amounts in a period of time. Therefore, paying the worker a total amount for a period of time looks like an employment relationship.

- ✓ Profit. Independent contractors have the opportunity to make a profit on work; employees get paid wages. If the worker has a potential to realize a profit or a loss, he is probably an independent contractor.

Type of Relationship. If there are parts of your working relationship with your worker that look like employment, then you look like an employer. This is a way of examining the facts in your arrangements to infer a truth.

- ✓ Written Contract. A written contract describing the relationship as an independent contractor relationship is helpful, but doesn't rule the ending.
- ✓ Employee Benefits. Independent contractors provide their own benefits; employees get them from their employer. If you pay your worker employee-type benefits, like insurance, pension, vacation, sick days, you look like an employer.
- ✓ Permanency. The IRS thinks that companies hire independent contractors to do projects and hire employers to work on a permanent basis. If the engagement goes on indefinitely, rather than for a project or period, you look like an employer. Similarly, the right to fire a worker without penalty makes you look like an employer.
- ✓ Services critical to business. The IRS thinks that the regular business activities of the company are done by employees. If services performed by the worker are a key aspect of the regular business of the company, you look like an employer.

You can also ask the IRS to make the decision for you by filing Form SS-8.

TWO OTHER RELATIONSHIPS – PARTNER AND LICENSOR

1. PARTNERSHIP OR JOINT VENTURES

There are rare occasions when you form a partnership with a service provider. A service relationship may convert to partnership when there is agreement that the provider will share the risks and rewards of the business and will have some control over his own performance and also over the business operations.

2. LICENSOR OR LICENSEE

Sometimes, a person who helps you could become a licensor. When a person has some asset – like software, a song or a patent – and you buy a right to use it, the owner becomes your licensor. If you hire the owner to customize the asset for you, the person could be your licensor AND your employee, independent contractor or partner, depending on your arrangement. (See Section 3, "Getting the Rights.")

INTRODUCING EMPLOYEES: AT WILL BY DEFAULT

Let's look a little closer at the employment relationship. In the United States, employment is, by default, "at will." That means that there is no guarantee to a job; you can fire or be fired without warning or reason. That's the basic rule and it's an easy one. The hard part is in the exceptions. These exceptions prohibit an employer from altering or pulling a job. Those exceptions are:

- ✓ employment contracts
- ✓ union contracts
- ✓ the right of an employee to uphold the law
- ✓ the right of an employee to reasonably complain about wrongs
- ✓ Laws that require notice during mass layoffs and mergers
- ✓ the right of an employee to not lose opportunities due to his race, sex, religion, national origin, disability or age, among others

CONTRACTS WITH EMPLOYEES

When you and/or your employee promise things to each other, you may have an employment contract. Employment contracts can be written after negotiation or formed by a verbal agreement. If the term is longer than a year, it may have to be in writing to be enforced.

Contracts can also be (1) made by mistake; (2) negotiated and then put in writing; and (3) made from collective bargaining.

1. CONTRACT MADE BY MISTAKE

Employment contracts are occasionally "discovered" even if the employer did not intend to make one. Employers can unknowingly create employment contracts by putting in their employee handbook or policy that employment will continue "for as long as performance is satisfactory," and termination will only be for "cause." This employment policy becomes, in effect, a contract. Or, employers may make broad statements – in writing or conversation – that promise the employee permanent employment. The idiosyncrasies of employment laws make it prudent to hire an employment lawyer when messing around with employment offers and contracts.

2. NEGOTIATED CONTRACT

Of course, you can also negotiate employment terms and then write them down in an employment contract that both you and your employee sign. Below are some standard categories of terms that people frequently include in written contracts with employees.

TITLE/RESPONSIBILITIES

You must describe the job title, job duties and the employee's immediate supervisor by title. The job duties, which form the basis for the employee's required standard of conduct, can also be attached to a sheet at the end of the contract.

COMPENSATION

The agreement should include a specific description of all of the compensation terms and payments.

Base Salary, Bonus and stock options or stock grants. The contract should include the rate of pay, eligibility for bonuses and descriptions of any stock options or stock grants.

Withholding. There should also be a statement that the company will deduct withholding and other payroll taxes.

Payment Timing. There should be a description on when the employee will get paid.

Expenses. Include a description of expenses that the company will reimburse and the rules for reimbursement.

Employee Benefits. These are non-wage compensations, such as insurance (health, dental, life, disability and long term care), retirement and pension benefits, perquisites (moving expenses, housing allowance, a company car, daycare and tuition reimbursement), sick leave, vacation and profit sharing.

Severance. Severance is money paid at or after the employment's end. If you agree to pay severance upon the employee's termination, that needs to be addressed here. The employee should not be entitled to the same level - or any - severance, if you fire her for cause. Make sure the severance section is reviewed by an employment lawyer.

TERM AND TERMINATION

Term of Employment. The "term" is the length of employment and the ways the employment can be terminated by either or both parties. Even if you have an employment agreement, you can still hire the employee "at will," rather than for a guaranteed period of time – but, you have to say, boldly and upfront in the contract that the employment is at will. Below is an example of language.

> Employee's employment is *at will* and nothing in this Agreement should be construed as a guarantee of employment for any period of time or at all.

Termination for Cause. "Cause" typically defines what actions would enable the company to rightfully terminate the employee. Typically, when a company fires an employee for cause, the company doesn't have to pay severance.

Termination by Executive. Sometimes, employees get the right to quit for "good reason." "Good Reason" often includes a demotion of the employee without cause, discrimination or hostile work environment.

Effect of Termination. It is a smart idea to define the employee's obligations after her termination. Common obligations are to return all material and equipment to the company, return all confidential information and business cards to the company, turn in access keys and security badges and sometimes help or get out of the way of a transition plan. In addition, you may want to provide a mechanism to get her to release the company from all claims she may have – if you do this, talk to an employment lawyer – this is tricky and filled with potholes (e.g.: Age Discrimination Act notices, compliance with company employment policies and history, etc.)

OWNERSHIP OF PROPERTY

Even though it may seem obvious, you should memorialize that all intellectual property and work she creates during her employment that relates to your business (a) belongs to you, (b) is a work made for hire, (c) is something she was hired to invent, and (d) in any event, she hereby assigns it to you. You also want to make sure there is an obligation for her to help you confirm your ownership of all related IP.

Executive's Property. You may also want to have her disclose the intellectual property she has created in the past, so that it is clear that it does not belong to you, <u>but everything else does</u>.

OLD EMPLOYERS

Someone Else's Property. You may be surprised at the number of problems and lawsuits that emerge from an employer using the property a new employee brings from her old employer. If your new employee brings a trade secret from the old firm to your company, you could be liable to the old firm. Try to avoid this. Adopt a policy that you won't use the confidential information or trade secrets of former employers. Memorialize that policy in your employee manual and in every employment agreement, and enforce it.

Old Restrictive Covenants. You should also have each new employee disclose in writing the existence of any employment agreements, confidentiality agreements, noncompetition agreements or other restrictive covenants to which she is a party. If you can, you should have your employment lawyer read them and help you manage your new employee's transition and the accompanying risk that the old firm will pick a fight with you. In some instances, employers get the employees to indemnify them for litigation costs and damages arising from suits from old employers. Though the indemnity may be fairly worthless, it may incentivize the employee to act appropriately.

RESTRICTIVE COVENANTS

A restrictive covenant is a promise to refrain from doing something for the benefit or protection of someone else. Restrictive covenants show up in employment contracts, owner agreements, merger or sale of business contracts, or in noncompetition contracts. Restrictive covenants are a big topic, so are discussed at length in the next section.

CONFIDENTIALITY

You need a good confidentiality provision obligating her to keep your secrets secret.

BOILERPLATE

There should also be standard interpretive provisions (e.g. entire agreement, no assignment, severability, governing law; submission to jurisdiction, rights of third parties, amendment, notices, counterparts and waivers). (See "Section 6, "Get Protection").

EMPLOYEE ACKNOWLEDGEMENT

In employment agreements, you need to have a statement that the employee has read, understands and agrees with the agreement and has had a chance to confer with her own legal counsel. And, if you have restrictive covenants, you need to include a statement that the employee understands and agrees that the restrictions are (a) necessary and critical for the company's ability to protect its valuable intellectual property and competitive position and (b) reasonably drawn. The employee must be given a bona fide and fair chance to read the contract with a lawyer and negotiate terms. You do not, of course, have an obligation to grant any request made during the negotiations.

3. UNION CONTRACT
(A/K/A "COLLECTIVE BARGAINING")

Contracts can also be the product of collective bargaining. **Collective bargaining** is a negotiation between an employer and a union of employees over the terms of employment. Employers can negotiate alone or with a confederacy of other businesses. The contract that results is the "**collective bargaining agreement.**"[6] Depending on the rules of the union, the contract may have to be approved by the represented union members.

For employees to be represented by a union, 30% of all employees must sign "authorization cards" asking for recognition of the union. If the employer won't recognize the union or less than 50% of the employees sign, then the employees ask the National Labor Relations Board ("NLRB") to hold an election of the workers. The election to form a union is held by secret ballot and requires majority approval for passage. If fifty percent of employees sign the authorization cards, the employer can voluntarily waive the secret ballot and recognize the union. However, if over 50% of employees sign the authorization cards and the employer has engaged in unfair labor practices that jeopardize fair elections, the NLRB may waive the election requirement.

Employers may not (a) discriminate, spy on, harass, or terminate the employment of workers because of their union membership; (b) retaliate against them for engaging in organizing campaigns or other "concerted activities" to form "company unions"; or (c) refuse to engage in collective bargaining with the union that represents their employees. Workers who have elected to join a union often are obligated to pay dues to the union, for instance 1-2% of pay, even if they don't agree with union representation. However, in 20 states, mostly in the South, requiring employees to pay union dues is illegal.

RESTRICTIVE COVENANTS

A restrictive covenant is a promise to refrain from doing something for the benefit or protection of someone else. Restrictive covenants show up in all types of contracts, such as employment contracts, company owner agreements, merger or sale of business contracts, or in noncompetition contracts.

There are essentially three types of restrictive covenants: (1) confidentiality agreements; (2) nonsolicitations; and (3) noncompetes;

1. CONFIDENTIALITY AGREEMENT

A Confidentiality Agreement (a/k/a "NDA") is a promise to keep someone's information secret. To create a confidentiality agreement, you will need to define 7 things: (a) Discloser; (b) Recipient; (c) Confidential Information; (d) Duration; (e) Recipient Obligations; (f) OK Use; and (g) Penalties.

DISCLOSER

The "Discloser" is the person who is giving and owning the information and is entitled to secrecy. Confidentiality agreements may enable one discloser, but they can also enable disclosure by more than one party.

RECIPIENT

The "Recipient" is the person who gets the information and must keep it confidential. Once again, confidentiality agreements may enable one recipient or multiple recipients.

CONFIDENTIAL INFORMATION

Defining "Confidential Information" is critical, because you want to cover as much as needs to be confidential without being so broad that it would not be respected.

DURATION

How long the Recipient must keep the secret should be defined. More specifically, when does the obligation start and when does it end?

RECIPIENT OBLIGATIONS

You should define what the Recipient is obligated to do. Often, confidentiality agreements say he can't use Confidential Information other than as listed in the confidentiality agreement, and that he can't disclose it to anyone, including employees, unless the employee has a reason to know (and often has signed a confidentiality agreement of his own).

OK USE

There must be a point to disclosing the Confidential Information — specifically, how, when and for what purpose the Recipient can use the Confidential Information must be carefully defined. For instance, many confidentiality agreements get signed to enable a business to disclose secret information to a potential consultant; the consultant is usually allowed to review the Confidential Information for the purpose of putting together a proposal for the potential client.

But, there are also often activities or conditions that get pulled out of the secret-information-bucket. For instance, most confidentiality agreements say that the Recipient can disclose Confidential Information if it is widely known in the public through no fault of the Recipient. Some confidentiality agreements will also allow disclosure of any information that the Recipient can prove he created all on his own. And, there is a frightening exclusion floating through the confidentiality agreements of big tech companies that says that a Recipient can use Confidential Information if he retains it in his memory.

PENALTIES[7]

Finally, you may want to define what happens if the Recipient breaches. First, you definitely want injunctive relief – the ability to get a court to stop the loudmouth from continuing to expose your Confidential Information. But, in addition to injunctive relief, you may want to estimate the amount of injury caused by a breach and stick that in the contract. Also, you may want to stick in a "fee shifting" paragraph that entitles the wronged party to reimbursement of his legal fees, paid by the bad guy.

2. NONSOLICITATIONS

Nonsolicitations are promises to not go after relationships with people. Typically, these prohibit asking employees to leave a company for new opportunities or asking customers to reduce or eliminate purchases with the company.

3. NONCOMPETES

Employees (and stockholders or members of management who cash out) sometimes agree to refrain from competing with the company for a period of years.

ENFORCEABILITY

Noncompetes are sometimes not enforced by courts, though enforceability varies state by state.[8] Noncompetes are viewed as restraints on trade.[9] Usually, noncompetes cannot be used to keep competitors out of the marketplace - when someone leaves, they get to take their skills and knowledge, even skills and expertise they acquired during their employment, with them.

Noncompetes are often enforceable if they protect a legitimate business interest[10] only to protect (a) trade secrets (and customer lists kept under lock and key) and (b) long term customer relationships.[11] In addition, noncompetes must be reasonable in time, territory and activity restrictions. 3-5 years is usually the outer limit of an enforceable noncompete following a sale of a business. For employees, the enforceable restrictive period is usually no more than 1 – 2 years. The reasonableness of the territory and activity restrictions is usually determined based on the facts and circumstances. Finally, noncompetes have to be supported by some exchange of consideration. That can mean a job, money or some substantial promise from you. It is smart to actually pay the employee something for the noncompete. It is even smarter to get the noncompete reviewed, negotiated and signed as part of the employee's employment commencement. Noncompetes are more easily enforced when given in a sale of a business.

CREATING A NONCOMPETE

To create an agreement where one person promises to not compete, there are four things that need to be defined: (1) What activities constitute "competition?" (2) What geographic region(s) are included in the competitive market? (3) How long will the noncompete period last? (4) What triggers the noncompete?

DEFINE "COMPETITION"

In a noncompete, you promise not to do certain things that would compete with the business. Defining what the business is and what would be competitive with the business is the first pull and tug. The buyer will want a very broad definition and the seller will want a very narrow definition.

Imagine you are the producer of the largest Star Trek convention in the American Midwest and you are hiring a new guy, Benjamin, to manage your relationships with your customers, including the people who rent booths at the show and the people who buy tickets to attend the show. You want to make sure that Benjamin cannot meet your customers and then quit your company and start an identical one, using your rolodex as a launch pad.

First, you have to define the boundaries of the industry - the definition of your industry will be the sandbox Benjamin can't play in for a while if he leaves. You may be inclined to try to exclude Benjamin from any trade shows or from consumer expos. Benjamin may argue that your business revolves tightly around Star Trek conventions and not much else so the sandbox should be limited to just those. The sensible thing for you is to draw the boundary tightly around what you actually do. If you stretch the sandbox too broadly, it may not be enforced by a court.

DIFFERENT WAYS OF DEFINING COMPETITION

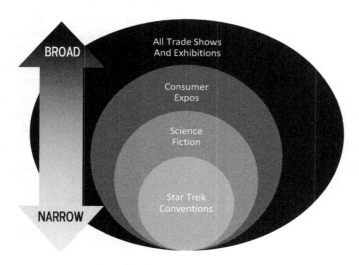

After defining the business Benjamin will stay out of, the next question is where in the world he will stay out of it. You may prefer that Benjamin refrain from competing all over the world, but most employees prefer something more tailored.

Let's say you hold your Star Trek convention in Milwaukee, Wisconsin (because of the cheese curds and beer). You may want Benjamin to stay away from working in Star Trek conventions all over the world, but demanding a territory much broader than where you actually operate could be problematic.

But, consider that the Star Trek convention market is a discrete, narrow and cohesive market – geography may be irrelevant. So, the struggle will be to find a balance between getting the whole world and getting just Wisconsin.

DEFINE DURATION OF NONCOMPETE

Next, you have to decide how long Benjamin is willing to stay out of the competitive marketplace. Typically, anything beyond 2 years is difficult to enforce, except in the context of company sales – for those, longer terms are more acceptable for two reasons. First, because it is regarded as an inducement to the buyer buying the business. Second, the sale of a business is relatively complex and, as a result, the seller is usually fully lawyered up and equipped to negotiate the noncompete.

How long to sit out of the market depends on a number of factors:

- ✓ How much Benjamin is getting paid
- ✓ The sales cycle
- ✓ Benjamin's other options for earning a living after you leave
- ✓ Estimated amount of time to transition his replacement

If the convention occurs only every two years, you may be able to reasonably insist that Benjamin sit out for at least one show without his competing force.

DEFINE NONCOMPETE TRIGGERS

A noncompete is designed to kick in when your employee leaves the company. But, in some cases, the departure isn't fair to the employee. The object is to trigger the noncompete only upon certain events.

NONCOMPETE TRIGGERS	MITIGATING FACTORS
On the employee's resignation	Unless he quits for a good reason (like discrimination)
If the employee is fired for cause	(and cause should be defined)
On his sale of stock in the company	Unless it is because your company goes public

OTHER WORKER PROTECTIONS

In addition to employment contracts, there are also laws that protect employees and effectively give them rights in their jobs. These laws forbid the employer to mistreat someone for reasons that go against our common values.

1. WRONGFUL DISCHARGE

In spite of the at-will-by-default rule, there are a few worker protections that have developed over the years. Employers can be liable for (a) breaching an implied promise; (b) terminating or altering employment to punish a whistleblower; (c) firing someone for making a worker's compensation claim or exercising a right; and (d) firing or treating workers in ways that violate public policy, such as serving on jury duty, for serving as a military reservist, for filing a workers' compensation claim, or for refusing to do an illegal act or whistle blowing.[12]

Tips to avoid retaliatory discharge. If you have to defend yourself against a wrongful or retaliatory discharge claim, having accurate and comprehensive documentation about all personnel and termination-related decisions would be invaluable:

- ✓ Set a regular schedule of employee reviews and stick to it
- ✓ Write, clearly and plainly, each employee's weaknesses and deficiencies (as well as good points)
- ✓ Treat all disciplines and warnings exactly the same
- ✓ Make sure the employee knows his employment is on thin ice, the steps he can take to fix the problem and why
- ✓ Evaluate and document specific reasons for termination
- ✓ Follow all review and termination policies
- ✓ Act in and reasonably document your good faith.

2. LAYOFFS

There are federal and state laws that require advance notice or severance payments to employees as part of a mass layoff or plant closing. For instance, the federal Worker Adjustment and Retraining Notification Act of 1988 ("Warn Act") requires employers to give 60 days' notice of plant closings and mass layoffs to workers, their union, the state dislocated worker unit and any other required government agency. All companies that have at least 100 employees with 6 months seniority are on the hook. This notice obligation gets triggered by a layoff of 50+ full time factory workers, a layoff of 50+ employees if that is 1/3 of all employees or a layoff of 500+ employees from a company of any size. WARN Act notices may also be triggered by sales of the business if they result in a big layoff. The WARN Act regulations and similar state laws are complex, so if you start to contemplate a reduction in force or a layoff, immediately check with a labor and employment lawyer.

CIVIL RIGHTS LAWS

Most companies are prohibited from treating individuals differently due to their identity. Specifically, the terms, conditions or benefits of employment cannot be affected by the employee's race, color, national origin, religion, sex, age, handicap or disability, and, in many areas, sexual orientation and veteran status. Each law affects companies that employ a certain minimum level of people – these minimums vary by law and by state.

Civil Rights laws include prohibitions against discrimination on the basis of (1) race & national origin; (2) religion; (3) sex; (4) age; (5) disability; and (6) sexual orientation.

1. RACIAL DISCRIMINATION AND NATIONAL ORIGIN

Discrimination on the basis of race means that due to an "ethnic characteristic," the terms, conditions, or benefits of employment were affected. Discrimination on the basis of national origin is also prohibited.

2. RELIGIOUS DISCRIMINATION

There are two kinds of religious discrimination: (1) "because of" religion, and (2) failure to accommodate religion. First, an employee cannot be discriminated against "because of" her religious beliefs. Second, employers must accommodate "legitimate" religious practices and beliefs as long as such accommodation does not create an unreasonable hardship on the business.

3. SEX DISCRIMINATION

Gender based sex discrimination occurs when an employment decision is made based on an individual's sex (the word "gender" has been increasingly used in this context). Sex discrimination laws apply equally to males as well as females.

SEXUAL HARASSMENT

The Supreme Court has said that sexual harassment is a form of sex discrimination.[13] There are two kinds of sexual harassment: (1) "quid pro quo" and (2) "hostile workplace." Both men and women may be victims of sexual harassment.

Quid Pro Quo. "Quid pro quo" harassment is when a superior uses his authority to gain sexual favors from an employee.

Hostile Workplace. A hostile workplace environment is when the victim is subjected to unwelcome conduct that is so severe or pervasive that it alters the conditions of employment and creates an abusive working environment[14]. As an employer, your responsibility is to take steps to prevent hostile workplace events and to process any complaints about them. Once you put in place an anti-harassment policy and procedures, the employees have an obligation to take the hard but necessary step of reporting any harassment. Talk to an employment lawyer about taking the following Anti-Sexual Harassment Steps.

ANTI - SEXUAL HARASSMENT STEPS:

1. Create a thorough anti-harassment policy and complaint reporting procedures and communicate it to all employees

2. Investigate all complaints thoroughly and confidentially

3. Take appropriate action following each and every investigation

4. AGE DISCRIMINATION

Employees over the age of 40 (usually) cannot be discriminated against on the basis of age.[15] But, (1) "bona fide executives in a high policy-making position," may be forcibly retired at 65 with retirement benefits, and (2) tenured employees in academia can be forcibly retired at 70.[16]

5. DISABILITY

The Americans With Disabilities Act of 1990 ("ADA") makes it illegal to discriminate against people with disabilities. Disabilities include physical or mental impairment that substantially limits one or more of the person's major life activities. The ADA prohibits employment discrimination only against qualified individuals who can perform the essential functions of the job with or without reasonable accommodation. "Essential" functions mean: (a) The position exists to perform the function; (b) the function is highly specialized; or (c) the person was hired for special expertise or ability.

Bottom line: if a qualified individual can perform the essential functions of the job, then he may not be discriminated against – employers must make reasonable accommodations for those qualified individuals. The ADA also prohibits all medical questions and examinations prior to an employment offer.

TIPS FOR EMPLOYMENT RECORDKEEPING

Under the ADA, employers must keep employment records for seven years. Those employment records should be kept under lock and key with access only given to supervisors with a need to know. In addition, many states require the employer to let the employee see his employment file at the employee's request. The types of records to be kept include:

✓ job applications and resumes

✓ incident reports, disciplinary proceedings and correspondence

✓ employment records, including pay and work records

✓ insurance benefits

UNDER THE ADA, YOU CAN:

1. Describe the job duties and ask the applicant how he/she would perform them

2. Give a test of physical agility, as long as they are given equally to all applicants. But, If these tests eliminate a large number of applicants, you may have to show that the test is job-related and part of a business necessity

Warning: One of my law partners (and friends) who specializes in employment law freaked out when she saw this box. She said, "THIS RARELY WORKS. DO NOT DO THIS WITHOUT GUIDANCE FROM AN EXPERIENCED EMPLOYMENT LAWYER." I can still hear her screaming. So, please follow her advice.

6. SEXUAL ORIENTATION

Many states and most cities prohibit discrimination on the basis of sexual orientation and, sometimes, gender.

SCREENING CANDIDATES

Various federal, state, county and local laws will probably require you to make your employment decisions based on individual merits, rather than because of an individual's characteristics, like sex, religion, national origin, age, disability, sexual orientation or veteran's status. So, when screening candidates, limit all questions to information that is job related.

Part of screening candidates includes (1) interview questions; (2) references; (3) background checks; and (4) drug and alcohol testing.

1. INTERVIEW QUESTIONS

Here are some helpful guidelines about questions you can and should not ask of a job candidate.

DO'S

Job-Related Questions. Interview questions should be job-related and focus on the candidate's academic preparation, related work experience, and depth of knowledge within the content area. Questions can also give the candidate a chance to discuss how he/she would handle job-related issues or events.

Disability Status. You can ask the candidate if she can perform the essential functions of the job, if there is anything that would prevent her from performing the job and how she will perform the essential functions of the job. But, don't ask about disabilities. If you ask about this, you should define, carefully and clearly, the essential functions of the job with your employment lawyer.

Dependability. You can ask about the candidate's previous records of tardiness and absences. You can ask the candidate if she can meet certain deadlines and schedules or if she has activities, commitments or responsibilities that would hinder meeting the job requirements. You can ask candidates about their expected duration in the position or anticipated absences, but only if you ask all candidates the same questions and weigh the answers equally.

Character. You can ask a candidate if she has been convicted of a crime if it is job related, the nature of the crime and the penalty, but you cannot ask about behavior or arrests.

Organizational Membership. You can ask a candidate about her clubs and memberships related to her ability to do the job, but not about her race, religion, national origin or ancestry.

References. You can request references.

Military Experience. You can ask a candidate about her military service, and his education and experience, but not his discharge.

Here are some things to avoid:

- ✓ her race, religion, gender, national origin, sexual orientation or age (except you can ask if she is over 18)
- ✓ her arrest record
- ✓ her marital status (including maiden name), family responsibilities, pregnancy or intent to have kids
- ✓ her health, family and worker's compensation history
- ✓ her military service record or lack thereof
- ✓ the applicant's financial condition, including troubles, liabilities or credit rating (except you can ask about his current or prior salary)
- ✓ the applicant's height and weight unless it is specifically job related
- ✓ if she has a disability, the prognosis of any medical condition and how often she gets medical treatment

2. REFERENCES

Get references to confirm the accuracy of the applicant's resume or job application. Former employers are less likely to actually provide a reference, other than to confirm dates of employment. Don't use the reference interview to get information about race, religion, gender, national origin, age, sexual orientation, etc.

3. BACKGROUND CHECK

Background checks into candidates are permitted, though there are restrictions on employer's use and disposal of information. For instance, if you want to do a credit check on a potential employee, you have to get written permission in a single document from the person to get the credit report and to use it in evaluating them. If you use information in the report to deny them something, you have to tell them the action taken, the name and address of the credit agency, that the credit agency didn't make the decision and that the applicant can get and contest the report.[17]

In some areas, if a reasonable background check on an applicant would have revealed a history of violent or bad behavior, but you don't do the background check, then you can be liable for the bad things your employee does while he works for you.

4. DRUG AND ALCOHOL TESTING

There are some laws prohibiting or limiting drug testing employees and these vary by state. The ADA prohibits discriminating on the basis of drug and alcohol addiction, as long as they are no longer using illegally. In addition, some industries actually require drug testing. For instance, the Department of Transportation requires drug testing drivers of commercial vehicles prior to employment, at any time for cause (good reason), post-accident, and periodically.

EMPLOYER OBLIGATIONS

Contracts and civil rights protections are just the beginning of employer obligations. There are also (a) wage and hour rules; (b) withholding; (c) workplace safety; (d) immigration verification; (e) family medical leave; (f) proprietary rights agreement; and (g) recordkeeping;

WAGES & OVERTIME

Wage and hour rules[18] are the rules that require (1) minimum wages and overtime pay after 40 hours; and (2) child labor restrictions.

1. MINIMUM WAGES AND OVERTIME

Here is the general rule: Each employee must be paid overtime once he hits 40 hours in a week, unless he is exempt. Employees not entitled to minimum wage or overtime pay are the exceptions, not the rule. So who is exempt?

TYPICALLY EXEMPT (SO NO OVERTIME)

In an example of the government's dreadful naming practices, a "nonexempt" employee has to be paid minimum wage and an "exempt" employee does not have to be paid minimum wage. Contrary to popular belief, salaried employees are not all exempt from wage and hour laws. Any worker performing repetitive tasks is most likely nonexempt and must be paid overtime. In contrast, exempt employees include executives, professionals, administration and outside sales, as well as computer software professionals and highly compensated employees.

Executive. Executives are people who make a salary basis of $455+ per week; and customarily and regularly direct the work of two or more employees, manage an enterprise, a department or departmental subdivision, have the authority to hire and fire; and use discretionary powers. An executive can also be a person who owns at least 20% of the enterprise and manages the business.

Professional. Professionals perform nonstandardized work that requires advanced knowledge acquired by a prolonged course, or original and creative efforts in a recognized field or artistic endeavor, exercising discretion and independent judgment (e.g. teachers, engineers and attorneys, highly skilled computer software workers).

Administrative. Administrative personnel earn a salary basis of $455+ per week, and primarily perform office or non-manual work directly related to management policies or general business operations, and customarily and regularly exercises discretion and independent judgment on significant matters.[19]

Outside salesperson. An outside salesperson sells goods or services offsite, regularly works away from the office and spends no more than 20 percent of their time in non-selling hours.

Computer Software Professional. A computer professional earns $455 per week or $27.63 per hour; and is employed as a computer systems analyst, programmer, computer engineer, etc., and primarily performs systems analysis regarding technology system specifications or operations.

Highly Compensated Employee. A highly compensated employee is a person who makes $100,000 per year or more in compensation (not including benefits); primarily does office work and typically performs duties of an executive, administrative or professional.

BASIC WAGE AND HOUR RULES

Minimum Wage. The federal government requires that all nonexempt employees get paid a minimum wage – currently $7.25 per hour for non-gratuity jobs. Some states have higher minimum wages – where there is a choice, the worker is entitled to the higher minimum wage.

⇨ An overview of minimum wages is at www.dol.gov/whd/minwage/america

Overtime. Nonexempt workers are typically entitled to 1.5x their regular rates for hours worked beyond 40 in a workweek. However, some states have overtime laws that offer better benefits to employees. When counting hours worked, include all hours the person worked and all hours that you or another supervisor of the employee knew or had reason to know he worked.

To figure out your obligations, check out:

⇨ www.dol.gov/elaws/overtime
⇨ www.dol.gov/elaws

Comp time. It is illegal for private employers to give nonexempt employees comp time (time off) instead of paying them overtime.

Breaks. Employers must follow federal and state law rules for providing employees with breaks.

2. CHILD LABOR

Federal and state laws have special rules about workers younger than 18, including type of work, wages, and hours that an employee can work. Under federal law, kids younger than 14 cannot work; kids 14 and 15 are restricted in hours of work and permitted jobs; and kids under 18 cannot do some hazardous activities.

PAYROLL AND PAYROLL TAXES

The easiest way to deal with payroll is to hire an outside service. Paychex, ADP and a variety of other companies take care of the whole burden of paying payroll and reporting and paying withholding to the federal government – you just have to supply information and money. You can also take advantage of the many software solutions that help companies manage payroll. The U.S. government also offers a free software program that allows you to check your W-2 reports for accurate compliance with withholding requirements. That software is called Accuwage and here is the link:

⇨ http://www.ssa.gov/employer/accuwage/.

WORKPLACE SAFETY

There are federal, state and local laws that require you to maintain a safe workplace.

The health and safety conditions of every workplace are subject to strict requirements. The Occupational Safety and Health Administration ("OSHA") is the main federal agency in charge of workplace issues. Under OSHA, employers engaged in interstate commerce with 10 employees are required to: (1) write down work place injuries; (2) keep records of employment; (3) post OSHA notice; and (4) have a plan for hazard communication, emergency action, fire safety, exit routes, walking surfaces and medical & first aid.

Occupational safety and health rules in the U.S are mostly standardized by OSHA which operates job safety and health programs in twenty-nine states, including conducting inspections and enforcing its standards. States with approved programs must set job safety and health standards that are "at least as effective as" comparable federal standards. Nearly every state will have their share of these types of regulations. State agencies may also require hanging posters (e.g. a wage payment rights poster).

⇨ Go to www.osha.gov for guidance and posters.

IMMIGRATION AND TAX FORMS

1. IMMIGRATION FORMS

Every employer has to get, examine and copy proof of the new employee's identity and his authorization to work. This information is collected through Form I-9, a standard Immigration form. Failure to get Form I-9 at the time of hiring is a violation of federal immigration law[20]. The penalty is "employer sanctions."

You can ask if the applicant is authorized to work in the US on a full time basis for any employer, but you can't ask his immigration status.

- ✓ Fill out the "Employment Eligibility Verification" form (INS Form I-9) http://www.formi9.com/
- ✓ Examine and make a copy of the employee's identification; the list of acceptable documents is on the last page of Form I-9
- ✓ Examine and make a copy of the employee's social security card or "qualifying documents" of their right to work

2. TAX FORMS

FOR EMPLOYEES

If you hire an employee, have the person fill out a Form W-4.

INDEPENDENT CONTRACTOR

If you hire an independent contractor, have the person fill out a Form W-9, which you can get from www.irs.gov. Through the W-9, you should get their Social Security Number or FEIN. If they do not give you a SSN or FEIN, you may be required to do "backup withholding," which is withholding the percentage of their pay at the IRS backup withholding rate. For 2011, the backup withholding rate is 28%. If you have to do backup withholding, then (a) deduct 28% of their pay; (b) pay the tax to the United States Treasury; (c) write down the amount you withheld on Form 10-99-MISC; and (d) give Form 1099 to the contractor by January 31 of the next year.

FAMILY MEDICAL LEAVE ACT ("FMLA")

Your employees may have a right to take a leave of absence due to illness, whether his or in his family. The big law in this area is the federal Family Medical Leave Act (aka "FMLA"), but there are also similar types of laws in about 15 states. These states have family and medical leave law: California, Connecticut, Hawaii, Maine, Minnesota, New Jersey, Oregon, Rhode Island, Vermont, Washington, and Wisconsin and the District of Columbia.

Under the federal and many state laws, companies with 50 or more employees (and all public agencies) have to give employees up to 12 weeks of unpaid, job-protected leave each year after the birth or adoption of a kid or for the serious health condition of the employee or of the employee's child, spouse, or parent. Employees are required to get permission for some leaves and to give advance notice of foreseeable ones. But, some states have laws more favorable to the employee. For instance, in Kentucky all employees get reasonable personal leave up to 6 weeks. Also, two states – California and New Jersey – have paid leave at reduced rates that is funded through special payroll taxes. Once again, another reason to have a good employment lawyer.

However, there are obligations on employees to get permission for some leaves and to give advance notice of foreseeable medical absences.

PROPRIETARY RIGHTS AGREEMENT & EMPLOYEE MANUAL

If you have an employee manual, provide a copy to the worker on the first day. This is also a good time to have the employee sign your proprietary rights agreement. A Proprietary Rights Agreement is a written confirmation and assignment of all intellectual property ("IP") created or developed by the worker. If you have chosen to have your workers review and sign agreements with Restrictive Covenants, provide the drafts to the worker before or on the first day. Make sure you give the worker a chance to review the document, get their own legal help to understand it and make a decision about whether to sign it or choose to not go forward with their work for you.

RECORDKEEPING

Finally, employers have a huge recordkeeping burden not only as good practice, but also under various statutes. There are recordkeeping obligations under the Fair Labor Standards Act, Americans with Disabilities Act, Family and Medical Leave Act, OSHA, tax, wage and hour, immigration and other laws. The state where your employee is located probably has different or additional recordkeeping requirements. Find out what they are and comply.

1. FAIR LABOR STANDARDS ACT

For instance, under the rules of the Fair Labor Standards Act ("FLSA"), every employer must make and keep records of non-exempt workers for 3 years, including:

- ✓ Employee's full name and social security number
- ✓ Address, including zip code
- ✓ Birth date, if younger than 19
- ✓ Sex and occupation
- ✓ Time and day of week when employee's workweek begins
- ✓ Hours worked each day
- ✓ Total hours worked each workweek
- ✓ Basis on which employee's wages are paid (e.g., "$9 per hour" or "$440 a week")
- ✓ Regular hourly pay rate
- ✓ Total daily or weekly straight-time earnings
- ✓ Total overtime earnings for the workweek
- ✓ All additions to or deductions from the employee's wages
- ✓ Total wages paid each pay period
- ✓ Date of payment and the pay period covered by the payment
- ✓ Any other payroll records
- ✓ Collective bargaining agreements

- ✓ Sales and purchase records
- ✓ Time cards, piece work tickets and wage rate tables (2 years)

These records must be open for inspection by the U.S. Department of Labor.

2. FAMILY MEDICAL LEAVE ACT

Under FMLA, employers have to keep records for 3 years, including:

- ✓ employee data, including name, address, occupation, rate or basis of pay and terms of compensation, daily and weekly terms of hours worked per pay period, additions to or deductions from wages, and total compensation paid. Hours worked records need not be kept
- ✓ Dates FMLA leave is taken by employees and designated in records as FMLA leave. If FMLA leave is taken in increments of less than one (1) full day, the hours of the leave.
- ✓ Copies of employee request for leave and copies of all supporting documents and notices given to employees.
- ✓ Any documents (including written and electronic records) describing employee benefits or policies and practices regarding the taking of paid and unpaid leaves.
- ✓ Premium payments of employee benefits.
- ✓ Records of any dispute with employee regarding leave.

3. OCCUPATIONAL SAFETY AND HEALTH ADMINISTRATION

Employers engaged in interstate commerce with 10 employees are required to: (1) write down work place injuries; (2) keep records of employment and maintain the following information:

- ✓ Injury and illness records.
- ✓ Accident investigation reports
- ✓ Workers' compensation claims and records
- ✓ Material safety data sheets (MSDS)
- ✓ Labels for hazardous chemicals in the workplace
- ✓ Chemical inventories
- ✓ Records of worker exposure to chemicals, noise, radiation, or other hazards

- ✓ Workplace inspection reports by a safety committee, safety and health personnel, OSHA, insurance carriers, fire departments, or other outside agencies
- ✓ Job safety analysis, including ergonomic evaluations of jobs or workstations
- ✓ Employee medical records or studies or evaluations based on these records
- ✓ OSHA standards and the background data on which they are based
- ✓ Resources to Help You figure out employment laws

4. TAX & COMPENSATION

Employers are obligated to keep records of worker compensation as well as copies of the worker's tax forms filled out at the beginning of the working relationship, such as Form W-4 and W-9.

5. IMMIGRATION

Every employer must keep copies of the worker's completed Employment Eligibility Verification" form (INS Form I-9) and acceptable identification document.

6. RESOURCES

There are resources available to help businesses figure out labor and employment laws. Below are some examples of these resources.

Business Relations Group. This resource helps businesses understand the workforce system, identify their key workforce challenges, and connect to federal, state, and local resources.

⇒ www.doleta.gov
⇒ www.doleta.gov/business

Office of Small Business Programs (OSBP). This resource administers opportunities for small businesses, small disadvantaged businesses, women-owned small businesses, HUBZone businesses, and businesses owned by service-disabled veterans. OSBP serves as the Department's Ombudsman for small businesses under the Small Business Regulatory Enforcement Fairness Act (SBREFA).

⇒ www.dol.gov/osbp

⇨ www.dol.gov/osbp/sbrefa/poster

⇨ www.dol.gov/osbp/sbrefa

Poster Advisor. Poster Advisor is designed to help employers comply with the poster requirements of several laws administered by DOL.

⇨ www.dol.gov/elaws/posters.htm

Note: You will also need to figure out the employee posters required by your state.

FirstStep Employment Law Advisor. This resource helps employers determine major federal employment laws apply to their business or organization.

⇨ www.dol.gov/elaws/firststep

HAP AND HAZ MEET SEYMOUR

When Gravity finished, Hazard said,

"Thanks, Gravity. Now, I know where to start."

"We do?" asked Hap.

"Yes. We do."

Still confused, Hap said,

"No, I'm confused."

"Hap, we just need to make a plan."

"But, how?"

"She just told us."

Exasperated, Hazard said,

"Gravity?"

Accustomed to losing people with her explanations, Gravity said,

"Look, it's very simple:

First, Specify. Write down what you want in your product as specifically as possible."

Search. Then, find groups interested in doing the same things you are — green technologies, sustainable businesses, computer accessory makers, solar power.

Study what they are talking about, go meet them and make friends. Ask them for referrals for engineers. And, do a little search for engineers who know something about your needs.

Consider locating an industrial designer who can help you with the product. Industrial designers are both engineers and artists. They focus on the usability and user experience of a product. They usually work with the engineers and marketing people on design of the product. They can be found through the Industrial Design Society of America.

Find 10 candidates you want to talk to. You can also include students if you want to take the risk on their expertise.

Solicit. Get a draft of a confidentiality agreement that prohibits the firm from using or disclosing your request or their designs. Only the candidates that (a) return your phone calls; and (b) sign a reasonable confidentiality agreement should stay on your radar. Submit your request for a proposal to these candidates. Ask for bids for production of designs. If a candidate asks for clarification, produce a restated bid request and send it to the other candidates, so that you are comparing apples to apples.

Solidify. Once you have narrowed your choices, confirm in writing the terms like price, quantity, specs and deadlines. They will come back with corrections — that's negotiating. Just keep working back and forth until you get a deal (or don't). Don't just base your decision on price — consider the professionalism and expertise. Make sure you work with me or another lawyer to help you with the engineering services agreement. And, don't forget to get ownership rights confirmed in writing if you can.

Start your designer.

Hap and Hazard did exactly as Gravity instructed. And that's how they found Seymour.

Seymour was a double whammy — a mechanical engineer and an electrical engineer. He also had a mild case of Asperger's Syndrome. Seymour spent his days alone, in a small workshop of tools and measures. He worked standing up at a tall, wide table that he positioned in the center of the room, under a domed skylight that provided heat and light. Seymour favored white short-sleeve dress shirts with brown ties and pleated pants. He was a genius.

SECTION ONE: GETTING ORGANIZED

Seymour had long ago adjusted to life on his own. With nothing – and no one - to distract him, he became the best solar power expert in the world. His blogs and columns about the future of mobile, renewable energy drove the leading edge of knowledge and experimentation.

As a subscriber to Seymour's blog, Hazard hung on his every word. He knew that Seymour would have the answer for how to build the MouseTrap, but he couldn't get up the nerve to reach out.

Finally, Hap said,

> "Haz, what about that guy you're always reading – the blogger guy who sees more."

> "You mean Seymour. I've thought about it, but I don't want to bother him."

> "Nonsense, Haz. He'd probably love to talk to his biggest fan."

> "I don't know, Hap. Why would he want to talk to me? He's a genius and I'm an accountant in the soap maker's workroom."

> "Haz, he's just a man. He would probably love to talk to you. And, what if he doesn't – what's the worst thing that can happen?"

> "He could yell at me. He could laugh at me. He could ignore me."

> "Then he's a dick."

> "Hap! Don't say that."

> "Seriously, Haz. Who cares?"

> "Then he wouldn't be my hero and I need heroes."

> "No, Haz. You just think you need heroes. What you really need are friends you admire."

> "Okay, Hap, I'll give it a try."

So, Haz spent 3 hours writing an email to Seymour.

Seymour, alone under his big skylight, saw the email, and rushed to his computer.

From: Hazard
To: Seymour
Subject: Your Biggest Fan

Dear Mr. Seymour:
I am familiar with your work. In fact, I subscribe to your newsletter, your blog, your podcast, your vlodcast, your forum, your FAQ, your Facebook page, your MySpace page and your fan club. I also follow your Tweets. You might say I am your biggest fan. My friend and I are trying to build a solar powered battery that can be embedded in a mouse or keyboard to power a laptop. Unfortunately, we don't know how.   I am interested in your thoughts. I know that if there is anyone in the world who can figure this out, it is you.

I hope that this email does not distract you from your work, and that you do not think it an imposition and that I didn't annoy you with my stupid questions, and that you don't mind taking the time to read this (although if you don't have time to respond, I completely understand, it's an honor just to send a note to your personal email address, so a reply would be nearly overwhelming, and anyway I told Hap you were too busy to respond, but he insisted, so really this is all his fault, because he made me send this.)

Thank you for your time.
Your fan,
Hazard

Seymour responded immediately:

From: Seymour
To: My Biggest Fan
Subject: Let's Talk

Dear Hazard:
Thank you for your email. I know that you are my biggest fan. I
recognize your email address from my Leonard Cohen Covercast.
I have very many ideas about how to help you. What you want to do
is possible and even scalable. But, you are right. You cannot
just hookup batteries to solar panels. It is more complicated
than that and it will take more of a patchwork of rights and
technologies.
I would be happy to talk with you about this. Perhaps we could
set up a Skype video conference. I have time later today.
Sincerely,
Seymour

"Hap! He wants to talk to us."

"Haz, I told you. He's just a guy. Maybe he'll become your friend instead of your hero."

And that is precisely what happened when Hap, Haz and Seymour got on a conference call.

During the call, Haz and Seymour talked a mile a minute, while Hap doodled and surfed.

"The key in portable, scalable solar technology is understanding solar energy itself. Sunlight hits a solar cell. Because of some unique structure of the solar cell, the sunlight charges the electron of the solar cell, severing it from its positive atom core. The severed electron is the electrical energy. A solar cell has a charge separation device that does the severing. One type of commonly used charge separation device is a photovoltaic cell. But, photovoltaic cells are both expensive and inefficient — they waste a lot of energy during the separation. This makes for expensive energy. What is critical is to discover or invent a new way to sever the electron from the atom. That new severing technology is a combination of nanoparticles and semiconductors that can be essentially spray painted onto a mouse. Once a stabilizer is applied, the nanoparticles create tiny solar panels that collect, transform and store the energy. The energy then recharges and powers the battery."

"That's all?"

"That's all. I have developed most of the technology you need. I even have patents. Maybe we could talk about some arrangement where you use my invention."

"Seymour, we do have a problem."

"What's that?"

Hap broke in.

"We don't have any money."

Seymour replied, "Oh. Well, you'll need some of that for manufacturing. But, I typically just take a royalty and stock."

Hap said, "Thanks, Seymour. We don't know how to make that happen, but we'll talk to our lawyer and get back to you. Maybe we could also take you to lunch?"

Seymour replied, "Of course. I'd like that."

Hap and Hazard danced a jig.

And then they went to see Gravity.

***

Gravity was very busy when they arrived (they hadn't made an appointment).

"Hello, Boys, is everything ok?"

"Yes, Gravity. Everything is terrific. We just need some advice. We have figured out that the MouseTrap is possible, but now we need to know the next step."

"I understand. You can wait in my office until I'm done, if you like. I'm in the middle of closing a deal, but as soon as we fund, I'll come in and talk with you."

Gravity returned a couple of hours later.

Hap and Hazard told Gravity about their progress, about Seymour and their plans.

"Excellent news. Have you worked out the terms of the license with Seymour?"

"Seymour says he gets a royalty and stock."

"That sounds fair, though we'll have to negotiate the royalty rate. You may want to lock down your ability to license his technology, just in case. You can do that by paying him something in exchange for an option to the license.

He may be willing to enter into a standstill agreement, which is a promise to not talk to anyone else until he gets some resolution with you."

"That sounds good, Gravity. Can you work that out for us?"

"I can try. If you get me the name of Seymour's lawyer, I'll give it a shot."

Within a week, Gravity had worked out a letter with Seymour's lawyer to secure a 120-day option on an exclusive license to Seymour's technology for use in a mobile computer accessory. The price for the option was $500.00, a paltry sum.

Hap and Hazard visited Gravity to sign the option letter agreement and to deliver a check for $500.

With check in hand, Gravity said, "Now that you are beginning to take on outside commitments, it is time for you to formally set up your company."

"We don't know how to set up a company. Can you help us, Gravity?"

"I CAN TRY."

SET UP YOUR COMPANY

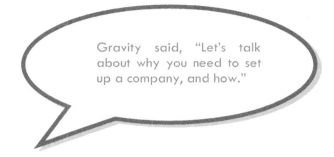

Gravity said, "Let's talk about why you need to set up a company, and how."

CHAPTER 03

WHY YOU NEED AN ENTITY

An "entity" is an invisible box that holds your business. It is like a Kevlar suit for your company – it gives you a professional appearance and a chance at safety from bullets. That is because many (though not all) entities have limited liability.

"Limited Liability" is a shield protecting owners of a company from liability beyond what they have invested. Without limited liability, you as the owner are personally on the hook for your business's debts. (Limited liability does not protect against liability for crimes, harassment, securities violations, failure to pay your employees' withholding to the IRS, fraud or environmental liability.)

Limited liability only comes with entities that you have to set up with a state government – corporations, limited liability companies ("LLC"), and limited partnerships ("LP"). It is regarded as a privilege and an incentive for business people – for the privilege you must authorize your state's Secretary of State to accept service of process on your behalf (plus pay an actual fee to the state each year).

HOW TO SET UP YOUR ENTITY

There are five steps to setting up your company: (1) Pick your tax treatment; (2) Pick your entity; (3) Pick a state; (4) Pick a name; and (5) File!

1. PICK YOUR TAX TREATMENT

Income in a business gets taxed.[21] Business income tax can be divided into two broad categories: (a) C-corporation tax treatment; and (b) pass through tax treatment. The first decision you need to make is to pick the tax treatment that is right for you.

A company that has **C-Corporation tax treatment** pays taxes on its profits and files its own tax return. The drawback to C-Corporation tax treatment is that the entity pays taxes on its profits and then when the entity sends cash to its owners, the owners pay tax on it again (that is called "double taxation.")

A company that has **pass-through tax treatment** is not a tax payer. Instead, the taxes due on the business's income get passed through to the business's owners. Business owners are responsible for their pro rata share of the businesses' taxes regardless of how much cash they get from the business; they can also use their share of the company's losses to reduce the tax they would ordinarily owe.

TAX TREATMENT OF ENTITIES	
PASS THROUGH	C-CORPORATION
✓ S-Corp	✓ C-Corporations
✓ LLC	✓ Any pass through entity that elects to be treated as a C-Corp by filing an election (Form 8832) with the IRS
✓ Partnerships	

Pass-Through Disadvantages. There are disadvantages to picking pass through tax treatment. The biggest one is that you may not have the cash to pay the tax when it is due. Remember that company owners pay taxes on the profits of the business. If you own 50% of a company, you have to pay 50% of the tax due on that company's profits. This risk usually gets managed with a promise to kick out cash to owners to cover taxes. But, sometimes, there is no cash to distribute to you to fund that tax. Much of the time, having income means your business had revenue. If there were big expenses that year that ate up cash, those expenses may be deducted from revenues, reducing how much tax you owe. But, if you have a year in which your business made capital improvements or paid down debt, your business could be profit rich, but cash poor. Worse, sometimes majority owners use the tax liability as a weapon to harass, bother or get rid of minority owners, by issuing a 1099 to a minority owner that has a tax liability, but then refusing to issue cash to cover the taxes.

C-Corp Disadvantages. There are also disadvantages to filing as a C-Corporation. First, the C-Corporation imposes two levels of tax on distributions of profits. Dividends are not deductible by the corporation which is the reason that closely held businesses often prefer to pay out officer salaries instead because salaries are deductible. The IRS and courts realize that taxpayers over-pay owner salaries, so they impose reasonableness tests on salary levels based upon the work performed by the owners. When salaries are over-stated, the salaries could be reclassified as dividends. Second, a separate return needs to be filed, each year (in contrast, a sole proprietorship or single member Limited Liability Company does not require a separate return to be filed). Third, losses may be trapped in the corporate entity and not allowed to offset an owner's tax on income from other sources.

2. PICK AN ENTITY

Based on your choice of tax treatment, the next step is to pick a business entity.

There are essentially five types of business entities being used today: (a) Sole Proprietorships; (b) Partnerships; (c) Limited Liability Companies; (d) Corporations; and (e) Trusts.

SOLE PROPRIETORSHIPS

A sole proprietorship is not an entity – it is a business operated by a single person without an entity. Cheap, no frills. It is the default form of business if you do nothing to form your company and you are the only owner. You report business taxes on your own income tax return on Schedule C or F. There is no limited liability. It is nearly impossible to get investors, because that would transform the entity into a partnership and the investor would be a partner without limited liability. And, you can't use "Inc" or "LLC" or the like in your company name.

PARTNERSHIPS

General Partnership. A partnership is two or more people joined together to operate a business for profit. It is the default form of business entity if you do nothing to set up an entity and you own your business with other people or companies. Partnerships have pass through tax treatment, and are not separate, taxable entities. The partners pay their pro rata share of the income and loss on their own income tax return. The advantages of partnerships are that they are cheap and easy to set up and partners usually have equal management rights, which can also be a disadvantage. To vary egalitarian management, you have to write a partnership agreement. Partnerships have no limited liability - a partner can be on the hook for all of the business debts, regardless of how small his ownership piece.

Limited Partnership ("LP"). A limited partnership is a special kind of partnership that must be formed by filing a document with a state. In a limited partnership, at least one owner has to be the "General Partner" and at least one owner has to be a "Limited Partner." The General Partner usually runs the business. Often, though not always, the limited partner is "silent," in that they invest in the business, but they don't work in or manage the business. The General Partner doesn't get limited liability – it is on the hook for the entity's obligations; but the limited partner does get limited liability. Limited partnerships have pass through tax treatment. Limited partnerships are a decent option for investors who have no real role in management. Further, if you have foreign partners, this may be the only option for limited liability and pass through tax treatment. LPs are losing a little luster in the age of LLCs.

Limited Liability Partnership ("LLP"). This is a combination of a corporation and a partnership, usually only for professional entities – like lawyers and doctors. Limited liability varies considerably from state to state. Owners have pass through tax treatment and some flexibility in the ability to structure management, profits, losses and cash to owners.

LIMITED LIABILITY COMPANIES

A limited liability company ("LLC") is a combination of a corporation and a partnership. LLC owners have limited liability and pass through tax treatment. The great advantage of an LLC is its flexibility. You can pretty much shape and reshape the inner workings of the LLC in a variety of ways, including structure of management and allocations of profits, losses and distributions of cash to members. If an entity can be hip, this is it. Its disadvantages are that it is still not desirable on the IPO market, so LLCs typically have to get converted to C-Corporations before the IPO. Because it has only been around since the 1990's, there is just a smattering of case law to look to for guidance. The filing fee is usually a little more expensive than other entity filing fees.

Single-Owner LLC. To the taxman, an LLC that has just one owner is a disregarded entity, a/k/a a "tax nothing." The owner of the company is looked at as the owner of the company's assets. The LLC is treated like a branch of the owner. As a result, the singly owned LLC doesn't have to file a tax return – the taxes get reported on the owner's return.

CORPORATIONS

A corporation is the graying workhorse of business entities – tough, weathered and predictable. It gives owners limited liability. The owners are "shareholders" or "stockholders." Shareholders elect directors who sit on a Board of Directors and direct policy and hire and supervise management. The entity may be closely held, where there are only a few Owners, or may be publicly held, where there are a large amount of Owners and the stock is sold on a public market. On the downside, corporations have to comply with

"corporate formalities," including annual votes by the Owners. A corporation can be either a C-Corporation or
S-Corporation, both of which are tax classifications.

C-Corporation. If you just setup a corporation (by filing articles of incorporation), you would have a "C-Corporation."

S-Corporation. An S-Corporation is a C-Corporation that has been converted to pass through tax treatment. You get that pass through tax treatment by filing an S-election on IRS Form 2553.

The tax man has lots of rules about what you can and can't do with an S-Corp. First, no business can own shares in an S-Corp – only people, some trusts and estates can own an S-Corp. That means that if you want to get funding from a venture capital firm or anyone who wants to invest through their company, you cannot be an S-Corp. Second, you can't have more than one class of stock, though you can have voting and nonvoting stock so long as all stock has equal rights to money. Third, you can't have more than 100 owners of an S-corporation. Fourth, there are limits to what the S-Corporation can do. For instance, S-Corporations cannot be internationally based, a financial institution or an insurance company. These limitations led frustrated business owners to demand the LLC.

TRUSTS

And, finally, there are trusts. A trust has four components: a trustee, a beneficiary, assets and rules. The rules come mostly from a document that establishes the trust and lays out it purposes and powers. The trust document names a trustee who controls and sort of owns all the assets. A trustee does everything with the assets solely for the beneficiary. The beneficiary is the person who gets all the good things flowing from the trust. For instance, if real estate investors set up land trusts to hold property, the beneficiaries probably get the distributions of cash from rents. Every trustee has a bunch of legal obligations to protect the assets, which demotivates the trustee from taking risks. Plus, the limited liability elements of a trust are funky and have to be put into the trust document in a way that doesn't violate a century of law. As a result, trusts are not good entities for running a business. However, trusts are used frequently by lawyers crafting sophisticated asset protection plans for rich people. Since that's not my purpose in life, I don't use them that often.

THOUGHTS ON ENTITY SELECTION

Flexibility & Creativity. If you need an entity that allows structural and governance changes or even creative arrangements, then you may want to stick with an LLC, a C-Corporation, or a Limited Partnership.

Money Split. In an S-Corp, you must split profits and losses by share ownership. In an LLC/partnership, you have more flexibility to divide profits.

Self-Employment Tax. Many experts believe that you pay more in an LLC for self-employment tax than in an S-Corp. That is because, in an LLC, you have to pay self-employment tax of 12.4% for Social Security on the first $106,800 of the business profits allocated to you plus 2.9% for Medicare of all business profits allocated to you. In contrast, in an S-Corp, you just pay self-employment tax on the money you get for compensation, but not on your share of the business cash distributions. If there will be income losses, the owners may want to start with pass thru tax treatment so that they can use the losses to offset other income, particularly if they work in the business.

Losses. Business and tax planners therefore typically advise new businesses that expect to have losses to elect pass through tax treatment so the owners can deduct losses currently against their other income from investments or another business. If there will be income losses, the owners may want to start with pass thru tax treatment so that they can use the losses to offset other income, particularly if they work in the business.

No Stock Options. An LLC can't give incentive stock options.

Sweat Equity. If someone is putting in sweat equity, and others are putting in cash, an LLC may be the best choice.

Investors and IPO's. The type of entity you pick may depend on your future finance plans. If you know you want pass through tax treatment but you are going to solicit venture capital, then don't go with an S-Corp (because S-Corps can only be owned by people). If you know for certain you are going to go public, then consider just starting with a C-Corp, because it is more preferred on the market.

Your Patience and Resources for Administration. Once you set up a company, there will be pain in the ass tasks you will have to do every month and year – taxes, filings, bank account monitoring and balancing, and holding meetings of your board, management and the owners. Sometimes, people spend way too much time and money in the beginning to get the entity perfect, draining resources from their launch; and sometimes people do too little, failing to make workable plans to avoid a catastrophe in the future. People also often create a complicated and hectic arrangement that requires more administrative attention than they want to or will give it. You should consider realistically how much complexity you (a) need; and (b) can handle, and don't do anything fancier than that. What constitutes fancy? Answer: more than a single class of shares, share vesting schedules, preferred shares, different levels of approval rights, guaranteed dividends and a first-paid-and-out rule, among others.

3. PICK A STATE

Before you can set up your entity, you have to decide where you are going to set it up. You may have heard that many companies set up in Delaware and Nevada. There are two reasons for that. First, states like Delaware have created an industry in their state out of providing a place for companies to organize. Delaware makes it easy, keeps the fees relatively low and maintains a very good infrastructure to handle organization. Second, Delaware law and courts are exceptional. The statutes are well written and relatively clear. These laws favor management, enabling enormous flexibility and, occasionally, some mayhem. The Delaware courts are highly regarded (not something you can say about all state courts), stocked with sober, smart judges and sensible procedures. Because of these things, lawyers and academics have an opportunity and a need to study Delaware statutes and cases, creating a snowball effect of incorporation. Incorporating in Delaware is a little like wearing an Armani suit – it shows you've got some savvy and you mean business.

But, if you do not live in Delaware, there are drawbacks to incorporating there. If you do business in a limited liability entity, you have to incorporate in the state you do business in and you have to register your company with every other state where you do business. This registration is usually called "Certificate of Authority" or "getting qualified." Like your incorporation, you have to re-up this registration every year with a report and a payment. Incorporating in Delaware will not relieve you of any obligations you have to pay fees or taxes in the state in which you have business activities. So, if you just need an uncomplicated organization, you may just want to file in your own state where you live and where you will locate your office.

4. PICK YOUR NAME

Each company needs to have a unique name. Once you identify a bunch of names as options, search the Secretary of State website for corporate filings in the state where you will organize for any entity name that is identical to the name you want to use.

In addition, in many situations, a company name should not be used if it is too similar to another company's name or trademarks. The name you want to pick should not violate someone's trademark.

DIFFERENT ENTITIES = DIFFERENT WORDS						
QUESTION	SOLE PROPRIETORSHIP	GENERAL PARTNERSHIP	LIMITED PARTNERSHIP	LIMITED LIABILITY COMPANY	CORPORATION	S CORPORATION
Owners are called...	Sole proprietor	Partners	Limited Partner and General Partner	Members	Shareholders or Stockholders	
Units of Ownership are...	N/A	Partnership interests	General Partnership Interest; Limited Partnership Interest	Membership Interests; Interests; Units	Stock or shares	
Governing documents are called...	N/A	Partnership Agreement	Limited Partnership Agreement	Operating Agreement or LLC Agreement	Articles of Incorporation and any Certificates of Designation; Bylaws; Shareholders Agreement	
Management is called...	Sole Proprietor	Partner; Managing Partner	General Partner (may also be an owner)	Manager (although can be managed by the Members)	Board of Directors: Directors, Chair Officers: CEO, President, Vice Presidents, other titles created	

You also may want a domain name that is relatively close to your company name. Sometimes, names are already taken, or it is difficult to get a domain name that is similar to your company name. It is smart to resist the tendency to make the name too long or containing letters of different cases and punctuation - those names get annoying to type.

5. SET-UP AND FILE

FILE AN ORGANIZATIONAL DOCUMENT

To set up an entity, you have to file a form. The form is usually on the Secretary of State website in the state in which you want to file. The form name differs from entity to entity (see Entity Comparison chart). Once the completed form is filled out, it gets filed, along with a filing fee, with the Secretary of State. Sometimes, the form will be rejected, but it's usually easy to fix and resubmit. Once the articles are filed and accepted, the entity is formed. The certificate will come back, stamped and with a state seal.

FILE A CERTIFICATE OF AUTHORITY

Any company doing business in any state where it is not organized may need to get a Certificate of Authority from the Secretary of State's office in that state.

REGISTER IN YOUR COUNTY

Some states, cities and counties require companies to file the organizational documents with the country recorder of deeds in the county where you will do business.

GET A BUSINESS LICENSE

Most cities and/or counties require businesses to get a business license.

STOCK REGISTER & CERTIFICATE

Owners need to buy stock in the Company. It is helpful (and required in corporations) to issue a certificate as proof of the stock. The certificate is merely a record of the owner's stock – it is not necessary for ownership. It is critical that if certificates are issued, they are prepared on the same, identical form of stock certificate. Blank forms of stock certificates should be attached to the first set of Board resolutions as the official certificate form. All stock certificates actually issued should be signed by the people required to sign them under the Bylaws or other governing documents.

The most important thing to do is to write down who owns the company stock and in which proportion. This writing is called an OWNERSHIP REGISTER, which is a simple table listing who owns what units of ownership, what they paid, when they paid and the certificate number of the certificate issued to them.

RESOLUTIONS

A company is like every other inanimate object: it can only act or move if a human makes it act or move. A new company needs to be instructed to get organized by the people who set it up and the people who will run it. These instructions are usually in the form of meeting resolutions or written consents. For instance, units of ownership need to be sold and the sale recorded; owners need to elect the Board or Managers; the Board or Managers need to hire officers, adopt banking resolutions (which you'll probably get from your bank) and adopt bylaws or an operating agreement.

BYLAWS

Every company should have a list of rules about how the company will hold meetings and who can act for the company. These rules can be in Bylaws, a Shareholders Agreement, an Operating Agreement, a Partnership Agreement or any other document. (See Different Entities = Different Words table.)

MINUTES AND MINUTE BOOK

All companies should have one big book, called a MINUTE BOOK, which contains the company's building block documents. Those documents include all state and tax filings, all resolutions of the Board and Owners, copies of stock certificates and the owner register. It can be a fancy leather bound thing or a 3-ring binder. Below are the contents which should be kept current:

- ✓ Articles or Certificate of organization
- ✓ Bylaws, Operating Agreement, Shareholders Agreement
- ✓ FEIN receipt
- ✓ S-election receipt from the IRS
- ✓ All written consents and minutes of meetings
- ✓ Business license
- ✓ All registrations and filings
- ✓ Copies of certificates of units of ownership
- ✓ Ownership (stock) register

Updates. Each year, you should update your minute book to include everything big that happened over the previous twelve months. Your company should have a yearly annual meeting of owners to elect the Board or other policy makers – the evidence and the results of these elections should be placed in the Minute Book. Then, any company actions that require Board approval should be approved and the approvals recorded and placed in the Minute Book. Any transactions or changes in the company's ownership or capital structure should be faithfully recorded and memorialized in the Minute Book. A good time to make sure this happens? When you receive your yearly notice from the Secretary of State to file your annual report with your state.

Get an FEIN. A company needs a Federal Employer Identification Number (FEIN), which is like your business's social security number. You get an FEIN by going to www.irs.gov, filling out and filing Form SS-4.

S-Election. If you want your company to be an S-corp, the S-election has to be filed no more than two months and 15 days after the beginning of the tax year the election is to take effect. An S-election is made by filling out and filing Form 2553 at www.irs.gov.

Entity Classification. If you want to select tax treatment different than the default or S-Corporation, you can file Form 8832.

State Department of Revenue. Most states require companies operating in their borders to register and pay state income taxes and sales and use taxes.

Most states require companies to register with whichever agencies regulate unemployment insurance and workers compensation and then to take out that insurance based on their laws and guidelines.

When the bank account is set up, the bank will require these documents:

- ✓ Copy of the Articles (the document that set up the company)
- ✓ Bylaws, Operating Agreement or Partnership Agreement
- ✓ Resolutions appointing officers and giving those officers the power to approve board resolutions and sign checks
- ✓ Your FEIN form and your S-Election

ENTITY COMPARISON CHART

QUESTION	SOLE PROPRIETORSHIP	(GENERAL) PARTNERSHIP	LIMITED PARTNERSHIP	LIMITED LIABILITY COMPANY	CORPORATION	S CORP
YOU ARE FORMED WHEN...	You do business all by yourself without any filing	You and another person do business together without any filing	You file a Certificate of Limited Partnership with a state's Secretary of State	You file Articles of Organization with a state Secretary of State's office	You file Articles of Incorporation with a State Secretary of State's office	You file Articles of Incorporation with a State Secretary of State's office AND file Form 2553 with the IRS
OWNERS INCLUDE...	One owner	Two or more Partners	The General Partner and the Limited Partners	One or more Members	One or more shareholders (percentage of ownership in proportion to shareholder's investment)	No more than 100 shareholders (percentage of ownership in proportion to shareholder's investment)
LIMITED LIABILITY?	No	No	Yes for Limited Partners; No for General Partner	Yes	Yes	
CONTROL	Sole Proprietor	Each partner has equal authority, unless partnership agreement states otherwise	General Partner	Can be member-managed or manager-managed Each member has equal authority, unless the Operating Agreement states otherwise	Shareholders elect directors who manage the company's affairs; officers manage day-to-day business activities	
OPERATIONAL EASE?	Easiest; no state requirements	Easy; little if any state requirements	Can be complicated	Easy by default; complicated by contract	✓ Formal recordkeeping requirements ✓ Annual meetings required ✓ Annual reports required	
TAXATION?	✓ Pass through taxation ✓ Subject to self-employment tax	✓ Pass through taxation ✓ Subject to self-employment tax	Pass through taxation (limited partners are typically exempt from self-employment tax)	✓ Pass through taxation ✓ Subject to self-employment tax	✓ Separately taxed at corporate income tax rates ✓ "Double taxation": Profits are taxed at corporate level, then taxed again when paid as dividends to shareholders	✓ Pass-through taxation ✓ Only salary is subject to employment tax (shareholder distributions are not subject to employment tax)

HAP AND HAZ PICK AN ENTITY

Hap, having drawn 18 replicas of his legal pad on his legal pad, said, "Wow, Gravity. That was fascinating."

"Thanks, Hap." Pointing at his work, she asked "Is that college or wide ruled?"

Haz rolled his eyes and said, "What do you think we should do, Gravity?"

Gravity replied, "I have some thoughts.

Create a Company. If you are going to be in business, you should pick an entity that gives you limited liability and create a company.

Tax Treatment. As for tax treatment, I think you should start with pass through tax treatment. You think you may have losses in the beginning, because it will be a huge cash drain to get to market so you can take these losses when you have them. (When every dollar will have to stay in the business, you can switch to C-corp tax treatment if that is more tax efficient.)

Entity. I think you should pick an LLC. An LLC will give you pass through tax treatment. Your investors can buy ownership through their own companies. If one of you has money to put in, but one of you must work for his equity, an LLC will enable you to contribute sweat equity without creating taxable income. An LLC will also allow you to set up something simple in the beginning, and change it later if you raise money from an investor. You can, but don't have to, hold annual meetings of the members. This is smart because Hap is bad at details and may forget to do his annual meeting minutes or sign annual consents. In the end, if there might be a disparity in your cash contributions, I'd advise you to select an LLC over a C-corporation.

State. I think you should set up your LLC in Illinois. You have a major city in your state, which means lots of law that is well developed. And, it will be cheaper for you to file your organization papers in just one state.

But, this is certainly your decision, so let me know if you disagree."

"I think your advice is good, Gravity."

"Me too."

"Would you like me to help you with this?"

"Yes please."

"Thanks, Gravity."

Gravity took care of all the filings and the minute book and the federal and state tax filings and city business license. At the end, she presented Hap and Haz with a pretty red leather Minute Book, which they asked her to store for safekeeping.

And, MouseTrap, LLC was born.

Gravity then said, "Boys, now that you have a real company, we should talk about the rights and obligations of owners, managers and Board members. It will be a big part of completing the process of getting you organized and getting you funded."

"How should we govern our company?"

"That depends."

"On what?"

"On what you want."

"Can you help us figure out our options?"

"I CAN TRY."

DECIDE FOUNDERS' RIGHTS

> Gravity said, "Let's discuss why you need to agree on how to work together, why you need an owner's contract, and the three big powers of a company."

CHAPTER 04

WHY YOU NEED TO AGREE ON HOW TO WORK TOGETHER

If you have partners and you are at the beginning of your venture, you all need to understand how you will work together. You need to have an honest conversation about how you and your partners want to go forward. This is important at the beginning of a venture, when it is just you and your co-founders, and you are all at your most optimistic. Your success will depend on your relationships with your co-founders. Just like a marriage, all of you need to feel that the divisions of control, labor, cash and credit are fair.

1. IN THE SHORT RUN

If you are not ready to formally organize your company, either because you lack the resources or the desire, you still have to be clear on each of your responsibilities to each other and to the new enterprise. You don't need to work out every tiny detail or come up with a lengthy agreement if you have neither the cash nor the need. But, you should at least agree on your individual and group obligations. And you should at least agree on who will be the boss.

MINIMAL DECISION POINTS ON FOUNDERS' RIGHTS

If your company has more than one owner, you should discuss and write down:

1. Which owner will be the boss?
2. How will voting get divided among owners?
3. Will one or more owners have veto power and, if so, over what?
4. How much money, property or time will each partner contribute?
5. Who will be the signatories on the bank accounts?
6. What will failure look like (so you know when to pull the plug)?
7. If you go out of business, what will you do with leftover assets?

2. FOR THE LONG RUN – THE OWNERS' CONTRACT

As owners of a company, you all should agree, in writing, about how you will own and run the business together, in a formal, written contract. The contract has many names, depending on the entity type, the state where you write it and the idiosyncrasies of your lawyer. Here, is a chart of typical contract titles.

ENTITY	CONTRACT TITLE
CORPORATION	✓ Shareholders Agreement ✓ Shareholders Agreement ✓ Buy-Sell Agreement
LLC	✓ Operating Agreement ✓ LLC Agreement
LIMITED PARTNERSHIP	✓ Agreement of Limited Partnership
PARTNERSHIP	✓ Partnership

Once you invest in a company, you ought to get stock in return, and rights and obligations, along with it. What you get back, how much control you have and how you can eventually cash out are all part of the business owners bundle of rights. These powers, which can be narrow or broad, can be divided into 3 categories:

1. MONEY
2. CONTROL
3. EXIT

MONEY

The right to money includes (1) Investor's contribution; (2) Investor's take away; (3) Dividends, Distribution, Allocations; and (4) Anti-dilution.

1. INVESTOR'S CONTRIBUTION

Whether you write a check for $1,000 or $10,000,000, you should get back ownership in the company (equity) or a promise by the company to repay the money (debt). Your investment is all negotiable, including (a) how much; (b) the form of payment; and (c) the timing of the payment.

The first thing to work out is what and how much you and your partners are putting into your company. Each owner of stock must contribute something as payment. How much you pay can be based on reason or expediency. You can pay for a percentage of the company based on a valuation of the business or based on what others contributed. You can pay based on what you have in your bank account or how much you need.

Arms' length investors typically invest some amount based on the value of your company, the value of the opportunity and the eventual value of the investment. Founders often invest what they have to invest and shape the business plan around that. And, many businesses simply target their investment needs towards how much it will cost to implement their business plans. Whatever is actually contributed should be listed on the owners' contract.

Your contribution can be in cash, property or sometimes a promissory note. It can also be in services, which is often called **"Sweat Equity."**

The Problem with Sweat Equity. Often, people want to give and take sweat equity. There are some legal and tax issues with sweat equity. First, if the idea is to take stock in exchange for services in the future, then some state laws may not allow that. Instead, the stock would probably be considered "owned" as it is earned through labor. Sometimes, you may want to pay a company for stock by giving a promissory note. This has the same issues as sweat equity – the safe bet is that only the stock that has been paid for will be owned. Second, there is a huge tax issue: if you get stock in exchange for services, it may be looked at by the IRS as income – and therefore taxable, so it should be discussed and structured with the help of someone expert in tax.

The due date for the investment may also be an issue. Your investment could be due now or in the future. That future date can be fixed (e.g., 30 days from now) or it can be triggered only after something happens (e.g., other investors put in at least $1 million). Also, there could be several due dates with contributions paid in installments.

Future Capital Calls. In the future, your company may need more money. You could create a power to require all co-owners to put in additional money. If you do, then you have to decide:

- ✓ Who has the power to make the other co-owners put in more cash?
- ✓ How will these payments be made? In installments? By a promissory note?
- ✓ What are the consequences of failure to meet a future capital contribution – forfeiture or mandatory redemption of membership interests, loss of control?
- ✓ Will the members be required to guarantee company loans? If so, are there limits to the amount to be guaranteed by any member?

2. INVESTOR'S TAKE AWAY

What an investor takes away for her contribution is another issue, particularly (a) the size of the share; (b) the type of share; and (c) special rights inside the share.

SIZE OF SHARE

How much you own after your investment depends on the amount you contribute, the amount others have contributed and the valuation of the company. Among founders, ownership in the company is often divided according to the amount of each owner's investment, but it can also be divided differently if by agreement. Among investors, ownership in the company is usually divided according to the valuation of the company and the amount of each owner's investment. (See "Valuing A Business," Chapter 25)

TYPE OF SHARE

Sometimes there is a need for multiple or different classes of membership with different rights or obligations - when that happens, you create different classes of ownership. For instance, founders may take common equity, but investors may take preferred stock. Whenever you have more than one class of common stock, you invite complexity, negotiation and legal fees. Remember also that you cannot have different classes of stock in an S-Corp.

Common Equity. By default, all equity is "common." Common equity has equal rights to everything, including cash and voting. It's simple and clean. If everyone just puts money in, what they take out is common equity.

Preferred Equity. Preferred equity is special equity. Unlike common, preferred equity has to be intentionally and specifically created to exist. To create preferred equity in a C-Corporation, you have to either create them in minute detail as an addition to the Articles or to embed a power of the Board in the Articles to create them and then have the Board create them in minute detail later.[22] To create preferred equity in other entities involves a combination of amending the owners' contract and the charter, depending on state law. Some preferred equity (and debt) can also be "convertible."

Profits Interest. If you have an employee or consultant of an LLC or partnership who you want to become an "owner" of the company, but not a voter, you may consider giving them a profits interest. A profits interest is the portion of stock in an LLC or partnership that entitles the owner to a portion of future profits, but not to ownership in the company as it exists today. Profits interests are often given to employees as compensation or a bonus. The great benefit of profits interests is that they can be given tax free to the employee, because they are worthless when given and only attain value if there is profits in the future. Unfortunately, once an employee gets a profits interest, he can no longer be an "employee" of the company because of tax laws – so the employee becomes "self-employed." Profits interests can take the place of employee stock options, which are not permitted for partnerships or LLCs under tax law.

Warrants. A "Warrant" – just like a stock option – is a contractual right to buy stock at a certain price with anti-dilution protections.

SPECIAL RIGHTS INSIDE STOCK

Different classes of stock usually have some rights that set them apart. Some of these rights are discussed below.

First Exit. You may want the owners of one class of stock to be able to get paid for their shares sooner than owners of other classes of stock if the company gets liquidated (a/k/a "liquidation preference"). If so, then decide the triggers and the terms for a first liquidation right.

Voting Rights. You may want a class of stock to have no voting rights.

Dividends, Distributions and Allocations. Your classes of stock may come with different rights to money or value.

Convertible. Convertible equity or debt can be exchanged for (a/k/a converted to) something else, like other preferred stock or common stock. Typical types of convertible securities include convertible subordinated debentures, subordinated debentures with warrants, convertible preferred units/stock, and preferred units/stock with warrants.

3. DIVIDENDS, DISTRIBUTIONS & ALLOCATIONS

Owners' shares of profits are called dividends or distributions. Owners' share of tax profits and losses are called allocations. Dividends are the portion of profits paid out to owners of a corporation. Distributions are the portion of profits paid out to owners of an LLC or partnership. Dividends or distributions happen only after the board or manager in charge of setting company policies declares them.

PARTS OF THE DIVIDEND

The Right to the Dividend. You or your investors may want to create rights to dividends or distributions. These rights often include the following:

- ✓ The right to a yearly dividend of a specific amount or a specific fraction of the owner's investment
- ✓ The right to a dividend in each year that the company has the cash to pay it (noncumulative)
- ✓ The right to a dividend that, if the company cannot pay it, gets added to the company's accounts as a debt (cumulative)
- ✓ A distribution of cash to cover each owner's taxes owed on the company's pass through income

The Rate is the size of the dividend. It can be described as an amount per share or as a percentage of the purchase price.

Payment Dates include when dividends have to be paid.

Commencement Date is when the dividend right starts.

Convertibility is when the investor can convert accrued but unpaid dividends into common stock (either at the existing conversion price or at the fair market value of the shares at the time of conversion).

Participation is the preferred shareholder's right to also get part of dividends given to common shareholders. Dividends can be participating (i.e., after payment of the stated rate, any dividend paid to holders of common stock would be paid to preferred holders as if they had converted.

Preference is the relative priority of various classes of preferred stock to dividends.

Remedies for Failure are the rights of investors if the company fails to declare and pay dividends. Options include ability to elect a majority of the board, an increase in dividend rate or a conversion of dividends into common stock or preferred stock.

LIMITS TO DIVIDENDS

Barring an agreement to issue a minimal dividend, business owners have no right to a dividend. Regardless of agreed to rights to dividends, it is usually unlawful to pay out a dividend if it would make your company insolvent. And, your bank documents or agreements with other investors may limit or restrict your ability to issue dividends or distributions.

ALLOCATIONS

An allocation is each partner's or member's share of profits or losses. "Profits" are the company's taxable profit. "Losses" are the company's tax losses.

4. ANTI-DILUTION

Anti-dilution is protection from dilution. Dilution is loss of value or ownership percentage due to stock sales. Anti-dilution rights can both preserve your ownership and limit your ability to exit the company. Anti-dilution usually comes in (a) preemptive rights; (b) right of first refusal; (c) right of first offer; or (d) preferred equity anti-dilution.

PREEMPTIVE RIGHTS

Preemptive Rights are rights to be able to buy additional stock from the company before a new owner can.

RIGHT OF FIRST REFUSAL

A right of first refusal is the right to be able to buy another member's stock before a new owner can.

RIGHT OF FIRST OFFER

A right of first offer is a right to be given the first chance to make an offer for someone else's stock.

PREFERRED EQUITY ANTI-DILUTION PROTECTIONS

If you own preferred equity, you may be able to convert it into common equity, either at your election or when the company goes public. But, how many shares of common equity should the company give for

1 share of preferred equity, particularly since preferred equity is more tricked out than common equity? Or, to put it another way, how many Toyota Camrys would you expect for your Lexus? If you agree that your Lexus is worth 4 Camrys, but before the trade, the Camry price drops by half, then your Lexus will now be worth 8 Camry's. Stock conversion prices get similar treatment.

Anti-dilution can adjust the conversion price when something happens to the common stock that diminishes the ultimate value of the preferred equity if you convert it right now. So, if your one Lexus is worth 2 Camrys, then if the 2 Camrys each have 2 babies (go with it), then one Lexus would be worth 4 Camrys. Anti-dilution can change when someone buys stock from the company for a cheaper price than what you paid.

CONTROL

The second major power is control over the company. Control includes (1) control among owners; (2) management; (3) the board; (4) baked in fiduciary duties of directors, officers and employees; and (5) personal liability of those in control.

1. CONTROL AMONG OWNERS

The owners of a company can come from different places. Owners can be founders, investors, employees who buy options or get shares as part of their compensation, or even the heirs of owners. Regardless of origin, it is smart to come to an agreement about the duties the owners owe to each other.

Every company has owner(s) who vote for policy makers. Policy makers, like a board or an LLC's manager, set up policies and hire management. Management runs the day to day operations. Owners, policy makers and operations can all be the same, single person or a bunch of different people.

If your company has more than one owner, you have to decide: (a) which owner will be the boss; (b) how will voting get divided among owners; (c) who will have veto power and, if so, over what and, (d) what happens when there is a deadlock.

Partners in new ventures often defer the question about who is in charge, insisting on unanimous approval. Unanimity can work, except when it doesn't. When partners can't agree, business can grind to a halt. Before you agree to unanimity, make sure you and your partner(s) are mature, accountable and reasonable. Because nothing is more destructive than a crazy tool with a veto.

The cornerstone of control is the right to vote as an owner. Whether shares are voting shares depends on the decisions made by the people who set up the company or run it going forward.

The big power in your voting rights is the election of the Board. By default (and democracy), majority rules and owners face off at a baseline with 1 vote per share, 50.1% of which is required to do things. When you set up a company, you have to decide how much you are going to move the baseline.

VOTING BASELINES AND VARIATIONS	
BASELINE	VARIATIONS
Each owner takes stock with one vote per share	Some co-owners take stock without voting rights
Each owner can vote as owners (generally to elect Board members and not much else)	Co-owners without voting rights don't get to vote and maybe don't even get invited to meetings
Whatever is being voted on is approved once it gets 50.1% of the votes cast	Supermajority (e.g. more than 50.1%) vote required for certain stuff
Whoever can amass a majority of votes, or who owns a majority of votes, will always win	Majority will not necessarily control. Minority retains some rights to control the company or to veto things

If you decide that some owners should have stronger or different rights than other owners, you have to decide these items are. Below is a list of things that co-owners often get veto and approval rights over.

Direction of Company. Changes in the company's focus, major products and services or markets are often subject to veto and approval rights.

Staff. Hiring or firing senior management or founders are often subject to veto or approval.

Additional Equity. Most people want to be able to veto additional sales of stock so they don't get diluted.

Amending the Owners' Contract Or Charter. Very few people (if any) should get to mess around with the documents that give you power without your authority.

Sale of Stock or Admission of Additional Members (for an LLC). Sometimes, an owner will sell his stock to someone that no one knows or likes. If the company is an LLC, the buyer does not necessarily become a member without the approval of Managers or co-owners. Owners may want a veto power over sale of stock or admission of new members.

Distributions. Owners and particularly investors will want the right to review and either approve or veto any cash distributions or dividends to owners.

Budget Ratification. The yearly or quarterly budget created by management and adopted by the Board is often subject to approval of a big investor or owner. Once approved, management ought to be free to run the company as long as they stay within budget.

Relocation. Some investors want veto power over relocation of the company's headquarters. If a company gets a new CEO who lives 45 miles away from the office, he may move the office to his town, and this right will probably get waived.

Debt. Debt or expenditures over a certain number are frequently subject to approval of some co-owners.

Merger, Sale or Consolidation. The basement of approval actions is the right to veto a merger or sale of the company. If you get any approval rights, this ought to be one of them.

A deadlock is when the people who need to approve or decide something cannot agree. Deadlocks and disputes among co-owners are common. Partners going the extra mile in organizing their company plan for deadlocks and disputes. Litigation to resolve deadlocks is cumbersome, expensive and unpredictable. The bad guy doesn't always lose - for all you know, you may turn out to be the bad guy.

Defining a Deadlock - What Does A Deadlock Look Like?
What is the difference between a resolvable disagreement and a deadlock? Usually, frequency or time. Here are some ways people have defined deadlocks:

- ✓ Difference of opinion over anything for 30 days
- ✓ Deadlock even after trying to work it out
- ✓ Deadlock over defined list of big issues
- ✓ Any of the above that occurred 3 or more times in a year

Options for Clearing a Deadlock. Here are some things people do to break a deadlock:

- ✓ Nothing - they just have to work it out
- ✓ A certain, prescribed period of time to try and work it out
- ✓ A right to make the company or other partners buy out shares
- ✓ An increase in the board seats for a party
- ✓ Appointment of an independent director to take control
- ✓ Mediation & arbitration

2. MANAGEMENT

You also have to work out who will manage the company. This may be the same or a different answer than your debate about which owner should be in charge.

Management is usually made up of Board members and officers. The officers need to be identified. Harder still, you and your partners need to decide a chain of command. Any miscommunications about who is in charge can - and will - lead to resentment, escalating hostilities and potentially a fatal deadlock.

OFFICER TITLES

Corporate titles can be a combination of authority, job description, hierarchy and ego. Corporate titles also vary among industries, entity types and founder whimsy. Sometimes corporate titles can be created to indicate succession and officers in training. For instance, some companies use the title Chief Operating Officer to identify the person designated as next boss. Executive Vice President often indicates a division head, however this position can also be known as Vice Chairman, or even President and CEO of a division or subsidiary.

COMPENSATION

You have to decide how much money each of you is going to get and how those amounts will be decided. Remember that in the beginning, you won't have much extra cash. And, nothing says "run" to investors more than a commitment to pay founders a big salary from the get-go. Be careful and be reasonable about how much money you plan to take out of the business in the beginning.

Some startups accrue compensation (or a part of it) until the business is cash flow positive. If you do this, talk to an employee benefits lawyer about potential tax penalties for 409A deferred compensation.

You may also be tempted to compensate people with stock or even a complicated stock option program with lengthy vesting schedules and forfeiture clauses. Setting up stock option plans takes legal time and money and should only be done when you have the attention span and cash to set it up properly.

ENTITY	MANAGEMENT IS CALLED...	MANAGERS INCLUDE...
CORPORATION	✓ Officers ✓ C-Level Officers	✓ Chairman of Board ✓ Chief Executive Officer ✓ President ✓ Vice President ✓ Chief Financial Officer ✓ Treasurer ✓ Secretary
LLC	✓ Managers ✓ Member Managers	✓ Manager ✓ Member ✓ Principal
LIMITED PARTNERSHIP	✓ General Partner	✓ Officer Titles for the General Partner
PARTNERSHIP	✓ Partnership ✓ Operating Group ✓ Executive Committee ✓ Board	✓ Partner ✓ Member of the Groups or Boards

3. THE BOARD

All corporations and some other entities have Boards. Boards set policy, govern big, organic changes and select and manage senior management.

The Board's effectiveness comes from accurate, candid and accessible information provided to the Board, management's enthusiasm for working with an engaged Board and each Board member's individual commitment and initiative.

MEMBERSHIP

The identity and number of Board members varies among companies. Technically, in most states you just need one director. But, in a perfect world, where your company is more than just you and a cat, your Board would have more than one member. The delicate part is making sure that your Board doesn't get too big or filled with people who are unreliable or extremely busy, because it can be difficult to gather enough of the members together to get stuff done. Typically, pubic company boards have an average of 12 members, most of whom are independent (i.e. not employed in the business). Smaller companies usually have boards with an uneven number of directors between 3-7.

Membership on the board matters. Certainly founders want a seat on the Board. Investors almost always want and get seats on the board. (Sometimes, as a substitute for Board seats, you can give out advisory or observer rights, which enables them to attend board meetings and review documents distributed to board members.) It is often helpful to recruit an independent professional to serve on your board to provide additional expertise, to avoid group think and to break ties. Getting people on a Board that have substantial finance and accounting knowledge is challenging at every kind of company, but beneficial.

MEETINGS

Boards should meet at least every quarter. Before each meeting, management should distribute agendas and materials supporting the agenda. There should also be some time built in to the meeting agenda for Board members to engage in a free flowing discussion about off agenda issues. Statute or bylaws will probably oblige you to have certain amount of members present to make up a "quorum."

ENTITY	BOARD IS CALLED...	BOARD MEMBER IS CALLED...
CORPORATION	✓ Board of Directors	✓ Director ✓ Board Member ✓ Member of Board of Directors
LLC	✓ Board of Managers	✓ Manager ✓ Board Member
LIMITED PARTNERSHIP	✓ General Partner	✓ General Partner
PARTNERSHIP	✓ Partnership ✓ Operating Group ✓ Executive Committee ✓ Board	✓ Partner ✓ Member of the Groups or Boards

Directors often get compensation for their services, from cash to stock or options. In setting compensation, the Board should base its decisions on surveys of other Boards in similarly sized companies. Hewitt Associates releases a yearly survey and report on director compensation, which you can find here:

⇨ http://www.hewittassociates.com/ MetaBasicCMAssetCache_/Assets/Articles/2010 /2010_Outside_Director_Compensation.pdf.

Other companies release reports that cost money.

⇨ For instance, Total Compensation Solutions at http://www.total-comp.com/ puts out reports and charges several hundred dollars for a copy.

COMMITTEES

Committees of the Board are a good way to make sure the Board supervises esoteric or sensitive matters. Below are some typical committees.

Finance and Accounting. You need a finance or audit committee to oversee the company's financial results, financial reporting and cash position. You also need this committee as a check on management and any tendency to present overly optimistic financial reports. Most importantly, you need at least one person with enough knowledge to read the financial statements and enough confidence to question them.

Compensation Committee. The comp committee is there to deal with management compensation and other sensitive employment matters of management. Management should not sit on this committee.

Special Committees. In big situations, the Board may set up a special committee to deal with things on the Board's behalf. Examples include evaluating offers to buy the company, an internal investigation, a legal problem or hiring top level management.

4. FIDUCIARY DUTIES THAT COME BAKED IN

There are some obligations of officers and directors that are so important, they are baked into the job – these are called Fiduciary Duties. Fiduciary Duties include the Duty of Care, the Duty of Loyalty and the Duty of Good Faith. [23]

The duty of care is the duty to do the job with reasonable care on the basis of adequate information. That means:

✓ Be diligent in your work; You have to do what a reasonable person in your shoes would do

✓ Do some level of examination and analysis where reasonable

✓ Make decisions based on the examination and analysis

The duty of loyalty is the duty to act in the best interests of the company and not for any other person. That means:

✓ Don't take a business opportunity that could reasonably be a part of the company's business for your own benefit, unless you get the company to knowledgably waive the opportunity

✓ You can't take money improperly, including putting through bogus expenses

✓ You must make decisions or take actions with the intention of benefiting the company, not yourself or a 3rd party

✓ Every transaction with the company, particularly ones where you have an interest, must be fair to the company

The duty of good faith is the duty to act with intention, in a manner he reasonably believes to be in or not opposed to the best interests of the company – a duty not to act in bad faith.

Someone acts in bad faith when he either:

✓ Has an actual intent to harm.

✓ Acts in a manner that is an "intentional dereliction of duty" or "conscious disregard for one's responsibilities.

But, these fiduciary duties do have a big, shocking limit: directors and officers are not obligated to be right. They can make mistakes, miscalculations and decisions that have terrible consequences, so long as they took the steps a reasonable person would do in their situation in formulating their decision. This is called the Business Judgment Rule and it protects directors and officers from mistakes. It does not, however, protect them from violating their duty of loyalty. How it works is another confusing part about the law.

Directors are presumed to act on an informed basis, in good faith and in the honest belief that the action taken was in the best interests of the company. The presumption can be rebutted with evidence that they breached their duty of care, duty of loyalty or acted in bad faith. Then, the burden shifts to the defendants to show that the act was entirely fair to the company and shareholders. If they can show that the transaction was entirely fair, the director or officer is probably off the hook.

5. PERSONAL LIABILITY

Officers, directors, employees and some owners are not shielded from all liability; they can be personally liable, if: (a) they violate a fiduciary duty; (b) they approve a distribution to co-owners that makes the company insolvent; (c) the company fails to pay the employees' withholding into the U.S. government or there is a violation of ERISA (federal law governing employee benefit plans); (d) they commit insider trading or another securities law violation; (e) there are material disclosure problems in reports filed with the SEC; and (f) the company has environmental liability or criminal liability. Further, some states (like New York) make owners liable for tax liabilities of the company.

Fiduciary duties among owners are heightened beyond what is normally required in companies where there are just a few owners. That is because they usually occupy positions that are interwoven with each other – owners, directors, officers, employees; and often friends, siblings, other relatives. With fewer people, it is critical that each of them do their part and it is more likely that one person can wreak more havoc on the other people, who are relying on each other.

Each company and its Board members and officers can take some measure to manage the risk of D&O liability through: (1) contracts; (2) insurance, and (3) vigilant due diligence.

Contract. Your company can agree to protect (indemnify) Board members and management from liability, but typically not from intentional bad acts, bad faith or if you guy didn't reasonably believe he was doing the right thing. The indemnification should be in bylaws, an agreement or the charter. It is better for you personally if the company's obligation includes an advance of lawyer fees and costs for defending an action (which has to get paid back if you are found to have done wrong). Some states let companies cancel in advance any liability of a Board member for breach of the duty of care and diligence, but not for breach of the duty of loyalty, intentional bad acts or issuance of bad dividends.

D&O Insurance. Many companies buy insurance to protect their Boards and management from liability. This also should kick in to fill in gaps where the Company cannot indemnify, particularly in OWNER derivative suits, securities law violations, or where a director cannot show he acted in good faith. However, D&O insurance will not cover:

- ✓ Intentional dishonesty
- ✓ Ungratified personal gain or illegal payments
- ✓ Bodily injury or property damage
- ✓ ERISA liability
- ✓ Some securities law violations
- ✓ Suits where a fellow insured is a plaintiff

Vigilant Due Diligence. Board member and officers can and must strive to limit their risk by doing the work necessary to identify hazards and take steps to avoid them. (See "How to Be a Great Board Member and Officer.")

HOW TO BE A GREAT BOARD MEMBER AND OFFICER

Board service is the subject of many treatises and seminars. New board members are encouraged to attend training on how to be a good board member and read white papers on their obligations. To save you some time, here are some quick tips to get you started.

1. SHOW UP

Seriously, showing up is a big part. You need to be present to carry out your obligations to the shareholders.

2. DO THE JOB

Do the job in three ways: Measure. Deliberate. Memorialize. In all things, drill down deeply.

Measure the impact of a transaction on the company. Drill down deeply. Read all materials you get. Keep a record of your review of the materials and any comments you have. Try and bring some doubt to the materials and assumptions behind them. Ask questions. Request and consider criticism from above and below. Probe and test management's statements, assurances, and recommendations.

Deliberate by having a comprehensive, debate and discussion about the benefits and detriments of taking the action. Drill down deeply. Never forget that the co-owners are depending on you to be a voice of skepticism and strength. You want to be tactful when you can, but you are not a rubber stamp for management. If you make decisions for the company that (1) you reviewed, analyzed and questioned; and (2) you made the decision that you thought was fair to the company and its shareholders, then your chances of beating a lawsuit goes way up.

Memorialize the board's work by crafting long minutes reflecting all arguments, each director's presence and position and highlighting the key points. Have your corporate lawyer drill down deeply.

3. BE FAIR AND LOYAL

Don't waste company assets. Don't take money or opportunities of the company. Don't repeat delicate or valuable information that you learn from your Board membership. Make decisions that are fair to the company and that you believe are in the best interests of the company and its shareholders (unless the company can't pay its bills when due – then make decisions for the benefit of the creditors.) And, if you must take opportunities from the company or sell a service or product to the company, make sure that it was approved by a majority of Board members who are not getting benefits from the deal.

4. SET CLEAR EXPECTATIONS

The job of a director and officer is to convey clear and strong expectations about safety, environmental compliance, good employment practices, forthright accounting, reasonable transparency, compliance with the Foreign Corrupt Practices Act and fixing mistakes immediately. The greatest danger to people and planet is a company that puts short term profits at the top of the priority list. Short-term profiteers tend to duck safety precautions, cut corners and disregard the future effects of current decisions. Hence, packaged mortgages and the credit market implosion; BP, the faulty pipe and no Plan B; and Madoff - all examples of businesses that grabbed the dollar today and ignored the crash tomorrow. Forget the morality, this approach is bad for business. Lehman Brothers, Bear Stearns and Merrill Lynch disappeared; BP's stock tanked; Bernie Madoff will die in jail. The costs to operate properly are expensive in the short-term, but cleaning up your name and reputation may be impossible in the long term. If your duty is to preserve and maximize shareholder value, "value" should be measured as a long term concept and not a short term deadline. Run a company that takes a profit, while it protects its customers, employees and universal prospects, allowing you to build your wealth steadily but fairly.

EXIT

The third major power is the ability to cash out and go away. The practical ability to sell your equity is called "liquidity." Equity in small companies is usually not liquid. First, because no one wants to buy it. Second, because securities laws limit the ability to sell it. Third, because the owners have usually already agreed to prohibit selling it.

Owners of a company can agree in advance on exit rights including contract terms that (1) keep owners from selling; (2) allow people to sell out; (3) force an owner to sell; and (4) govern how to price shares of a departing owner.

1. KEEP OWNERS FROM SELLING

Equity, on its own, is property of the owner, freely transferable - owners can sell their stock to anyone they choose for any price they choose, unless the owners' contract says otherwise. Frequently, owners are prohibited from selling all or any part of their stock. Those prohibitions are called "Restrictions on Transfer," they essentially lock the doors, barring an owner's exit.

There are some standard mechanisms to keep people from selling stock: (a) Right of First Refusal; (b) Right of First Offer; (c) Drag Along; and (d) Tag Along.

RIGHT OF FIRST REFUSAL

Under a right of first refusal, an owner cannot sell stock unless other people (or the company) have the option to buy it first. The right of first refusal often excludes transfers to family members and estate planning trusts as triggers. Any owner who wants to buy usually has to match any outstanding offer. Rights of first refusal can be divided into rights offered only to particular groups of people or to groups of people in a certain order. For instance, you can limit the right of first refusal to founders. Or, you could give the right, first, to founders, and anything left over to employees. The right of first refusal not only provides ownership continuity, it also provides comfort to founders about their ability to preserve the company. If the price is low, the existing co-owners can snap up the stock.

There is one primary drawback: they impair the ability to negotiate with potential 3rd party purchasers. As a result, it is common to permit a 5% reduction in the price without having to go back to the owners.

RIGHTS OF FIRST OFFER

Under a right of first offer, an owner must first offer her shares to her partners at terms she would accept for her stock. Those other owners then have to accept the offer or reject the offer; if they reject the offer, she can market her stock for a certain period of time, usually 6 months on the terms offered during the offer period. The right of first offer allows an owner to sell without a chilling effect on potential buyers because of a right of first refusal.

DRAG ALONGS

A drag along is a right of an owner to make the other owners sell their stock along with her. They are neat little inventions of corporate lawyers that often go into documents and rarely get used. But, they are good in that they give an investor comfort that other owners can't get in the way of her exit strategy. The main disadvantage is that owners, who could be founders, could be forced to sell on undesirable terms; this effect can be improved if all parties are given a meaningful opportunity for negotiation.

Key Questions for Drag Alongs.

- ✓ What should be the trigger for a drag along?
  - o Majority owner sells all of his stock
  - o Majority owner sells some of his stock
  - o Any owner sells all of his stock
  - o Any owner sells some of his stock
- ✓ On what basis do the remaining owners get to tag along?
  - o Percentage interests?
  - o Fully, thus reducing the total payment to original seller

TAG ALONGS

A tag along is a right of an owner to force himself into another owner's share sale. If your partner sells his shares to a third party, you could force the third party to buy your shares also, as long as you sell on the same terms. Once again, they are neat little inventions of corporate lawyers that often go into documents, but rarely get used. They are also usually badly written and confusing as hell.

Sometimes, the love is gone. The sight of your business partner makes you want to throw knives or up and neither one of you is willing to surrender. If no solution is found, you go to court. This is a terrible option. Litigation is expensive, unpredictable and painful.

If you must go to court to resolve disputes, then there are basically three options that the court will take: (1) appoint a custodian; (2) intercede; or (3) dissolve the company.

Appoint A Custodian. Most state statutes authorize a judge to appoint a custodian over a company in event of a deadlock. The custodian could be an agent of the court, a member of the board of directors or a member of management. For good and bad, the fights behind the deadlock are out of everybody's hands now and at the mercy of the custodian.

Intercede. In most states, the court can just order someone to do something, including:

- ✓ injunctive order to do or stop doing something
- ✓ remove a member of management or the board
- ✓ amend a bylaw
- ✓ issue a dividend
- ✓ pay damages

Dissolve the Company. In many states, a court can force the dissolution (termination) of the company, particularly if there is a deadlock; the directors acted illegally or there is big waste or mismanagement. In dissolution, the property will either be sold to pay off creditors or distributed to the owners (if no creditors). If the assets get sold, the price will be liquidation value – a low price – so your work and investment may be lost. That is why it is prudent to provide a way to buy each other out.

2. RIGHTS TO GET OUT

There are rights that unlock the doors and open them wide, facilitating an owner's exit. These are usually negotiated parts of contracts, including (a) Puts; (b) Registration Rights; and (c) Liquidation Preferences.

A put is an owner's right to make the company buy back her stock. A put right usually gets triggered on big events, like an owner's death or disability, departure of a key manager or owner, retirement or termination without cause. Put rights can also be written to allow the owner to "put her stock to the company" after the passage of a certain amount of time.

Registration rights give an owner of stock the right to register her shares with the SEC. Registration rights are usually given in a separate registration rights agreement. There are two main kinds of registration rights: (1) Demand; and (2) Piggyback. Demand rights empower the owner to force the company to take the owner's shares public. Companies should and do resist granting these – they are expensive and get in a company's way of raising money from directly selling new shares to the public. Piggyback rights empower the owner to ride along on the company's public offering of shares belonging to the company or someone else.

A liquidation preference is a right of an owner to get paid for her stock before anyone else.

Amount. The amount of the liquidation preference is how much the holder is entitled to get before any other owner of equity. Numerous, but common options include 100% of investment (a/k/a 1x), 200% (a/k/a 2x), or return of investment plus 10% per year.

Participating. If preferred is participating, the preferred stock owner will likely get the liquidation preference and will share in any proceeds available to common stock on an as-converted basis.[24 & 25] The conversion price will be determined by a formula.

Events triggering Liquidation Preference. There are many possible triggers for a liquidation preference, but the most common are sale of the company and insolvency.

POSSIBLE TRIGGERS FOR BUYING OUT AN OWNER	
(IN ORDER OF THE BADNESS OF THE REASON FOR THE DEPARTURE)	
REASON FOR DEPARTURE	NOTES
Disability Death	What constitutes "disability" should be defined
Retire at or after 65	What constitutes "retirement" should be defined
Quit before 65	Before or after a certain date or at any time; this can also be a very bad thing
Terminated from Employment without Cause	Usually, the parties negotiate a settlement; sometimes, the parties go to court
Terminated from Employment for Cause	"Cause" should be defined. Examples of "cause" include: ✓ violation of owners agreement ✓ divorce ✓ insolvency/bankruptcy ✓ company dissolution (if owner is an entity) ✓ failure to maintain eligibility requirements, including licenses (if applicable) ✓ breach of the owners' agreement or of a fiduciary duty ✓ prison ✓ using the company as a piggy bank

3. POWER TO KICK OUT AN OWNER [26]

And, then there are the rights of the company and the other owners to literally eject an owner from the company, forcing the departing owner to sell his stock. Often this right is called a "call" or a "mandatory redemption." The right to eject a member can be triggered by a big, bad event or by a positive, happy development. You have to pick the happenings that will trigger the company's right to kick out the owner and/or buy back his stock (see the chart "Possible Triggers for Buying Out an Owner").

Shootout. For instance, one ejection trigger is the "shootout." A shootout is when you have two partners sort of shoot it out. One partner makes an offer for the other guy's shares, which gives the guy who got the offer the exclusive right to buy the first guy out on the terms he suggested. So, if you offer to buy out your partner for $1 million, then your partner has two choices: (1) he can accept your offer and sell out for $1 million; or (2) he can buy your stock for $1 million. His right to buy out your shares on terms proposed by you should make you quote a fair price – if the price is too low, you can get bought out for less than market price. Often, the offeror actually has deeper pockets than the offeree, and the offeree then has to sell.

Ejection – Right or Obligation. Typically, buy sell terms vary depending on why the guy left. So, whether a departing owner must sell his shares back to the company or may keep them; and whether the company must buy the shares back from the Owner or may buy them (or not), will change with the reasons for departure. For instance, an Owner who departs at 70 because he retired with plenty of notice may be able to keep his stock; but if he departed the company for prison, he may be obligated to sell them back, regardless of his wishes. The table below shows a typical arrangement.

RIGHT OR OBLIGATION TO SELL OR BUY DEPARTING OWNER'S STOCK		
REASON FOR DEPARTURE	COMPANY	HOLDER
Quit before 65	May Buy	Must Sell
Retire at or after 65	May Buy	May Sell
Disability	Must Buy	Must Sell
Terminated for Cause	May Buy	Must Sell
Terminated without Cause	Must Buy	May Sell
Violated fiduciary duty to the company or owners agreement	May Buy	Must Sell
Death	Must Buy	Must Sell

QUESTIONS FOR THE MANDATORY EXIT

You have to decide:

- ✓ How many partners does it take to kick out a co-owner? All of the other co-owners? One particular person? Vote of a certain percentage of ownership? The Board or Manager? All or a couple of the above?
- ✓ What will you give the guy you kick out? Anything? Nothing? Capital Account? Money back? Some formula?

4.   BUYING SHARES OF A DEPARTING OWNER

CALCULATING "VALUATION"

One of the hardest questions – for everyone – is how you will calculate the purchase price for a departing partner's ownership interests. The possibilities range from very simple to very complex.

The purchase price may depend on why the guy is leaving. Again, if an Owner retires at 70, he may get a relatively higher purchase price than if he departs for prison. See "Valuation Basics," Chapter 25.

HAP AND HAZARD HAVE AN HONEST TALK

At that point, Hap started to snore.

Haz shook his shoulder. "I think she's done." Hap sat up and smiled.

Haz asked, "What should we do, Gravity?"

"You need to have an honest conversation and you need to agree on how to organize your company."

Hap and Hazard sat down over a beer.

Haz said, "Hap, I think I should be the boss."

"I agree," Hap replied.

"Oh. Great. That was easy."

"But, I also think voting should be 50/50."

"What if we can't agree?"

"One of us overruling the other could be just as damaging as not agreeing."

"Good point. Okay, 50/50. Hap, I have to tell you something."

"What's that?"

"I have a little money, so I can put in some cash."

"Haz, I have something to tell you."

"Yes?"

"I have no money."

"That's okay, Hap. We'll work it out. I'll put in $150,000 and you can contribute over the years."

"Thanks, Haz. We'll probably have to raise another $250,000. If we can't raise enough money or we can't get to market with just your investment, we should call it quits. And, you get all the assets since you are putting in the cash."

"Hap, it's a deal."

"Ok, let's go see Gravity."

Hap and Haz explained their agreement to Gravity. Gravity asked questions in return. In the end, the terms included:

1. MONEY

Hazard agreed to contribute $150,000. No upfront capital contribution by Hap. To mitigate the difference, on liquidation of the company, Hazard would be entitled to return of his capital contribution before Hap and Hazard begin to evenly divide the leftover assets.

Hap and Hazard would each take 50% of the equity.

Hap and Hazard would each get preemptive rights and a right of first refusal to buy the other owner's stock.

2. CONTROL

Hap and Hazard would be the sole managers and officers of the company (though they agreed that in the near future, it would be helpful to bring in another advisor to serve on their board).

Hazard would be President and Chief Financial Officer

Hap would be Chief Operating Officer and VP of Sales and Marketing.

The company would indemnify Hap and Hazard. The company would also take out directors and officers liability insurance, particularly when their products go to market.

3. EXIT

Hap and Hazard decided not to adopt a drag along or a tag along, because they decided they did not want to include coercive measures in their agreement. But, they did include a Shootout to provide a way to divorce if they really could not agree in the future. They also agreed to include a right to call the equity of a disabled or deceased owner for a purchase price of fair market value calculated by a single appraiser chosen by the company's accountant using appropriate and commercially prevalent methods.

Gravity said, "That all makes sense. Would you like me to write it up?"

"Yes, please."

A few weeks later, Hap and Hazard returned to Gravity's office to sign the completed Operating Agreement of MouseTrap, LLC. After they had signed the contract, Hazard asked,

"Gravity, I know there are things we need to do to put a little more discipline to our operations. But, we could use some guidance on initial steps we should take to get going. Can you help us?"

"I CAN TRY."

SET UP OPERATIONS

Gravity explained, "There are things you should do, both as a new company and as an ongoing business, to operate your business prudently."

CHAPTER 05

ACCOUNTING AND FINANCE

Finance and accounting make up a big part of running your business. "Finance" is the prediction of future expenses and revenues. "Accounting" is the calculation of past, actual expenses and revenues down to the penny. Accounting and finance functions begin with (1) setting up your finance and accounting system, (2) getting comfortable with financial statements and (3) financial ratios.

1. SET UP YOUR FINANCE AND ACCOUNTING SYSTEM

To get started, you can (a) pick your software; (b) obtain a good accountant; (c) pick your tax year; (d) pick your accounting periods; and (e) identify any industry business cycles. Setting up systems to record and monitor the financial aspects of your business is important for two major reasons. First, because cash is the lifeblood of every business and if your business runs out it probably dies. Second, because maintaining separate accounts is required to keep the limited liability of your business entity – if you treat your personal money and your company money like it sits in a common pool, you may be denied limited liability when you really need it.

PICK YOUR SOFTWARE

There are hundreds of software products that either easily or automatically collect and organize financial information. Some of these products are for download and some are hosted on the Internet. Pick one and use it to help you monitor your financial position.

HIRE A GOOD ACCOUNTANT

A good accountant is an integral resource. The tax and accounting rules are complex and changing. These rules require a fine attention to detail and also a wide angle lens to see the big picture. A good accountant ought to keep up with the rules and keep your tax and financial reporting in compliance. A really good accountant will find you legitimate ways to avoid some tax and provide a voice of reason to your decision-making.

PICK YOUR TAX YEAR

A business year is a period containing one or more business cycles and ending on a business cycle. Under IRS Tax Regulations, the business year cannot exceed twelve months and individuals, sole proprietorships, partnerships, and S-Corporations must choose 12/31 as the end or their year unless they get IRS permission to adopt a different year end.

IDENTIFY ANY ACCOUNTING PERIODS

An accounting period is a division of a business year. Accounting periods should be long enough to accommodate not only ordinary business activities, but also extraordinary ones, to give management a good picture of the company and an opportunity to respond and adjust. Accounting periods should also be equal to or less than a business cycle and should correspond to the amount of time it takes to prepare, analyze and act on reports of the accounting period's results. Each accounting period should match as closely as possible each other accounting period, so the information produced during the period can be compared to previous accounting periods. For example, the accounting period in July should have the same number of selling days, the same number of Thursdays and Saturdays and same holidays each year. Accounting periods need to be adjusted to accommodate the fall of holidays on different days in different years. Accounting periods allow management to break up the financial performance of the company into manageable chunks to enable more precise and reliable accounting and monitoring. At the end of an accounting period, management has to reconcile the bank accounts, run reports and close the books.

IDENTIFY INDUSTRY BUSINESS CYCLES

A "business cycle" is the amount of time it takes for a business to perform all of its functions. For instance, the retail business cycle is the amount of time beginning in a sales season to the end of the sales season. A retail apparel business cycle is the six-months ending on July 31 or January 31, called a season. (February 1 - July 31 is the Spring Season; August 1 to January 31 is the Fall Season). The retailing business cycle includes the buying period, sales peaks and valleys, clearance sales, and inventory peaks and valleys. Also, peak times are Holiday season, Travel season, Transitional season, and Back-to-school season. Many retail businesses use the **4-5-4 Retail Accounting Calendar**. The 4-5-4 Calendar enables management to prepare more accurate sales forecasts and budgets. Management is also able to take and maintain more accurate inventories because each week ends on a Saturday and inventory can be taken at the end of each week or month. The 4-5-4 Retail Accounting Calendar consists of four 3-month quarters. Months 1 and 3 are 4 weeks each. Month 2 is 5 weeks each. Each month begins on a Sunday and ends on a Saturday. Each month has the same number of selling days as that month in the previous year. The 4-5-4 Accounting Calendar begins with the month of February, the start of the Spring Season.

2.   FINANCIAL STATEMENTS

Financial statements show you where a company's money came from, where it went, and where it is now.

Financial Statements are made up of four components: (1) balance sheets; (2) income statements; (3) cash flow statements; and (4) statements of owners' equity.

Balance sheets show what a company owns and what it owes at one moment in time. Income statements show how much money a company made and spent over a period of time. Cash flow statements show the exchange of money between a company and the outside world, also over a period of time. The fourth financial statement, called a "statement of owners' equity," shows changes in the interests of the company's Owners over time.

THE BALANCE SHEET

A balance sheet shows a snapshot of a company's assets, liabilities and owners' equity at the end of the reporting period (though it does not show the flows into and out of the accounts during the period.)

Assets. Assets are things that a company owns. Assets is a broad category that includes physical property (like plants, trucks, equipment and inventory), intangible stuff (like trademarks, patents and copyrights), and cash and investments. Liquid assets such as bank accounts, certificates of deposits, stocks and bonds are generally reflected at fair market value whereas long term assets, such as computers and buildings, are reflected at their original purchase price less an accumulated depreciation allowance.

Liabilities. Liabilities are the company's obligations to pay money or provide something of value to third parties. Liabilities is also a broad category that includes money borrowed from a bank, rent, cash owed to vendors for supplies, payroll, environmental cleanup costs and taxes owed to the government, as well as obligations to provide goods or services to customers in the future.

Owners' Equity. Owners' equity is the money left over if a company sold its assets and paid off all its liabilities.

Balance Sheet Layout. All balance sheets are essentially this formula:

ASSETS = LIABILITIES + OWNERS' EQUITY.

The company's assets have to equal, or "balance," its liabilities and owners' equity. A company's balance sheet is usually set up like the picture above – assets on the left side and liabilities and owners' equity on the right side, although they can also show the assets at the top, then the liabilities and ending with owners' equity at the bottom. Assets are usually listed in order of speed to cash. *Current assets* are assets the business predicts will convert to cash within a year. Inventory is a "current asset," because companies plan to sell their inventory in less than a year. *Noncurrent assets* are assets that a business predicts will not be cashed out in a year. Examples of "noncurrent assets" are fixed assets, which are assets used to run the business not up for sale, like vehicles, furniture and computers.

Liabilities are usually listed in ascending order of due date, with next due date listed first. Liabilities can be either current or long-term. <u>Current</u> liabilities are obligations a company expects to pay off within the year. <u>Long-term</u> liabilities are obligations not due within a year.

Owners' equity is the amount owners invested in the company's stock plus or minus the company's earnings or losses since inception. Sometimes companies distribute earnings, instead of retaining them.

The Balance Sheet Footnotes. Footnotes are critical sources of information:

- ✓ Generally Accepted Accounting Principles (GAAP) require companies to disclose their material accounting policies used in preparing the financial statements

- ✓ Footnotes usually discuss the company's income taxes at the federal, state, local and foreign level and the activities or items that drove the taxes

- ✓ Footnotes usually discuss pension and retirement plans, and whether those plans are over or under funded

- ✓ Footnotes usually discuss any stock options granted to management, employees and directors

An income statement reports a company's revenues and costs spent earning those revenues during a particular period of time. Then, the bottom line of the income statement shows the net earnings or losses – how much the business earned or lost during the period. Then, the income statement calculates the earnings per share – how much shareholders would get if the company distributed its net earnings to the owners. Income statements are laid out like walking down a flight of stairs. The top step contains all sales made during the period – gross revenues or gross sales. Gross means no expenses have been deducted yet. Each step down is a deduction for a cost or expenses associated with the making the sale. Finally, at the bottom of the stairs, the bottom line contains the amount of earnings or losses during the period.

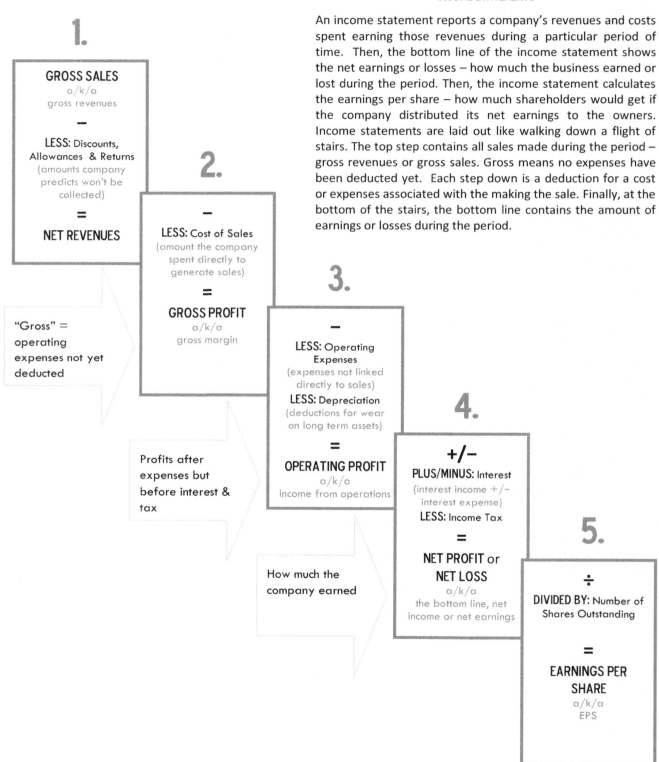

1.

GROSS SALES
a/k/a
gross revenues

–

LESS: Discounts, Allowances & Returns
(amounts company predicts won't be collected)

=

NET REVENUES

2.

–

LESS: Cost of Sales
(amount the company spent directly to generate sales)

=

GROSS PROFIT
a/k/a
gross margin

"Gross" = operating expenses not yet deducted

3.

–

LESS: Operating Expenses
(expenses not linked directly to sales)
LESS: Depreciation
(deductions for wear on long term assets)

=

OPERATING PROFIT
a/k/a
income from operations

Profits after expenses but before interest & tax

4.

+/–

PLUS/MINUS: Interest
(interest income +/– interest expense)
LESS: Income Tax

=

NET PROFIT or NET LOSS
a/k/a
the bottom line, net income or net earnings

How much the company earned

5.

÷

DIVIDED BY: Number of Shares Outstanding

=

EARNINGS PER SHARE
a/k/a
EPS

Cash statements show the company's net cash flows. The income statement shows profits and losses, but the cash flow statement shows cash generated or expended. The cash flow statement is not a snapshot, but a report of movement over the period, made up of parts of the balance sheet and income statement.

The bottom line of the cash flow statement shows the ultimate increase or decrease in cash. Cash flow statements usually include 3 parts: (1) cash from or for operating activities; (2) cash from or for investing activities; and (3) cash from or for financing activities.

sales of assets shown as inflow of cash

cash from stocks & bonds and bank loans shown as cash inflow

OPERATING REVENUES
examines cash flow from net income or loss, by comparing net income vs. actual cash received or spent

INVESTING ACTIVITIES
purchase or sale of long term assets; e.g. machinery, plants, equipment, investments

FINANCING ACTIVITIES

adjust net income for:
-noncash items
-depreciation
-cash used by other assets or liabilities

purchases of assets shown as outflow of cash

cash paid for debt shown as outflow of cash

BOTTOM LINE
net increase or decrease in cash

STATEMENT OF OWNERS' EQUITY
(STATEMENT OF RETAINED EARNINGS)

Owners' equity represents money invested and profits retained. The Statement of Owners' Equity shows changes to the retained earnings in a particular period of time. The Statement of Owners' Equity takes information from the Income Statement and calculates information for use on the Balance Sheet.

3. FINANCIAL RATIOS FOR THE MILDLY MATH PHOBIC

Financial ratios can be a black hole for the financially untrained. Below is a quick rundown of some of the big ones.[27] Be aware that ratios used may vary by industry.

DEBT-TO-EQUITY RATIO

The Debt to Equity Ratio compares a company's total debt to OWNERS' equity. Both of these numbers can be found on a company's balance sheet. To calculate debt-to-equity ratio, you divide a company's total liabilities by its OWNER equity, or

Debt-to-Equity Ratio = Total Liabilities / Owners' Equity

If a company has a debt-to-equity ratio of 2 to 1, it means that the company has two dollars of debt to every one dollar Owners invest in the company. So, the company is taking on debt at twice the rate that its owners are investing in the company.

OWNERS' EQUITY

Owner's equity is an owner's pro rata portion of company assets after all liabilities are paid off. Owner's equity is negative if the company's liabilities exceed its asset values. Owners' equity (or risk capital, liable capital, owners' equity, owners' funds, owners' capital employed) is this interest in remaining assets, spread among individual owners of common or preferred stock. At the dissolution or bankruptcy of a business, the owners of the business come last. The creditors come first, ranked in order, to their share of the assets.

INVENTORY TURNOVER RATIO

The inventory turnover ratio compares a company's cost of sales on its income statement with its average inventory balance for the period. To calculate the inventory turnover ratio, you divide a company's cost of sales (just below the net revenues on the income statement) by the average inventory for the period, or

Inventory Turnover Ratio = Cost of Sales / Average Inventory for the Period

If a company has an inventory turnover ratio of 2 to 1, it means that the company's inventory turned over twice in the reporting period.

OPERATING MARGIN

Operating margin compares a company's operating income to net revenues. Both of these numbers can be found on a company's income statement. To calculate operating margin, you divide a company's income from operations (before interest and income tax expenses) by its net revenues, or

Operating Margin = Income from Operations / Net Revenues

Operating margin is usually expressed as a percentage. It shows, for each dollar of sales, what percentage was profit.

P/E RATIO

P/E ratio compares a company's common stock price with its earnings per share (really only applies to public companies). To calculate a company's P/E ratio, you divide a company's stock price by its earnings per share, or

P/E Ratio = Price per share / Earnings per share

If a company's stock is selling at $20 per share and the company is earning $2 per share, then the company's P/E Ratio is 10 to 1. The company's stock is selling at 10 times its earnings.

WORKING CAPITAL

Working capital is the money leftover if a company paid its current liabilities (that is, its debts due within one year of the date of the balance sheet) from its current assets.

Working Capital = Current Assets − Current Liabilities

BRINGING IT ALL TOGETHER

Although this discussion examines each financial statement separately, keep in mind that they are all related. The changes in assets and liabilities that you see on the balance sheet are also reflected in the revenues and expenses that you see on the income statement, which result in the company's gains or losses. Cash flows provide more information about cash assets listed on a balance sheet and are related, but not equivalent, to net income shown on the income statement. And so on. No one financial statement tells the complete story. But combined, they provide very powerful information for investors. And information is the investor's best tool when it comes to investing wisely.

TAXES

Business needs roads, bridges, sanitation, sewers, police, firefighters, courts and everything else you need to make the immediate world run smoothly. Without things running smoothly, business can't ship packages, get its employees to work, stay safe from thieves or enforce its contracts. But, keeping things running smoothly takes money - each citizen and business owes their fair share. So, every level of government needs you to pay them some cash for using, depleting and benefiting from the infrastructure. These payments are usually in the form of a license, access or registration fee and taxes on transactions and income. Licenses, access and registration fees will vary depending on your location, industry and regulatory umbrella. Taxes on transactions and income apply to us all.

Let's discuss some of the things that get taxed, including (1) income; (2) transactions; (3) payroll;

(4) a bunch of other things; and (5) some deadlines for tax filings.

1. TAXES ON INCOME

When you set up your entity, you chose your company's tax treatment for your business income taxes. (See "Pick Your Tax Treatment.") You tax rate will vary depending on your entity's tax treatment and tax rates in effect when you incur your tax liability. Work closely with a tax professional with expertise and experience in business tax.

State(s) Department of Revenue. Most states require companies operating in their borders to register and pay state income taxes and sales and use taxes. However, if you sell a product or service into a state, the state's department of revenue may take the position that you owe tax there. For instance, an Illinois architect needed to file in Minnesota because although the architect may never have stepped foot in Minnesota, the drawings were for a project in Minnesota[28]. A C-Corporation may need to file in that state for its business, but the owner does not. However, an owner of a pass-through entity may need to file in that nonresident state as well as the business, because there may also be non-resident withholding requirements.

2. TAXES ON TRANSACTIONS

SALES TAXES

Any state where you have a physical presence will require you to collect and pay sales tax from customers in that state. Sales tax is due on sales of goods and, in some states, on sales of services. If you typically buy stuff to re-sell, you may be able to get a sales tax reseller's certificate from your state's department of revenue.

Contrary to popular wisdom, sales tax is due on all purchases by customers in your state (if you state has sales taxes), whether they buy from you at your brick and mortar store or at your internet website. Internet sales are not really exempt from sales tax – if you buy a computer as a customer on Amazon and you don't pay sales tax, you actually owe use tax in your state.

Certainly if you have an office or a store in a state, you owe sales tax in that state. The physical presence is called "nexus." However, if you do not have a physical presence in a state, you are not required to collect sales taxes from customers in that state.[32] But, many states have a fiercely aggressive definition of nexus. To figure out where you have nexus, you should consult a tax lawyer, an accountant and, as a last resort, the applicable state's revenue agency.

Alaska, Delaware, Hawaii, Montana, New Hampshire and Oregon do not have a sales tax; some states also exempt food or clothing. To figure out sales tax on your website, you may want to use a good online shopping cart, which may calculate sales tax rates for you.

TRANSFER TAXES

Transfer taxes are taxes on the passing of title to property. Transfer taxes vary depending on the location of the property. Most of the time, only the outright sale of property will get taxed, but sometimes there is a tax on leasing property (for instance, in Florida).

3. PAYROLL AND OTHER WITHHOLDING TAXES

You know that employers need to withhold federal and state income taxes on employees. If you do not have a proper social security number of FEIN on file, you also need to withhold federal and state income taxes on independent contractors. In some states, the state may require withholding tax on profits of pass-through entities regardless of whether the profit is distributed to the owner. The federal government also imposes withholding requirements on non-US resident owners, unless certain exceptions are met.

Unemployment, Worker's Compensation, FICA and Medicare payments may also need to be paid on employee wages. Be careful about trying to circumvent employment laws by classifying employees as independent contractors – there are penalties to pay if the government comes along and reclassifies the independent contractor as an employee. Seek professional assistance in such classifications. You are usually safer classifying a service provider as an employee when in doubt.

UNEMPLOYMENT INSURANCE AND WORKERS COMPENSATION

Most states require companies to register with whichever agencies regulate unemployment insurance and workers compensation and then to take out that insurance based on their laws and guidelines.

4. MISCELLAENOUS TAXES

The federal government also imposes some special taxes particular to certain industries. For instance, imported inventory may be taxed by import duties and tanning bed rentals may be subject to certain taxes.

5. FILE TAX RETURNS ANNUALLY

If you do not file a tax return, the government can audit and penalize you anytime – there is no statute of limitations if you don't file a tax return. Sometimes penalties and interest are imposed on the tax amount due, and other times the penalties are based upon the number of months the return has not been filed. Make sure you keep good records of your income, expenses, tax returns and back up documentation. An automatic extension can be filed to allow additional time to gather and complete the return, but the extension does not extend the time to pay the taxes.

TAX TREATMENT OF ENTITY	RETURN TO FILE	RETURN DUE DATE
C-Corporation	1120	March 15
S-Corporation	1120S	March 15
-Pass-through partnership return (a business entity with 2 or more partners) -Limited Liability Company -General Partnership -Limited Partnership	1065	April 15
-Pass-through return with only one individual owner -Sole Proprietorship -Single member LLC	Schedule C to be filed with that individual's 1040	April 15

Most taxpayers estimate the tax liability and pay this amount with the extension to avoid penalties and interest.

SET UP A WEBSITE

Business in the 21st century requires a website. To set up a website, you need (1) a domain name; (2) a host; (3) to build a website.

1.   GET A DOMAIN NAME

To set up a **w**ebsite, you need a domain name. You get a domain name by registering one with an accredited domain name registrar. Domain name registrars are accredited by the Internet Corporation for Assigned Names and Numbers ("ICANN"), which is the group in charge of internet addresses. Registrars catalogue and collect records about domain names and publish that information using WHOIS. WHOIS is the Internet database storage and retrieval method for all domain names. Domain names are actually leased by site owners, rather than purchased. Registries and registrars charge fees, usually small, for their services. Find an ICANN-accredited registrar, like POW WEB or Go Daddy.

When registering your domain, you will need to supply several pieces of information, including:

- ✓ **Administrative contact**. The administrative contact has the highest level of control over a domain. Information about who is responsible for domain names is publicly available but it is possible to register a domain in someone else's name or privately through your registrar if they offer the service
- ✓ **Technical contact**. The technical contact manages the name servers of a domain name (that leads to the accessibility of the domain name)
- ✓ **Billing contact.** The billing contact gets the bills and processes them for payment
- ✓ **Name servers**. Name servers are the file locations of your site. When you pick a host, your host's name servers will be used to fill this space; however, if you are registering a domain name before you've picked a host (likely), take the name servers offered by your registrar to start and you can change it later

WHAT'S A DOMAIN NAME?

A domain name is part of a Uniform Resource Locator ("URL") used to access web sites. For example:

URL

`http://www.hapandhaz.com/index.html`

TOP-LEVEL DOMAIN NAME

`.com`

SECOND-LEVEL DOMAIN NAME

`hapandhaz.com`

HOST NAME

`www.hapandhaz.com`

SUBDOMAIN NAME

`mousetrap.hapandhaz.com`

There is a big and lucrative market for holding and re-selling domain names. According to Guinness World Records and MSNBC and Wikipedia, the most expensive domain name sales on record were:

- ✓ Business.com for $7.5 million in December 1999
- ✓ AsSeenOnTv.com for $5.1 million in January 2000
- ✓ Altavista.com for $3.3 million in August 1998
- ✓ Wine.com for $2.9 million in September 1999
- ✓ CreditCards.com for $2.75 million in July 2004
- ✓ Autos.com for $2.2 million in December 1999
- ✓ Bank.ht for $1.4 million in March 2010
- ✓ Inn.im for $1.8 million in December 2009

2. PICK A HOST

Your domain name gives you an address, but you still have to get a place to put your website and its files and contents. The place is a web host. Web hosts provide space and access on computer servers. There are hundreds of web hosts, some cheap and some not. Some web hosts are perfect for small blogs or static brochure sites. Some web hosts are better for extensive, dynamic sites with lots of traffic and bandwidth needs. Your plans will drive your needs. There are reviewers who provide ratings of web hosts, including their customer service and reliability to help you select the right one.

3. BUILD YOUR SITE

In the beginning of the Internet, websites were magical products of genius. Today, websites can be created by anyone. You can (a) code from scratch, (b) pick a website builder program or service that is designed to make it easier for non-technical folks to make a site by giving you a choice of modules to throw into your site, (c) build your site out of an open source website platform; and/or (d) just hire someone to do it all for you.

CODE FROM SCRATCH

You can learn and/or use HTML, Java, PHP, ColdFusion or other software systems and languages. God Bless. Coding from scratch may be the best way to make a website. In the short run, it's probably the most expensive.

PICK A WEBSITE BUILDER

The internet is filled with software packages that will allow you to build a website. Some of these software packages are neato! Your web host will probably offer other software that gives you the ability to make your site. Here are some resources and packages.

⇨ www.squarespace.com
⇨ www.yola.com
⇨ www.officelive.com
⇨ www.google.com/sites

⇨ www.simplespark.com for a catalogue of web based services or software
⇨ http://www.go2web20.net/ for a catalogue of web based services or software

OPEN SOURCE WEBSITE PLATFORM

There are software programs that are open source and designed to help people make websites. "Open Source" means that the source code – the guts or secret ingredients of the software – are available for viewing and use (though not necessarily ownership or free use). Open source software is often supported by vibrant communities of developers and activists who work out the bugs, provide support and grow the software. Open source is an astonishing and beautiful world of collaboration and creativity. The software offerings are extensive, from easy to use to difficult and technical. Below are some of the biggies:

✓ Wordpress
✓ Joomla
✓ Drupal

JUST HIRE A DEVELOPER

If you have no skills or time, but you have some cash, hire someone. It is exceedingly difficult to find a reliable, competent and affordable web developer, but it is not impossible. If you encounter one, let me know. And, here are some spaces to look:

⇨ www.Elance.com - Post projects and receive bids. Review profiles, reviews and portfolios for vendors
⇨ www.Craigslist.org - Local classifieds from around the world
⇨ www.AgentsofValue.com - Agency that specializes in webmasters and traffic generation
⇨ www.GetFriday.com - The agency featured in The Four Hour Work Week[33]
⇨ www.Rentacoder.com - Excellent for finding software programmers
⇨ www.Guru.com - Another marketplace for finding a wide variety of freelancers

INTERNET WEBSITE COMPLIANCE

As the internet grows, so do the laws that govern it. When operating a website, you need (1) a privacy policy; (2) a security policy that protects information; (3) terms of use; (4) to try to protect user content (if you take it); and (5) to protect kids' information.

1. PRIVACY POLICY

A growing area of law requires websites to post a written notice on your site that tells visitors how you collect their personal information, how you store it and what you do with it. There is a discussion about privacy policies in Section 4.

2. SECURITY MEASURES

REASONABLE SECURITY PROCEDURES

For your website, you must maintain **reasonable security procedures** to protect personal information and notify users when the security of their personal information has been compromised. Reasonable security procedures are measures that ensure the confidentiality of personal information, protect against reasonably foreseeable threats, and ensure personnel compliance.[34] You can divide your security measures into administrative, physical and technical measures.[35]

Administrative. Administrative efforts include business practices to manage security:

- ✓ a risk analysis and risk management assessment of potential risks
- ✓ policies & procedures to handle information and to reduce risks to a reasonable level
- ✓ specific personnel designated to be in charge of privacy and security
- ✓ periodic personnel training
- ✓ contingency plans for fire, vandalism and system failure

Physical. Physical efforts include a plan to protect computers and files, such as:

- ✓ access controls
- ✓ computer security policies
- ✓ device control policies

Technical. Technical efforts include technical measures to limit and monitor information access and human error:

- ✓ encrypt data
- ✓ firewalls, automatic logoffs, password systems
- ✓ industry best practices for the current standard of care

3. TERMS OF USE

Most websites have rules of the road for using the site. These rules can be encapsulated in a contract, which can be called "Terms of Use," or some other similar name. The Terms of Use should include:

- ✓ Description of what people can do on the site
- ✓ Order and payment terms
- ✓ Reasons why the user can get thrown out
- ✓ Prohibitions
- ✓ Terms for posting content (if any)
- ✓ Boilerplate (e.g. entire agreement, no assignment, severability, governing law; submission to jurisdiction, rights of third parties, amendment, notices, counterparts and waivers).
- ✓ Copyright and trademark notices
- ✓ A DCMA policy (see below)

The Terms of Use is a legal contract, subject to the rules of formation for all other contracts – if the user can't see the contract and manifest an intention to agree to it, it ain't a contract.

To form an Internet-based contract, do these things:

- ✓ Stick links to the Terms of Use, the Privacy Policy and your Copyright Notice, in a readable font, <u>on every page</u>
- ✓ If there is no moment when a user has to present his information or sign up for a membership, then the Terms of Use needs to say (a) that the user's use of the site constitutes agreement to the Terms of Use; and (b) if the user cannot agree to the Terms of Use, he should stop using the site immediately
- ✓ If there is a moment when a user gives his name, then have the Terms of Use pop up on a separate page and require a clicked acceptance of the agreement to continue using the site; even better, make the user page down through the Terms of Use to get to the "I Accept" button

✓ When you make changes to the Terms of Use, (a) send them out to users by email and alert them to the change; and (b) post a notice on the site about the changes. If feasible, you can also make the user click through the revised terms marked to show your changes the next time he logs on

4. USER GENERATED CONTENT

User generated content can cause all kinds of problems. Content that your users post could be defamatory, stolen, pornographic, harassing, unlawful or criminal. There are a couple of things you can do to manage the risk, including a DMCA policy and a CDA policy.

DMCA POLICY

The Digital Millennium Copyright Act ("DMCA") was created to extend copyright protection to digital technology and the Internet[36]. Essentially, DMCA keeps websites free of copyright infringement liability for their user's posted content as long as they didn't coax or solicit posting of the content.[37] DMCA puts the burden on the owner of the copyright to police the pirating of their work and protect it "with specificity." [38]

To comply with DMCA:

1. Adopt a policy to (a) refrain from soliciting or coaxing infringing content; and (b) comply with the DMCA

2. Designate an employee to serve as the DMCA agent and register that person with the U.S. Copyright Office (it's $30.00)

3. On your site and/or Terms of Use, request that any claims of infringing content should be sent to your DMCA agent and your agent's address and email address

4. When you get a demand to take down content that describes the content, take the content down and post a popup in its absence that says, "Content removed at request of content owner"

5. If the user whose content is taken down sends you a demand to restore the removed content, you have to send a copy of the demand to the party that originally requested the removal; you have to restore the content if the complainer doesn't get a court order to keep the content off your site.

COMMUNICATIONS DECENCY ACT

The Communications Decency Act of 1996 ("CDA") keeps websites safe from liability for the acts of its users if the website didn't originate or specifically select the content.[39] The CDA does not keep you safe if user generated content is in some way criminal or infringes someone's intellectual property. And, you can screen and remove content to "in good faith restrict access ... to obscene, lewd, lascivious, filthy, excessively violent, harassing, or otherwise objectionable content." However, once you start making content decisions, you lose your immunity under CDA. One way websites deal with the CDA is to include "offensive content" buttons that empower users to police the site and alert the website owner to content that is "objectionable," so it can be removed without running afoul of the CDA.

5. PROTECT KIDS' INFORMATION

If you operate a website that knowingly collects personal info from kids under 13, you have to comply with The Children's Online Privacy Protection Act ("COPPA"). COPPA protects the privacy of kids and their information. Please see the COPPA discussion in Section 4.

WAR STORIES

EXPEDIA

THE WAR

Expedia.com's user agreement specifically said expedia.com would not be responsible for the quality of hotel rooms users book through the website. An expedia.com user sued Expedia over a shoddy hotel room, claiming he wasn't bound by the user agreement because he didn't read it.

THE WINNER

Expedia.com won. Why? Because the user agreement, which stated that users consent to be bound by the agreement by accessing and using the Web site, was linked at the bottom of every page and he could have and should have read it.

THE MORAL OF THE STORY

Stick links to your privacy policy and terms and conditions on every page. (Burcham v. Expedia, Inc., 2009 WL 586513 (E.D. Mo. 2009).)

NEGOTIATE AN OFFICE LEASE

When you find space you like, negotiate, negotiate, negotiate, for the best deal you can. Be polite and respectful, but unafraid. If the potential landlord is hard to deal with, you may want to walk away. It's only going to get worse later. And, make sure you have a good lawyer on your side reviewing and negotiating your lease.

Let's discuss some of the parts of the lease you will need to negotiate, such as (1) the term; (2) the rent; (3) furniture; (4) security deposits; (5) permitted use; and (6) improvements on the space.

1. TERM

The term is the period of time when you have the right and the obligation to pay for the space. Because commercial space sits vacant for an average of five months between tenants, landlords usually seek longer terms (3-5 years). You may also want a longer lease term if you think the terms are favorable compared to the market. If you want an out clause, you may be able to negotiate termination rights coupled with a rent termination payment (usually 3-6 months of rent).

ASSIGNMENT AND SUBLETTING

You should negotiate enough flexibility in the assignment and subletting clause to allow for mergers, reorganizations, and ownership changes.

RIGHT OF FIRST OFFER OR FIRST REFUSAL FOR ADDITIONAL SPACE

A right of first offer obligates your landlord to show you space that opens up in the building before marketing it to third parties. A right of first refusal on space obligates the landlord to give you a chance to match any third party's bona fide offer for space in the building.

OPTIONS TO RENEW & EXPAND

A renewal option gives you the right to renew the term of your lease. Expansion option gives you the right to grow your space as your business grows. Renewal options are best for the tenant if the renewal rent is fixed and predetermined, rather than subject to negotiation.

MOVE IN DATE

If a space has been vacant for a long time, you may be able to negotiate a move in date earlier than the beginning of your lease term, provided that you pay your first rental installment before you get the keys.

2. RENT

The landlord will start with an asking price for rent. Always negotiate the asking price downwards. Typically a downward adjustment of 5-10% is reasonable, but you may be able to argue for a deeper reduction based on current rates in the market.

FREE RENT

For longer terms, landlords may give a few months' rent free. Your ability to negotiate free rent will depend on the vacancy rate in the surrounding area, your riskiness as a tenant and the length of the lease. A lease of less than 2 years probably will not generate free rent. A lease term of 5 years may get you 3-5 months of free rent. Free rent is usually provided as an incentive to cover moving costs.

COMMISSIONS

If you are not represented by a leasing broker, you could try to negotiate a deduction of your missing broker's share of the commission as a deduction from the rent.

UPFRONT COSTS

For long term leases in a market with commercial vacancies, landlords may be willing to kick in upfront move-in costs.

RENT ESCALATIONS

Most leases contain rent increases throughout the term. Optimally, the increases will be predetermined. These rent increases should be calculated based on some market index, like Consumer Price Index. You may be able to negotiate a 2 or 3 year delay in rent increases and/or a cap on yearly increases or total rent.

NET LEASES & CAM

Common area maintenance is a collection of operating costs that the landlord passes on to the tenant ("CAM"). These should be carefully negotiated. For instance, you should ensure that your share of CAM equals your share of the building. If you have to pay property taxes, you should negotiate a right to either fight or have the landlord fight any property tax increases. And, you can try to get a cap on the total amount of CAM. There are standard names in the commercial real estate industry for different sets of costs passed on to the tenant.

SINGLE NET LEASE

A single net lease (a/k/a Net or N). This type of lease makes the tenant pay the property taxes.

DOUBLE NET LEASE

A double net lease (Net-Net or NN). This type of lease (a) makes the tenant pay the property taxes and building insurance; and (b) the landlord pays expenses incurred for structural repairs and common area maintenance. "Roof and structure" is sometimes calculated as a reserve and often equal to $0.15 per square foot.

TRIPLE NET LEASE

A triple net lease (Net-Net-Net or NNN). This type of lease makes the tenant pay property taxes, building insurance, and maintenance (the three 'Nets'), plus all costs associated with the repair and maintenance of any common area. A triple net lease is often used for freestanding buildings.

BONDABLE LEASE

A bondable lease (a/k/a **absolute triple net lease** or a "hell-or-high-water lease"). This type of lease makes the tenant liable for everything including the obligations to rebuild after damage, and to pay rent even after condemnation. These leases are not terminable by the tenant, nor are rent abatements permissible. An example of this type of lease would be a leaseback arrangement in which a retailer leases back the building it formerly owned and continues to run the store. Putting all risk on the tenant is an exchange for giving the tenant all of the upsides of the space.

3. FURNITURE

Make sure you specify up front whether the furniture is going to be left after your lease expires and if you will be responsible for purchasing the furniture.

4. SECURITY DEPOSITS

Security deposits reflect the landlord's fear that you will destroy the space or stiff him on the rent. Security deposits range from 1-12 months; commonly, though, the security deposit is 1-3 months.

5. PERMITTED USE OF THE PREMISES

A lease usually lists the things you can and cannot do in the premises. Make sure the permitted uses capture how you intend to use the space. Also, look for any prohibitions on competing with co-tenants that may keep you from operating your business.

6. WORK & IMPROVEMENTS

All spaces may need improvements or alterations. Make sure that you can make improvements or alterations with the landlord's consent and that consent won't be unreasonably withheld or delayed. If you sign a long lease, the landlord may be willing to pay for and/or perform the work. You should certainly test your landlord's willingness to take care of the improvements you want made.

HAP AND HAZARD SET UP THEIR OPERATIONS

Hap and Hazard took copious notes of everything Gravity told them about getting organized (except that Hazard rolled his eyes a lot during the finance and accounting portion). They left with all kinds of excitement.

"What should we do first, Hazard?"

"First, we should finish our business plan and budget. Along the way, we should figure out what we really need to bring the MouseTrap to market."

"Good idea, Haz."

With renewed vigor, Hap and Hazard continued to work nights and weekends (and many afternoons).

Hazard bought a commercial license to QuickBooks, but one version back to reduce the cost. Hazard then set up his accounting system just the way he liked, which included the four main financial systems plus a "dashboard" view of cash ins and outs specifically for Hap.

Hazard also registered the business with the commercial credit agencies and took out a phone number to begin building credit.

Hap began to plant a stake on the web. First, he bought the domain name www.thesolarmousetrap.com and a bunch of variations. Then, Hap set up a simple single page website using Microsoft Live. The small website foreshadowed the MouseTrap and invited interested people to sign up for email newsletters. The website also began to establish a presence in the web crawlers and search engines.

Finally, Hap and Haz decided to get an office, but a small, cheap one. First, they looked at coworking offices. A coworking office is an office suite shared by a bunch of different businesses. Grass roots and entrepreneurial, they can give a young business a starter home, a community and a copier for a reasonable price. The coworking spaces that Hap and Haz visited were either filled or filthy.

Then, they looked at renting office space in a business center. Business centers are like coworking offices, but are usually run by bigger companies. In their price point, they could afford a closet without windows or unassigned desk space.

Frustrated, Hap said, "Hazard, let's just find our own space. Something we can clean and decorate."

"Okay, but remember: cheap, cheap."

They looked at space after space, all too tight, too expensive or too remote. Finally, they found it.

Hap was walking down a hot, dirty street, when he looked up above the doorway to a drugstore and he saw a sign that said "office for rent" on a partially opened window. Thrilled by the prospect of opening a window after a decade of working in a hermetically sealed office, he wrote down the number.

Later that day, he toured the building, and the available office: two rooms with a sink, bumpy walls, stained carpet and 3 windows overlooking a McDonald's arch. But the monthly price: $450.00. He took it. Then, he showed it to Hazard.

Hazard took note of the building's business offerings. Massages, herbal treatments and many nameless offices. He blanched.

Hap said, excitedly, "It's low rent."

"It certainly is."

"Look, Haz," Hap said. He opened the window and a breeze blew in.

"I love it," Haz agreed.

"Good, because our first payment is due Monday."

Hazard took over negotiations. By the time the lease was signed, the landlord agreed to repaint the office, let them move in early, keep the rent stable for 2 years and give them a right to terminate early with 3 months payment.

Following a trip to IKEA and Home Depot and three days of work, Hap turned the office into, not a palace, but a creative, functional space. And a place to call their own. They invited Gravity to see it.

Gravity said, "I love it, boys. You look like you're serious."

"We are," Hazard answered. "In fact, we're ready to get to the next stage. We need to raise some money. Can you help us? We don't know where to start."

"I CAN TRY."

END NOTES

1 In his terrific book, *The Art of the Start*, Guy Kawasaki commands the reader to create a business mantra instead of a mission statement. I recommend a read.

2 Internal Revenue Code Section 3121 is the focal point for tax definitions of employees.

3 §3121(d) of the Internal Revenue Code (IRC)

4 IRC §3102

5 IRC §3403, IRC §6672

6 The National Labor Relations Act ("NLRA") adopted in 1935 as part of the New Deal. 29 U.S.C. § 151 is the major statute that governs collective bargaining agreements. The National Labor Relations Act trumps state law and is administered by the National Labor Relations Board.

7 I know, Counselor – they aren't penalties, because penalties are prohibited. But, "Remedies" is confusing to the uninitiated.

8 For instance, in California, noncompetes are pretty much unenforceable unless they arise out of the sale of a business.

9 Noncompetes are regarded enforceable if they (a) have adequate and separate consideration for the covenant; (b) are ancillary or related to an employment contract; (c) are reasonable in duration and geography; (d) are reasonably necessary for the protection of the employer, and (e) do not impose undue hardship on the employee or disregard the interests of the public.

10 *Carter-Shields v. Alton Health Institute*, 317 Ill. App. 3d 260, 250 Ill. Dec. 806, 739 N.E. 569 (Ill. App. 5 Dist 2000).

11 These long term customer relationships are typically referred to as "near permanent customer relationships" which are long term customers of the business that the employee would not have known but for his employment with the business. There is also a 7 factor test (1) the number of years required to develop the clientele, (2) the amount of money invested to acquire clients, (3) the degree of difficulty in acquiring clients, (4) the extent of personal customer contact by the employee, (5) the extent of the employer's knowledge of its clients, (6) the duration of the customers' association with the employer, and (7) the continuity of the employer-customer relationship. *Agrimerica, Inc. v. Mathes*, 199 Ill. App. 3d 435, 443, 557 N.E. 2d 357, 363 (Ill. App. 1 Dist. 1990).

12 Claims under contact law are considered wrongful discharge. Claims under tort law are retaliatory discharge. Most discrimination claims are not wrongful discharge claims.

13 *Meritor Savings Bank v. Vinson* (1986); Title VII of the 1964 Civil Rights Act.

14 The EEOC factors for a hostile work environment are: (a) whether the conduct was verbal or physical, or both; (b) the frequency of the conduct; (c) whether the conduct was hostile and offensive; (d) whether the alleged harasser is a supervisor or a co-worker; (e) whether the harassment is directed at more than one individual.

15 U.S. Age Discrimination and Employment Act of 1967 (ADEA)

16 29 CFR § 1625.12.

17 Fair Credit Reporting Act (FCRA). Sections 604, 606, and 615

18 Fair Labor Standards Act, 29 USCA 201 to 219; state wage payment laws.

19 Executive assistants who have been delegated authority over significant matters may be exempt (like Joan from *Mad Men*).

20 The Immigration Reform and Control Act of 1986 ("IRCA"), Pub.L. 99-603, 8 USC 1 et seq.

21 Corporate income tax is a big issue and billions of dollars have been spent trying to figure out how to reduce or escape it.

22 The minute prescription is called a "Certificate of Designation."

23 There is also a duty to provide "honest services" which federal prosecutors use to bust elected officials and corporate officers who get caught with their hand in the cookie jar. (18.USC 1346). However, following the Supreme Court decision to limit application of the crime in *Skilling v. US*, No. 08-1394 (2010), its application is unclear.

24 If you are reading or negotiating conversion prices and triggers based on anything in this book, please please go get a lawyer. If you are a lawyer trying to figure out conversion price from this book, please please go ask your mentor.

25 The absence of similar footnotes appended to every sentence like the immediately preceding is not (a) an indication that you should use this book as a replacement for getting qualified legal counsel; or (b) grounds for your shoddy law suit.

26 A/K/A "mandatory redemption

27 This is a reproduction of an excellent article entitled "Beginners' Guide to Financial Statements," sec.gov, http://www.sec.gov/investor/pubs/begfinstmtguide.htm. I borrowed it, because it seems to be a government publication, so I assume it was created by a government employee and thus is not copyrightable.

28 Minnesota Revenue Statute section 290.191(j).

29 States cannot require mail-order businesses (and thus online retailers) to collect sales tax unless they have a physical presence in the state, because compliance with 7,500 tax jurisdictions was too complex for sellers to manage, and would put a strain on interstate commerce. *Quill v. North Dakota*, 504 U.S. 298, (1992).

30 Ferriss, Timothy (2007). *The 4-Hour Workweek: Escape 9-5, Live Anywhere, and Join the New Rich*. Crown Publishing Group, (2007).

31 These procedures follow the Health Insurance Portability and Accountability Act (which, with Gramm-Leach-Biliely Act, are the most well developed American laws on privacy). See Milewski, Anthony D. Jr., Compliance with California Privacy Laws, 2006.

32 Under the HIPAA regime.

33 The Digital Millennium Copyright Act, 17 U.S.C. § 512 (the "DCMA").The DMCA protects websites from copyright infringement for content posted by users if: (a) the website does not "receive a financial benefit directly attributable to the infringing activity;" (b) it does not have "the right and ability to control such activity;" (c) it has registered an agent of service with the U.S. Copyright Office; and (d) it maintains a DMCA policy. You don't have to monitor your website, but you have to terminate repeat offenders. There is a fine line being drawn between safe and unsafe business practices.

34 Consider two cases. YouTube users posted hours of Viacom's content and YouTube management knew about it, though didn't actively ask for it. As soon as Viacom sent a letter listing all of the pieces of content that belonged to them and ordering their removal, YouTube took it all down – as a result, YouTube was not liable to Viacom. Viacom v. YouTube, 2010 WL 25 32404 (SDNY 6/23/10). In contrast, consider Gary Fung, who operates a Bit Torrent site, but he's been shut down by a court of law. Mr. Fung apparently kept a list of top 20 movies in theaters next to a link for users to upload (presumably pirated) films. The Motion Picture Association of America sued and a federal judge put Mr. Fung out of business. Columbia Pictures et al v. Fung, 2:06 – cv – 05578-SUM – JC CD Cal 10/21/09 & 5/20/10

35 Viacom.

36 "[n]o provider or user of an interactive computer service shall be treated as the publisher or speaker of any information provided by another information content provider"

section two

GETTING FUNDED

CHAPTERS IN THIS SECTION:

6) Funding Options
7) Equity
8) Debt

FUNDING OPTIONS

Gravity continued, "Let's discuss why you need to understand funding options."

CHAPTER 06

WHY YOU NEED TO KNOW ABOUT FUNDING

Most businesses need cash from the outside for several reasons. First, most businesses need money in greater quantities than the founders have in the bank. Second, many business starters believe that using a lot of their own money in the business clouds their judgment; instead, they prefer to use other peoples' money. Third, even if the business is profitable, cash could be needed because of seasonal or cyclical cash dips.

EQUITY AND DEBT

When people invest in a company, they expect to get something in return. What they get for their money is either **Equity** or **Debt.** Let's talk about the difference between (1) equity; and (2) debt.

1. EQUITY

Equity financing is money (or property) that someone gives you for a piece of ownership of your company. Equity investments are often funded by friends, relatives, employees, customers, or colleagues. However, the most common source of professional equity funding comes from private equity firms. Equity is governed by a purchase agreement and agreements among the owners of the company.

EQUITY	
ADVANTAGES	DISADVANTAGES
✓ No personal guaranty ✓ Could be a bigger amount than debt ✓ Usually no obligation to pay back the investment ✓ Investors often join board, providing expertise and counsel, as well as discipline	✓ "Securities Laws," a painful spider web of red tape ✓ Equity will dilute (reduce) your total ownership in your company ✓ Investors often join board, providing expertise and counsel, as well as discipline ✓ Investors have a right to see the books and records of the company at their request ✓ You will have "fiduciary" duties to your investors (like ethics and diligence)

2. DEBT

Debt is money that has to be paid back, usually with interest. It can come from friends and family and complete strangers, as well as banks, credit unions and credit card companies. Debt is usually governed by a loan agreement and a separate promissory note.

BOOTSTRAPPING

You can't talk about 21st century startups without mentioning bootstrapping. "Bootstrapping" is starting and operating a business using a slight amount of your own cash and then only expanding when and if there is enough cash from operations. Bootstrapping is a fantastic way to start a business. You don't mess around with investors, you keep control and you take the business higher and higher only when you have proven your concept. Eventually, capital needs may force you to abandon bootstrapping. If you want to bootstrap, you should still treat yourself as an investor. Record your investments in a stock register. If you loan money to your company, have your company give you a promissory note in return. Your company is not you – it is a separate entity, with separate risks and exposures, and should be treated separately.

DEBT	
ADVANTAGES	DISADVANTAGES
✓ You don't have to give ownership in the company in exchange for the money ✓ The bank probably won't join your board and they pretty much stay out of the running of your business ✓ You don't have to give them a cut of your profits ✓ You don't have to give them a cut of your tax losses ✓ You repay the loan over time – once it's repaid, your obligations are over ✓ You may be able to deduct your interest payments as a business expenses ✓ The people who lend money are usually easier to figure out than people who buy ownership in your company	✓ Remember Goodfellas - "fuck you, pay me"; even if you don't have the cash, or you need your cash for payroll or anything else, you have to pay the bank, on time ✓ Your lender will probably stick "loan covenants" into your loan contract that say that they can call their loan if you get certain bad financial results or do something major without their approval ✓ Your lender may demand you sign a personal guaranty

EQUITY

Gravity said, "Let's talk about sources of equity and parts of an equity deal."

CHAPTER 07

SOURCES OF EQUITY CAPITAL

Sources of equity capital include friends and family, and professional investors.

3. FRIENDS AND FAMILY

The first and most obvious sources of capital are friends and family. Friends and family may be the most convenient and accessible investors and the most willing. Friends and Family are friends and family members who give you money to start a business. The securities laws still apply. But, now there is guilt and Thanksgiving involved. Going into business with friends and family can also change the relationships, so proceed with caution. And, get everything in writing.

4. PROFESSIONAL EQUITY INVESTORS

The most common source of larger investments is professional investors. A professional investor is someone who invests cash in ventures they don't work in or didn't start. There are millions of them. Professional investors are largely professional risk takers, made up of rich people, government backed groups, insurance companies, pension funds or financial behemoths.

Many private equity professionals actually specialize in a particular industry, so they know a lot about the industry's products, revenue models, prospects and landscape. That expertise makes them a valuable resource to you and a tough opponent in negotiations.

The Exit rights we talked about earlier are absolutely critical to professional investors. Investors must see a clear path to converting their investment to more cash than they invested.

Professional investors fall into a bunch of categories from small scale to big scale: (a) incubators and accelerators; (b) angels; (c) venture capitalists; (d) private equity, and (e) strategic buyers.

INCUBATORS AND ACCELERATORS

Incubators and accelerators are entrepreneurial honors programs for promising startups. They have started cropping up around the country and can take the place of friends and family investors. You typically have to apply, but once in, you get a little seed capital, coaching and networking. The typical investment is between $15,000 and $50,000.

ANGEL INVESTORS

An angel investor invests in startup or early stage ventures. Angel investors are often retired business owners or executives. Some angels organize in groups or networks to share access, opportunities and due diligence. These angel groups may focus on a common type of investment or a common geographical area. Angel networks are usually referral sources or matchmakers for angels and startups.

Angel deals are less rigorous than VC deals because they are usually just investing their own money or the money of a group of angels. Angel capital fills the gap between money raised through friends and family and money raised through venture capital.

Particularly since it is hard to raise more than $100,000 from friends and family and VCs won't invest under $1 million, angel money can be critical to the early stages of a business. Angels also may invest in ventures that are too risky for banks but lack the upside required by a VC. Angel capital is common as a second round of financing, particularly while the founders seek bigger rounds from VCs.

Angel financing can be expensive capital. Because the risk is high, the return must be high. Angels may prefer to take debt or a combination of debt and convertible equity. Like VCs, angels will want an exit strategy to cash out, including a buyout, a put option or an initial public offering ("IPO"). Angels might expect a five-year exit and a return of 3-5 times initial investment. There is also a subset of Angels called "Super Angels," who invest in larger amounts (up to $1,000,000.)

VENTURE CAPITAL

Venture capital is investment in a new or emerging company. Typically, venture capital firms raise money from other people and then invest it in businesses. A venture capital firm ("VC") sets up a fund and identifies a target amount of money to raise and an investment target for the money. The VC then collects promises to invest from investors and later draws down on the promises as needed. The investors in venture capital firms are usually institutional investors or high net worth individuals, because these two groups have more money to invest and require less disclosure and hand holding under the securities laws. When the fund reaches the target amount it "closes" and the fund's lifespan begins. The fund's lifespan is often 10 years.

PRIVATE EQUITY

Private Equity ("PE") firms are often set up like a VC. They invest in advanced, mature companies with some cash to squeeze out. Private equity typically buy companies using new debt that they take out on the assets of the company they are buying (aka "leveraged buyouts"). The PE guys then install new management, cut costs with a hatchet and sell the company either back to the public markets or to another private equity firm. Some private equity firms may specialize in leveraged buyouts, growth capital and distressed capital. Hedge funds can also walk and talk like private equity funds.

AMOUNT OF CAPITAL

Incubators and Accelerators may invest between $15,000 and $50,000. Angels typical investment is between $20,000 and $500,000. VCs on average typically will only invest in chunks of $500,000 and up in companies with $2 million of revenue and $1 million of prior capital, though there are exceptions. Private Equity guys usually describe companies that do deals of $100 million in companies with revenues in excess $500 million. Angels, VCs and Private Equity folks hear lots of pitches, but only invest in a fraction of the pitches they hear. Typically, 1/3 of investments fail, 1/3 of investments underperform and less than 1/3 meet expectations by returning 10-30 times the investment. [1]

Since we're talking about companies that get bought into or out, we should mention strategic buyers. Strategic buyers are companies that buy other businesses for strategic reasons. Those reasons can include buying competing or complimentary products, buying a customer list or even just taking a competitor out of the market.

VC/PE Compensation – Two and 20. VCs and Private Equity managers typically charge management fees and a carried interest (a "two and 20" arrangement):

Management fees – this is usually an annual management fee of 2% of all assets under management.

Carried interest – this is a portion of the fund's yearly profits (usually 20%, but can be higher depending on demand).

There is some wisdom to only resorting to VC/PE capital in situations where bank debt or institutional debt is not possible or attractive due to balance sheet (debt to equity) inadequacies or the large amount of capital needed. In some cases, large capital needs may require use of bank debt, mezzanine debt (debt subordinated to another lender) and venture capital together.

PROFESSIONAL INVESTOR CAPITAL		
INVESTOR	ADVANTAGES	DISADVANTAGES
VC	✓ Your credibility takes steroids ✓ Deep well of cash (if you can get it) ✓ The contacts and expertise of the VC	✓ Very expensive money – half your company, caps on compensation, approval rights ✓ The deal to get the money won't be pleasant ✓ The legal fees to get the money won't be pleasant or small ✓ They push for an exit (maybe before you are ready) ✓ Very formal May be forced to expand too quickly[1]
ANGEL	✓ Advice and counsel ✓ Gap filler in startup capital ✓ Contacts of angel ✓ Angels may take a more personal and mentoring role	✓ Expensive money ✓ Exit strategy

PARTS OF AN EQUITY DEAL

There are a million ways to build an equity financing deal. (There are also thousands and thousands of books and multi-book sets on everything having to do with equity.)

Once an investor buys equity, he is a business owner, so he will have the same concerns as you did when you formed the business in the first place. But now, the investor, particularly if he is a VC, may be a crafty fellow, with fancy lawyers and even fancier investors of his own; his demands may sting a little. The framework – the powers over (1) money, (2) control and an (3) exit – remain the same.

PERVERSITY IN FINANCE
TOO MUCH MONEY CHASING TOO FEW DEALS

There is a strange syndrome that affects the world of private equity that few outside of finance and big law understand: there is too much money chasing too few deals. All sorts of funding sources – people and companies who could seed new businesses or help existing businesses grow or survive – simply will not participate in investments below at least $500,000 (and that's on the very low end), because the transaction costs are too high and the payoff too low. Typical VC deals are in the many millions. It is an odd and perverse cruelty of the American world of money that the people with the cash to spend have not figured out more models for investing in equity at low dollar amounts.

MONEY

The investor's right to money includes (1) investor's contribution; (2) investor's take away; (3) dividends & distributions; and (4) anti-dilution.

1. INVESTOR'S CONTRIBUTION

The (a) amount; (b) form; and (c) timing of payment of the investor's contribution are all subject to negotiation.

HOW MUCH

How much the investor puts in will be interlaced with (a) how much you are seeking to raise; (b) the valuation of your company and opportunities presented by your business; and (c) the market.

FORM OF PAYMENT

The form should be cash, because you need it to fund your operations.

TIMING OF PAYMENT

The investor may want to pay his investment in installments and then only on the condition that you meet targets. Try and push back on this (because a hand in the bush…). Get all the cash you can as quickly as you can before they run out of money, get tired of your act or head to rehab.[2]

Future Capital Calls. There should be some discussion or arrangement about the investors' obligations to contribute more cash if necessary.

2. INVESTOR'S TAKE AWAY

The (a) size of stock; (b) type of stock; and (c) special rights inside the stock are also subject to negotiation.

SIZE OF SHARE

Expect an investor, particularly a VC or an Angel, to take a big bite out of your equity. Investors build deals on a concept called "pre money valuation." Pre-money valuation is the value of your company seconds before your investor puts in his money. Once the investor puts money in, your company has a "post money valuation." When you add the pre-money valuation to the amount invested by the VC, you get the post-money valuation. The percentage increase in the value equals the percentage of stock the VC will take. A VC firm might typically receive anywhere from 10% to 50% of the company in return for its investment. More or less is possible, but that's a typical range. The original shareholders are diluted in the process. (See Chapter 25, Valuing a Business). The method of valuing your company and the number itself must be agreed to by the VC. You may spend more time and heartache than you would like arguing about the pre money valuation of your company.

Vesting of Your Stock. Sometimes, investors may want to limit founder ownership by making founder's stock forfeitable or subject to a vesting schedule. Resist this demand if possible.

TYPE OF SHARE

Investors often insist on taking a different class of shares than founders, because those different classes of stock can give them priority to money, each year and on liquidation or sale. Often, debt convertible into equity is created and issued to them. This puts them ahead front of others for dividends and payment on liquidation, but with the power to convert to common stock of the company.

SPECIAL RIGHTS INSIDE THE SHARE

Different classes of stock usually have some rights that set them apart. Some of these rights are discussed below.

First Exit. Investors will likely want the right to get paid sooner than owners of other classes of stock if the company gets liquidated. If so, then decide the triggers and the terms for a first liquidation right.

Voting rights. Most investors will want voting rights,

except for silent partners who may be willing to buy a type of limited interest.

Convertible. Professional investors will probably want convertible securities, such as (1) convertible subordinated debentures; (2) subordinated debentures with warrants; (3) convertible preferred units/stock; or (4) preferred units/stock with warrants.

QUICK GUIDE TO ODD INVESTMENT ADJECTIVES

Common means the automatic, default type of equity created just by incorporating or organizing a company.

Convertible means the equity or debt can be transformed into another type of equity or debt.

Debenture means a document that creates or evidences a debt. Debentures in the U.S. are usually corporate bonds that are unsecured and medium to long term in duration.

Preferred means a separate class of equity that has some right(s) bigger or more valuable than other classes and more so than common equity.

Subordinated means that there is some loan or share that has to be paid off first before the subordinated loan or share can get paid.

Warrant means a right to buy shares of stock at a particular price.

3. DIVIDENDS AND DISTRIBUTIONS

Your investors may also have investors to please and they need to produce yearly numbers showing that they made smart investment decisions. As a result, VCs usually demand an annual return of 20%-40% and/or a yearly dividend that adds up if they can't be paid every year. VCs also typically insist on financial and other covenants, with real remedies for breach (such as increased dividend, accelerated redemption rights, more board seats or control, more "free" equity).

4. ANTI-DILUTION

Investors will want preemptive rights – the right to buy a pro rata amount of stock sold by the company to maintain their percentage ownership. Typically, pre-emptive rights should terminate on an IPO and exclude issuances of options and stock to employees. Investors will also want any conversion price for convertible stock or warrants to automatically reduced if the stock gets sold for much less. The best anti-dilution protection for the founder is "pay to play" anti-dilution, which means if the investor doesn't put more money in the company in later rounds, he forfeits the anti-dilution protection. The worst anti-dilution for the founder is "full ratchet." The compromise position for anti-dilution is weighted average anti-dilution protection. Make sure to carve out shares or options issued to you and your employees from anti-dilution triggers and calculations.

CONTROL

Part of the sacrifice for taking outside cash is the control you will fork over to the investor. These types of controls include: (1) voting and protective provisions; (2) Board seats; and (3) management.

1. PROTECTIVE PROVISIONS

Investors typically want voting rights and the power to influence management. However, in larger private placements, you may be able to bring in "silent" investors who act as limited partners, with no control whatsoever. These types of arrangements are typical in real estate funds and Broadway shows.

Investors who come in as active participants often demand an open pipeline of information and regular engagement (and second guessing) with management. These investors usually also grab rights to approve or blackball big actions, like the budget, sale or purchase of businesses or expenditures over a certain amount.

2. BOARD SEATS

Investors will usually demand and get seats on the Board. If they insist that you and your other founders give up control of the Board, then try and get a mutually agreed upon slate of one or more independent people to sit on the Board.

3. MANAGEMENT

Investors may also get the right to approve or initiate the hiring or firing of key management. As part of this, investors may insist that new management get hired. That will lead to two particularly dicey issues. First, what authority will new management have (particularly over you)? Second, how does the new officer get his stock or options, how does it vest and how much will it dilute your stock.

Employment Agreements & Compensation. Investors may want to limit compensation payments to management to just what is required to keep management around. They will probably insist on approval and veto power over the terms of your employment and compensation. Typically, investors also want key members of management to sign noncompetes. You should have a lawyer who represents you personally to help you with these issues.

EXIT

Investors need an exit strategy. For instance, VCs will usually insist on an exit within three to seven years with a total return of five to ten times the original investment. The company will need to consider and negotiate these rights to assure that they will not adversely affect any future rounds of financing.

Investors have three options for exits:

- ✓ Sale to the public
- ✓ Private Sales to outsiders
- ✓ Resales back to the company.

Investors have a bunch of weapons to accomplish this. To get a sale to the public, investors need to be able to force the company to facilitate the sale. So, they want registration rights (both demand and piggyback) which empower them to force the company to go public in an IPO or to have a special registered offering that includes the investor shares.

To get a private sale, investors can make the company agree to help the investor get out. For instance, they can demand tag along rights, which are rights to participate in any sale of stock by other shareholders; they can demand drag along rights, which are a right to force the other shareholders to sell out to a third party; they can also insist that any restrictions on transfer get lifted. Any of which can grease a sale to private equity or a big dog buying for strategic purposes.

Investors may also want the right to make the company by back their shares. To accomplish this, investors demand a put right which is a right to force the company to redeem their stock under certain conditions.

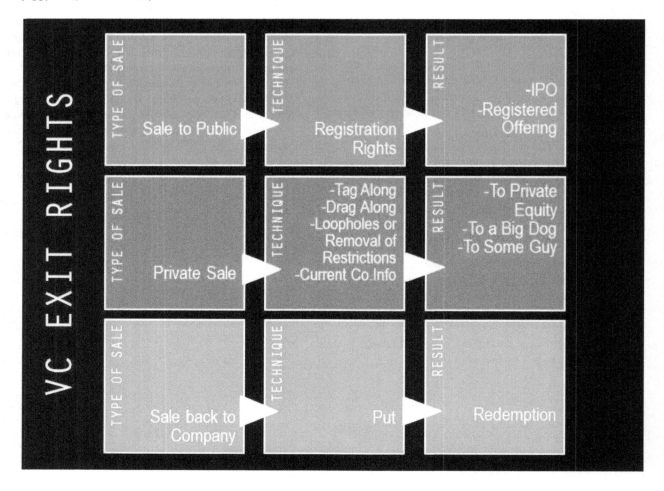

THE DOCUMENTS & THE DEAL

There are a variety of rights, phases and documents that make up an investment deal, including (1) lock up rights; (2) due diligence; (3) term sheet; (4) stock purchase agreement; (5) certificate of designation; (6) stockholders agreement; and (7) registration rights agreement.

1. LOCK-UP RIGHTS

Increasingly, investors insist on a lock-up period during which the investors have the exclusive right, but not the obligation, to make the investment. The lock-up period (usually 30-90 days) allows the investors to complete due diligence without fear that other investors will pre-empt their opportunity to invest in the company.

2. DUE DILIGENCE

Due diligence is a thorough examination into a possible deal. Due diligence includes business due diligence and legal due diligence. Business due diligence starts with an examination of financial statements and products, and proceeds to an examination of a business's nitty gritty. Legal due diligence is an examination of all of a company's contracts and obligations.

The buyer is looking for 3 things:

- ✓ Problems, including phony accounting or sales, looming litigation, labor and employment strife, weaknesses in products or services, warranty issues, cancellations by suppliers or customers, environmental dangers, ownership issues, weakness in intellectual property protections, security holes or tax problems
- ✓ Integration and synergy
- ✓ Information necessary to raise the financing for the deal

Due diligence is just horrible. Find a good, dependable, honest person to provide the information. Don't disclose even a Post-It Note without a good Nondisclosure Agreement ("NDA") in place. Seek to disclose everything that you would want to know if you were the investor.

3. TERM SHEET

Term sheets are very helpful. They allow you to come to agreement on the big points of the deal, without messing around with the minutiae. They can either list just the bare essentials or they can list all points that need to be negotiated, depending on the preferences of the parties and the deal. A short form makes negotiating easier but drafting the contracts harder. A long form makes the term sheet harder, but drafting the contracts easier.

4. STOCK PURCHASE AGREEMENT

The Stock Purchase Agreement is the umbrella contract that governs the deal. It describes the deal, lists the purchase price, what is being purchased and all conditions for the deal. It also serves as the major vehicle for disclosures and information about the company through the representations and warranties, and will establish conditions that must be satisfied prior to the investment being made. Finally, and somewhat surprisingly, it may contain rules for operating the company in the future through both affirmative and negative covenants, particularly if some of the purchase price gets paid based on future results ("earn outs"). Structurally, all other agreements ought to hang off the Stock Purchase Agreement as exhibits.

REPRESENTATIONS AND WARRANTIES

The representations and warranties serve as the primary disclosure mechanisms. Sometimes breaches of representations and warranties trigger self-executing remedies, such as a change in the conversion ratio of preferred stock to common stock. More often, though, breaches of reps and warranties are remedied by indemnification or obligations for the breacher to unwind the deal or pay damages.

COVENANTS

Following funding, the company is often obligated to promise to do some or all of the following:

Information Rights. To keep and provide access to books and records.

Financial Statements. To provide financial statements (at least quarterly; sometimes monthly; sometimes accompanied by certificate of CEO or CFO). You may want to put off being required to produce audited financial statements until the cost will not be material to your budget.

Annual Budget. To provide the annual budget and to have it approved by the Board and/or the investor before it gets adopted.

Operation. To comply with laws.

Insurance. To obtain life insurance for critical managers ("Key Person Life Insurance").

Protection of Proprietary Rights. To do everything prudent and reasonable (or sometimes possible) to protect the company's intellectual property rights.

Taxes. To pay taxes and claims when due.

Negative Covenants. To NOT, without investor approval, conduct mergers, acquisitions, dispositions, liquidations, dissolutions, related party transactions, change in business, amendment to Charter or Bylaws, to issue dividends or redemptions, to issue Issuance of Equity, to grant liens, to take on debt over a certain amount, to set management compensation. These protective provisions can be placed in the agreement among the owners or in the charter.

CONDITIONS TO CLOSING

Before you can get the money, you typically have to take care of the following:

Representations and Warranties. The reps and warranties must still be true.

Compliance and Contract Checklist. All licenses and permits necessary must be obtained and any consents to transfer company contracts must be obtained.

Securities Law Compliance. All securities laws must be complied with.

Opinion of Company Counsel. In formal transactions, an opinion of counsel of the company's lawyer may be required. An opinion of counsel is a lengthy, painstakingly worded letter written by the seller's law firm to the buyer promising them that they don't know of a reason why the transaction will violate a law, contract or document. These are very expensive to get because it takes so much time to prepare.

REPRESENTATIONS & WARRANTIES & COVENANTS -OH MY!

What are the differences among representations, warranties, and covenants? Lots of paper and blog bytes have been shed debating this question. I think it is sort of simple:

"REPRESENTATION"	a promise informing someone about a fact
"WARRANTY"	a promise informing someone about the condition, ingredient or level of quality of something
"COVENANT"	a promise to do something

---

5. CERTIFICATE OF DESIGNATION

The Certificate of Designation lists the special rights embedded in preferred equity, which is part of the charter, Board resolution or owners agreement.

6. STOCKHOLDERS AGREEMENT & OPERATING AGREEMENT

The rights of the equity owners will be either defined in the Stock Purchase Agreement or in another document that is hyperlinked. For instance, in an LLC, the document would be an Operating Agreement; in a corporation, the document would be the Stockholders Agreement. This contract would memorialize the agreements regarding all owners' rights to Money, Control and an Exit.

7. REGISTRATION RIGHTS AGREEMENT

The Registration Rights Agreement contains the rights of the investor to have his stock registered on a public exchange so he can sell it. Typically, an investor gets two to three demand rights and unlimited piggyback rights. These rights are usually limited to common stock and require the conversion of the preferred stock prior to exercise of rights. These rights are usually junior to the Company's stock registrations and subject to the decision of the managing underwriter to cut back the number of shares to be registered pro rata with other holders of piggyback rights.

SECURITIES LAWS

All sales of securities are governed by Federal and securities laws. The securities laws seek to make companies keep people about to trade in their stock knowledgeable about the risks.

Let's skim the surface of the securities laws by discussing (1) the values behind the securities laws; (2) the big rules; and (3) exemptions from registration.

1. THE VALUES BEHIND THE SECURITIES LAWS

The securities laws are built on a few value statements, which help make sense of them.

- ✓ An investor can only make a good decision if he is well informed about his investment
- ✓ The market does not elicit people to provide the necessary information on its own, so the market needs an active police force
- ✓ Investors with lots of experience and expertise in investing, or an inside view of the company, need less information than investors with less experience, expertise and inside knowledge
- ✓ It is the responsibility of the person selling the securities to provide enough information so that the particular buyer can make an informed decision

From these values, the securities laws flow. If you sell stock to one person who is employed by the company or who is ungodly rich, you really have to tell him just a little bit about your company.

But, if you sell to twenty people who don't know your company and have never bought stock before, you have to tell them as much information as you have in the simplest language you can find. The rub is in the nitty, annoying, skull-numbing rules about how and when you tell the information. And, God help you, if you ever have to employ or have lunch with a securities lawyer – like couples and masters/pets, they begin to resemble the laws they live with.

2. THE BIG RULES OF SECURITIES LAW

The Securities Exchange Commission was created under the first major securities law to supervise the capital markets.

REGISTRATION

All sales of (non-exempt) securities must be registered unless an exemption can be found for the sale. Most of the time, companies have to register with the SEC, but sometimes they also have to register with the states under state securities laws called "blue sky" (a pretty name for a wretched set of laws)). .[3]

REPORTING

Once you register, you must make the public reports throughout the year and when things happen that are required by the Exchange Act of 1934 and other federal securities laws and exchange rules.

ANTIFRAUD

You may not make a misstatement or omission of facts that are relevant for someone to make a fully informed investment decision. The penalties for violating this rule are terrible.

3. EXEMPTIONS FROM REGISTRATION

Remember that without an exemption, you have to do an IPO to sell stock to anyone at any time. Thankfully, there are many exemptions.

Private Placement.[4] Private placements - sales made without a public offering - are often exempt.

Private placements include:

- ✓ Sales in offerings that are obviously private to sophisticated investors who have lots of information about the company and agree to keep the stock for awhile[5]
- ✓ A security offered, bought and sold, all within a single state (intrastate)[6]
- ✓ Stock offered for less than $5 million to accredited investors[7]

"Sophisticated Investors." These investors have sufficient knowledge and experience so that they understand the risks and merits of the investment, or the issuer reasonably believes the investors have these qualifications. To determine their qualifications, investors usually fill out an accredited investor questionnaire.

Limited Offering.[8] There is another class of offerings built on limitations on how much you raise or how many people participate. (Regulation D)

- ✓ Sale of up to $1 million of securities in the last 12 months. No disclosure document required, but the offering may not include general ads or solicitations to reach buyers. (Rule 504)
- ✓ Sale of less than $5 million of securities to less than 36 unaccredited (not rich) persons and any number of accredited investors (Rule 505)
- ✓ Selling to less than 36 nonaccredited investors if they are also "sophisticated investors" either alone or with an advisor. Disclosure document must be delivered to any unaccredited investors, so sale to even a single unaccredited investor makes this much more expensive (Rule 506)

"Accredited investors" are: (1) company insiders (e.g., officers and directors); (2) persons with more than $200,000 individual annual income in each of the two most recent years or joint income with their spouse in excess of $300,000 in each of those years and a reasonable expectation of reaching the same income this year; (3) persons who, individually or jointly with their spouse, have a net worth of at least $1 million, excluding the value their primary residence[9,10]; or (4) institutional investors (e.g., banks, brokers and dealers, insurance companies) and charities and trusts with $5 million.

THREE DANGER AREAS FOR PRIVATE OR LIMITED OFFERINGS

There are three danger areas for private offerings: (a) disclosure; (b) restrictions on resale; and (c) offering must be private and contained.

Disclosure. The level of disclosure that must be given depends on the size of the offering and the nature of the investors.

- ✓ For offerings up to $2 million, you must provide information required under Part II of Form I-A under Reg A plus an audited balance sheet no older than 120 days prior to the start of the offering[11]
- ✓ For offerings up to $7.5 million, you must provide information required under Part 1 of Form SB-2, (roughly 23 items) plus financial statements and an audited balance sheet no older than 120 days prior to the start of the offering[12]
- ✓ For offerings in excess of $7.5 million, Part 1 of a registration statement[13]

You must also be available to answer questions by prospective purchasers and you must give unaccredited investors the same information you give to accredited investors.

Even though there may be no specific disclosure requirements, all information you deliver to investor must be free from false or misleading statements; similarly, you should not exclude any information if the omission makes what you do provide investors false or misleading.

Finally, as part of a limited offering, you have to file a Form D reporting the offering with the SEC within 15 days of the first sale.

Restrictions on Resale. After you sell stock under an exemption from registration, the stock is "restricted." Consequently, you must inform investors that they may not sell for at least a year without registering the transaction. These "restricted securities" may not be transferred without registration or a resale exemption.[14]

Offering Must be Private and Contained. In a private offering, you cannot use an ad, article or other communication in any newspaper, TV or other broadly disseminated medium, or have an event where attendees have been invited by a general solicitation or advertising. You are obligated to have a substantive relationship with an investor that would allow you to ensure that the investment is suitable for him.

REGULATION A OFFERING

A "Reg A" offering[15] is selling up to $5 million in 12 months of stock off of an offering circular and a prospectus filed with the SEC. However, unlike an IPO, you don't have to file audited financials or make periodic reports until you have $10 million in assets and 500 shareholders. Shareholders can also use Reg A to re-sell up to $1.5 million in stock.

SMALL COMPANY OFFERING

There is a questionnaire that may be used as a proxy for creating a detailed private placement memorandum. That questionnaire is the Small Company Offering Registration (a/k/a "SCOR") on Form U-7, created by the North American Securities Administrators Association, ("NASAA") and the American Bar Association. SCOR is used for state registrations of offerings exempt under Rule 504. In addition, SCOR can form a big part of an offering under Regulation A. SCOR may not be suitable or available for you and your investment plans or needs, but it may be worth exploring.

NASAA has the Form U-7, an "Issuer's Manual" and regional reviews to assist small business offerings. See:

⇨   www.nasaa.org

TYPES OF SALES OF SECURITIES

By fact and under law, there are a few different types of sales of securities: (1) private placements; (2) public offerings; and (3) Resales.

1.   PRIVATE PLACEMENT OF SECURITIES

A private placement is a sale of securities that is exempt from registration.

2.   IPO AND PUBLIC OFFERINGS

An initial public offering ("IPO") is a first sale of stock to the general public. An IPO is a long process where every aspect of your company is scrutinized and described, including all of your business risks and foibles. In an IPO, you get an investment bank to "underwrite" or sell your securities to the public. Then, you and your expensive lawyers go through a lengthy, painful process drafting a disclosure document about everything about you and everything that's wrong with you. That document gets filed with the SEC for review. In the meantime, any registration rights previously given to your VCs or other investors get triggered. And, you apply for listing on an exchange. At some point, the SEC weighs in on your disclosure documents and gives you lots of comments. You and your lawyers do another painful round of revisions and re-file. You may get more comments. The SEC may eventually give you the all clear (which simply means that the words in your disclosure documents seem to answer the questions in the securities rules).

Then, you go public. Your disclosure documents get filed as final on EDGAR, the SEC's mini-internet. You sell stock to the public and make a billion dollars – but only on paper. You then become subject to the myriad, tiny, agonizing disclosure obligations under the Exchange Act of 1934 and the Securities Act of 1933. Your securities lawyers will spend hours of time (on your dime) analyzing cryptic but impactful SEC rules and letters. Securities plaintiff law firms have access to your public reports to build a case to sue you.

Later, you can also sell stock to the public through a registered offering, provided you comply with many of the same rules as in an IPO.

IF YOU WANT TO GO PUBLIC SOMEDAY...
✓   Be a corporation – it is most accepted form for going public
✓   Grow - generate sufficient net revenues to justify the expense
✓   Treat the administrative works seriously – keep good and accurate financial statements and maintain clear, accurate and comprehensive corporate records

TYPES OF SALES		
TYPE	ADVANTAGES	DISADVANTAGES
PRIVATE PLACEMENT	✓ Flexible – can be any amount ✓ Flexible – can be any form – debt or equity ✓ Investors more patient than VC's ✓ Investment demands reduced – frequently, 10-20% return over 5-10 years ✓ Cheaper transaction costs	✓ Investors may be hard to locate ✓ May have less capital to invest
IPO	✓ Your investors (and you) get a big exit ✓ Access to giant pool of funding ✓ Your footprint takes steroids ✓ A market is created in your stock, so it is easier to raise money and compensate employees	✓ Hugely expensive for the IPO – legal fees, lost time for management and accounting staff ✓ Hugely expensive for continued reporting – cost can be $50,000 - $500,000 per year ✓ Scrutiny and obligation to comply with securities laws ✓ Administratively burdensome

3. RESALES OF SECURITIES

People who buy stock, particularly in private companies, may have a hard time selling it. Sales of unregistered securities by a person that is not the issuer, someone who controls the issuer (an "affiliate") or a dealer, and had no intent when he bought the stock to turn around and re-sell it (an "underwriter")[16] are also exempt from registration. But, to get the exemption and to pass along unrestricted stock, you may have to comply with the dreaded RULE 144.

If you buy stock in an unregistered, private sale from the issuer or from an affiliate of the issuer, that stock will probably be "restricted securities." Restricted securities will have a legend stamped on the back of the certificate indicating their re-sell must be registered or exempt from registration.

Let's pretend there is a company director who has some stock in the company he works with that he wants to sell. If the director sells stock through an IPO, the stock lands without restriction. But, if the director buys stock on the open market, he is limited in what he can do with the stock because of his "affiliate" status. If he re-sells the stock in the open market, he must comply with Rule 144 – failure to comply with Rule 144 would make the sale not exempt from registration.[17] Once he complies with Rule 144 and sells his stock on the open market, the stock lands without restriction.

If the director sells the stock in private to his neighbor, the stock becomes "restricted" in the neighbor's hands, because he bought it from an affiliate and not on the public market. That neighbor now has to comply with Rule 144 to resell the stock without having to go through a public offering.

The Neighbor. The neighbor who bought restricted stock has to hold the stock for a certain amount of time – how long he has to hold the stock depends on whether the company has filed status reports and updates with the SEC for the last 3 months (a/k/a a "reporting company"). If the stock is issued by a "reporting company," then the neighbor has to hold the stock for six months. [19] If the stock is issued by a non-reporting company (most companies), the neighbor has to hold the stock for 1 year. After the neighbor holds the stock long enough, he can sell and the stock will land without restriction.

The Director. For stock issued by reporting companies, the director cannot sell for the six months after his purchase. For stock issued by a non-reporting company, the director cannot sell for one year after his purchase. And, after he has held the stock long enough, he then can only sell if his sale does not exceed the volume limitations, complies with the manner of sale requirements, properly files a Form 144 with the SEC and the issuing company has put out enough current public information. [20]

This little explanation of Rule 144 is necessarily simplified. Rule 144 is terribly complicated. Plus, there may be other avenues to sell stock if Rule 144 is a bar. In any event, when dealing with stock, get help from a good and experienced securities lawyer.

HAZ IS RAPT

Gravity took a breath. Haz broke in:

"Gravity, I had no idea that the federal government had changed the definition of "accredited investor." That seems like a sensible change, though. I also found it interesting that you can avoid expensive disclosures by selling to only accredited investors. Fascinating, just fasc...Hey, Hap, what are you doing?"

In Gravity and Hazard's excitement over securities laws, neither noticed that Hap had found Gravity's stash of yellow "Sign Here" tabs, which he had used to cover every square inch of Gravity's bookshelves, sofa and front door.

Shaking his head, Haz said, "Gravity, I'm so sorry. I don't know what to say."

But, Gravity just shrugged. "It's fine. Taking them down may keep Hap occupied while we talk about debt."

"You mean it's not over?" wailed Hap.

"Sorry, Hap. We're about half way through."

Hap replied, "I'll take down the sticky tabs. But, Gravity, could you give us just the highlights of debt?"

"I CAN TRY."

DEBT

Gravity said, "Let's talk about sources of debt and parts of a loan."

CHAPTER

08

DEBT IS...

Debt is money that has to be paid back, usually with interest. It can come from friends and family and complete strangers, as well as banks, credit unions and credit card companies. Debt is usually governed by a Loan Agreement and a separate promissory note.

SOURCES OF DEBT FINANCING

There are some typical sources of debt financing, including (1) friends and family; (2) banks; (3) credit unions; (4) finance companies; (5) trade credit; (6) factors; (7) leasing companies; and (8) government backed debt.

1. FRIENDS AND FAMILY

Friends and family remain the biggest source of startup loans, principally because they are more lenient than arm's length lenders. Borrowing money from friends and family will probably change your relationship – after all, you owe them. It is natural for them to look upon you as a debtor and even look judgmentally at your actions as an indicator of your ability to repay them. Treat any loan like a business transaction. Get a lawyer to document the loan and be clear about your roles in your business.

2. BANKS

Banks may be the loan source that first comes to mind. Banks are in the business to make loans to businesses they know will get repaid. If you have a limited or a bad operating history, they don't know

that you will repay their money, so they will be very reluctant to loan to you.

3. CREDIT UNIONS

Credit Unions are in business to help their members make deposits, collect interest and get loans. As a result, members of a credit union may have an easier time getting a loan, though the available amount will probably be lower than at a commercial bank.

4. FINANCE COMPANIES

Finance companies are businesses that provide debt financing, usually at higher interest rates than banks. This type of debt is usually secured with some type of collateral. As a result, if your company has heavy equipment and inventory, you may be a good candidate for a loan with a finance company, because you have the collateral to pledge. Be sure to not confuse commercial finance companies with consumer finance companies. Insurance companies also make loans to companies with collateral.

5. TRADE CREDIT

Trade Credit is simply when a supplier doesn't make the customer pay in advance or up front, but gives them a bit of time until the purchase price is due. Trade credit is extremely common; the most frequent type is "Net 30," which means payment is due on the invoice 30 days post receipt (whether that is 30 days post receipt of the invoice or the goods/services may be negotiable). Suppliers may deny you trade credit for a variety of reasons. For instance, if you pay later than your competitors, they have reason to think your business is in trouble, suspicious or cash starved, or if they just think you're a schmuck, your suppliers may require cash on delivery or even in advance. If your supplier is cash starved, they could demand cash up front. Or, if the economy is shaky or your industry is in decline, your suppliers may also make you pay upfront. Alternatively, your suppliers may condition their trade credit on your grant to them of a security interest in your assets (like your receivables or inventory).

Sometimes, suppliers will use trade credit to incentivize you to pay early. For instance, a supplier's payment terms may be "2% 10, net 30," which means you can take a 2% discount if you pay within 10 days, but if you don't, the whole amount is due in 30 days.

6. FACTORS

A Factor is a bank or financing company that buys receivables at a discount to provide the seller with some cash in advance of collection. The amount of the discount depends on the riskiness of the receivables. The Factor then collects on the receivables and the seller has an obligation to turn over any money it gets on the receivables.

Factors could make you guarantee payment on the receivable (recourse) or assume the whole risk (nonrecourse); if they take more risk, they will pay you less upfront.

7. LEASING COMPANIES

Leasing companies help companies finance equipment in a clever way. After you locate some asset you want to get for your business, a leasing company could step in front of you (metaphorically), buy the equipment (or guarantees its payment) and lease it to you. The leasing company would take a security interest in the asset and may then have the asset to sell at the end of your lease term. Although you may have to go out and find your own leasing company, frequently equipment suppliers will have one or more leasing companies available at the point of purchase for you to engage.

8. GOVERNMENT BACKED DEBT

The federal government and the states have created many financing programs for business. Although the most prominent includes the U.S. Small Business Administration, every state and most cities have economic development and commerce groups.

OUR GOVERNMENT

A big function of government is empowering people to start and run businesses and employ people. The government at every level may have ways to help you. This is not welfare – the government probably won't give you and your business a handout. But, it could point you towards funding sources with fair terms, mentoring and networking opportunities and access to information. Nearly every official that represents you keeps a staff in their home office dedicated to helping people. That staff, called "Constituent Services," exists for one reason: your prosperity and well-being. Don't be shy about asking for their help.

If you don't know who your member of Congress or Senators are, go to:

⇨ http://www.govtrack.us/congress/findyour reps.xpd.

Small Business Investment Companies ("SBICs"). SBICs are private companies licensed by the SBA to make loans guaranteed by the federal government to small businesses. SBICs may tend to take on slightly more risk than a commercial bank. SBICs are sort of like mini-VCs - they pick companies to back with loans and do better if those companies do better. Frequently, an SBIC may make loans in return for a promissory note and warrants (right to buy stock in your company) or even loans convertible into stock.

The master list of SBICs are on the SBA website at:

⇨ http://www.sba.gov/aboutsba/sbaprograms /inv/INV_DIRECTORY_SBIC.html.

U.S. ECONOMIC DEVELOPMENT ADMINISTRATION

The U.S. Economic Development Administration not only has programs that provide funding for businesses, it also maintains a bunch of web pages that list government sources of business funding.

⇨ The list of government sources of funding is located at: http://www.eda.gov/Resources/Resources.xml.

THE SBA

The United States Small Business Administration exists to support small business and entrepreneurs. A big part of SBA's support is enabling financing for small businesses. But, the SBA doesn't cut the check – it guarantees the loan made by a bank. So, if you fail to pay, the government is obligated to repay a big portion of the loan.

QUALIFICATION FOR SBA LOAN

SBA loans are limited by a bunch of qualifications. For instance, only small businesses, that are for profit, that do not already have the resources (business or personal) to provide the financing, and can demonstrate the likelihood of repayment are eligible for an SBA-backed loan. The proceeds from a loan can be used to buy equipment and land, to fund working capital and to purchase an existing business. However, SBA loans cannot be used for refinancing where the loan is a loss, to buy out an owner if it does not help the business, pay back owner loans, to pay taxes or for non-sound businesses purposes.

SBA PROGRAMS

7(a) Loan Program. The 7(a) Loan program is the SBA's primary and most flexible loan program, with financing guaranteed for a variety of general business purposes. It is designed for start-up and existing small businesses, and is delivered through commercial lending institutions. There are several types of 7(a) loan programs.

Express Loans. Express loans are expedited loans for small businesses in general.

Community Express Program. The Community Express program includes loans of $25,000 or less to finance businesses in impoverished communities. Eligible communities include SBA's Historically Underutilized Business Zones (HUBZones) and areas identified as distressed through the Community Reinvestment Act (CRA). To encourage small business start-ups, SBA makes eligible loans of $25,000 or less, regardless of where small businesses are located.

Patriot Express. The Patriot Express program provides loans for small businesses owned and controlled by veterans or military members.

SBA Export Express. SBA Export Express helps small businesses develop or expand their export markets. SBA Export Express loans are available to manufacturers, wholesalers, export trading companies and service exporters that are small businesses in business for at least 12 months and show that the loan proceeds will enable them to enter a new export market or expand an existing export market. The maximum line of credit/loan amount is $250,000 and the term is usually for 5 – 10 years (though revolving lines of credit must end at 7 years).

CDC/504 Loan Program. 504 loans are long term loans to buy brick and mortar stuff - real estate or fixed equipment. 504s are brokered by Certified Development Companies, which are private companies set up to provide 504 loans.

Microloan Program. Microloans are loans of $35,000 or less for working capital or inventory, supplies, furniture, fixtures, machinery and/or equipment. Microloans are brokered by specially designated intermediary lenders (nonprofit organizations with experience in lending and technical assistance).

Disaster Assistance Loan Program. This program provides low-interest loans to homeowners, renters, businesses of all sizes and most private non-profit organizations to repair or replace real estate, personal property, machinery and equipment, inventory and business assets that have been damaged or destroyed in a declared disaster.

THINGS LENDERS CARE ABOUT (AT A MINIMUM)

Borrowing is common, but getting qualified is hard. Below are things banks look at to determine if they want to give you a loan.

1. EQUITY

Equity is the amount of cash in your business. You can build equity by keeping cash in the business (instead of paying it out to the owners) or by payments of cash for stock. The bright line rule is that banks recoil from companies with a debt to equity ratio of 4 to 1 (i.e. your total liabilities divided by your equity should not exceed 4).

2. CREDIT HISTORY

Credit history is your and your partners' personal history of paying your bills on time.

3. CREDITWORTHINESS

Creditworthiness is your company's ability to pay back the loan. Banks want you to have at least two avenues of repayment: (1) cash from your company's sales and (2) collateral (just in case your company's sales plummet).

4. SKIN IN THE GAME

All investors and lenders want to know that the founders have invested their own cash in the company – that they have "skin in the game." Your failure to put in cash may signal a lack of confidence in the business plan by the very people who should have the most confidence. In addition, if the founders contribute cash in the form of a loan to the company, the bank will always insist it gets paid back before the founders.

5. EXPERIENCE

A lack of experience in a particular business usually discourages investment.

THE PARTS OF A LOAN

Loans and loan documents usually have the same types of terms, though the terms themselves will differ wildly depending on you, your creditworthiness, your bank, how much you are taking, the type of loan or note you are giving and the world around you. Every loan will have (1) a loan amount; (2) interest rate; (3) maturity date; (4) security (if it is a secured loan); and (5) loan covenants.

1. LOAN AMOUT

The first part of a loan is how much the lender is lending and when the borrower can take possession over the proceeds. Most loans are paid in one lump sum, but in some instances (like construction) the loans can only be "drawn down" in stages or on milestones.

2. INTEREST RATE

Interest is a charge for borrowing the money. Interest is usually a percentage applied against amounts outstanding under the loan. If interest is applied against just the principal balance, the interest is **"simple."** If interest is applied against the principal and interest, the interest is **"compounded."** The percentage – called the interest rate - is picked based on the duration of the loan, the amount of the loan, the riskiness of the loan and the borrower, the demand in the market for other loans and governmental monetary policy. The interest rate can also be fixed or variable. If it is **fixed**, it is a definite percentage and it doesn't change during the loan (unless there is a default). If it is **variable**, it changes based on other market rates.

3. TERM OR MATURITY

A loan usually has a definite end that is predetermined. (Just like a mortgage that ends on its 30th anniversary.) The term or maturity determines how long the loan will go on.

Short-Term Loans. These last less than a year and are used for working capital.

Intermediate-Term Loans. These usually run from one to three years, and are used for new equipment, expansion or an increase in working capital.

Long-Term Loans. These usually run from three to five years, and are used for real estate, improvements, fixed assets, or other big expenditures.

A Line of Credit. This is a pool of cash to which you have access, for periodic cash needs. A line of credit is critical for cash management, particularly for businesses that experience seasonal fluctuations.

4. SECURITY AND COLLATERAL

Debt can be secured or unsecured. Secured debt is backed up by some kind of assets (called "collateral"). In a secured loan, the borrower pledges some asset (e.g. a car or property) as collateral for the loan. Collateral includes assets that can be sold to fund repayment of the loan. Most debt is secured, because most commercial or business lenders insist on it.

There are two reasons why debt gets secured. First, if secured debt doesn't get repaid when due, the lender can try to grab the collateral to fund payment of the debt. Second, secured debt has a higher priority in right to payments from a company going out of business. For example: if you owe $10,000 under your car loan, which is secured with your car as collateral, and another $500 to your doctor's office, and you go bankrupt with $3,000 in your bank account, your car loan company will probably get all $3,000, because a secured creditor gets paid before unsecured creditors get paid.

For secured debt to have any real legal teeth, you have to grant a security interest all in accordance with a little statute we like to call the Uniform Commercial Code or "UCC"). The UCC is a standard set of laws that a bunch of relatively smart lawyers write – that set of laws then gets adopted by most state legislatures around the country. Specifically, you have to comply with Article 9 of the UCC. The security interest is really about giving your lender a tiny handhold on the property you are using as collateral – if you default, the security interest gives

HOW COLLATERAL GETS VALUED[21]		
COLLATERAL TYPE	BY SBA	BY BANK
House	75% (Market value minus debt)	85% (market value minus debt)
Car	0	0
Truck & Heavy Equipment	Half of depreciated value	Half of depreciated value
Office Equipment	0	0
Furniture & Fixtures	Half of depreciated value	Half of depreciated value
Inventory (Perishables)	0	0
Jewelry	0	0
Other	10-50%	10-50%
Receivables	75% of Accounts Receivable less than 90 days old	Half of Accounts Receivable less than 90 days old
Stocks & Bonds	50-90%	50-90%
Mutual Funds/IRA	0	0
CDs	100%	100%

your lender the right to seize the collateral and sell it. However, the UCC requires that security interests be publicly disclosed.

There are essentially four things you have to do:

1. Grant the security interest in writing
2. Make sure the writing actually attaches to the property being used as collateral
3. Describe your security interest on a form called a UCC-1
4. File your UCC-1 with the Secretary of State of the state where your business is organized

If you fail to do these steps, your security interest will be nearly worthless. Of course, since in this case, the security interest is in your lender's interests, you may want your lender to bring this up.

Warning: If you have existing lenders, then adding secured creditors to your balance sheet and public notices may anger or spook them. Also, your loan agreements with your existing lender may obligate you to get their permission.

COLLATERAL TYPE & VALUE

The value of collateral to the bank is not fair market value; it's liquidation value, which includes a discount for what is lost if you have to sell the asset in a hurry. The table, "How Collateral Gets Valued," gives a general approximation on how different forms of collateral are valued by a typical bank and the SBA.

5. LOAN COVENANTS

If you borrow money, you may expect that the terms of the loan, including the loan amount, payment terms, interest rate and all other terms, are listed in the cover letter. The rest of the documents may look like inaccessible lawyer filler that have no bearing on your conduct, but, in fact, they do. Business bank contracts usually have "loan covenants." Loan covenants are minimum standards and prohibitions for you and your business to meet. Loan Covenants can be "affirmative" covenants to do something and "negative" covenants to refrain from doing something.

TYPICAL AFFIRMATIVE LOAN COVENANTS

Affirmative covenants obligate a borrower to:

✓ Get and keep liability and property insurance with minimum coverage amounts
✓ Get and keep "key man" life insurance on top management
✓ Pay all taxes and state fees on time
✓ Deliver certificates of insurance to the bank
✓ Subordinate all other loans to the bank's loan
✓ Prepare and have "reviewed" or "audited" financial statements each year, and then deliver them to the bank
✓ Maintain liquidity and performance ratios
✓ Deliver annual corporate tax returns

NEGATIVE COVENANTS

Negative covenants obligate a borrower to not:

✓ Change management
✓ Merge with another business
✓ Take other loans
✓ Issue dividends
✓ Increase management salaries
✓ Sell assets

Loan covenants are the bank's weapon against bad management or economic downtimes. The bank uses the loan covenants to pressure the borrower into keeping enough cash flowing to pay its debts, to keep growing and to protect the bank's investment and collateral. Small businesses do breach loan covenants. Banker leniency depends on the overall economy and condition of business.

BUILDING BUSINESS CREDIT

Your business begins to establish a credit history from the beginning.

Your business's creditworthiness will be partly evaluated using your business's credit score. Business credit scores run from 0 (bad) to 100 (excellent) – a score of 75 is a very good score. Your score is influenced by when you pay your bills, your available business credit, the length of time you've had a credit footprint and the number of inquiries about your credit score.

STEPS TO BUILD BUSINESS CREDIT

You can build your business credit by taking these steps:

1. Credit transactions are compiled by business credit bureaus and used to form a business credit report. Register your business with the business credit bureaus. Business credit bureaus include Dun & Bradstreet, Experian, Equifax and Business Credit USA.

2. Get a dedicated phone line.

3. Get a business license.

4. Keep your financial statements and business plan up to date to provide upon request.

5. Use your business information – and not your personal information – when applying for business credit.

6. Pay your bills on time.

7. Get credit lines, even if small, to build credit history.

8. Report your own payment history to the business credit bureaus.

TIPS ON LOAN COVENANTS

✓ Read and understand every page and every clause before you sign

✓ Don't be afraid to negotiate any clause you don't think is fair; that includes financial ratios and obligations to get audited financial statements

✓ Once you sign, make sure you get at least one folder of all documents

✓ Give copies of your financial covenants to your accounting professional to make sure you stay vigilant on compliance (particularly beware of the positive cash flow covenant)

✓ If you have to produce audited financials, reserve plenty of time and cash for the audit fees

✓ Calendar the due dates for delivery of financial statements or other reports

✓ If you have to sign a personal guaranty, negotiate limits and terminations so if you leave or things change, the guaranty ends

HAP & HAZ LEARN TO PITCH

"There's a lot more to cover, but that's a good start," Gravity said.

Haz said, "What should we do, Gravity?"

Gravity said, "You said you need to raise $250,000. That amount is too small for a VC. But, you may be able to find an angel or another debt source who specialize in your industries — computer accessories, renewable energy, socially responsible business — and pitch them. You are going to get turned down, but that's okay. Just keep going. You are just as capable and talented as anyone else. Even if you aren't, incompetence and lack of talent isn't the bar you'd think.

But, be prepared:

- ✓ Do your homework. Know your business cold.
- ✓ Make sure your business plan is fool proof and reasoned.
- ✓ Practice your pitch.
- ✓ Be ready to give up a big portion of your stock.
- ✓ Stick some skin in the game — any money you can put in, put in.
- ✓ Don't expect a big salary in the beginning — it signals a lack of maturity.
- ✓ Whatever you do, don't talk about a company plane."

Hap and Hazard began to call all of their contacts, old and new, looking for opportunities to talk about the MouseTrap. Their goal was not initially to get the money — it was to give the pitch, to take the hard questions and struggle through the answers. Good thing, too. Because of the first 10 people they talked to, 9 of them said Hap and Hazard were wasting their time. The 10th was nicer, but still uninterested. Hap and Hazard went back and forth between hope and dejection. Just when one of them wanted to surrender, the other one would urge him on.

Along the way, they got better and better. Initially, everyone asked the same three questions:

1. How will it work?
2. How will you make it and sell it?
3. Why you?

Learning to answer these questions - often posed skeptically, sometimes caustically, with confidence and cheer took many attempts. First, they stumbled. They stuttered. Once, Hap cried. Finally, having traveled to Atlanta to meet a potential investor on a layover, they gave their pitch in the doorway to baggage claim. The investor, pressed, pursed and focused on his Blackberry, cut them off mid-sentence.

"This is a problem that billion dollar companies can't solve. Why you?"

Haz dropped his shoulders. Hap stepped forward.

"Giants don't innovate. For that, you need the new, the small and quick. That's us. We live in Chicago. We're in Atlanta for a 40 second pitch. If you aren't interested, then we have a plane to catch. You have a coffee spot on your tie."

Hap grabbed Haz and propelled him back towards the terminal.

"Hey, hang on," the investor called after them. "You got a book?"

Hap turned briefly, tossed him a prospectus and marched Haz back to Chicago.

After that, it got easier, and they got smarter. Haz and Hap stopped looking at the whole world and started looking for people who supported renewable energy and sustainable business practices. They also started participating in Seymour's podcasts, talking about their plans, their product and their vision for the MouseTrap.

With a narrower focus and more targeted, but aggressive and uncommon outreach tactics, they got an offer from a small business investment company to make a loan of $200,000 backed by the federal government. Hazard made adjustments to the budget to reduce costs by $50,000. Then, they took the offer to Gravity.

"This looks good, Boys. A nice clean deal. These are the terms they are offering:

- ✓ $200,000, paid in two tranches: the first, on execution to fund the prototype and the second on completion of prototype for manufacturing
- ✓ Interest at 12%
- ✓ Monthly interest payments
- ✓ Yearly principal repayment
- ✓ Maturity in 3 years
- ✓ Note convertible to common stock
- ✓ Preemptive rights and right of first refusal on future investments in company with 90 days' notice
- ✓ Note secured with assets, inventory and proceeds"

"What do you think, Gravity?"

"I think it's an excellent start and they are not trying to gouge you from the start. But, what is most important is what you think."

"I think the interest is a shade too high," Hazard answered.

"I agree. Since prime is so low right now, 12% is high. But, you guys are relatively high risk and the market for debt is terrible. What if we negotiated to 9%?"

"I like that."

"Me too."

Haz continued. "I also think that monthly interest payments hurt our cash flow. I'd rather ask for quarterly interest payments. And, to the extent we have to pay any principal, I'd rather it be a set amount that is less than the total principal outstanding."

"Ok. What else? What about the term?"

"The term?" Hap asked.

"That's the lifetime of the line." Haz explained. "5 years is preferable."

"Fine. I also suggest we make the right of first refusal period much less. If you have to give them 90 days to put more money in when you need the money, you'll be out of business by the time you get it. I'd go with 15 or 30 days."

"What about the security interest?"

"Haz?" asked Hap.

"A security interest is a hold on assets that solidifies if there is a default. Here, they are saying that they want to have a hold on our assets and revenues that they can grab if we fail to make payments or breach other parts of this loan."

"That sounds scary."

"That's finance. Be thankful they aren't demanding we personally guarantee the loan. Gravity, we're okay with that."

"Okay, then I'll send the investor's lawyer our comments."

After some to and fro between Gravity and the other lawyer, the final terms were:

ITEM	THE OFFER	OUR COUNTER	THEIR RESPONSE
PRINCIPAL AMOUNT	$200,000	N/A	N/A
INTEREST	Interest at 12%	8%	9.5%
INTEREST PAYMENT	Monthly interest payments	Quarterly interest payments	OK
PRINCIPAL REPAYMENT	Yearly principal repayment	Principal paid in balloon at the end	Principal of $25,000 each year, balloon at end
TERM	Maturity (final due date) in 3 years	5 years	4 years
CONVERTIBILITY	Note convertible to common stock	N/A	N/A
ANTI-DILUTION	Preemptive rights and right of first refusal on future investments in company with 90 days' notice	30 day notice	45 day notice
SECURITY INTEREST	Note secured with assets, inventory and proceeds	N/A	N/A

Hazard studied the chart, nodded and said, *"Done."*

"Hap?"

"Yes. Good. Is that it? Do we get the money?"

"Not yet. We still have to write the documents. But, we'll be very careful not to mess up your deal. Hopefully their lawyer will be reasonable and quick."

Gravity's wish was granted; the documents were drafted in 5 drafts. The legal bills were, for Gravity, "$12,500" and for the lender's lawyer, "$32,000."

At closing, the lender's lawyer tried to deduct the lawyer bills from the payment to Hap and Haz, but Gravity rejected it. The lender wired the money and Hap and Haz were in business.

"Gravity, I think we need to finish our deal with Seymour."

"And, you also need to make sure you have all of the intellectual property rights you need from any source."

"We don't know how to do that. Can you help us?"

"I CAN TRY."

END NOTES

1 Fred Wilson, Union Square Ventures, http://unionsquareventures.com/2007/11/why-early-stage.php. Mr. Wilson in a later post indicated that businesses that succeed are (1) nimble; (2) monitor and limit their burn rate; and (3) continue to figure out how to make money

2 I'm just kidding. VCs go to treatment, not rehab, and only rarely.

3 Securities Act of 1933 and the Exchange Act of 1934.

4 Securities Act

5 Securities Act, Section 4(2).

6 Securities Act, Section 3(a)(11) and Rule 147.

7 Securities Act, Section 4(6).

8 Regulation D

9 Exclusion of primary residence from net worth under accredited investor calculation was prescribed by the Dodd-Frank Wall Street Reform and Consumer Protection Act, July 21, 2010, Public Law No: 111-203. Dodd-Frank also authorizes the SEC to review and revise the definition of Accredited Investor sometime before 2015.

10 Pending implementation of the SEC's rules required by Dodd-Frank, the related amount of indebtedness secured by the primary residence up to its fair market value may also be excluded. Indebtedness secured by the residence in excess of the value of the home should be considered a liability and deducted from the investor's net worth. [July 23, 2010]

11 17 CFR 230.502

12 17 CFR 230.502.

13 17 CFR 230.502

14 In other words, investors cannot turn around and sell the securities right away. Instead, you should get a promise from the investor that they are not an underwriter, and stick a paragraph "legend" on the back of the stock certificate to put potential purchasers on notice that the securities were issued in a transaction exempt from the registration requirements of the 1933 Act.

15 Regulation A under Securities Act 3(b); 17 CFR 230.251-263.

16 Securities Act, Section 4(1)

17 The buyer would probably be entitled to return the stock.

18 Rule 144, as amended effective February 15, 2008

19 One more safety tip: if the neighbor was an affiliate in the last 3 months, he can't sell like this – he has to do what the director would have to do.

20 **Current Public Information**. Reporting companies must (1) be registered under the Exchange Act for at least 90 days and (2) have filed all required reports (other than 8-Ks) during prior 12 months (or such shorter period of its Exchange Act registration). **Volume Limitation**. Amount sold, together with all sales of any restricted and other securities of the same class sold within the preceding three months, must not exceed the greater of: (a) 1 percent of the outstanding shares of that class or 10% of debt securities; or (b) the average weekly reported trading volume during preceding four weeks. **Manner of Sale**. equity must be sold in broker's transactions or directly with "market maker" and may not be solicited by seller. **Form 144**. File for sales over 5,000 shares or $50,000 in last 3 months.

21 Small Business Administration http://www.sba.gov/smallbusinessplanner/start/financestartup/SERV_BORROW.html

GETTING THE RIGHTS

section three

CHAPTERS IN THIS SECTION:

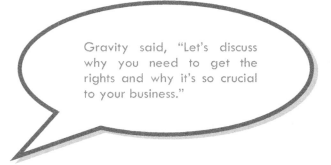

GET THE RIGHTS

Gravity said, "Let's discuss why you need to get the rights and why it's so crucial to your business."

CHAPTER 09

WHY YOU NEED TO GET THE RIGHTS

Before you can really get going, you need to see about getting the rights to all of the necessary Intellectual Property ("IP").

IP is a right to a creation of the mind. IP includes **TRADEMARKS, COPYRIGHTS, PATENTS, AND TRADE SECRETS**. A **TRADEMARK** is a marker on a thing or service that tells the world who it comes from. A **COPYRIGHT** is an unprecedented expression of an idea. A **PATENT** is like calling dibs on a particular invention used in a particular way. A **TRADE SECRET** is an actual secret that gives a business an advantage over its competitors. For an overview, see the chart on the next page. Each of these IP rights is covered in the following chapters.

The stakes for failing to secure your IP rights are high. If someone thinks you are violating IP rights, they could simply demand that you stop with a cease and desist letter or they could sue you. Dealing with a cease and desist letter takes time and money. Going to court can be expensive, debilitating and depressing. If you cannot resolve the problem, you may be forced to re-brand, re-invent, re-write and re-craft products, processes, packaging, copy, websites and letterhead. If you lose in court, you can be charged with financial penalties, including your profits, loss of adversaries' profits/value and even punitive damages. You could even be entirely shut down by a court of law.

On the other hand, you could spend years, creativity and money establishing your intellectual property only to have someone steal it and use it

(maybe better than you do). In that case, you would have to pay a lawyer to go sue the bad guy – that's incredibly expensive without any guarantee of success. Therefore, there are two essential questions in dealing with intellectual property.

1. Can you use it?
2. Can you protect it?

To really answer these questions, you need a solid understanding of the different branches of intellectual property, their variations, what they cover and how they work.

Let's dig in. (Alternatively, you can skip the next 4 chapters and go right to Chapter 14: Clear the IP - though you'll be missing all the fun).

IP PRIMER

	WHAT IS PROTECTED?	WHAT RIGHTS DO YOU GET?	HOW DOES PROTECTION START?	HOW LONG DOES PROTECTION LAST?	DAMAGES/REMEDIES FOR INFRINGEMENT?	REGISTER & ENFORCE?
PATENT	Invention (process, machine, article of manufacture, composition of matter or improvement thereof) that is: ✓ Novel ✓ Non-obvious ✓ Useful	Right to exclude others: ✓ From making ✓ From using ✓ From selling ✓ From importing the claims in the patent	✓ Registration required; takes 1.5 - 4 years ✓ Protected on patent issuance, but as of earliest filing date ✓ Pre-Reg. notice: Patent Pending ✓ Post-Reg. notice: Patent [+Patent No.]	✓ 20 years from earliest filing date ✓ 14 years for design patent	After a lawsuit filing, damages incurred during the prior 6 years, including: ✓ Lost profits ✓ Reasonable royalty ✓ Costs and interest ✓ 3x damages for willful infringement ✓ Injunctive relief	✓ Patent and Trademark Office ("PTO") handles registration ✓ All enforcement by private litigants ✓ Federal court
COPYRIGHT	Original works of authorship fixed in a tangible medium: ✓ Literary ✓ Musical ✓ Dramatic ✓ Choreographic ✓ Pictorial, graphic, sculptural ✓ Motion pictures ✓ Sound recordings ✓ Architectural ✓ Computer programs	Exclusive right to: ✓ Reproduce ✓ Prepare derivative works ✓ Distribute copies ✓ Perform publicly ✓ Display ✓ Perform publicly by a digital audio transmission	✓ Protection begins when work is fixed in a tangible medium ✓ Apply for registration w/in 3 months of 1st publication; takes up to 1 year; effective as of filing date ✓ Notice: © + year of 1st publication + owner Eg: © 2007 Coco Soodek	Currently, life of the author plus 70 years, except: ✓ For works made for hire, the shorter of 95 years from publication or 120 years from creation ✓ Varies depending on when work was fixed or published	Registered copyright: ✓ Actual damages plus profits of the infringer, or ✓ Statutory damages ($750-$30,000 per work) ✓ Innocent infringer: $200 ✓ Willful infringer: $150,000 Unregistered copyright: ✓ Proven damages/profits Equitable Relief: ✓ Injunction/Impoundment	✓ Copyright Office handles registration ✓ All enforcement by private litigants ✓ Federal court
TRADEMARK	A word, name, symbol or device (or even smell or sound) used in trade to indicate the source of goods and distinguish them from others	✓ Exclusive right to use the mark with products or services in the territory of use or registration ✓ Right to exclude use of the mark that is likely to cause confusion in the market or that dilutes a famous mark	✓ Protection starts on use in commerce ✓ Federal registration takes 9 months to 2 years, effective as of filing date ✓ Pre-Reg. notice: [MARK]™ ✓ Post-Reg. notice: [MARK] ®	As long as it remains in use and renewal fees are paid: ✓ Between the 5th and 6th year after registration ✓ Between every 9th and 10th year after registration	Infringement: ✓ Defendant's profits ✓ Plaintiff's damages ✓ Costs and attorney's fees for willful infringement ✓ 3x damages for bad faith ✓ Injunctive relief Dilution: ✓ All above damages if dilution was willful	✓ PTO handles registration ✓ All enforcement by private litigants ✓ FTC enforces false advertising of another's trademark ✓ Federal or state court
TRADE SECRET	A formula, pattern, process or device which is: ✓ Kept secret by reasonable measures ✓ A competitive advantage	✓ Right to prevent misappropriation through breach or wrongful act ✓ Does not prevent independent creation	As soon as it satisfies the legal elements. ✓ Notice: Confidential & proprietary material of [your name here]	As long as it satisfies the legal elements	✓ Varies by state ✓ Profits & royalty ✓ 2x damages if willful malicious ✓ Injunctive relief	✓ All enforcement by private litigants ✓ Usually state court

TRADEMARK

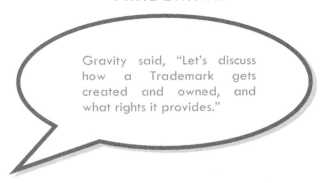

Gravity said, "Let's discuss how a Trademark gets created and owned, and what rights it provides."

CHAPTER 10

A **Trademark** is a word, logo, marker or name that identifies the source of the products or services.[1] Technically, service marks describe services and trademarks describe products, but often the terms get smashed together under the "trademark" or "mark" umbrella. A trademark can be a word, name, symbol, device, color, sound, or a scent, or any combination of these things. For instance, UPS registered its shade of brown; Veuve Clicquot registered its shade of orange; MGM registered its lion's roar.

HOW A TRADEMARK GETS CREATED AND OWNED

The rule of trademarks is: use it or lose it. A trademark gets created only when someone uses it to identify a particular product or service. If two people use the same mark, for the same products, in the same geographic area, the owner will probably be the person who used the mark in the area first. Once that person stops using the mark, his rights in it start to evaporate.

The owner of a mark that has not been registered with the U.S. Patent and Trademark Office ("PTO") only gets rights to areas where they have marketed their products (with the marks) or where they have a reputation. But, the owner of a mark that has been registered with the PTO automatically gets rights to the whole country. An unregistered mark can trump a registered mark, but only in the regions where it has been used before the application to register the mark was filed. That is one of the reasons why the best thing to do is get a federal registration for all of your trademarks.

TRADEMARK RIGHTS

Your trademark gives you rights to distinguish yourself as the source of your products and services. These rights give you the right to (1) exclusive use; (2) freedom from trademark dilution for famous marks; (3) freedom from passing off; and (4) freedom from unfair competition.

1. EXCLUSIVE USE

Your ownership of your trademark gives you the exclusive right to use your mark. It also gives you the right to keep others from using a trademark that may confuse your potential customer about your products and services.

2. NO TRADEMARK DILUTION FOR FAMOUS OR VALUABLE MARKS

Your ownership of your trademark gives you the right to keep others from using your mark in a way that dilutes the distinctness of your famous mark through blurring or tarnishing your mark. "Blurring" happens when your mark is weakened by association with other, different products. "Tarnishment" happens when your mark is presented in an unflattering light, often due to associations with inferior or embarrassing products. For instance, Toys R Us, Inc. successfully sued www.adultsrus.com, a porn site, for tarnishing its mark. Strong trademarks are protected from losing their singular association in the public mind with a certain product. But, only owners of famous marks are protected from dilution under Federal law. Owners of all trademarks are protected from dilution under state laws, so long as (1) the mark has "selling power" or, in other words, a distinctive quality; and (2) the two marks are substantially similar.

3. NO PASSING OFF

You have the right to keep others from passing off products or services. Passing off happens when someone tries to pass off his product as your product or your product as his product; essentially, piracy. Passing off is illegal for the manufacturer and any seller that knowingly helps.

4. UNFAIR COMPETITION

Unfair Competition in intellectual property is when a bad guy's actions probably make your customers think that your products are the bad guy's products, that the bad guy's products are your products or that you endorse the bad guy's products.[2]

WAR STORIES

BURGER KING VS. BURGER KING

THE WAR

Gene and Betty Hoots opened a restaurant called "Burger King" in Matoon, Illinois in 1957. Then, in 1959, Gene got a trademark registration – but just in Illinois. Meanwhile, Burger King ("Big BK"), a much bigger company, got federal registration and opened its first fast food store in Illinois, both in 1961. By 1967, Big BK had 50 stores in Illinois. That's when Gene and Betty sued Big BK for trademark infringement.

THE WINNER

Big BK won, because its federal registration entitled them to nationwide protection except for the parts of Illinois where Gene and Betty operated their restaurant. Since Gene and Betty only had one restaurant in Matoon, Big BK has exclusive right to use BURGER KING all over Illinois except for the 40 mile radius around Matoon. And Matoon has no Big BK.

MORAL OF THE STORY

This rule remains a whopper. You only get exclusive trademark rights where you actually do business unless you get federal registration. But, federal registration may not empower you to get a prior user to stop using the mark completely.

Burger King v. Hoots, 403 f.2d 904 (7th 1968).

THE TRADEMARK CONTINUUM

Trademark strength runs along a "spectrum of distinctiveness," a sliding scale of protectability, where the more distinct and unique the term, the easier it is for the owner to claim and be granted exclusive trademark rights for it.

MARKS THAT CAN BE REGISTERED

STRONG

FANCIFUL MARKS have a marker or sign that was invented just to set the product or service apart – there is no association to anything in the dictionary. They don't describe the product, but indicate the source of the product. Examples: EXXON (oil) and KODAK (cameras).

ARBITRARY MARKS have a common meaning that has no relation to the product or service it is used with. Examples: APPLE (computers) and SUN (computers).

SUGGESTIVE MARKS have a marker or sign that has an element that reflects or suggests a quality or attribute of the product; as a result, some imagination, thought, or perception leads you to comprehend the nature of the goods. Examples: COPPERTONE (suntan oil) and CHICKEN OF THE SEA (tuna).

Inherently distinctive

MARKS WITH SECONDARY MEANING are marks that consumers recognize as a source for a product, have acquired a "secondary meaning" and can get registered even though they are generic or descriptive. This is an exception to the rule against registering generic or descriptive marks. It is intended to protect very famous or very valuable marks. Secondary meaning is earned through long term use or lots of publicity and ads. You have to be able to prove secondary meaning (e.g. through consumer surveys). Examples: SHARP (televisions), WINDOWS (windowing software), and INTERNATIONAL BUSINESS MACHINES (computers and other business machines).

MARKS THAT CANNOT BE REGISTERED

DESCRIPTIVE MARKS literally describe the product or something about the product. Many people think that they get more protection by picking a mark that perfectly describes their product, but the opposite is true. The use of an obvious and common place mark is not eligible for exclusive registration because it describes all other competing products too, unless the mark has obtained secondary meaning. Examples: PARK N FLY (airport parking lot) and COMPUTERLAND (computer store).

GENERIC MARKS either describe the category of goods or services (instead of their source) or become common ways to identify something. If a mark becomes generic, it can lose its protection. And, no generic mark can be registered. Examples: CELLOPHANE, ASPIRIN and ESCALATOR.

SURNAMES, on their own, are not eligible for registration, unless they obtain secondary meaning. Examples: JIM BEAM (whiskey), CALVIN KLEIN (jeans), and LOUIS VUITTON (luggage).

GEOGRAPHIC MARKS have some geographic location in them. A geographic mark cannot be registered, unless it obtains secondary meaning. Example: PHILADELPHIA (cream cheese).

MISDESCRIPTIVE MARKS that disparage or falsely suggest a relationship with a person, an institution, a belief, or a national symbol are not registrable.

WEAK

CONFUSINGLY SIMILAR MARKS that are likely to cause confusion, mistake or deception with someone else's mark cannot get registered. Marks can cause confusion if they sound, look or "feel" the same as a preexisting mark. Note that because common law marks have limited geographic scope, it is possible that the existence of a common law mark may prevent the federal registration of a mark without prohibiting its use.

NOT YOUR MARK - a government's flag, a name, portrait or signature identifying a particular living person without their consent cannot be registered; a name, portrait, or signature of a U.S. President during the life of the President or the President's widow, without her/his consent, cannot be registered.

FEDERAL REGISTRATION

Federal registration is a pain, but a necessary one. Let's discuss (1) the benefits of federal registration; (2) disqualifications for registration; (3) qualifications for registration; and (4) the application.

1. BENEFITS OF FEDERAL REGISTRATION

The Registration of a mark with the PTO gets you:

- ✓ First blush exclusive use of your mark with your products and services throughout the U.S.
- ✓ Nationwide notice that you own the mark
- ✓ 5 years after registration, your mark becomes "incontestable" – not foolproof, but impervious to attacks of descriptiveness

2. DISQUALIFICATIONS FOR REGISTRATION

Only certain marks can be registered. The PTO reviews every application to see if it falls into one of the following categories - if it does, it can't be registered. Marks that describe the goods, describe a quality or feature of the goods, describe the geographical location or include a surname are usually not able to be registered (See "The Trademark Continuum").

3. QUALIFICATION FOR REGISTRATION

Only marks <u>used</u> in <u>interstate</u> <u>commerce</u> can get federal registration.

"USED IN INTERSTATE COMMERCE"

"<u>Use</u>" in interstate commerce means to use the mark to identify and distinguish your product or to sell or advertise services. Specifically, for products, put the mark on the product, label, tag, packaging or displays around the product, or if you can't do that because of the product, then on documents provided with the product; for services, put the mark on material selling, promoting or advertising the services.

Use in "<u>interstate</u>" commerce means to use the mark across state lines or with another country, in good faith (as opposed to "token" use for the sake of grabbing the trademark). Use of a mark in purely local commerce within a state does not qualify as use in interstate commerce. Here are specific steps to satisfy the "interstate" requirement:

- ✓ Make actual sales to buyer in another state or country
- ✓ Use means or methods regulated by Congress under the Commerce Clause (phone lines, mail, etc.)
- ✓ Advertise your product or service out of state
- ✓ Solicit customers in markets in another state or country
- ✓ Advertise to the interstate traveler or list in a travel guide, travel magazine or other publication
- ✓ Keep articles from out of state or national publications mentioning your product or service
- ✓ Keep a record of out of state customers
- ✓ Accept credit cards and have a phone reservation policy (because they are a part of interstate commerce)

Use in interstate "<u>commerce</u>" means all commerce that may lawfully be regulated by the U.S. Congress, for example, interstate commerce or commerce between the U.S. and another country. The use in commerce must be a bona fide use in the ordinary course of trade, and not made merely to reserve a right in a mark. Use in commerce does NOT mean putting your mark on business cards or letterhead or showing it in presentations to company employees, advertising agencies, investors or potential partners.

4. APPLICATION FOR FEDERAL REGISTRATION

To register your mark, you have to file an application for registration with the PTO on its website. Here are three ways to apply for federal registration.

Use Application. Remember that you can only own a trademark you use. So, if you have already started using your mark in commerce, you file a "use" application.

Intent to Use Application. You can file an application for federal registration based upon a bona fide intention to use the mark in commerce (an "intent-to-use" application) as long as you file proof of actual use within six months (or up to thirty months with extensions).

Foreign Registration. Some international agreements allow you to file a trademark application based on an application or registration in another country. The time limit to file the application for international registration is six months after you file your basic trademark application.[3]

THE APPLICATION

You will need to supply the following contents in the Application:

- ✓ Applicant's name
- ✓ The mark
- ✓ A description of goods and services with which the mark will be used
- ✓ The International Classes of Goods and Services. The International Class of Goods and Services is a 42-point list of types of goods and services; the application fee is actually pegged to the numbers of classes you claim on your application
- ✓ Dates of first use of the mark
- ✓ A "specimen" of the mark in use – copies of actual use of the mark
- ✓ The fee, which changes all the time, but as of May 1, 2012, is $275-$375 per class, depending on how you file. You will need to consider filing for goods, services and your website

PRINCIPAL REGISTER VS. SUPPLEMENTAL REGISTER

There are actually two lists of federal trademark registrations: the Principal Register and the Supplemental Register.

The Principal Register. This is the Broadway of trademark registration avenues. It grants all the really good benefits of registration. It's the big show everyone wants to see.

The Supplemental Register. This is the Branson, Missouri of trademark registration avenues. It's an option, but it's not as great. The Supplemental Register is for marks that are descriptive and could be admitted to the Principal Register once secondary meaning is established. An application for Supplemental Registration must be based on actual use of the mark.

There are some benefits to getting on the Supplemental Register:

- ✓ The mark will appear in trademark searches
- ✓ You can use the ® symbol with the mark
- ✓ It will help you get registered abroad
- ✓ It can help prove exclusive use of a mark for a five year period, which is a way of proving acquired distinctiveness and secondary meaning

The major distinction between Principal and Supplemental Registers arises if you end up in litigation. In litigation, marks on the Principal Register are <u>presumed</u> to be valid marks and all mark users are presumed to have constructive notice (nation-wide) of the registration. On the other hand, marks on the Supplemental Register are often challenged in litigation as not being strong enough marks to support a claim. You would have to prove your use of the mark and the distinctiveness you acquired as a single source for things identified with your mark. In addition, you would have to prove confusion in the marketplace and damages.

EXAMINATION AT THE PTO

On filing, the application is assigned a serial number. An examining attorney at the PTO reviews the application. Sometimes, the examiner has no objections, but, usually, the examiner will identify problems with the application through a document called an "office action." An office action lists reasons for refusal and requests for more proof or argument that your mark should be registered. You have six months to respond to the office action. The examiner can then either issue a final office action denying registration or it can submit it for publication. If the examiner denies it for registration, you can appeal with the Trademark Trial and Appeal Board. Once the application passes muster with the examiner, it gets published in the Official Gazette, a weekly publication of the PTO. The point of publication is to give the public an opportunity to denounce and oppose your mark application. Oppositions must be filed within 30 days of publication.

LIFETIME OF YOUR TRADEMARK

Your trademark ought to last as long as you use it as a trademark, but sometimes trademarks slip away. Let's discuss (1) the time period of the trademark registration; (2) accidental loss; and (3) opposition and cancelation.

1. TIME PERIOD

Trademark registrations last 10 years. Between the 5th and 6th anniversaries of registration, you have to check in with the PTO and tell them you are still using the mark. Every 10th anniversary of the registration, you have to renew your registration. But that is not the end of the story.

2. ACCIDENTAL LOSS

Your trademark can last forever – unless you accidentally give it away, abandon it or let it become generic.

GIVING IT AWAY ON ACCIDENT

Sometimes, owners of trademarks accidentally give away their mark. This happens when the owner gives someone a license to use the mark, but then does not keep a right in writing to police how the mark is used or accidentally "assigns" it by contract.

ABANDONMENT

Trademark rights can also be lost if abandoned. Not using your mark for 3 to 5 consecutive years is usually treated as having stopped using your mark. Since use = ownership, no use = no ownership.

BECOMING GENERIC

If your mark becomes so widely used to identify both your products and everyone else's competing products, your mark has become "generic." This is a curse of success. For instance, Bayer owned the trademark to ASPIRIN to identify its acetylsalicylic acid tablets, until Aspirin became the common name for any acetylsalicylic tablets regardless of the giver. Then, ASPIRIN was declared generic.

Anytime your trademark could appear in a dictionary to describe a type of product, your mark is at risk for becoming generic. There are a couple of solutions. First, use the mark like a mark, not like a name of a product. For instance, Rollerblade refers to its types of products as "inline skates" rather than "rollerblades." Second, conduct marketing efforts to shore up the name of your product, and associate your mark with that product type.[4]

3. OPPOSITION AND CANCELLATION

Even if no one files an opposition and your mark gets registered, it is still vulnerable to challenge. Third parties can bring a cancellation proceeding arguing that the mark is confusingly similar to a mark owned by them, while the other party disputes that claim.

THE TRADEMARK SYMBOL - ®

This symbol - ® - is the symbol for a registered mark.

This symbol - TM - is the symbol for an unregistered mark (you can also use "SM" for services). Once the mark is registered, you should place the registration symbol adjacent to the trademark. You should use the ® because your ability to get damages and lost profits in an infringement suit may be limited unless the infringer had actual notice of your registration[5]. The public is also notified that the mark is federally registered. Until the mark has been registered, the user should use "TM" for trademarks or "SM" for service marks.

TRADEMARK FIGHTS

If someone violates any of your rights, you may sue them for infringement or dilution. However, the person you sue will likely have defenses. In addition to attacking the validity of the trademark itself, there are also defenses that are based on the defendant's use of the mark, including (1) fair use; (2) parody; and (3) prior use.

1. FAIR USE

Fair use occurs when a trademark's use is not likely to cause confusion or dilute the brand. So, using words of description that happen to be like someone's trademark is fair use. Fair use also includes "nominative use" – when using the mark is necessary for clarity.

2. PARODY

Parody is a First Amendment defense that protects commentary of marks. Generally, parody is protected as long as use of the mark is not tied to commercial use.

3. PRIOR USE DEFENSE FOR LOCAL CONTINUOUS USE

A defending trademark owner may be able to claim that it used the mark before the filing of the trademark application or before the registered mark owner began using the mark.

HAP COMES ALIVE

"So, if we pick a name for our product that describes it exactly as it is, other people could use the name?"

"Yes, in the beginning, they could."

"What about "MouseTrap" for a mouse that doubles as a solar powered battery. Is that *descriptive*?"

"It might be, Hap. We have to do a little research, but we can probably make enough arguments that MouseTrap is more suggestive than descriptive. But, time will tell. We could make the arguments to the PTO while you plan to use MouseTrap as your trademark – then we could lose at the PTO.

If we were not able to get MouseTrap registered, you would have some choices. You could abandon the mark and pick a new one. You could appeal the decision of the trademark examiner. And, you could apply for registration on the Supplemental Register."

Haz asked, "Hap, does any of this make you want to dump MouseTrap?"

"Nope. Not a bit. Gravity, can you tell us a little about copyrights now?"

"I CAN TRY."

COPYRIGHT

Gravity said, "Now, let's launch into Copyright and what it protects."

A **Copyright** is ownership over the tangible result of your creativity.[6] Copyright protects the creator of a work by embedding exclusive rights to copy, sell, show and change the work within the work itself.

Not every creation is covered by copyright. Only "original works of authorship" are entitled to copyright protection. "Original" and "authorship" mean works that contain a minimal degree of creativity – something distinctly your own. At the extreme, a work is not original if it is copied or borrowed from someone else. The threshold for "originality" is low – originality will usually be found except for "works in which the creative spark is utterly lacking or so trivial as to be virtually nonexistent."

Your dominance over your expression lasts only for a limited period of time - at the end of your copyright, other people get to use it as source material for their own creation. Your ability to keep people from using your work does not include stopping people from commenting on your work or reporting on it. To encourage you to create, and to encourage other people to create, you get dominance - in use and exploitation - over your expressions, but with serious limitations. First, your expression has to be sufficiently "creative" - that is, it must contain something that springs essentially from you - otherwise, it isn't your work and you aren't entitled to protect it. Second, copyright does not apply to ideas or to utilitarian things.

COPYRIGHTABLE WORKS

Literary Works: books and other textual matter, such as magazine articles, computer programs and databases

Musical Works and Accompanying Words: lyrics and music to songs

Dramatic Works and Accompanying Music: plays and musicals

Motion Pictures and Audio Visual Works

Pictorial, Graphic & Sculptural Works

Works of artistic craftsmanship in form (but not mechanical or utilitarian aspects)

2D and 3D works, including Fine, Graphic & Applied Art (ornamental designs of useful objects, such as lamps)

Photos

Pantomimes and Choreography: ballets and dances

Sound Recordings

Architectural Work

Maps

Charts

Models

Prints and Reproductions

Globes

Diagrams

Technical Drawings

Architectural Plans

HOW A COPYRIGHT GETS CREATED AND OWNED

Copyright springs to life in the hands of the author. The author is either the human being(s) who created it or the business entity that employed someone to create it. Let's discuss (1) things you can copyright; and (2) your copyright rights.

1. THINGS YOU CAN COPYRIGHT AND REGISTER

Expressions that are original works of authorship "fixed in a tangible medium of expression" – captured so you can see, hear or sense them again in more than just memory – get copyright protection.[7] Typing, writing, electronically recording, photographing, painting or sculpting all are usually sufficient. A tangible medium of expression can be paper, a CD ROM or DVD, digital or photo film, canvas, clay, or stone.

2. RIGHTS – WHAT YOU GET AND WHAT YOU DON'T WITH A COPYRIGHT

Copyright is like a bouquet of flowers – one object made up of many parts, which you can give away, never look at, rip up and waste to wither. Part of the bouquet of rights includes rights to things that are tangible and some things that are just in the air.

Your ownership of the copyright to your work of authorship gives you the exclusive right to:

1. Reproduce in copies or records
2. Prepare derivative works
3. Distribute copies to the public by sale, rent, lease, lend or license
4. Perform publicly any literary work, musical, dramatic work, choreography or mime
5. Display publicly any literary work, musical, dramatic work, choreography, mime, and pictorial, graphic, or sculpture
6. Perform publicly a sound recording by digital audio transmission

THINGS YOU CAN'T COPYRIGHT

-Slogans
-Standard Calendars
-Height & Weight Charts
-Tape Measures
-Ideas
-Procedures
-Rules
-Govt. Publications
-Processes
-Systems
-Concepts
-Titles
-Mere Words
-Short Phrases

FEDERAL REGISTRATION

Unlike trademarks and patents, registering copyright is relatively easy. Let's discuss (1) benefits of registration; (2) the application; (3) examination at the copyright office; and (4) duration.

1.   BENEFITS OF REGISTRATION

Not only does getting federal registration for your copyright have benefits – not having a registration hurts you. Here are the reasons you should register your copyright:

You May Not Be Able To File A Copyright Infringement Suit In Federal Court.   If someone copies your unregistered book, you may not be able to sue (this has long been the rule, though a March, 2010 Supreme Court case may have weakened this).[8]

Quickly File, Get Better Damages. If you file within 3 months of your work's publication or before someone rips you off, you can get statutory damages and lawyers' fees; if you don't, you only get the amount of damages you can prove.

Record.   Registration creates a public notice of your copyright.

Proof of Validity.   If you file within 5 years of your work's publication, copyright registration will be prima facie proof that your copyright is valid and accurate.

Anti-Piracy.   Copyright registration allows you to record your copyright with U. S. Customs Service as protection against the importation of pirated copies.

2.   THE APPLICATION

To register a copyright, you have to file an application. You get the application form on the website for the U.S. Copyright Office. You can also file your application online. Go to http://www.copyright.gov and click "How to Register a Work."

There are three things you will need to submit:

The Application.   You will need to fill out the application, including describing the work, describing the authors (the creators) and describing the owners/claimants of the copyright.

Fee. You will need to pay a nonrefundable filing fee for each application. As of 2010, the fee ranges between \$35 and \$50.

A Copy. You will also need to submit a copy of your work, which the Copyright Office calls a "deposit." A deposit is usually one copy (if unpublished) or two copies (if published) of the work to be registered for copyright. If you file online, you have to be ready and able to upload a copy of your work onto the U.S. Copyright site.

3.   EXAMINATION

The application will be reviewed by an examiner at the U.S. Copyright office and will either be accepted or rejected. Typically, the application is accepted. However, sometimes the examiner rejects the application if he concludes that it does not qualify for copyright registration. In that case, you can appeal (though your appeal may fail).

4.   DURATION

A copyright's life depends on when it was created and/or published. Why? Because Congress has monkeyed with the copyright law several times, most recently to extend copyright duration to protect the copyrights in cartoon characters that were about to expire.

For works made today, the duration depends upon the status of the author. Works made by humans (as opposed to business entities) last for the authors' lives plus 70 years. Works made by business entities (called "work made for hire") last 95 years from the date of publication or 120 years from the date of creation, whichever expires first. For an excellent resource for copyright duration, see:

http://www.librarycopyright.net/digitalslider/

COPYRIGHT FIGHTS

Many people, including some lawyers, are unclear on when you can use another's work and still not be liable. (For instance, according to one urban legend, you can use another's artistic creation as long as you use less than 30 percent of it.)

Here is the general rule: Use of all or any part of someone else's copyrighted work is copyright infringement. This includes copying and making derivative works from another's work, as well as distributing, displaying and selling someone else's work. A work is "copied" if it was made using the original as a "model, template or even inspiration," or if the new work shows a substantial similarity to the old work and the artist had access to the old work. Judges also frequently regard "substantial similarity" as an indication of an impermissible copy if a new work includes copyrightable elements from an original work, and not merely ideas, then it may be infringing on that copyright. For instance, George Harrison's "My Sweet Lord" was found to infringe on the Chiffons' "He's So Fine" because of an overlap of three notes.[9]

Similarly, any transformation of an original work into a new work can be considered a "derivative work." The bottom line is that when borrowing content, you make a copy.

If someone violates a copyright, the copyright owner can sue him in court. Copyright fights are very, very fun, unless you are a party. Let's discuss (1) what you have to prove in an infringement claim; and (2) defenses to infringement claims.

1. WHAT YOU HAVE TO PROVE IN AN INFRINGEMENT CLAIM

You own a valid copyright. Your copyright must be (a) for an original work of authorship; and (b) fixed in a tangible medium. Registration of the copyright gives you the benefit of the doubt.

The bad guy copied your work. This can be through direct or indirect evidence. Direct evidence means an admission or a witness. Indirect evidence means (a) a "striking similarity" plus (b) access and use of access (e.g. wide geographical distribution or testimony that the defendant owned a copy of the protected work).

The part the bad guy copied is a misappropriation of your work. First, that the part of your work used was protectable (e.g. not ideas, facts or public domain). Second, the intended audience will recognize substantial similarities between the two works. Two methods are used to determine if unlawful appropriation has occurred: the subtractive method and the totality method. In the subtractive method, the unprotected elements are subtracted and the remaining portions are examined for substantial similarities. In the totality method, the entire work is examined for substantial similarity.

2. DEFENSES TO INFRINGEMENT

INDEPENDENT CREATION

Independent creation is a defense to infringement since it shows that the defendant did not merely copy. The key is to disprove that the defendant had access to the work (that is why studios won't take or keep unsolicited manuscripts).

TRIVIAL USE (A/K/A/ DE MINIMIS COPYING)

Trivial use is a defense, but only when the use is obscured, short, meaningless to the action or accidental. The Beastie Boys won a sampling case — the court said that using 3 notes in Pass the Mic was de minimis (i.e. no big deal). However, contrary to popular wisdom, there is no 3 note free zone in sampling; some courts don't even let music samplers claim de minimis use.

FIRST SALE

The first sale defense allows a bona fide purchaser of a work to resell it. This is a defense to the right to distribute, but not to copy. So, if you buy a painting by a local artist, you can resell the painting, but you can't sell T-shirts made from the painting. And, you can sell items purchased legitimately, as long as you don't change them.[10]

FAIR USE

Fair use[11] is a defense that allows people to use copyrighted works for comment, study or criticism.

It is not a golden ticket to stealing other peoples' works; it is a narrow defense, which has no bright line.

In much of law, there is no bright line. Instead, you ask a bunch of questions. The answers to the questions will be: yes, and, yes, but, no and, and no but. You take the answers and make a judgment about whether the sum total of the answers makes something more than something else. Instead, you have to ask several questions to decide if copyright use is not infringement because it is fair use. Here are the questions:

- ✓ What was the purpose and character of the use?
- ✓ What was the nature of the original copyrighted work?
- ✓ What was the amount and substantiality of the portion used?
- ✓ What was the effect on the market for the original copyright?

Let's take them one by one.

Purpose and character of the work.
The purpose and character question seeks to identify how the defendant used the work. Did he transform it to make a statement or did he really just convert it to a commercial product for financial gain. Use tilts towards fair use, and away from infringement, if the one who borrowed either transformed the portion he used to comment on the original work or else he did not use the portion for very commercial purposes. But, the question weighs against the borrower if he didn't comment on the original work or he sold his use of it for cash money.

Nature of Copyrighted Work.
The nature of the copyrighted work question really looks at the quality and strength of the copyright in the original work. The borrower's use tilts towards fair use if the original copyright is weak.

Amount and Substance Used.
The amount and substance used looks at how much the defendant used – was it just enough to make his point or did he take more than he needed (or the whole thing). The borrower's use tilts towards fair use if he had borrowed just a smidge or no more than necessary to make his point. However, the

question weighs against the borrower if he borrowed the central figures of the original, taking "the very heart of his work."

Harm to Original Owner's Market.
Harm to the original owner's market looks for signs that the defendant's use of the work hurt the original owner in his native or predictable market. The borrower's use tilts towards fair use if the market for his works was vastly different than the copyright owner's.

AUTHORSHIP

The author of the work is the one who made it. The author has the initial right to register the copyright and to transfer ownership of the copyrights to some third party, who then becomes the "owner" of the copyright. Permanent transfers of exclusive right in copyright must be done in writing. Authorship has many facets and includes (1) works for hire; (2) joint works; (3) derivative works; and (4) the right to cancel old copyright deals.

1. WORK FOR HIRE

Usually, the work's author is the owner. But, if a work is created by an employee in the course of her employment, the employer owns the copyright. Works created by independent contractors are more complicated. Works that fit into particular categories <u>and</u> are declared "**works for hire**" in writing are owned by the employer.

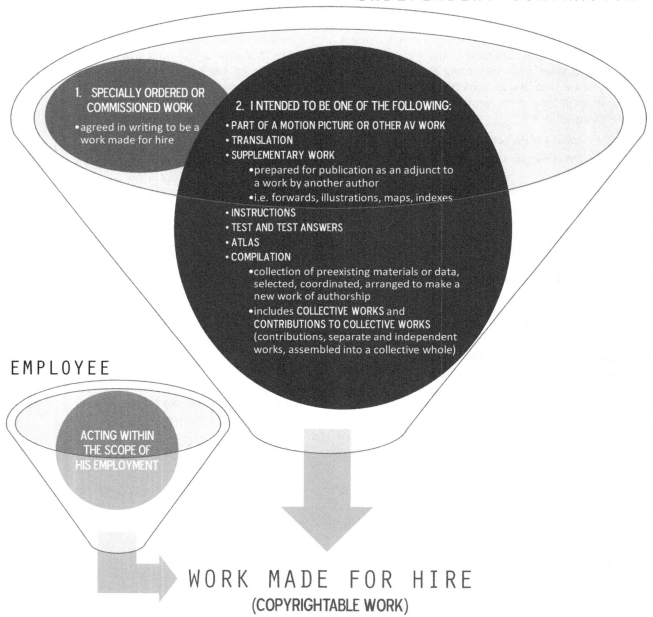

INDEPENDENT CONTRACTOR

1. SPECIALLY ORDERED OR COMMISSIONED WORK
   • agreed in writing to be a work made for hire

2. INTENDED TO BE ONE OF THE FOLLOWING:
   • PART OF A MOTION PICTURE OR OTHER AV WORK
   • TRANSLATION
   • SUPPLEMENTARY WORK
       • prepared for publication as an adjunct to a work by another author
       • i.e. forwards, illustrations, maps, indexes
   • INSTRUCTIONS
   • TEST AND TEST ANSWERS
   • ATLAS
   • COMPILATION
       • collection of preexisting materials or data, selected, coordinated, arranged to make a new work of authorship
       • includes COLLECTIVE WORKS and CONTRIBUTIONS TO COLLECTIVE WORKS (contributions, separate and independent works, assembled into a collective whole)

EMPLOYEE

ACTING WITHIN THE SCOPE OF HIS EMPLOYMENT

WORK MADE FOR HIRE
(COPYRIGHTABLE WORK)

2. JOINT WORK

If two or more people create works, intending to put them together in a single, cohesive work, the resulting collaborative piece is a "joint work."

The division of rights in a joint work can be re-made in a written contract. Without a contract saying otherwise, co-authors have equal, individual rights to control and exploit the work, particularly in four areas: (a) Ownership, (b) Control, (c) Accounting and (d) Transfers.

OWNERSHIP

No matter the size of the contribution, the joint work's author owns an undivided interest in the entire work and all its elements. Similar to a joint bank account, each party to the account can withdraw funds, even beyond amounts he or she deposited.

CONTROL

Traditionally, an author has the exclusive right to use, reproduce or make new works inspired by the original work.[12] An author of a joint work shares that control with other joint authors. As such, one joint author can exploit the joint work without the other authors' permissions. One joint author can exploit any individual element of the joint work without the other authors' permissions — even, with limitation, if the non-consenting author contributed the element in question.

Joint authors cannot sue each other for infringement.[13] For instance, imagine a painter contributes a painting and a photographer contributes a photo to a collage. Without consulting the painter, the photographer may license the collage for a calendar and may permit the calendar company to sublicense the collage for a mouse pad.

There are some limits to this control. The law will not permit a joint author to "destroy" the work.[14] However, it may be difficult to prove any particular use or license has lowered the value of the work so much that the work has been "destroyed."

ACCOUNTING

Joint authors are accountable to each other for any profits generated from the joint work. All such profits must be disclosed and divided equally among all joint authors.

TRANSFERS

A joint author may sell his or her ownership to a third party. The buyer will "step into the shoes" of the original joint author, as if the transferee is the joint author with respect to all of the rights discussed above.

3. DERIVATIVE WORK

The right to make a derivative work is one of the rights in copyrights. Only the copyright owner can create or authorize the creation of a derivative work. A "Derivative Work" is a tangible result of creative expression based on or including another copyrightable expression.

A work is not "derivative" merely because it is inspired by the first work. For a work to be a "derivative work", it must include a substantial amount of the previous work — enough that an average person would think it had been based on or adapted from a prior work. An average person must be able or likely to recognize the copy job. [15]

A Derivative Work can be an infringing derivative work or it can be a copyrightable work all on its own. But, only derivative works that have new, original material have some level of copyright protection for the author of the derivative work. The copyright only covers the additions. Use of a piece of a work that does not have sufficient transformation to be a derivative work is an infringement. So, taking a small sample is a simple infringement. A major sample is an infringing derivative work.

4. THE RIGHT TO CANCEL REALLY OLD COPYRIGHT DEALS.

Authorship matters. Authorship creates a permanent right in the work. If a work is a work made for hire, the employee or independent contractor who made it can't ever take it back - the boss is the author. But, if a work is not a work made for hire, and the actual author sold or licensed it, the author can take it back even from the person who hired her to make it in the first place. Most of the time, people don't put anything in writing and the boss just thinks he owns it. The other half the time, people put it in writing that it's a work made for hire. And, the contract also says that if it fails to be a work made for hire, the contractor assigns it to the boss, which is the right way to handle it, but not perfect.

Here's why. In 1976, Congress amended the Copyright Act to allow copyright authors to revoke old sales or license grants of their copyrights during the 5-year period starting on the 35th anniversary of the sale (or publication).[16] This was meant to right the wrongs done to struggling musicians and artists who often sold their works for peanuts. The impact of this amended law starts in 2013. That's because the termination right is effective on the 35th anniversary of the sale or publication and the law went into effect in 1978.[17] At the same time, the work made for hire rules were rewritten to narrow the class of works that can be authored by companies who hire independent contractors to make content. The author (or the estate) has to send a notice of termination at least two years (but not more than 10) years before the termination date and file the termination notice with the US Copyright Office. The author or estate should also be ready to show that the author was not an employee and the work was not a work made for hire.

Hazard asked, "Will we have copyrights, Gravity?"

"Sure," Gravity answered. "You'll have the prototype designs, your brochures and ad copy if it's longer than a short phrase. You'll have images you take of your product, your website content and website art. And, you'll have Hap's three-foot sculpture made entirely of binder clips."

Hap blushed. "Sorry, Gravity. I'm listening, really. This part is interesting. I just have so many brains, I need to keep them all activated."

Haz continued, "What's next, Gravity?"

"Patents."

"I've never really understood patents," Haz admitted. "Can you go slowly?"

"I CAN TRY."

PATENT

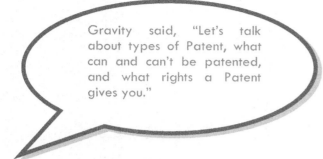

Gravity said, "Let's talk about types of Patent, what can and can't be patented, and what rights a Patent gives you."

A **Patent** is the power to exert limited, exclusive dominance over a new and useful process or thing.[18] A patent is a bigger right than copyright. Copyright protects the way someone expressed an idea. Patent protects ways to use the idea. But, those ways must be new, novel and not obvious.

THREE TYPES OF PATENT

There are three types of patents: (1) design; (2) plant; and (3) utility.

1. DESIGN PATENTS

Design Patents are inventions of new, original, and ornamental designs for articles of manufacture.

2. PLANT

Plant Patents are inventions or discoveries of new asexual reproducing varieties of plants.

3. UTILITY PATENTS

All other patents, other than design and plant patents, are Utility Patents.

See the chart on the following page.

THREE TYPES OF PATENT

	UTILITY				DESIGN	PLANT
	MACHINES	ARTICLES OF MANUFACTURE	COMPOSITIONS OF MATTER	PROCESS		
DEFINITION	A concrete thing, with parts or a combination of devices, that interact with one another.[19]	Tangible things made from raw materials using labor or machines all artificial items that are not found in substantially the same form in nature, and that are neither machines nor compositions of matter	The intermixture of two or more ingredients. Usually means new compounds created by humans	A new, novel and nonobvious method or process that produces something valuable	New, original, nonobvious and ornamental design for a product (article of manufacture)	A distinct and new variety of plant that has been invented or discovered and asexually reproduced other than a tuber or a plant found in an uncultivated state.
EXAMPLES	An engine, a pump, an electrical appliance, or most any sort of mechanical or electrical devise which has any sort of operation	A tool, a kitchen implement, a container, a fastening device, a toy, a game, an electronic component, software, or most any sort of useful object that might have some sort of physical function.	Chemical compounds, mixtures, alloys, and drugs, as well as improvements on such compositions or composite articles	One click purchase by Amazon.com	Form must be dictated by ornamentation. A design patent is about ornamentation rather than functionality. Thus, a design patent is its own category because An invention may support both a utility patent and a design patent but the scope of protection under each type of patent will vary	Includes 3 types: 1. sports (from bud variation, not seed variation) 2. mutants (from seedling variation by self-pollination), and 3. hybrids (cross-pollinated seed from 2 species or a species and variety)

HOW A PATENT GETS CREATED AND OWNED

Because of a patent's strength and breadth, it only springs into existence if the government says it should. The Patent and Trademark Office has the sole authority to grant a patent. To get a patent in the U.S., an inventor must submit a lengthy application describing the invention and how it can be used, so that other people can learn from it. Like any other property right, patents may be sold, licensed, assigned or transferred, given away, or simply abandoned.

A second generation of a patent, called an "improvement," can be a wholly patentable invention that still constitutes infringement. An improvement follows the same analysis of patentability. However, if using the patent requires using the first patent, it is infringement.

WHAT CAN AND CAN'T BE PATENTED

Patents are very complex. Not only is the law tough, but the application of the law to an invention is also difficult. I will tell you, candidly and proudly, that most pure patent lawyers have at least 20 I.Q. points more than me. Let's take it easy and discuss (1) what can be patented; (2) what does not qualify for patent; and (3) a little guidance.

1.   WHAT CAN BE PATENTED

Patents are only granted to things that: (1) have a patentable subject matter; (2) are useful; (3) novel; and (4) not obvious.

SUBJECT MATTER

Any new and useful invention that is made by man can be patented, including a process, machine, manufacture, or composition of matter, or any new and useful improvement of them.

Process. "Process" means a process, act or method, typically industrial or technical. [20] A business method patent is a patent for a method of doing business or a process that solves a real world problem or produces a "concrete and tangible result." [21]

In other words, the business method must be new and novel and produce something that has a value in the real world, rather than just a theory or a fantasy.

Business methods can include (1) a process that transforms an "article" from one state into another; or (2) a process that requires a particular machine. Business method patents are in flux and have not been well defined by Congress, the courts or the PTO. The PTO has a bunch of factors that its examiners look to in deciding whether a method is patentable, which you can get at:

⇨   http://www.uspto.gov/patents/announce/
bilski_qrs.pdf

Machine or Article of Manufacture. "Articles of Manufacture" means any articles that are made or manufactured by man.

Composition of Matter. "Composition of matter" means chemical compositions, mixtures of ingredients, as well as new chemical compounds.

USEFUL

The invention must be useful for current use by a person of ordinary skill in the art. Use must be identified, demonstrated and demonstrable. The use must conform to scientific principles and be possible. And, the invention must work as promised in the application. Theoretical use is not enough.

NOVEL – INVENTION MUST BE NEW AND NOT ANTICIPATED

Must Be New and Not Anticipated. The invention must actually be new – neither known nor used in the U.S. and neither patented nor described in print anywhere in the world. The invention must also be different from any prior device or process and not anticipated.

Prior Art. To know if an invention is new and anticipated, you have to look at all of the information that has been made available to the public before your patent application filing date that may overlap with this patent – that information is called "prior art." If there is prior art that lists all of the elements of a claim of your patent, then the prior art anticipated your patent and it is not novel.

Prior art can be anything – both old patents and patent applications as well as the inventor's own discussion. The list of information types that can be prior art include: earlier patents, earlier published patent applications, scientific publications, textbooks, newspapers, lectures made to people located in the US[22], demonstrations made publicly to people in the US, and Internet publications that can be shown to have been publicly accessible before the filing date, among others. Similarly, offering the patent for sale or exhibition publicly before the patent application is filed makes it not novel[23], even if the invention was hidden inside a product.

Any information made available to the public in the past can be prior art – even if no one read it or most people could not understand it. A single copy of a dissertation in a small university library is sufficient. Information is considered available to the public if the public could access to it without violating a confidentiality obligation. However, disclosures made in confidence, such as under a confidentiality agreement, are not made publicly.

However, in the U.S., there is a one year grace period for an inventor's own activity. That means that once you or one or your co-inventors makes a public statement of any kind about your invention, you have one year to file your patent application. Most other countries are not so forgiving and provide no grace period.

Prior art, then, trumps your patent if it:

- ✓ was described in printed publication before invention or 1 year prior to application
- ✓ was known or used by others in the US before it was invented by the applicant
- ✓ was in public use or on sale in the US 1 year prior to application

You can blow your U.S. patent by publicly writing about, discussing or using the invention more than a year prior to filing. And, you can blow your international patents by writing about, discussing or using the invention at any time prior to filing.

NOT OBVIOUS

A patent cannot be obvious. "Obvious" means that the invention would have been obvious to someone in the area of the invention. Whether a patent was obvious when made is factual and includes analysis of:

- ✓ Prior art (knowledge prior to invention in the field that is directly applicable to the invention)
- ✓ The differences between the prior art and the patent claims at issue
- ✓ The level of ordinary skill in the pertinent art
- ✓ Commercial success of the invention as evidence of long expressed, unresolved needs

2. PATENTS ARE NOT GRANTED FOR:

- ✓ Inventions used solely in the utilization of special nuclear material or energy in an atomic weapon[24]
- ✓ Laws of nature, physical phenomena, and abstract ideas are not patentable subject matter
- ✓ Tax avoidance or tax limitation strategies
- ✓ Any claim to a human organism
- ✓ A mere idea or suggestion
- ✓ Anything not new
- ✓ Anything not demonstrably useful
- ✓ Anything obvious

3. GUIDANCE

During the year following public disclosure of your invention, you must file a patent application. If you have not filed, get a nondisclosure agreement signed before you discuss or disclose your invention. Even chatting to a group of friends more than 1 year prior to filing may blow your ability to get a patent. Although the United States gives you one year to file, other countries don't. So, you should file a patent application before you publicly disclose your invention, i.e. before public release or announcement.

PATENT RIGHTS

The rights that a patent gives you are like the end of the movie *No Way Out* – you just don't see it coming. Let's talk about (1) what a patent gives you; and (2) what a patent does not give you.

1. WHAT A PATENT GIVES YOU

As a patent owner, you are granted the exclusive right to prevent others from making, using, offering for sale, or selling the invention or certain components of the invention, defined by the patent grant. The boundaries of what the patent includes are defined by "claims" in the final patent application.

2. WHAT A PATENT DOES NOT GIVE YOU

A patent does not give a right to actually make the invention or to supplant an existing patent. A patent can be subject to an earlier patent. For instance, if you invent an improvement to an earlier device that is also patented, your rights to your improvement are limited to the rights of the inventor of the original inventor. If its claims are sufficiently broad, this prior "dominating" patent may prevent you from making your invention.

PATENT FIGHTS

If someone makes, uses, sells or offers to sell your patented invention without your permission, that person has infringed on your patent rights. You can sue an infringer in Federal court for infringement. However, the infringer will probably try and invalidate your patent and also claim he was not infringing on your patent. Your patent fight can be helped or hurt by (1) the inconveniently invalid patent; and (2) other defenses.

1. THE INCONVENIENTLY INVALID PATENT

Patents are presumed valid, though this is rebuttable. Below are some ways a patent is proven invalid or unenforceable.

Prior Patents, Prior Art. Prior patents, prior commercial use, prior art or publications can trump a patent.[25]

Not New. Proof that the invention was in public use or on sale in the U.S. more than a year prior to the date of the application may break the patent. The patent can also be broken by showing that the inventor derived the invention from an earlier invention.

Overbroad claims. Claims that stretch beyond a reasonable basis may be invalid.

Inequitable Conduct in Obtaining the Patent. Inequitable conduct committed to get the patent can be grounds for invalidity. Inequitable conduct can include: (a) failure to submit known material prior art; (b) failure to explain foreign references translations; (c) misstatements of fact or concerning patentability; and (d) mis-description of inventorship.

2. ADDITIONAL DEFENSES TO PATENT INFRINGEMENT

EXHAUSTION (SIMILAR TO FIRST SALE DOCTRINE IN COPYRIGHT)

The first unrestricted sale of a patented product exhausts the patent owner's control over that product. When you let go of the physical embodiment of an IP right, it's gone.

Exhaustion doctrine issues are especially a problem for parallel imports. A parallel import is a non-counterfeit product imported from another country without the permission of the intellectual property owner. Parallel imports are often referred to as grey product, and are implicated in issues of international trade, and intellectual property. The practice of parallel importing mainly occurs for two reasons: (1) Different versions of a product are produced for sale in different markets and get bootlegged to another country; and (2) companies, either the manufacturer or the distributor, set different price points for their products in different markets.

INDEPENDENT INVENTION NOT A DEFENSE

Independent invention is not a defense to patent infringement. But if you reasonably fear being sued for patent infringement, you can file suit for a declaratory judgment that the patent at issue is invalid, or that the conduct in question does not constitute infringement.

CHALLENGES

There are a number of avenues for attacking the validity of a patent at its core. For instance, before a patent issues, anyone can file prior art with the PTO to challenge the patent application within six months of publication or before the first rejection of a claim. A prior inventor can challenge a patent application on grounds that it is derived from the prior inventor's invention. Anyone can request PTO review of an issued patent within nine months of the patent grant. And, a defendant in a business method patent infringement suit can ask PTO to review the patent if the patent is in the financial services for management of a financial product.

FEDERAL REGISTRATION

To get a patent, you have to file a patent application within twelve months of commercial exploitation. "Commercial Exploitation" includes disclosure of the invention in a printed publication, public use of the invention, or offering the invention for sale. Around the world, you have to file the patent application before you publicly disclose the invention. The patent application must describe your invention so that a person with some skill in the applicable area can make and use the invention. Some countries require specific descriptions of the usefulness of the invention, the best way to perform the invention known or the technical problem or problems solved by the invention. Drawings illustrating the invention should also be provided. The application will have one or more claims, which define what the inventor wants to protect and exclude others from making, using, selling or importing. The claims prescribe the limits and boundaries of the patent. Some countries charge annual or periodic renewal fees for the duration of the patent.

As part of registration, you will need to (1) identify the inventor(s); (2) identify the patent owners; (3) have an application completed; (4) file the application; and (5) consider a foreign filing; (6) get the patent issued and pays for it; and (7) include a patent notice on the products of your patent; and (8) be aware of the duration of the patent.

1. THE INVENTOR

In the United States, only the inventor(s) may apply for a patent although it can be transferred to a company after filing the application, or the employer will be listed as the owner of the patent.

Employers may apply for a patent for a missing inventor. Estates and heirs can apply for a patent for a deceased inventor. In most countries, both natural persons and companies may apply for a patent. To be an INVENTOR, you must have contributed to the subject matter set out in a claim of the patent, such as conceiving the invention or having had some intellectual dominion over the invention.[26] The inventors are people who conceived a definite and permanent idea and reduced it to practice;[27] the ones who identified a problem and solved it.

Inventors cannot be the actual inventor's boss, the person who just reduces the idea to practice or followed the inventors' instructions. Financial investment does not constitute inventing. Falsely claiming inventor status could invalidate the patent unless made in good faith.[28] If two or more people jointly made an invention, they go should down on the application as joint inventors. Patents can and often do have "JOINT INVENTORS" or "CO-INVENTORS."

2. THE PATENT OWNERS

The patent's inventors may be different than the patent's owner. A patent's owner starts off as the inventors and then can be transferred to someone else.[29] Patent assignments must be made in writing. Joint owners of a patent have equal rights to make, use, offer to sell, sell the invention without consent of the other owners and without accounting to the other owners.[30]

As an employer, you should get written assignments of all intellectual property, including inventions, from your personnel. Although it is wise for you to get an assignment of inventions from all personnel, there are two situations where you may get rights to the inventions under law. First, if an inventor was specifically "hired to invent," the thing he invented, then you may come to own the rights to the invention. Second, if your personnel invent something using your time, resources and facilities, you may get SHOP RIGHTS – a perpetual license to practice the invention.[31]

3. THE APPLICATION – UTILITY PATENT

The application must contain: (a) the Specification; (b) claims; (c) drawings; and (d) an oath and declaration.

WRITTEN DESCRIPTION (A/K/A/ THE SPECIFICATION)

The Specification is a written description of the invention that enables the use of the patent and describes the best methods for using the patent. Enablement includes 4 things: (1) the enablement requirement; (2) the best mode requirement; (3) the written description requirement; and (4) abstract and art.

Enabling Requirement. The language must specify and describe the invention so clearly that anybody in the invention's profession could use the invention without "undue experimentation." This language should also differentiate it from old inventions (a/k/a prior art).

Best Mode Requirement. The language must also disclose the best mode of practicing the invention, and the inventor's preference if it materially affects making or using the invention.

Written Description. There should be uniformity between the description of the invention and the invention attributes listed in the claims. It is possible for a specification to meet the test for enablement, but fail the written description test. All claims must be supported by the written description.

Abstract and Art. The Specification also includes the invention's title, an abstract of the invention, an initial summary of the invention being claimed, and a description of the drawings. The ABSTRACT must be 150 words or less and be part of the Specification. The application can include figures, but they are not required.

PATENT CLAIMS

The heart of the patent application, and the patent, is the "claims." Claims are essentially what the inventor is calling "dibs" on. Claims are the exclusive rights that the patent gives to the owner of the patent. They list the essential features necessary to distinguish the invention from old inventions.

During its examination, the PTO will focus on the claims to ensure that they are different than old inventions and sufficiently narrow. Claims are both technical and legal – they are also critical – so get a patent lawyer to write this for you.

DRAWINGS

Drawings will usually be included to illustrate the invention of a mechanical or electrical invention. These may require a professional draftsperson. For instance, biotech applications can include protein gene sequences set out in a specialized software program.

THE OATH

Inventors must make an oath about the accuracy of the application, which is notarized. The oath or declaration of the applicant is required by law.

4. FILE AND REVIEW

The application will be reviewed by an examiner at the PTO. It typically takes somewhere between one to three years for an application to be reviewed. Often, the examiner will reject the application by sending an Office Action. The rejection may be overcome by narrowing and revising the claims and arguing with the examiner. An application could go through a couple more rounds. If it is actually rejected, there are avenues for appeal.

5. FOREIGN FILING

Within one year of filing an application with the PTO, you can file a patent application in a foreign country and claim priority to the original filing date under international treaties. Alternatively, you can also delay filing the application for up to 30 months by first filing an application under the Patent Cooperation Treaty ("PCT") within twelve months of the initial patent application filing date. This allows you to postpone incurring the filing costs until you figure out whether it is worth the money to make the filings.

Regardless of these filing guidelines, most foreign countries do not provide a grace period, and must be filed before publishing or commercializing the invention. If you talk about your patent publicly or display it or put it up for sale, you must apply for a patent before one year has gone by, otherwise your right to a patent will be lost. You must file on the date of public use or disclosure, to preserve patent rights in many foreign countries.

6. PATENT ISSUE AND FEES

Patents aren't free – you have to pay when you get the patent and over the years.

PATENT FILING FEES

Utility Patent fees are convoluted and a la carte. Currently, the filing fee is $530 for companies of fewer than 500 employees, which consists of a $98 application fee (for an electronic filing), a $310 search fee and a $125 examination fee. Then, if you win and you get a patent, you have to pay a patent issue fee of $870. Therefore, the lowest amount of patent fees – just fees – is $1,400 These fees will increase depending on the type of patent, the number of claims, the size of the application and a bunch of other factors.

Some lightly funded patent owners (called "small entities") get discounts on patent fees. Small entities that have 500 or less employees and have not assigned or licensed any rights in the invention to a larger entity get a 50% discount on patent fees.[32] In the future, if a small entity qualifies as a "micro entity," it gets a 75% discount on patent fees.[33]

WHEN YOU GET THE PATENT

When a patent passes the application process, the PTO sends out a Notice of Allowance to the inventor or inventor's lawyer. Once you get a Notice of Allowance, you have to pay the issue fee. Following payment of the Issue Fee, the patent will "issue."

OVER THE YEARS

You have to pay maintenance fees for all utility patents; if you don't pay on time, your patent will expire. Conveniently, all of these fees are due during the 6 months prior to the following anniversaries of the issue date:

- ✓ 3.5th anniversary
- ✓ 7.5th anniversary
- ✓ 11.5th anniversary

7. PATENT NOTICE (A/K/A PATENT MARKING)

If you make or sell patented products, you must put "Patent" and the patent number somewhere on the product. You can only get damages for infringement if you properly mark the products or the bad guy was notified of the infringement and continued his badness anyway. Many people use "Patent Pending" or other phrases on their products, but that has no legal impact. However, it is illegal to falsely mark a product as patented or patent pending.

8. DURATION

The patent will end:

1. If the application was filed after June 8, 1995, for utility patents, 20 years from filing + 5 year extension for drugs, medical devices and additives; for design patents, 14 years from filing.
2. If the application was filed before June 8, 1995, the greater of 17 years from issuance or 20 years from filing.

The term of the patent may be extended up to five years for particular disputes with the PTO on patentability that the patent owner wins. After the expiration, the invention can be practiced by the public.

SPECIAL TOPICS IN PATENT

There are a few other things to discuss about patents, such as (1) design patents; and (2) provisional patent applications.

1. DESIGN PATENTS

Design patents protect only the ornamental appearance of something. That ornamental appearance had to be intended merely for ornamentation – the way it looks – and not the way it works. Any ornamental design that was created to work well or be cheaper can only be protected by a utility patent. A design patent lasts for just 14 years. In contrast to copyrights, design patents protect the ornamental parts of useful objects that cannot be severed from the object's utility. For example, a design patent could cover a computer's appearance or the shape of a shoe (such as the Crocs shoes). However, an ornamental feature could be protected by both a design patent and a trademark. A shape of a package can be a trademark, but may also be protected under a design patent. However, the protections are different. A design patent allows the owner to prohibit others from making, selling or using a product with the design. A trademark would prohibit use of the design if it were likely to cause confusion in the consuming public.

In a fight over a design patent, the question is whether the accused product would appear "substantially the same" as the patented design by an ordinary observer.

To apply for a design patent, drawings showing numerous views of the article are carefully prepared. The specifications are short and you can only state one claim, which reads, "A design as shown in the figures." Design patents are currently popular because of the much higher registration success rate than utility applications.

2. PROVISIONAL PATENT APPLICATION

Inventors can file a "provisional patent application." People, mistakenly, file provisional patent applications to avoid or put off the expense of hiring a patent lawyer to complete a real application. A provisional patent application can be an inventor's notification to the world that it claims its invention and it promises to maybe file a real patent application within a year. The provisional patent application is meaningless unless you actually file a patent application within the 1 year period following the filing of your provisional patent application.

Description of Invention. The description must satisfy the enabling requirements and the best mode requirements of the regular patent application.

Drawings. Drawings necessary to understand the invention must be included.

The applicable filing fee. Filing fees for the provisional application change, but are currently $220 ($110 for small entity). If the specification and drawings exceed 100 sheets of paper, an application size fee is also due, which is $270 ($135 for small entity) for each additional 50 sheets or fraction thereof.

Cover. The application must include a cover sheet, which you get from the PTO's website.

BAD THINGS ABOUT THE PROVISIONAL PATENT APPLICATION

PTO review usually identifies inadequacies in describing or defining the patent. On a provisional patent application, there is no PTO review, so these inadequacies may not be discovered. Further, it is more likely for a non-patent lawyer to inadequately describe an invention. If the provisional patent application fails, it cannot be relied on by the regular patent application. If the regular application is filed more than one year after public disclosure of the invention in reliance on the (now failed) provisional patent application, the inventor will miss the filing window.

BENEFITS

But there are benefits to filing a provisional patent application, including:

- ✓ Getting something on file while you prepare the regular patent application
- ✓ Proving who was the first inventor of an invention
- ✓ As of March, 2013, the first to file a patent application wins – filing a provisional patent application is a way to plant your flag
- ✓ Extending the patent duration by one year
- ✓ Getting something on file while the inventor raises money for legal fees

HAP IS HOPEFUL

Hazard interrupted.

"Gravity, are we going to have patents to file?"

"Probably not, Hazard. Because you are licensing inventions from Seymour, it is not likely that you will invent anything. However, you may want to discuss with Seymour getting him to assign to you ownership of inventions that you pay him to develop."

Hazard said, "I think he likes his patents. If anything, maybe he would let us use them."

Hap jumped in, "Will we have anything else to protect?" His tone indicated he was hopeful they were near the end.

Gravity replied, "You may have some trade secrets."

"Oh." He paused. "I don't know what those are. Can you tell us about trade secrets?"

"I CAN TRY."

TRADE SECRETS

Gravity said, "Finally, let's talk about Trade Secrets."

CHAPTER 13

A trade secret[34] is a double secret way of doing something that gives you a competitive advantage because you have it and your competitors don't.

TRADE SECRETS

Specifically, a Trade Secret is a formula, pattern, device or compilation, program, method, technique or process which is used in your business, that gives you an advantage over your competitors and that is unknown and unknowable by your competitors and kept secret by your efforts.[35] A trade secret becomes stronger with more investment in money and effort. Trade secret protection includes protection over ideas, not just tangible information.

1. DURATION

A trade secret lasts as long as it is "secret" and provides an economic benefit. For example, the formula for Coke is a trade secret.

2. WHAT IS NOT A TRADE SECRET

The boundaries of trade secrets are critical. Below are some things that do not qualify as trade secrets:

- ✓ Something widely used throughout the industry or that is easy to develop or get through reverse engineering
- ✓ Something known by all employees, regardless if they need to know it or not
- ✓ If nothing or too little is done to keep it secret
- ✓ No value to information or advantage from the information

- ✓ A patent cannot be a trade secret, because you have to disclose the invention; anything not disclosed in the patent could be a trade secret (But remember you must disclose the best mode to obtain a valid patent.)
- ✓ Little or no resources put into developing it

PROTECTING YOUR TRADE SECRETS

You must take reasonable actions to keep your trade secret a secret – otherwise, it is not protectable.

- ✓ Keep the trade secret a secret by keeping it under lock and key (and behind a password)
- ✓ Segregate it from other, non-secret files
- ✓ Only disclose it to people who have a real need to know it and sign an NDA obligating them to keep it secret
- ✓ Create an internal policy about trade secrets and security measures
- ✓ Schedule and conduct regular audits of your IP to identify trade secrets.
- ✓ Periodically schedule and conduct checkups and training on efforts to keep it secret
- ✓ Place a notice or legend on trade secret materials, (though it is neither a total solution nor a requirement), such as:

This document contains confidential and proprietary trade secret information which is the property of _____. Its contents may not be copied, reproduced, distributed, or otherwise disclosed without the express permission of _____."

CLEAR THE IP

Gravity said, "Remember, when doing anything as it relates to IP, the essential questions are *Can you use it?* and *Can you protect it?*"

CHAPTER 14

CAN YOU USE IT?

There are three steps to figuring out whether you can use the IP:

1. Search for potential problems
2. Examine potential problems for real problems
3. Either get the right to use it or abandon it

1. SEARCH FOR POTENTIAL PROBLEMS WITH...

You have to search for potential problems with (a) trademarks; (b) copyrights and trade secrets; and (c) patents.

...TRADEMARKS

If there is a trademark that is similar to your mark in any way, you could be in danger of infringing that other trademark. Specifically, you need to know if there is a trademark, slogan, logo or name that: (1) is in use or is registered with the U.S. government; (2) is for similar goods or services; (3) is used in your geographic territory; (4) is in your marketplace of customers; (5) is similar in look, feel, aural tone, spelling, etc. to what you plan; and (6) would cause your trademark to have a likelihood of confusion in the public as to who makes and sells the product or service.

You need to know if there is a preexisting trademark in use that could trump your mark, so you need to gather the possibilities. Because trumping trademarks can be registered and unregistered, it is not enough merely to search the database of the PTO. You must do a broad search to collect all potentially trumping marks.

Search Options. Broad searches include:

- ✓ Internet and online law website "knock-out" searches; this is the first step and only tells you if you should find another mark, not if you should stick with the one you want to use
- ✓ USPTO federal government registries for U.S. trademarks: the USPTO is a good website, but the searching isn't necessarily comprehensive
- ✓ Third-Party Search Reports + opinion of counsel analyzing the reports (the gold standard); this is an expensive option, but it is the most comprehensive

...COPYRIGHTS & TRADE SECRETS

For copyright, you need to know if there is a work of authorship that you got from someone without obtaining ownership or a license. To find this out, gather every copyrightable work you are using. Don't forget:

- ✓ Software
- ✓ Business plans
- ✓ Manuals
- ✓ Ad copy
- ✓ Brochures
- ✓ Website copy
- ✓ Website design
- ✓ Music (both the song and the recording)
- ✓ Pictures, graphics, art and images
- ✓ Presentations
- ✓ Internal procedures

If your product treads on a preexisting patent, you're at risk, even if you've never heard of the patent. You need to know if there is a preexisting patent that could trump your rights, so gather the possibilities. Do a search of the registries. Search options include:

- ✓ U.S. Federal government registries for U.S. patents
- ✓ International patents: European, World (WIPO), and unexamined Japanese patents
- ✓ Third-Party Search Reports and opinion of counsel

This can be much more complicated than it seems. Get a lawyer, with experience in doing and looking at patent searches, to help you. And, consider getting a formal opinion from your lawyer about risks.

2. EXAMINE POTENTIAL PROBLEMS FOR REAL PROBLEMS WITH...

You have to examine potential problems with (a) trademarks; (b) copyright and trade secrets; and (c) patents.

...TRADEMARK

Once you identify potentially trumping trademarks, you have to assess whether they really trump your mark.

1. **Similarity of Mark**. If the mark is similar in any way, including the way it sounds when spoken, be on guard.

2. **Class of Goods and Services**. If the goods and services that the older trademark identifies are in the same international class of goods and services, you've got a problem. If they are in a related class of goods and services, or ones that their customers could see as an overlap, then you may have a problem. Some companies do market research to quantify the likelihood of confusion.

3. **Very Famous Mark**. If the mark you want to adopt is identical or close to a very famous trademark, then it may be dangerous to use it. And, if you want to use the mark because

it reminds people of the very famous mark, then you probably shouldn't use it.

4. **Invalid Mark**. If you see things that make you or your lawyer conclude that the mark has been abandoned (not used in the last 3-5 years) or has become generic, then you may have an indication that the mark poses a low risk.

5. **Challenge Registration**. You may also choose to take an aggressive position by challenging the use or registration of a trademark based on any of the requirements for a registered and/or strong mark. As long as you are aware of the risks and willing to take them, fight on.

...COPYRIGHT & TRADE SECRETS

Once you have identified and gathered works of authorship potentially owned or controlled by others, you have to assess whether they actually belong to another.

1. **Owned by Another**. Survey the work you are using in light of the contributions of people who helped you, particularly in the early stages. Could it be the work of another company or another person who did not make this for you? Could it be a sequel to an older work? Could it include even the smallest amount of someone else's creation? If you don't have proof that you own it, you may need to get that proof.

2. **Work Made For Hire.** For small businesses who do not employ people in permanent positions to do necessary, but specialized jobs (logo design, prototype molding, even the drafting of an employee handbook), making sure the products produced by people you pay get classified as a "work made for hire" is very important. Alternatively, if you were hired to produce something, consider whether it is owned by the person who paid for it as their "work made for hire."

3. **Joint Work.** If it was made by more than one person with the intention of creating an

integrated work, then it may be partially owned by its co-creator.

4. **Documents**. Is there a document that gives you or someone else a right to use it?

...PATENTS

Once you identify and gather potentially problematic patents, you have to assess whether they really trump your use.

Duration. A patent lasts 20 years from the registration date – if the patent registration term has ended you may be in luck.

Claims. A patent is made up of "claims" – applications of the patent and uses of the patent. If the challenging patent's claims (protected activities) don't overlap with what you intend to do, you may not have a problem.

Navigate the Rights. It may be possible to engineer "around" the rights. But, this is not advisable if the opposing party has the resources and is willing to defend its rights. This should not be done to basically steal another's invention. A patent attorney can determine with a reasonable level of certainty the boundaries.

WAR STORIES

A "DESIGN AROUND" INVENTOR WAS SUED

THE WAR

This is the story of competing, lime-busting water heaters. A.O. Smith Corporation invented a water heater totally inspired by its examination of a competitor's water heater. A manager from A.O. Smith Corporation even admitted to buying the Plaintiff's product, deconstructing it, and then designing his own product to meet the same function. So, the original manufacturer sued for willful patent infringement – and lost.

THE WINNER

A.O. Smith Corporation won, because it had devised its own, different structure. The judge said, "One of the benefits of a patent system is its so-called "negative incentive" to "design around" a competitor's products, even when they are patented, thus bringing a steady flow of innovations to the marketplace."

THE MORAL OF THE STORY

A purpose of patent law, in granting a limited monopoly to inventors, is to spur competition to design around patents to increase products and further challenge/incentivize new innovation. You can use this to your advantage (though you still may have to stomach a lawsuit). If you are the inventor, be aware that you may be the victim of someone doing your invention better than you did. (State v. A.O. Smith, 751 F.2d 1226 (Fed Cir 1985).

WAR STORIES

WORK MADE FOR HIRE

THE WAR

A nonprofit community organizer called the Community for Creative Non-Violence ("CCNV") hired the artist James Earl Reid (Reid) to make a sculpture dramatizing the plight of the homeless. There was no written agreement. Reid finished the work with CCNV's input, delivered the sculpture and took his check. Then, CCNV and Reid filed competing copyright applications with the U.S. Copyright Office. The fight over who owned the copyright to the sculpture went all the way to the Supreme Court.

THE WINNER

Reid won. Here's why: Reid was not an employee and there was no written contract calling the sculpture a "work made for hire," as is required by copyright law. However, since CCNV gave input into the creation—fabricated the pedestal, had the idea for the design, and gave input on posing the figures—potentially a court could find it has copyright rights if a determination is made that the work should be considered a "joint work."

MORAL OF THE STORY

Get it in writing. Any time you hire anyone to make anything for you, hire them based on a written document.

Work Made For Hire. Make sure the contract includes language calling the deliverables a "work made for hire," and that even if not a work made for hire, the maker of the deliverable assigns all rights, title and interest in and to the deliverable and the copyright to the deliverable.

WORK MADE FOR HIRE

In a "work made for hire" the work created belongs to the person who paid for it. Creations made by employees and many independent contractors belong to their employer. But the work made for hire rules are slippery.

3. GET THE RIGHTS OR FORGET IT

If there is intellectual property that you want to use that someone else owns, you need to either get the right to use it or abandon it. (You can also take the risk of using it, but that's a much broader conversation). If you choose to get the rights, you can either try to buy the IP outright or get a right to use it. The easier path is to license the IP.

BUY THE IP

You may be able to just buy the IP from the owner or the company as a whole, though this is a big commitment. If you buy the IP, you want to make sure the seller owns it and has the right to sell it to you. You also want to make sure you can snap it up for a fair price.

FACTORS IN THE PRICE

Valuing IP as an asset (not just to calculate royalty payments) follows the same patterns as valuing other businesses or assets. Below are some variables that impact and are figured into the valuation of IP:

- ✓ The potential market
- ✓ The IP's fit in the business technology, markets, distribution channels and supply chain
- ✓ Exposure to new markets and potential downside to current market
- ✓ Stage of development of the technology (gleam in the eye, engineered plans, prototype, tested & functional units, scaled up and market ready)
- ✓ Competition for the technology
- ✓ The strength and scope of the IP protections and ease of monitoring infringement
- ✓ Profit margins of the industry
- ✓ Economic feasibility
- ✓ Market demand
- ✓ Follow-on opportunities, extensions and multiple applications

VALUATION METHODS FOR IP

There are 3 common methods[36] for valuing intellectual property: Cost, Market and Income.

Cost Method. The cost method values IP based on what it cost to develop or buy it. This can be good and bad. The cost may produce an artificial ceiling for the buyer and an artificial floor for the seller. Instead, a better method may be what the IP can generate in cash over its life. Alternatively, the licensor could get "cost plus" where the seller gets a premium for his troubles.

Income Method. The income method values IP based on a prediction about the value it generates. That value can be in the form of (a) revenues and (b) savings.

Market Method. The Market Method values IP based on the value of comparable IP. The key to this method is to determine available, accurate data. The similarity or suitability of comparisons is based on their industry, efficiency and protectability.

LICENSE THE IP

A right to use someone else's intellectual property is called a license. Licensing is a foundation of modern commerce. A license usually includes a right to use something, for a certain period of time, in a certain geographic area, with limitations, for money. Licenses are typically governed by "license agreements" that have (1) license terms; and (2) license fees.

1. LICENSE TERMS

A License Agreement can be built around various concepts, or combinations of concepts.

Licensed Property. The Agreement should include a clear explanation of the property being licensed.

Parties. The parties to the license agreement are the LICENSOR – the one giving the right away - and the LICENSEE – the one getting the right and paying for it.

Territory. Licenses usually enable the licensee to exercise the licensed rights in a certain geographic region. That region can be the universe or it could be Topeka. In any event, it should be defined.

Exclusivity. If the license is exclusive – meaning no one else can get a similar license or right to the property – that should be spelled out. Exclusivity can be defined as the sole right for a period of time, the sole right for a period of time in Topeka, the sole right for a period of time in the Hardware Store market, or any other way you can slice and dice the world.

Performance Requirements. License Agreements often include milestones, minimum payments, covenants to adhere to marketing plans, and even sanctions. These standards are easier to enforce with quantitative minimums.

2. LICENSE FEES

Licenses are typically granted for license fees, royalties and other forms of compensation. The structure of the license fees, royalties and compensation is negotiable. Broken down, the royalty is usually:

Licensor's Share x Sales = Royalty Amount

CRAFT A ROYALTY

A royalty is a payment for continued use of intellectual property; a "royalty interest" is the right to collect royalties, which is a property right all on its own. A royalty is typically some percentage of gross or net sales generated from use of the IP or a per unit price.

Determining the royalty is usually a controversy to define two things: (1) Licensor's Share; and (2) Sales.

1. LICENSOR'S SHARE

How much the Licensor needs to get to continue to let you use the IP determines the "Licensor's Share."

STRUCTURES FOR LICENSOR'S SHARE

There are different ways to structure licenses.

Percent of sales. You can simply pay a percentage of sales. Here are some examples:
- ✓ 3-10% of wholesale price
- ✓ 10% of net revenue
- ✓ 5% - 8% of gross revenue

Units Sold. You can pay a certain amount of money for each unit sold. – so for example - $0.50 per unit.

Step Deal. You can pay different share amounts through a step transaction. In a step transaction, the Licensor's Share changes based on things that happen. The Licensor's Share can increase or decrease upon:
- ✓ Passage of time
- ✓ Sale of a specific number of units
- ✓ Achievement of milestones or sales targets
- ✓ Timely or early delivery of product or information
- ✓ Breach by a party
- ✓ Number of warranty claims or defects

The events that trigger changes to the Licensor's Share depend on the incentives necessary to get the parties to do the deal in a certain way or at all. For instance, if a licensor is particularly nervous because you are new in business, you may have to pay him a higher Licensor's Share up front, retaining more profit at the end for yourself.

An example of a simple step deal is:

10% of net revenues for first $10,000,000, 5% thereafter.

STANDARD FORMULA

The 25% Rule. The 25% Rule is commonly discussed as a lazy benchmark for royalties. The 25% Rule actually has at least two different meanings.

First, experts in the economics of royalties[37] have concluded that a common rate in royalties is 25% of gross profits (pre-tax profits).

Second, the 25% Rule is also used to divide 25% of profits each among (a) the inventor; (b) the developer; (c) the manufacturer; and (d) the distributor – if one person serves multiple roles, he gets multiple quarter shares of the profits.[38]

The 5% Rule. The 5% Rule is another discovery of economists – that the average royalty is 5% of net sales.[39] For instance, one study determined that the absolute median of royalty rates is 4.5% (from 2.8% for low margin food products to 8% for media and entertainment properties at the high end).[40] In industries with high profit margins, the royalty rates are higher.

MINIMUM PAYMENTS

The licensor may insist on minimum payments. These minimum payments can be structured in four ways:

1. **Flat Amount**. You (the licensee) have to pay the Licensor a certain amount of money regardless of how much you actually sell or make yourself. Sometimes this minimum payment could be recoupable against (i.e. deductible from) future payments.

2. **Strike Price**. You have to pay the licensor some amount up front just to get the license plus a Licensor's Share of sales over time.

3. **Per Unit Minimum**. You have to pay the licensor a certain amount on each sale — then, you can keep whatever is left over.

4. **The Greater Of**. You have to pay the licensor a minimum payment or the Licensor's Share of the sale price, whichever is greater.

FACTORS IN LICENSOR'S SHARE

Expectation v. Will. The see-saw between the licensor's cash expectation and the amount the licensee is willing to pay influences the amount of the license fees. Frequently, the licensor has racked up costs developing the IP, which helps create his expectation. Similarly, rates for other licenses may establish the licensor's expectation. On the other hand, the licensee has expectations about what he is willing to pay up front, early in commercialization and then through the years.

Stage of Development. The Licensor's Share may fluctuate depending on the stage of development. The more advanced the development, the higher the Licensor's Share. And, IP in an earlier development phase will require more in expenses from the licensee, which could be deducted from the ultimate amount paid to the licensor.

Exclusivity and Territory. An exclusive license may generate a higher price than one that is nonexclusive, depending on the potential revenue stream of the property. For a lucrative license, the broader the market, the higher the price.

The Market. The market for similar products or similar licenses will be a critical driver of a fair price. The royalty rate will vary by industry and by industry average profit margin.[41] Reliable information on current market rates for royalty rates can be hard to find. However, there are a few excellent resources (See "Resources for Market Rates" at the end of this chapter under the heading.

Incentives. There may be results or conduct one party wants to coax out of the other by incentivizing them with the promise of more cash or earlier payment.

2. SALES

In a license, you also have to create the unit of value that the licensor gets a share of.

The Royalty Trigger. You should decide what event or step in the order process will trigger the licensor's right to money (i.e. when is a unit considered to have been "sold") — after order, delivery, invoice, or payment?

Counting Licensor's Share – Product v. Money. You have to define the pool of proceeds from which the Licensor's Share will be taken – typically this is either units of product or money (which can be gross or net). If product sold, then the licensor could get his Licensor's Share for every unit of product regardless of sale price. If money, then the licensor gets his Licensor's Share of dollars from a customer.

Money – Collected v. Promised; Gross v. Net. The pool of cash out of which you will owe the Licensor's Share can include cash you have collected or IOUs for orders. IOUs will fill up the pool quicker than collections, so the licensor will prefer to apply his Licensor's Share to IOUs.

Gross v. Net. Before you pull the Licensor's Share out of the pool of cash, you may want to pull out expenses first. Remember that the licensor gets his share applied against everything in the pool of cash

– if the pool is falsely higher because it includes all money paid for sales before expenses are paid back, the licensor is not bearing the expenses. To complicate matters further, gross can mean all sale prices or all prices minus "cost of goods sold." So, you should also be clear about whether Sales will be gross – meaning right off the top, or net – meaning after you deduct expenses. And, if net, you should list which expenses you can deduct to get to net sales, which will be the unit of value the licensor gets a share of.

Discounts and Returns. You also have to decide how returns and discounts will be handled. Often, the licensor allows Sales to subtract returns, but only up to a certain amount or percentage of sales.

Share of Sublicense. You also should determine whether the licensor is entitled to a portion of revenue obtained from reselling – or sublicensing, the intellectual property (if that is permitted under the license agreement).

RESOURCES FOR MARKET RATES

There are some resources that catalogue market rates and recent rates for royalties and license fees.

- ⇨ www.fvginternational.com
  (The Financial Valuation Group)
- ⇨ www.ausinc.com (Royalty Source)
- ⇨ www.pl-x.com (PLX Systems)
- ⇨ www.consor.com
  (Consor Intellectual Asset Management)

Also, there is a terrific book called "Licensing Royalty Rates," by Gregory Battersby and Charles Grimes that stays current on royalty rates across industries and products. If you need market values or comparison royalty rates, search the Internet for recent surveys, or look at Wikipedia, which stays mildly current on royalty rates.

ROYALTY RATES

Below are some past "going rates" for licensing products:

Golden West Brewing Co., Inc. & Mateveza USA, LLC (From GWB 10Q Sept. 30, 2007)

In November, 2006, the Golden West entered into a License, Production and Distribution Agreement with Mateveza USA, LLC, a California limited liability company to manufacture, sell and distribute Mateveza's proprietary yerba mate ales within an exclusive territory consisting of the states of California, Oregon, and Washington. Under the terms of the arrangement, the GW agreed to advance production costs and sell under a jointly-developed marketing plan.

The Royalty. 50% of the net profits generated from the sale of the Mateveza yerba mate ales.

GW agreed to maintain a minimum manufacturing capacity of 1,000 barrels per year, and has a right of first refusal with respect to any required capacity in excess of that amount.

TRADEMARK FOR JEANS

Joe's Jeans & JD Holdings (From Joe's Jeans proxy statement for annual meeting Nov. 6, 2008)

On February 7, 2001, Joe's acquired a license for the rights to the Joe's® brand from JD Design LLC, which was subsequently merged with and into JD Holdings.

The Royalty. 3% on net sales of licensed products to JD.

CHILDREN'S CLOTHES

In October 2005, Joe's granted JD Holdings the right to develop the children's branded apparel line under an amendment to the master license agreement.

The Royalty. 5% royalty on net sales of those products to JD.

CARE BEARS AND STRAWBERRY SHORTCAKE IP

Cookie Jar Entertainment, Inc. & American Greetings Corporation (agreement filed with SEC)

Cookie Jar (COOKIE JAR) and American Greetings (AG) entered into a letter agreement setting forth the terms of the acquisition by COOKIE JAR of the Strawberry Shortcake ("SSC") and Care Bears ("CB") properties (collectively, the "Properties") owned by AG and its affiliates. AG got a right of first refusal and "last match" provisions upon any license relating to the Products that is similar to certain product categories in their deal. Categories included: greeting cards, party goods, calendars, stickers, and "digital photo IP product use." AG and COOKIE JAR agreed to a ten year exclusive inbound licensing agreement for the Properties from COOKIE JAR to AG on certain categories reserved for AG.

The Royalty. 10% royalty to COOKIE JAR.

HAND SANITIZER

Skinvisible, Inc. & DermalDefense, Inc. (From Skinvisible 10Q, June 30, 2008)

In March 2004, Skinvisible entered into a letter of intent ("LOI") with Dermal Defense, Inc. for the exclusive marketing and distribution rights to its patented Antimicrobial Hand Sanitizer product for North America.

The Royalty. 5% on product sales of the Antimicrobial Hand Sanitizer. Terms of the LOI also require Dermal Defense, Inc. to pay a fee of $1 million comprising of a non-refundable deposit of $250,000 with the balance of $750,000 payable as to $75,000 per calendar quarter or 5% of product sales (whichever is greater) until the entire $750,000 is received.

CAN YOU PROTECT IT?

In deciding whether to use any intellectual property, you also need to consider if you can protect it from other people's use or theft.

Let's start with the cruelest rule: you cannot protect your ideas. You may have a terrific way of using a garbage can or an idea for a book, but the ideas are not protectable. People may copy you, imitate you and execute your ideas better than you do. People may steal from you – unlawfully – and the cost to go after them may be more than you can afford.

You want to protect your IP as best you can. You want to look like a threat to discourage people stealing from you. And, there may be times when you can and need to challenge someone's theft of your intellectual property.

Other than litigation, there are essentially three ways to protect your IP: (1) by Contract; (2) by Registration; and (3) by Vigilance.

1. BY CONTRACT

Every piece of content, every idea and everything you make or have made for you, you should own. Get written agreements from all employees, consultants, contractors and partners to confirm your business's ownership of intellectual property and all results of projects or efforts.

CONFIDENTIALITY AGREEMENTS

Get confidentiality agreements with all who see your information, particularly your trade secrets. Anyone you are doing business with who balks at signing one is someone you may want to avoid. That goes for strategic partners, investors, employees, and consultants.

ASSIGNMENTS

You should get written proof of your ownership to IP through assignments and agreements. Every assignment and agreement should contemplate trademarks, copyrights and patents.

Patent. For patents, get an assignment of all inventions and improvements on those inventions, and patents, patent registrations and applications for registration. Get the document notarized.

In addition, employees should be required to (1) disclose all inventions that relate to your business; (2) assign the inventions to you/your company; and (3) keep records on their invention work and progress.

Joint Research Agreement for Patent. If you have collaborated on research or development work with third parties, you may want to put in place a Joint Research Agreement so that your collaborator's research does not render your invention "obvious" and thus not patentable.[42] The patent application must be made for parties to the agreement, the invention must have resulted from the activities under the agreement, and the parties to the agreement have to be disclosed in the patent application.

Trademark. For trademarks, get an agreement that all use of marks "inures to your exclusive benefit", which means that anyone else's use of your trademark is really your use. Also, get a written promise to not use or register the mark and an assignment of any goodwill associated with marks, to you. Get the document notarized.

Copyright. For copyright, get an agreement that all works of original authorship and all derivative works of them are "works made for hire," solely owned by you, and include language that, in any event, assigns the works to you.

Further Assurances/Cooperation. Always get an agreement to do anything you ask in the future to confirm these rights, including signing any documents and registrations (plus a power of attorney coupled with an interest to sign their name on those documents and registrations, if you can).

2. BY REGISTRATION

Budget for the expense of registering your IP everywhere appropriate. Get a good IP lawyer and have her conduct the registration process.

3. BY VIGILENCE

Once you have the rights to IP, it is up to you to use them correctly and to watch the world to make sure your rights are respected.

Document Patent Development. Until March, 2013, out of two inventors competing for a patent, the one who invented first wins. Having accurate and careful records that establish the dates of your invention could be invaluable.

Database. Keep a list or database of all the IP you own, its stage of development, the people who worked on it and the registration dates. Attach pdf copies of all assignment and license agreements in the database. This will facilitate your management of your IP and it would also be extremely valuable if you go on the block for an acquisition.

Monitor. Schedule time to police the use of your marks and potentially infringing inventions (if you have patents).

Trade Secret Policy. Implement a trade secret policy; make sure it is followed.

Meet and Train. Conduct yearly meetings and training sessions on the company's trade secret policies and proprietary rights procedures; make sure these are part of all personnel and contractor intake procedures.

Lawyer Up. Make sure you have a good, tough, but sensible lawyer who knows IP and can advise you.

GRAVITY'S ADVICE: LICENSE TO SEYMOUR'S PATENT

Gravity laid out her advice:

Seymour's Technology. First, you need to make a deal with Seymour. You said Seymour is willing to take a combo of stock and royalties on sales. So, let's propose just that. Offer Seymour a:

5 and 5 License. 5% of stock and 5% of net profits. We should be prepared to increase the royalty rate to obtain exclusivity for five years. Our proposal should be very fair and reasonable. We should also encourage Seymour to work with his lawyer; if he doesn't, it is possible he could have your agreement thrown out down the road.

Patent Search in General. We have to make sure that none of the technologies you use in the MouseTrap violates anyone else's patent. We should do a "Freedom to Operate" patent search. For that, I'll get one of my IP lawyers to talk with you and run and review the search. The IP lawyers will also need to talk to Seymour. Part of our search is going to include Seymour's technology. Even though we are going to ask Seymour to promise that his technology doesn't violate anyone's patent, I think we should assume that if Seymour is wrong, he won't have the resources to support you. As a result, we want to manage your risk by doing some due diligence and also taking out IP insurance.

Assignment of Inventions and Work. We also want to give you a proprietary rights agreement that all of your employees, independent contractors and vendors must sign. This way, if anyone does or makes anything for you, it will be assigned to you.

Trademark for the MouseTrap. We need to do a trademark search for MOUSETRAP. If we find that it is in use, we need to revisit using the mark and maybe pick a new one. However, if it is not used for consumer electronics or green technology solutions, then we should apply for registration.

License for Mouse. Finally, we should take a look at whether you should structure a deal with a mouse maker for the design or whether you should just hire them for the manufacturing. But, let's handle the other IP matters first. Then, we can come back to this.

Following a brief negotiating period, Seymour signed a license agreement with MouseTrap, LLC. The trademark search revealed many trademarks similar to MouseTrap, but not related to solar powered devices or mobile computer accessories. The patent search revealed a potentially troubling patent, but numerous inquiries of the owner proved fruitless.

> Gravity said, "You should manage the risk of the potentially troubling patent as part of your risk management strategy, which we'll discuss a little later (in Section 6). For now, you may have enough knowledge, money and rights to get your prototype made."
>
> "Can you help us figure out our prototype, Gravity?"
>
> "I CAN TRY."

END NOTES

1 Trademark law is a creature of federal and state law. The heart of the federal law is the Lanham Act, 15 USCA 1051 et seq, plus its 1988 and 1999 amendments. At the state level, unfair competition, state trademark statutes and trademark case law shapes trademarks.

2 Section 43A of Lanham Act prohibits using a mark that is likely to cause confusion, cause mistake, deceive on affiliation or association, or as to origin, sponsorship, approval or commercial activities; or which misrepresents the nature, qualities, geographic origin of goods or services.

3 The Madrid Protocol Relating to the Madrid Agreement Concerning the International Registration of Marks (Madrid Protocol) is an international treaty that allows a trademark owner to seek registration in any of the countries that have joined the Madrid Protocol by filing a single application, called an "international application." The International Bureau of the World Intellectual Property Organization, in Geneva, Switzerland administers the international registration system.

4 "Did You Know There's a Trademark Graveyard?" Timothy J. Lockhard
http://www.hamptonroadschamber.com/blog/index/view/id/2

5 1 5 USCA §1111.

6 Law Note. Copyright gets its rules from the Constitution and from the US Copyright Act at 17 USCA 101 et seq.

7 A work of authorship must be sufficiently permanent or stable to be "perceived, reproduced, or otherwise communicated for a period of more than transitory duration." 17 USCA §102(a).

8 *Reed Elsevier, Inc. v. Muchnick*, 130 S.Ct. 1237 (2010).

9 Terrible result - "He's So Fine" is cute; "My Sweet Lord" is sublime.

10 *Lee v. A.R.T. Company*, 125 F.3d 580 (7th Cir. 1997).

11 "Narrow Exception to an Old Rule," John Paul Benitez and Coco Soodek, originally published in Art Calendar Magazine.

12 17 U.S.C. §106 (2007).

13 Alleged infringers may claim that they either 1) are joint authors themselves or 2) received a valid license or assignment from a joint author. See *Shady Records, Inc. v. Source Enterprises, Inc.*, 73 USPQ2d 1954 (S.D.N.Y. 2005) (Eminem's friend's presence during a recording session did not make him a joint author).

14 *Shapiro, Bernstein & Co., Inc. v. Jerry Vogel Music Co., Inc.*, 73 F.Supp. 165 (S.D.N.Y. 1947).

15 *Rogers v. Koons*, 960 F. 2d 301 (2d Cir. 1992).

16 17 U.S.C.A. §§ 304(c) and 304(d).

17 Assignments and licenses to the renewal term of a copyright signed by the author in 1977 or earlier can also be terminated under 17 U.S.C.A. §§ 304(c) and 304(d). The author can grab it back 56-61 years after the copyright vests. There is also a right to terminate for pre-1978 works during the 75-80th years after the transfer.

18 Patents are governed by the U.S. Constitution and the Patent Act at 35 USC 1 et seq.

19 *Burr v. Duryee*, 68 U.S. (1863).

20 Business method patents have been included since 1998 after United States Court of Appeals for the Federal Circuit in *State Street Bank and Trust Company v. Signature Financial*, 149 F.3rd 1368 (Fed Cir 1998) confirmed that business method patents are appropriate subjects of patentability.

21 *State Street Bank (*though the State Street test was sort of thrown out by the Supremes in *Bilski v. Kappos*, 561 U.S. __ (2010), it is still the best test around for the patentability of a business method patent).

22 35 USCA § 102(a)

23 35 US Code 102(b)

24 42 U.S.C. 2181 (a).

25 Sometimes, the patent's "file wrapper" at the PTO, which has copies of the application and the communications between the applicant and the PT, may show you what claims the PTO rejected, the grounds for rejection and the prior art that was relevant to the examination.

26 Remus, Edward W. Esq. Personick Laura M., Esq., Clearing Up The "Muddy Metaphysics" Of Patent Inventorship (Or -- How To Conduct An Inventorship Determination); http://www.mhmlaw.com/article/Muddy%20Metaphysics%20rev-2-2%20-%20Remus-Personick.pdf (2006-07).

27 Manual of Patent Examining Procedures, Section 2138.04.

28 35 USC §256.

29 Id at § 301, 37 C.F.R. § 3.73(a) ("The inventor is presumed to be the owner of a patent application, and any patent that may issue therefrom . . . .").

30 35 USC §262.

31 *Wommack v. Duram*, 715 F.2d 962 (5th Cir. 1983).

32 35 USC 4(h)(i).

33 35 USC Section 123.

34 Trade secrets are largely governed by the Uniform Trade Secrets Act ("UTSA"), which has been adopted in most states (except for Massachusetts, New Jersey, New York, North Carolina, and Texas.)

35 Reverse engineering is okay as long as it doesn't violate another obligation.

36 Zaharoff, Howard G., Setting Values and Royalty Rates for Medical and Life Science Businesses, Journal of Biolaw and Business, Vol. 7, No. 4, 2004.

37 Robert Goldscheider, John Jarosz and Carla Mulhern, Use of the 25 Per Cent Rule in Valuing IP, 37 LES NOUVELLES 123 (December 2002). Goldscheider was apparently one of the first licensing experts to write about the rule, which he notes had been in use, in some form, since at least 1938, id at 124. But see Kemmerer, Jonathan E, CPA, Lu, Jiaqing, PhD., CFA, Profitability and Royalty Rates Across Industries, 2008.

38 Valuate Manual, Association of University Technology Managers, 12/1/00.

39 Zaharof.

40 Id.

41 Id.

42 35 USC 103(c)(3).

GETTING IT MADE

section four

MAKE A PROTOTYPE

Gravity said, "Let's discuss why you need to have a prototype made."

CHAPTER 5

WHY YOU NEED A PROTOTYPE

Make a prototype, even an early and clumsy one, to begin the process of executing your vision. It may show you that your idea is completely nuts and ought to be abandoned, or it could allow you to work the kinks out of your product before you make thousands. It will also give you something tangible to hand to people when you explain your business. Although it may seem exotic to have something manufactured out of metal and multi-materials, all kinds of businesses, from very big to very small, make things every day.

5 STEPS TO MAKE A PROTOTYPE

To get your prototype made, you have to pick someone to make it. The process of picking someone to make your prototype is exactly the same as when you found technical help – Seymour. Remember, there are five steps and, though cheesy, they all start with "s."

1. Specify (what you need)
2. Search (for candidates)
3. Screen (for interest and qualifications)
4. Solidify (for terms)
5. Start (the work)

1. SPECIFY SPECS FOR PROTOTYPE

Write down what you want in your prototype – be as specific as possible. It is best to use an engineer's designs and drawings when you approach the business that makes the prototype. It is also best to have your engineer involved in the process, so that he can talk with the manufacturer, learn about what works and what may not, and then revise the designs and drawings.

Tooling. You may discover that you need special tooling to make the prototype (or prototypes) or ultimate product, particularly If the product to be manufactured is going to have custom parts that need to be molded or stamped. The tooling may not exist and you may need to have it made.

2. SEARCH FOR PLACES TO GET YOUR PROTOTYPE MADE

There are a variety of routes to make your prototype.

ALL BY YOURSELF

You could put together a prototype yourself. That may be the cheapest option, but if you need a fully functioning prototype to base your broad manufacturing off of, this may not be the most efficient final method. Though, it may be a good start.

ELECTRICIAN REPAIR GUY

You can approach electricians, car repair shops and other businesses that have tools and skill.

TOOL AND DIE

Tool and die makers manufacturer tooling, fixtures, dies, cutting tools, gauges and other manufacturing stuff. Though they have been disappearing in the U.S., there are still some tool and die companies around.

164   SECTION FOUR: GETTING IT MADE

FABRICATOR

Fabricators are manufacturers that make things out of other things. Some fabricators specialize or work in developing prototypes. A fabricator may also help you find a manufacturer or even do the manufacturing on site.

STEREOLITHOGRAPHY

Stereolithography uses 3D engineering drawings and a 3D printer to create a prototype. For instance, a Fab Lab (fabrication laboratory) is a workshop containing computer operated tooling to make almost anything. Fab labs are the brain child of MIT and are an emerging method of making things. Some of the equipment in a fab lab includes:

- ✓ Laser cutter, plasma cutter and water jet cutter to cut sheet metal
- ✓ CNC machines, which are computer operated mills and lathes
- ✓ Rapid prototype, which is a 3D printer
- ✓ Circuit board milling

- ⇨ Look for a fab lab in your area or contact the Center for Bits and Atoms to find a convenient fab lab; go to http://cba.mit.edu/
- ⇨ For an excellent demonstration of this, watch the video: http://www.ted.com/talks/neil_gershenfeld_on_fab_labs.html

Some businesses that possess this technology for their own use may be willing to let you use their equipment for a price if it's sitting idle –it makes for a quicker payback on their investment (these machines are very expensive), and you may get a lower price than you would at a business that specializes in making prototypes. Look for a similar but non-competing business perhaps, or a larger company that makes products out of similar materials.

WEB RESOURCES

The web is filled with resources to make things, including:

- ⇨ www.crowdspring.com
- ⇨ www.ponoko.com
- ⇨ www.coroflot.com
- ⇨ www.99designs.com
- ⇨ www.scriptlance.com
- ⇨ www.hackerspaces.org/wiki
- ⇨ www.emachineshop.com
- ⇨ www.quickparts.com
- ⇨ www.redeyeondemand.com
- ⇨ www.bigbluesaw.com
- ⇨ www.becausewecan.org

3. SCREEN

Submit requests for bids to the potential manufacturers you identify and use the bids to screen out candidates.

4. SOLIDIFY THE TERMS

Once you have narrowed your choices, confirm in writing the terms like price, quantity, specs and deadlines. Before you get just beyond the talking and soliciting stage with any prototype maker, you should make sure they sign a confidentiality agreement to protect your ideas and the work they do for you. The NDA should also contain a couple of sentences (a) calling the product a WORK MADE FOR HIRE; and (b) assigning all work they do for you to you.

5. START THE WORK AND REVISIONS

You will probably need to do more than one version of your prototype, so build in time, planning, cash and patience. Now is the last moment for you to refine and test your prototype and put it through the ringer. During the process, take and keep pictures of models and samples, detailed notes and send clear written instructions back to the factory with each sample. In the end, have twelve prototypes made and be prepared to give the manufacturer one to three samples.

If you hope to patent an invention related to your product, be careful not to blow it. Remember, that in the U.S., you must file within 1 year of publicly discussing or marketing the invention. And, if you want to get patent protection around the world, most countries have no 1 year grace period. Make sure you consult with a patent lawyer as you go through development of your prototype and product.

HAP AND HAZ MAKE A PROTOTYPE

Hap and Haz specified what they wanted in function, while Seymour made drawing after drawing until they were satisfied. First, Hazard (with Seymour's help) cobbled together a handmade prototype, which looked good as long as you didn't drop it or touch it. Hap's neighbor's cousin owned a small grocery next to a guy who repaired lamps, radios and razors. So, Hap had him make a prototype. Hap and Hazard went to the Museum of Science and Industry and played in the Fab Lab, next to dozens of excitable children making puppy puzzles. Hap and Hazard also hired a local tool and die manufacturer to retrofit a store bought computer mouse.

Using these prototypes, Hap and Hazard had Seymour revise his designs for the MouseTrap. Hap and Hazard then sent requests for proposals to ten manufacturers in the United States, several of which already made computer mice and accessories.

Hap and Haz, preferring speed and efficiency, picked a manufacturer that uses additive fabrication technology, a/k/a 3D printing, to build their prototype. They also chose to pay a bit more to work with a maker located in their own city limits for two reasons. First, to control quality, they wanted a presence around the manufacturer — lacking resources or time to travel or hire an agent, they decided to do it themselves. Second, all things being equal, they wanted to work with a local, privately owned company and workers, to support their community. So, they picked USA Prototype, a small blink and you can miss it manufacturer in Chicago, their home town.

With Gravity's help, they put together a minimal term sheet. Once USA Prototype received the term sheet, they came back with comments, which Hap and Haz believed were, in most cases, reasonable, so they accepted (see table on next page).

Gravity wrote up a relatively simple letter agreement listing the terms and Hap, Hazard and the prototype manufacturer signed it instantly. Hap and Hazard sent off the package of materials; two weeks later, they were dismayed to see a completely screwed up and nonoperational model of a mouse. At first incensed, and then inzensed, they prepared and sent a detailed list of comments and changes. Two weeks later, they got a new model; this one was terrific, though there were still problems with the shape and usability. Following another round of comments, they obtained a final version that was fully operational. Along with this version, they also obtained a description of the contents of the MouseTrap.

At Gravity's request, they brought the packing manifest and a sample back to their lawyer.

> Holding the MouseTrap, Gravity said, "Beautiful, boys, just beautiful. Now that you have the ingredient list and the actual specifications, we can begin to source your regulations."

> Hazard responded, "Sorry, Gravity, 'source' our regulations? I don't understand. Can you explain?"

> "I CAN TRY."

TERM SHEET FOR PROTOTYPE			
ITEM	HAP AND HAZ'S OFFER	USA PROTOTYPE'S COUNTER	H&H'S RESPONSE
ENGAGEMENT	H&H will hire USA Prototype to make prototype	OK	N/A
ORDER SPECS	5 units of finished solar-powered computer mouse with USB connector.	5 units of finished solar-powered computer mouse with USB connector, subject strictly to designs and plans H&H provide	OK
PRICE	$1,200 set-up and $250/unit	$1,500 set up and $300/unit	OK
DELIVERY	10 days following order date	14 business days following order	OK
IP OWNERSHIP	Hap and Haz own all IP	OK	OK
CONFIDENTIALITY/ NONCIRCUMENTION	(1) MFG may not disclose designs, plans, schemes or contract; (2) MFG may not make similar device	(1) OK (2) MFG may not make similar device based on or referencing H&H's plans	OK
QUALITY CONTROL	MFG will make up to 3 versions, will work with Hap, Haz and Seymour in refining design	MFG will make up to 2 versions, additional versions at additional per unit charge MFG will work with Hap, Haz and Seymour in refining design	OK
WARRANTY	Prototype will be fully functional	Prototype will receive a solar charge and power a laptop computer for up to 1 hour	OK

SOURCE YOUR REGULATIONS

Gravity said, "Let me explain why you need to source your regulations."

WHY YOU NEED TO UNDERSTAND YOUR REGS

Nearly every service, product and material has laws or rules about it that you should (and often have to) follow. Governments regulate products and services that have the capacity to injure: restaurant refrigerators, mutual fund ads and lawyers are all examined, more or less, for weaknesses or malfunctions.

The regulations over products and businesses can sometimes be easily identified, but sometimes they are hard to discover. Regardless, you'll be very sad (and maybe ruined) if you make something or sell something and <u>then</u> find out there is a big rule you needed to follow.

THE 7 TYPES OF REGULATIONS

Regulations typically require you to do 7 different things (in the trade, this is called "compliance").

PERMIT
• Get a license or a permit to do something. (e.g. restaurants need a license to sell liquor)

MATERIAL
• Limit use of, or don't use, a material (e.g. heroin, lead)

PRODUCTION
• Manufacture a certain way. (e.g. waste disposal rules)

INSPECTION
• Get something inspected or tested and/or prove it complies. (e.g. kid's products)

LABEL
• Stick a label or warning on product and packaging. (e.g. warning: gasoline not for drinking)

FIX
• Fix it, clean it or pay for it to be fixed or cleaned. (e.g. owner must shovel snow outside store)

REPORT
• Disclose information to the public and/or the government. (e.g. SEC filings for public companies)

IDENFITY THE REGULATIONS THAT GOVERN YOU

Government regulations over products and services can come from many places: the federal government; the state(s) where you operate or sell; other countries where you operate or sell. There can also be product requirements and standards issued by an industry group, or a customer, particularly big box retailers with standardized rules for vendors. Here are some questions you can ask yourself to identify where to begin to look for regulations that may apply to you. This list is by no means exhaustive.

1. Are there industry standards for your business?
2. Is your industry specifically regulated by government?
3. Are you in a profession?
4. Do you handle private information?
5. Do you sell equity?
6. Do you handle other peoples' money or credit?
7. Do you make a product?
8. Could your product have defects?
9. Is your product intended for consumers?
10. Is your product intended for kids?
11. Do you sell a product?
12. Do you have employees?
13. Could your product or service hurt the environment?
14. Do you do business outside the US?
15. Are you bringing goods across a national border?

Now, let's look at each question in more depth.

ARE THERE INDUSTRY STANDARDS FOR YOUR BUSINESS?

There may be voluntary standards and certification information developed or coordinated by industry groups associated with your product, business or activity. In many cases, industry standards create the threshold for performance – called the "standard of care." Sometimes, government even coaxes industry to come up with standards so government does have to pass the regulations – that is the current government plan for ratcheting up the privacy rules. Compliance with industry standards is also an excellent way of managing risk.

Consider the little UL label on the back of your electronics. That UL label gets here from Underwriters' Laboratories, which creates standards for electronic equipment and appliances. Underwriters' Labs get their accreditation – their market authority – from ANSI which is the American National Standards Institute, the big American standards accreditation group. And, ANSI works with ISO, the International Organization for Standardization, which is an international standards writing umbrella.

To search for industry standards, look at these resources:

⇨ http://www.cpsc.gov/volstd/vslinks.html
⇨ http://ts.nist.gov/Standards/Conformity/request.cfm
⇨ http://webstore.ansi.org/
American National Standards Institute (ANSI) (examples: all-terrain vehicles, furnaces, gas appliances, turkey fryers)
⇨ http://www.comm-2000.com/default.aspx
⇨ http://www.nssn.com/
⇨ http://www.asrcreviews.org/
The Advertising Self-Regulatory Council (ASRC) for advertising standards, review and some adjudication.

⇨ http://www.astm.org/Standard/index.shtml
ASTM International (examples: children's products, bunk beds, playground equipment, toys)

⇨ http://database.ul.com/cgibin/XYV/template/LISEXT/1FRAME/index.htm
Underwriters Laboratories (UL) (examples: electrical products and appliances, batteries, smoke alarms)

IS YOUR INDUSTRY SPECIFICALLY REGULATED BY GOVERNMENT?

Some industries produce so much risk that they are regulated as a whole.

1. HEAVILY REGULATED INDUSTRIES

Heavily regulated industries include: accounting, aerospace, alcohol, cars and trucks, boats, chemicals, construction, cosmetics, defense, dry cleaning, consumer goods and services, energy, financial services, firearms and explosives, food and beverage, health care, law, manufacturing, medical devices, mining, pharmaceuticals and biotech, printing and publishing, real estate, telecommunications, tobacco, toys and transportation and logistics. If you operate in or near these industries, you should look around for regulations.

2. FEDERAL LICENSE REQUIRED

Some businesses are required to get licenses to operate. Below is a sample of businesses that must get **licenses** from the federal government but, make sure to watch for state, city and county licensing requirements.

FARMS

You need a permit from the U.S. Department of Agriculture ("USDA") to import and transport animals, animal products, biologics, biotechnology and plants.

ALCOHOL BEVERAGES

You have to register with the Alcohol and Tobacco Tax and Trade Bureau ("TTB") to make, sell and import booze. Alcohol and tobacco businesses above the retail level (i.e., manufacturers, wholesalers, importers, exporters, etc.) have to get an operations permit from TTB before engaging in business. You'll also have state and local requirements for your alcohol beverage business, including bars, nightclubs, restaurants, and retail liquor stores.

AVIATION

Licenses from the Federal Aviation Agency are required for airmen, aircraft, airports, airlines, medical aviation services, pilots and plane mechanics.

FIREARMS, AMMUNITION AND EXPLOSIVES

Manufacture or sale of guns, ammo and things that blow up must be licensed by the Bureau of Alcohol, Tobacco, Firearms And Explosives ("ATF"). Licenses required to carry a concealed weapon are issued by state or local governments if permitted.

FISH AND WILDLIFE

If you do any wildlife related activity, including the import/export of wildlife and derivative products, you may need a permit from the U.S. Fish and Wildlife Service.

FOOD

Federal law requires food to be safe to eat. So, there are thousands of regulations about what are, and what are not, acceptable ingredients in foods.

FOOD PROCESSING

The U.S. food processing sector, as with other industrial and commercial sectors, faces increasingly stringent environmental rules, many of which have their roots in federal statutes and are implemented through state laws and regulations by various agencies. Most of these rules relate to the treatment and disposal of food processing wastes. Often, permitting, monitoring, reporting and other regulatory requirements are implemented by multiple agencies (e.g., composting operations may be regulated by the environmental protection agency, department of health and department of agriculture). Food processors and manufacturers are also subject to a lot of safety and inspection rules.

THE LIMITS OF REGULATION: ACCEPTABLE FOOD CONTAMINATION

Food has to be free of critters – but only up to a point. See this list? This is the upper limit of how much filth CAN be in your food. Bon Appétit.

- ✓ Asparagus – 9.9% infested with beetle eggs; 39 thrips or 4 insects in 100-gram samples
- ✓ Chocolate – 59 insect fragments in 100-gram sample or 2 rodent hairs
- ✓ Coffee beans – 9.9% insect infested, damaged, or molded
- ✓ Fish – 4.5% of fillets or fish with "definite decomposition" 25% of the area, or 19% with "slight decomposition" 25% of area
- ✓ Pepper – 1% insect infested; 1 mil. of excreta per pound
- ✓ Popcorn – one rodent pellet or hair per 12-oz samples, 19 gnawed grains per lb. or 4% by weight
- ✓ Spinach – 49 aphids, thrips, mites or 7 leaf miners in 100-gram sample
- ✓ Strawberries – mold count of 54% in half the samples
- ✓ Tomato paste (added to pizza & sauces) – in 100 gram samples: 29 fly eggs, or 14 eggs and one larvae, or two larvae, or mold count averaging 39% (only 29% in pizza sauce)

(First appeared in Spy Magazine (date unknown) and reproduced in The Fun Side of Man, 1/3/08).

COMMERCIAL FISHERIES

If you do some commercial fishing, you may need a permit from The National Oceanic and Atmospheric Administration ("NOAA").

MARITIME TRANSPORTATION

Water based carriers probably need a permit from the Federal Maritime Commission.

MINING

If you are involved in drilling for natural gas, oil or other mineral resources on federal lands, you may be required to obtain a drilling permit from The Minerals Management Service ("MMS"), a bureau in the U.S. Department of the Interior.

NUCLEAR ENERGY

The U.S. Nuclear Regulatory Commission licenses commercial nuclear reactors and fuel cycle facilities, distribution of nuclear materials, and nuclear waste disposal facilities.

RADIO, TV AND PRODUCTS THAT EMIT RADIO WAVES

If your business broadcasts information by radio, television, wire, satellite or cable, or emits radio waves through products, you may be required to obtain a license from The Federal Communications Commission ("FCC").[1] A device which has obtained the FCC certification is granted FCC ID which is shown on the product. Every electronic device could emit radio waves. Devices that unintentionally emit radio waves are called "unintentional radiators". Devices are not permitted to emit a level of radio waves in excess of FCC limits for uncertified devices.[2] To avoid liability, electronic products should be tested to detect the level of radio wave emissions, if any. Typically, the product is tested during the prototype phase by a certified testing lab.

TRANSPORTATION AND LOGISTICS

The United States Department of Transportation requires registration, inspection and permits for commercial truckers and transportation companies, as well as the interstate transport of hazardous materials. This also includes oversized vehicle permits. Each state also have a department of transportation that regulates the use of its roads by commercial truckers.

For more information, go to: http://www.business.gov/register/licenses-and-permits/

ARE YOU IN A PROFESSION?

The professions – medicine, law, accounting, engineering - are filled with requirements for entry, operation and continuing education. These professional regulations are usually issued and controlled by states and are designed to keep the quality of the professions high and the professionals trustworthy.

In addition, other vocations may require licensing. For instance, ticket brokers, talent agents and hair stylists are just a few examples. These regulations are usually created by state and local authorities.

DO YOU HANDLE PRIVATE INFO?

More and more regulations emerge to protect peoples' private information[3]. Of course, your obligation is to keep sensitive information private – but that is just the beginning. As the web becomes bigger and less stable, everyone – governments, consumers and your partners – will demand you take reasonable security measures to protect sensitive information. Plus, good safety is good business.

1. WHAT INFORMATION ARE WE TALKING ABOUT

What information you have to protect varies based on the particular law (of course it does). Data should be protected if it can be reasonably linked to a person, computer or device. Historically in data breach laws, you had to protect "sensitive information" which was often defined as personally identifiable information. Increasingly, the pieces of information that you have to treat as "sensitive" or private belong in a broad list including:

- ✓ Social Security Number
- ✓ Driver's license number
- ✓ Bank account number
- ✓ Financial information
- ✓ Health information
- ✓ Child information, which includes audio, video, images, persistent identifiers

(Internet Protocol addresses, customer numbers held in cookies, processor or device serial number and unique device identifier) and geolocation information

2. GROWING LIMITS ON SHARING WITH 3RD PARTIES

It is usually not considered disclosure of sensitive data if you just use the information inside your company. You may also be able to permit your sister companies to use the data if they share your brand so your relation to the sister company is evident to the consumer. But, for all other 3rd parties, without permission from the user, you should only provide aggregated, de-identified data if (a) your company publicly commits to not try to reidentify it; and (b) you only disclose it to companies who contractually agree to not re-identify the data.

3. THE FOUR PRIVACY OBLIGATIONS

Privacy rules are complex, but they basically obligate you to do four things:

a. **Protect**. Take reasonable and appropriate security steps to protect sensitive data that you collect and keep.

b. **Disclose**. Tell people what you do with their data. A smaller minority of states have these.

c. **Alarm**. Notify the public about sensitive data security breaches. Breach notification statutes have been passed in 48 states.

d. **Dispose**. Get rid of the information so it is completely gone.

These obligations are enhanced when you are dealing with certain kinds of information, including: (a) Health Information; (b) Financial Information; and (c) Information about Kids.

PROTECT

You have to protect the information in your possession. To protect sensitive information, you have to adopt reasonable and appropriate security measures and adopt a written information security policy.

ADOPT REASONABLE AND APPROPRIATE SECURITY

Reasonable security procedures are measures that ensure the confidentiality of personal information, protect against reasonably foreseeable threats, and ensure personnel compliance. [4] Like privacy policies, California and to a greater extent Massachusetts are on the leading edge of laws requiring sites to take steps to protect the personally identifiable information of its users. [5] There are some basic procedures you should adopt, follow and enforce at a minimum.

Limit. Only collect sensitive info you actually need - not if you think you can make use of it in the future.

Encrypt. You must transmit and store sensitive info in encrypted form. Encryption means to transform data into a form unintelligible without a confidential process or key. Segregate servers with sensitive information from servers without sensitive data.

Lock. Use common, smart technical tools to protect information: firewalls, automatic logoffs, password systems, password protocols. Require and implement access controls, computer security rules, device control rules, building alarm systems, locked offices, screens shielded from secondary viewers. Follow industry best practices for the current standard of care.

Personnel. Designate specific personnel as a privacy officer to be in charge of privacy and security. Schedule and conduct periodic, mandatory training of personnel on sensitive data, allowed uses, storage procedures and protections to keep it all safe. Put procedures in place to secure sensitive data from former employees. Finally, give access to sensitive information to just the employees who need it.

Test. You have an independent obligation to test software developed by a 3rd party[6] to make sure it (a) collects only the information you say you collect in your privacy policies; (b) collects and stores sensitive information in encrypted form; (c) doesn't and (d) collects the information you actually need and no more.

Improve. Conduct periodical risk analysis and management assessment of potential risks and make any improvements to your security measures.

Appoint. Designate specific personnel as a privacy officer to be in charge of privacy and security. Schedule and conduct periodic, mandatory training of personnel on sensitive data, allowed uses, storage procedures and protections to keep it all safe. Put procedures in place to secure sensitive data from former employees.

Contract. Plan for 3rd party contract compliance and review by requiring vendors sign agreements respecting the confidentiality of PHI. Make sure web hosts employ security procedures.

ADOPT A WRITTEN INFORMATION SECURITY PLAN ("WISP")

Some laws obligate the receiver to adopt a written plan about how it will deal in sensitive information[7]. Certainly if you collect financial information about any person in the United States or if you collect sensitive information about residents of Massachusetts, California, Nevada and other states that adopt WISP laws you have to adopt a plan.

The obligation is to implement *"appropriate security measures to* protect *such personal information."* The Massachusetts WISP statute obligates websites collecting private info about Massachusetts residents to create a written information security policy, which: (a) designates privacy employees to manage the WISP; (b) provides for training of all employees on WISP compliance; (c) requires review of policies periodically; (d) requires documenting responsive actions; (e) contingency plans for fire, vandalism and system failure and for breaches and breach notifications; and (f) includes policies for storage, transport access, disciplinary procedures for violation of the WISP policies and measures to keep old employees away from sensitive data.

DISCLOSE (WITH OPTIONS)

A growing area of law requires websites to post a written notice on their site that tells visitors how you collect their personal information, how you store it and what you do with it. The leading law is actually a state law in California; because the Internet is everywhere, websites comply with that law. Once a company promises to comply with the industry guidelines, they are held to that standard.

PRIVACY POLICY

The privacy policy is your promise to users about how and when you collect information about them and what you do with it. Here is what should be in your privacy policy:

- ✓ Effective date and/or date of last change
- ✓ How you notify people of changes to the privacy policy
- ✓ Categories of information that you collect
- ✓ Why you collect that information
- ✓ How and when you collect that information
- ✓ How you protect the data in your possession
- ✓ How, when and why you use and disclose that information
- ✓ Likely 3rd parties with whom you may share sensitive information
- ✓ Specifically, who should users contact to review or destroy their information or to opt out of further notices from the site

Stick the links to the disclosures and opt in or opt out forms on every page of your site, including your home page. Make sure the language is clear and simple. Most importantly, make sure the language is accurate. The minute the privacy policy no longer accurately describes your collection and use of personally identifiable information, change your policy and notify users of the change.

GET OPT IN OR OPT OUT

The FTC and various states are pointing privacy obligations towards something currently called "do not track." "Do not track" is the right of a consumer to tell the whole web world to stop tracking and recording her movements and activities around the Internet. Industries will soon start to develop guidelines for giving consumers easy, effective ways of turning off tracking cookies and other technology. But, even before the laws and guidelines evolve, the FTC and some states have expressed their preference that you get a user's permission before you share or sell information about them.

This is done through a process called "opt in" which just means that the user has to check a box you set up for them to give you the right to collect their information.

Before you collect and use a user's information, you need to give her notice and either get her permission (opt-in) or at least don't get her veto (opt-out). If you require a user to approve your collection and use of her information, you have to give her – technically and logistically – a way to opt in. If you just want to alert her to your intentions around her information and allow her to tell you to knock it off, then you need to give her – technically and logistically – a way to opt out. The easiest way to deal with this is to use just about any credible commercial email service, like Mailchimp.

GIVE USERS ACCESS TO THEIR INFO

You should give users access to their information to see it, correct it and make you destroy it. For instance, under California's "Shine the Light Law," at a California customer's request, websites must notify them when they have released personal information to third parties for marketing purposes within the twelve months prior to the request. [8]

ALARM

Security breaches happen. If you experience a security breach, you will be obligated under various laws to notify the people whose information was compromised. Breach notification statutes have been passed in 48 states. There are also breach notification obligations in HIPAA (thanks to Hitech) and other statutes[9]. You may also be able to mitigate your liability if you (a) notify affected users within two weeks of discovering the breach; (b) try not to lose financial data; and (c) offer credit monitoring services to affected customers.

DISPOSE

There is a final obligation to destroy the sensitive information when you are done with it or when the user requests it back. For instance, if you use a consumer report for a business purpose, you have to get rid of it under the Disposal Rule created by the FTC[10]. Personal information must be disposed of in a reasonable and appropriate way to prevent unauthorized access to or use of the information. Reasonable measures for disposing of consumer report information could include establishing and complying with policies to:

✓ Burn, pulverize or shred the information so that the information can't be read

✓ Destroy or erase electronic files so that the information cannot be read or reconstructed

✓ Hire a document destruction specialist, but only after you have done due diligence on the specialist, including investing independent audit, references, certification by trade associations and the specialist's security policies[11]

Most of the law obligates you to protect, disclose, alarm and/or dispose as a package depending on the source or type of sensitive information.

4. HEALTH INFORMATION

The U.S. Health Insurance Portability & Accountability Act (HIPPA) protects the confidentiality of a patient's personally identifiable information and medical records; whenever there is any disclosure of health related information, you should be on guard for HIPPA issues. There are additional laws at the federal and state levels about protecting health information.

5. FINANCIAL INFORMATION

Handling financial information for your customers brings responsibilities to safeguard that information. Below is just a sample.

HIDE CREDIT CARD INFORMATION

The Fair and Accurate Credit ("FACTA") requires that all merchants with credit card machines hide all but the last four or five digits of the account number on the customer's receipt.

IDENTIFY RED FLAGS OF IDENTITY THEFT

If you lend money or extend credit, you could be subject to a variety of laws. For instance, financial institutions and creditors have to adopt policies to identify red flags that alert your staff to possible identify theft, ways to detect those red flags, procedures to mitigate the damage from identify theft and to police your program regularly. Banks, savings and loans, credit unions or any other business that allows consumers to write checks or pay are on the hook for the rule. Any business that often bills after delivery of goods or service or defers payments are also on the hook, including utility companies, health care providers, phone companies, finance companies, mortgage brokers, real estate agents, automobile dealers, and retailers that offer financing or help consumers get financing from others, as well as debt collectors.

EMPLOYERS WITH CREDIT REPORT

If you want to do a credit check on a potential employee, you have to get written permission in a single document from the person to get the credit report and to use it in evaluating them. If you use information in the report to deny them something, you have to tell them the action taken, the name and address of the credit agency, that the credit agency didn't make the decision and that the applicant can get and contest the report.[12]

6. INFORMATION ABOUT KIDS

There are laws that protect the privacy of kids and their information. The big, federal law is "COPPA." I wish Congress and the FTC could make "COPPA" more complicated – I'm not sure they can. "COPPA" is The Children's Online Privacy Protection Act[13] and it requires a web site directed at children under 13 years of age to obtain "verifiable parental consent" before collecting personal information online from children.[14]

WHO'S ON THE HOOK

If you operate a website that knowingly collects personal info from kids under 13 through your site or through some subcontractor or partner, you have to comply with COPPA. If you operate an ad network, a plugin site, a web app or any other service you know gets used to collect kids information, you are on the hook for COPPA. However, one main collector – the "primary operator" can do the complying and serve as the single disclosed collector.[15]

Funked up Exceptions. Allegedly, sites that provide access so that others can collect kids information are not on the hook - in practice there will be a whole lot of hair splitting so be very cautious in deciding COPPA doesn't apply to you. In addition, if you are just collecting the data to use internally ("internal operations"), then you don't have to comply with COPPA. What is included in "internal operations" is fuzzy but does include: contextual advertising, frequency capping, legal compliance, site analysis, and network communications. The second you start contacting people, using the information to build a kid's profile or disclosing the kid's information to anyone else, you don't get this exception. If you do something you think is internal, but it's not listed, you can ask the FTC for permission to treat it as an "internal operation."

KID'S INFO YOU HAVE TO PROTECT UNDER COPPA

The bucket of kid's information you have to protect is deep.

Online contact information: email address, any other substantially similar identifier that permits direct contact with a person online, IM Name, Video Chat Name, VOIP Identifier (e.g. Skype name) and Screen names or user names - (not internally used member names); images, audio files or videos depicting a kid's image or voice.

Persistent identifiers: Internet Protocol addresses; customer numbers held in cookies; processor or device serial number; and unique device identifier. Identifiers also include data that connect a kid's activities across different websites, particularly if the info can be gathered over time to profile or deliver behavioral ads to the kid.

Geo-location information identifying the kid's whereabouts.

5 STEPS TO COMPLY WITH COPPA

To comply with COPPA, you have to take these 5 steps: (1) Create a COPPA Privacy Policy and post it on your homepage and link to it where ever info is collected; (2) Send a COPPA notice to parents about your site's information collection practices; (3) Get Verifiable Parental Consent to collect information about their children; (4) Give parents access to kids' information, as well as control over further use of

that information; and (5) Don't condition participation on site on the kid's provision of unreasonable information. This is merely a summary of the steps – for more detailed information, go to http://www.ftc.gov/ for more information on COPPA. Or, you could take the shortcut and sign up with one of the FTC-approved Safe Harbor Programs: Here is the link:

⇨ http://business.ftc.gov/content/safe-harbor-program.

DO YOU SELL OR PROVIDE EQUITY OR STOCK?

We talked earlier about just a couple of federal securities laws. These laws require companies and sellers of stock to provide sufficient information that allows someone to make a fully informed investment decision. A big part of the securities laws is regulation of the people who buy and sell stock.[16] If your company sells its own stock, you have to comply with the securities laws that apply to the issuer. If you sell another company's stock, you have to comply with securities laws on broker-dealers and maybe even exchanges. If you recommend stocks or provide investment advice, you have to comply with the laws around investment advisors (and act as a fiduciary to your client).[17] If you sell pieces of investments in other companies, you may have to comply with the laws around investment companies.[18] In all events, you will need to comply with the antifraud rules under 10b-5 and probably some unpleasant, cryptic state laws.

DO YOU HANDLE OTHER PEOPLE'S MONEY OR CREDIT

Every possible permutation of handling other peoples' money or credit has a hornet's nest of regulations. Banks (commercial, consumer/retail and investment), credit unions, credit card companies, stores that extent credit and layaway plans are all subject to these regulations. Many of these regulations obligate you to act fairly and in good faith by clearly communicating the terms of credit; by protecting the secrecy of consumer information;

by giving your customers the benefit of their bargain. Banks have much deeper regulations that really drill down to both the fact and the transparency of their stability. An entire new agency – the Consumer Finance Protection Bureau - was just established to regulate consumer finance. There are even regulations about how merchants handle gift cards and group discounts. Anyone dealing with consumer credit or consumer money should tread carefully and honestly.

DO YOU MAKE THINGS?

In the course of making things, you may have to (1) properly measure and (2) label your products.

1. SIZES, WEIGHTS AND MEASURES MUST BE STANDARD

The U.S. government has set up a committee to create standard units of things so that everyone measures their product sizes in the same way. The standard units are the "Uniform Laws and Regulations" adopted by the National Conference on Weights and Measures.[19] Though these are federal standards, most states have adopted them. States also often operate testing and inspection activities to make sure that scales, measures and dispensers conform to the standards. Go see the National Institute of Standards and Technology:

⇨   http://www.nist.gov/index.html

2. PRODUCTS MUST BE LABELLED

Labels and packaging are both advertising and promises about the product inside. The contents of packaging have to give information required by law (and be truthful). For instance, labeling requirements are specifically targeted at food, vitamins, appliances, health products, cosmetics, diet and fitness, tobacco, electronics and textiles. The Food and Drug Administration ("FDA") is in charge of labeling for foods, drugs, cosmetics, and medical devices. The Environmental Protection Agency ("EPA") is in charge of labels for insecticides and fungicides. The Federal Trade Commission ("FTC") is in charge of labeling many other products. In labeling the contents of your product, you need to

figure out which standard applies to your product. This is a question for an engineer and a lawyer (or better yet, find an engineer and a lawyer in the same body). For some specifics, go to:

⇨   http://www.business.gov/business-law/advertising-law/labeling/

Consumer Products. By law, you have to disclose the contents of what you are selling.[20] The purpose is to help people compare products, including value comparisons, to enable people to make informed choices.

On most consumer products, you have to list the following[21]:

1.   Identity of commodity (e.g. detergent, sponge)

2.   Description of ingredients

3.   Package size in metric and inch/pound units[22]

4.   Name and place of business of the product's manufacturer, packer, or distributor

5.   Country of origin

Country of Origin. Every imported product must have a conspicuous and indelible mark in English to indicate to the ultimate purchaser the product's country of origin. The "ultimate purchaser" is the last U.S. person who will receive the article in the form in which it was imported. So, stuff coming into the country in retail-ready packages has to have the mark. But, stuff on its way to a U.S. processor for substantial transformation does not need the mark.[23]

COULD YOUR PRODUCT HAVE DEFECTS?

All products must be free from defects. The obligation and potential liability belongs to everybody along the chain of manufacture and sale.[24]

The depth of a maker or supplier's responsibilities vary depending on where they or the injury were. Some states (like Virginia) will make a manufacturer responsible only if the injury happened because he did something that was sloppy, stupid or worse (negligence states). Some states (like California) will make a manufacturer responsible if his product's unreasonable level of danger caused the injury (strict liability states).[25]

There are three types of product defects: (1) manufacturing defects, (2) design defects and (3) defects in marketing.

1. MANUFACTURING DEFECT

A manufacturing defect is a flaw in the way the product got made, such as shoddy materials or workmanship, missing or loose parts or any deviation from the design specifications. If your product has a manufacturing defect that injured someone, you will probably be liable even if you took reasonable care.[26]

2. DESIGN DEFECT

A design defect is a baked in design flaw that makes the product unreasonably dangerous to use. Design defects are defined differently among the states. In some states, a product's design is defective only if there is another design that (a) would have lessened the risk of injury; (b) would not have impaired the product's utility; and (c) was technically and economically feasible. In other states, a product's design is defective if its dangers outweigh the product's usefulness.[27]

3. MARKETING DEFECT (A/K/A FAILURE TO WARN)

A marketing defect is where the warning signs or instructions on a product fail to adequately guide the user around the hidden dangers in the product. If a user would have needed better, clearer or sharper instructions or warnings than what was provided to ward off danger, the product's warnings were defective. Manufacturers are also responsible for addressing foreseeable misuses – in other words, a manufacturer can be held liable even if a product is used in a way that it was not intended to be used if that misuse was foreseeable.[28]

IS YOUR PRODUCT INTENDED FOR CONSUMERS?

If your product is intended for consumers, then you have to look at the universe of laws and agencies that protect consumers. Commercial customers are assumed to have more power, access and ability to negotiate purchase terms and to look out for themselves, but consumers need special care. Consumers lack the practical access, time and resources to monitor the safety of products. A healthy and robust market requires the consumer to depend on the general safety and reliability of the things they buy. So, consumers get much more protection than commercial buyers.[29] This is not about big daddy government getting in the way – it is about recognizing that you don't have a beaker, centrifuge and lab coat to test a quart of milk before you throw it into your cart.

There are many government entities that oversee consumer regulations, including the Federal Trade Commission and the Consumer Product Safety Commission at the federal level and each state Attorney General at the state level.

Let's discuss (1) the Consumer Product Safety Commission and the obligations it imposes to (2) report product hazards; (3) not sell recalled products; (4) limit, test, certify and label consumer products.

1. CONSUMER PRODUCT SAFETY COMMISSION

Some consumer protection laws apply to all consumer products across the board and some consumer protection laws or rules apply to specific products. The Consumer Product Safety Commission ("CPSC") is an agency specifically created to make rules about many consumer products and to enforce them, though some products may be under other Federal agencies[30]. For information about the jurisdiction of products, go to:

⇨ www.cpsc.gov/businfo/unreg
⇨ www.cpsc.gov/businfo/regsbyproduct

⇨ www.cpsc.gov/businfo/notcpsc[31]
www.cpsc.gov/businfo/reg1
(for a list of regulated products)

CPSC talks to the public through media coverage, brochures and alerts, the CPSC website, the CPSC hotline, the National Electronic Injury Surveillance System, and www.saferproducts.gov, which is a CPSC website that makes all kinds of information available about dangers in products. The NATIONAL ELECTRONIC INJURY SURVEILLANCE SYSTEM collects reports from hospital emergency rooms on injuries from products. You can actually search different injuries at the website.[32]

Manufacturers[33], assemblers, wholesalers, importers, donors, distributors and retailers are all obligated to comply with consumer safety laws and regulations.[34] So, if you make, sell, import or give a consumer product, you must (1) report dangerous or defective conditions in the product; and (2) not sell recalled products (in addition to ensuring that your products are safe and lawful).

2. REPORT HAZARDS

For all consumer products under CPSC, you have to report dangerous products[35] within 24 hours of getting information that your product has a defect that could create a substantial risk of injury or unreasonable risk of serious injury or death. Further, you also have to report settled or adjudicated product injury lawsuits. This obligation applies to retailers and distributors as well as manufacturers, and includes voluntary safety standards that the CPSC relies on.

3. DON'T SELL RECALLED PRODUCTS

It is illegal to sell recalled products, so if you are a retailer or distributor, check the "List of Recalled Products" on the CPSC website, which you can get at:

⇨ http://www.cpsc.gov/cpscpub/prerel/prerel.html

⇨ https://www.cpsc.gov/cgibin/NEISSQuery/home.aspx

4. LIMIT, TEST, CERTIFY & LABEL CONSUMER PRODUCTS

If you are a manufacturer (or a seller), the CPSC may require you to: (1) limit or eliminate materials the government says are hazardous; (2) test your product for compliance; (3) certify that the test was done appropriately and your product passed, and label your product.

Governments frequently limit or ban dangerous materials, such as asbestos, lead and phthalates.[36] For instance, rhinestones and crystals, which often contained lead, have had to be replaced with lead free materials instead. The amounts you can use, if any, will be technical and may change from time to time.[37]

Flammable textiles in clothing. There are some fabrics that are illegal for use in clothing – these prohibited fabrics burn too quickly to be safe to wear. The government divides all fabrics into three classes, with Class I being the safest, Class II being less safe and Class III being the most unsafe and prohibited. Examples of fabrics in Class III are pure fleece, chenille and some pure silks. So, if you operate a store, don't buy 1,000 fleece bathrobes until you make sure they aren't unlawful. For more, check out the CPSC website to see which stores, designers and manufacturers have had clothing recalled.

If you make or import into the U.S. a consumer product that is regulated by the CPSC, you have to implement a reasonable testing program for lead content and other materials as required by the CPSC. You can also test components of representative samples. A reasonable testing program means annually testing your products. But, kids products have to be tested by a 3rd party approved by the CPSC and listed on the CPSC website for your product and/or test[39]. All makers have to test regardless of size, though there is now a registration process and some exemptions for companies that qualify as small batch manufacturers. [40] For a list of products that must be tested and certified, go to:

⇨ http://www.cpsc.gov/businfo/unreg.html

All "manufacturers" of consumer products regulated by the CPSC have to provide a certificate that promises the products comply with the materials restrictions. "Manufacturers" include agents, brands, importers of record, and "private labelers." "Private Labelers" includes owners of a brand or trademark on the label of a consumer product which bears a private label. This certificate, called a "General Conformity Certificate" must state that: (1) the product has been tested either through unit testing or a reasonable testing program; and (2) the product complies with all safety rules. The GCC Certificate must be in English and must cite the rule, ban, standard or regulation.

A list of retail products that require a GCC is available on the CPSC website:

⇨ http://www.cpsc.gov/businfo/reg1.html.

If you are a distributor, retailer or someone who contracted out the manufacture, make sure you get any required certificates and test results. Be careful about testing prior to modifications, because the changes could trigger another round of testing. The absence of a testing or certification requirement for a product is not necessarily a free ride: distribution and sale of banned or hazardous substance or a misbranded substance is against the law. Any person who violates that law may be guilty and subject to fines and prison.

IS YOUR PRODUCT INTENDED FOR KIDS?

Products for kids must comply with a lengthy and detailed body of regulations. These regulations evolve over time, so you should get together with a lawyer to identify which ones particularly relate to you and the product you make when you make it. But, here is an overview of at least how the regulations work today, including (1) what kid's

products include; and (2) the CPSC obligations to limit, test, certify and label kids products.

1. KIDS PRODUCTS INCLUDE...

Any products designed or intended PRIMARILY for kids 12 years old or younger are children's products. To determine whether a consumer product is intended primarily for kids, consider: (a) the manufacturer's statement about the intended use of product, if reasonable;[41] (b) if the product is represented as appropriate for kids 12 and under; (c) if the product is commonly recognized by consumers as intended for kids 12 and younger; (d) Age of Determination Guidelines issued by CPSC (which defines kids in categories); and (e) if the products are not for general use.

The CPSC has operated with a particular focus on toys and children's safety in the past, earmarking about half of its annual budget to the safety of children's products. Because of this, toys sold in the U.S. are the most highly regulated and monitored in the world. [42]

2. THE CPSC 4: LIMIT, TEST, CERTIFY AND LABEL

Just like for all consumers, there are four things you may have to do if you are a manufacturer or importer of kids products:[43] (a) limit or eliminate materials identified as hazardous by the government; (b) test your product through a 3rd party accredited tester; (c) certify that the test was done appropriately and your product passed; and (d) label your product.

There are a number of limitations on the materials or characteristics of your product. For instance, there are lead limits, which are different for the paint and for all other parts of your product. There are limits on how flammable the material in kids clothing can be; there are also rules against using specific, flammable materials in kids' sleepwear. There are limits on the contents of buttons, fasteners and kids jewelry or clothing decorations. There is a "small parts" limit that prohibits you from providing products for kids under 3 if they have or can break up into small parts that fit into a child's throat. Toys with small parts, small balls, and marbles each require their own specific warning label. Balloons also require a specific warning label[44]. There are also limits on phthalates. The FTC enforces these rules and is vigilant around items of greatest risk, such as squeezable bath toys.[45]

TEST FOR COMPLIANCE BY A 3RD PARTY

Kid's products may have to be tested, but only by a *recognized* 3rd party lab. All recognized labs are listed on CPSC's website with their approved scope; a lab may be approved by CPSC for one standard but not another. Anyone who, in the previous year, made less than $1 million in sales and 7,500 products can register as a Small Batch Manufacturer to potentially get out of the 3rd party testing requirement. You can search for recognized labs nearest your location at:

⇨   http://www.cpsc.gov/cgi-bin/labsearch/

CERTIFY TESTING AND COMPLIANCE

You may have to certify that the test was done, it was done correctly and your product passed, meeting all the limits for your product. The certificates must be provided by the manufacturer or by the one who imported the product into the USA.

LABEL PRODUCTS

There are also extensive regulations about the labels and tags you have to stick on your product or packaging. Kids products have to have a permanent tracking label on the product, or, if not possible on the product without damaging it, on the packaging. The tracking label has to say (a) the source of production; (b) the date of manufacture; and (c) the batch or run number. You also have to include the country of origin or manufacture on the product[46]. This is a manufacturing challenge, so leave time for it. You'll need a system for keeping track of the labels. Some manufacturing trade associations offer a digital system on the web.

DO YOU SELL THINGS?

Sellers and suppliers can also be liable for defects in the product, particularly if the defect is a breach of warranty. A breach of warranty arises from a mismatch between the actual or implied promises made about the product and the product itself, which results in an injury. Breach of warranty is just another way of holding a maker or supplier liable (based on a contract right). Warranty regulations come from states. But, warranties on consumer products also come from the federal government, which we'll talk about a little later. (See Section 6, "Getting Protection.")

PAYMENT RULES

Sellers of products also have to be aware of things that manufacturers don't, like payment laws and rules. Rules about how you can collect money from a customer, what information you can collect when you take the money and how you have to alert the customer to the terms of sale come from government and from your private deals. Some states (like California and Texas) have detailed rules prohibiting you from writing down someone's drivers license information if he pays by credit card. And, there are limits to your ability to even refuse to put the transaction through if he refuses to produce his I.D. There will also be hundreds of pages of rules laid down by whichever credit card companies and payment processors you engage. If you have a brick and mortar store in a single state, you will have an easier time figuring out your obligations. But, if you have stores in many states, including California, you need to find a lawyer with a particular expertise in consumer protection. Or, you could wait for complaints to build up at the FTC and just hire a lawyer when you are under investigation or hit with a class action suit.

DO YOU HAVE EMPLOYEES?

There are regulations designed to get employers to create a safe workplace for employees. (See Section 1, "Getting Help.")

COULD YOUR PRODUCT OR SERVICE HURT THE ENVIRONMENT?

One area of substantial regulation is the environment. Environmental laws usually either protect people from unnatural poisons (a/k/a pollution); or protect natural materials from people (a/k/a conservation). Pollution laws focus on limiting and cleaning up poisonous emissions into and from the air, water and soil. Conservation laws focus on preserving forests, minerals, animals, and natural treasures. Pollution and conservation laws often crossover – for example, one law may ban dumping poison and riding jet skis in the same lake.

Environmental laws are controversial because they impose limits on what people can do and what business can take from the earth. Environmental laws emerged to clean up the air and water, because people were getting sick from overflowing toxins. Pollution laws keep business from taking shortcuts that poison people. Conservation laws protect natural resources from people taking too much out of the earth for the quick profit, leaving nothing left. How those laws get catalogued, implemented and enforced provides a whole area for continuing, robust debate.

RESOURCES

There are numerous resources to gather and grasp environmental regulations:

⇨ http://www.envcap.org/
⇨ http://www.business.gov/business-law/environmental-regulations/general-info.html
⇨ www.assistancecenters.net
(assistance centers for environmental compliance)

Getting started. Look out for the regulations you have to satisfy whenever you have or use any of these things: waste, hazardous substances, emissions, construction, toxics, water, litter, and noise.

1. WASTE

By the 1970's, there was so much solid waste – particularly paper, oil and tires – that our dumps were both overrun and polluting our environment. EPA, under a law called Resource Conservation and Recovery Act ("RCRA") a/k/a Solid Waste Disposal Act,[47] began to put out rules to collect, store,

transport, treat and dispose of solid waste. This waste excludes waste from sewage and irrigation, which is usually regulated by state and local governments.

If you produce waste, you have to be responsible for it. Those responsibilities include registering with the EPA or your state environmental agency, getting dumping permits, complying with dumping restrictions and keeping active records of your waste activity. Below are some types of waste.

TYPES OF WASTE

Solid Waste. Waste is discarded materials. Solid waste is waste without enough water to flow freely. Solid waste is garbage, refuse, salvageable material, solids, liquids, semisolids, contained gasses, paper, wood, yard debris, food wastes, plastics, leather, rubber and other combustibles, and noncombustible materials such as glass and rock.

Waste Water Discharge. Waste Water Discharge is pollutants flushed through the septic or public treatment systems. This is common from car washes, food processors, cleaning solutions, factories, and boats.

Storm Water Runoff. Storm Water Runoff is runoff from buildings and sidewalks which collects pollutants that then dumps into waterways. Pollutants include: oil and grease from car repair, construction site sediment, pesticides, car wash soaps and hazardous liquids from leaking aboveground storage tanks.

Universal Waste. Universal Waste is common hazardous waste, such as batteries, pesticides, florescent bulbs, thermostats.

Regulated Medical Waste. Generators of regulated medical waste usually have to register, provide a management plan to store and dispose of medical waste in accordance with regulations.

Construction and Demolition Debris ("C&D Debris"). C&D debris includes materials from construction like concrete, asphalt, wood, gypsum wallboard, paper, glass, rubble, and roofing materials. Land clearing debris, such as stumps, rocks, and dirt, are also included in some state definitions. In most cases C&D debris is nonhazardous and is regulated by states and local governments rather than by EPA. An exception would be where C&D debris contains hazardous waste, such as removed asbestos insulation.

2. HAZARDOUS WASTE

Hazardous Waste is solid waste that is hazardous. Something is considered "hazardous" if it is characteristically hazardous or listed by the EPA as hazardous.[48] Characteristic hazardous wastes are: (1) ignitable; (2) corrosive; (3) reactive (in that it reacts violently with water or generates toxic fumes); or (4) toxic (alone or in mixtures of hazardous waste with other substances).[49] Listed hazardous wastes are wastes that EPA thinks are always hazardous.[50]

If you create, hold, or handle hazardous waste, you will have a monster set of regulations to comply with. You will need to identify the types and amounts of hazardous waste and how it is being generated. Then, you will need to notify your local hazardous waste offices. You may need to register with the EPA as a generator, report on the type and amount of waste, and take actions to reduce the amount and toxicity of the waste. There are limits to how long and how much waste you can store in your facility. There are also requirements about how to store your waste. You have to have emergency plans in place, fully train your staff in handling waste, and try and minimize or reduce waste. You must frequently inspect the storage facilities. You must keep records of all waste activities. Finally, you will need to comply with regulations about the shipment and disposal of your hazardous waste. Industries that may qualify as generators of hazardous waste include chemical manufacturing sandblasting operations, metal fabrication pesticide applicators, fiberglass fabrication laboratories, chemical formulation vehicle repair and maintenance, wood products manufacturing furniture refinishing, textile manufacturing dry cleaning, metal plating and finishing printing and related industries.

Because so many hazardous waste sites have been abandoned, the federal government created the Comprehensive Environmental Response, Compensation, and Liability Act ("CERCLA").[51] Under CERCLA, EPA identifies polluted sites and tries to figure out who did it (also called "potentially responsible parties"). Potentially responsible parties ("PRPs") can be owners and operators of the site where hazardous material was dumped. PRPs are jointly and severally liable – they are all on the hook separately for the whole liability. When the bad guys can't be found, the federal government pays for the remediation from funds paid by TSDs into a federal account called the Superfund.

3. HAZARDOUS SUBSTANCES

Hazardous substances are things that cause or significantly contribute to mortality or illness or pose a substantial threat to human health or the environment when improperly used, stored, transported or discarded.[52] Some hazardous substances are harmless when used, but become dangerous when released. Hazardous substances have different levels of danger - substances with higher levels of acute and chronic toxicity have more severe and demanding regulations. There is a group of hazardous substances considered even more dangerous and these are called "Toxic Pollutants." Toxic Pollutants are materials that will cause death, disease, behavioral abnormalities, cancer, genetic mutations, physiological malfunctions or physical deformations in organisms who encounter, ingest or inhale them.[53] Toxic pollutants include arsenic, asbestos, benzene, cyanide, DDT, lead, mercury, nickel, silver. Hazardous pollutants that may not be toxic include acetic acid, ammonia and cobalt.

Substances that have an unreasonable risk of injury to health or environment are regulated by the EPA.[54] Manufacturing hazardous chemicals is governed by the Toxic Substance Control Act ("TSCA").[55]

Under TSCA, you cannot make a new chemical until you have given EPA ninety days' prior notice (although there are exceptions). You also can't import or make chemicals if they are not preapproved on the TSCA inventory of existing chemicals. You may have to test substances and mixtures of substances which present unreasonable risk of injury. EPA can inspect any plant where chemical substances or mixtures are manufactured, processed, stored, or held.

There are also separate regulations for how certain packaged chemicals must be labeled and handled when they're shipped. These regulations are created and governed in part by the US federal Department of Transportation. You can find some of those regulations here:

⇨ http://www.fmcsa.dot.gov/

Material Safety Data Sheets. Some federal regulations require businesses to maintain information on hazardous substances under OSHA's Hazard Communication standard.[56] Under this rule, businesses must make and supply Material Safety Data Sheets ("MSDS") that describe the potentially hazardous materials that could be toxic to a person who comes into contact with them. Good resources for which chemicals need to be disclosed are (a) OSHA's listed chemicals in the Air Contaminants regulations; (b) the National Toxicology Program or International Agency for Research on Cancer's lists of carcinogens; (c) the Threshold Limit Values for Chemical Substances and Physical Agents lists published by the American Conference of Governmental Industrial Hygienists.

If your employees may be exposed to hazardous chemicals, you must provide information to those employees through MSDSs, and container labels, training and written hazard communication program. These MSDS should also be included in all packaging materials.

The MSDS must cover the substance identity and ingredients, physical and chemical characteristics, physical hazards, such as fire and explosion, health hazards and symptoms, main routes of entry into the body, legal exposure limits (by OSHA and other agencies), if it is a carcinogen, instructions for safe use and handling, ventilation, protective equipment, emergency and first aid procedures, the date the MSDS was prepared, the name, address, and phone number of the manufacturer and if it is listed as a hazardous material by EPA. You also have to keep an active inventory of all hazardous chemicals used in the workplace. However, you can omit the chemical composition if it is a trade secret, as long as you say so on the MSDS and disclose the possible effects of it.

There are also obligations to make this type of information available to the general public.

Community Right to Know. Americans have a legal right to know the chemicals they may be exposed to throughout their day to day life.[57] EPA maintains a database called the Toxics Release Inventory, which you can access online, to see which toxic materials are released around you. Businesses that handle or make any chemical that EPA sticks on its EPCRA Section 313 list may need to report its disposal and release activities to EPA under EPCRA section 313. EPA assembles the data submitted through these reports into the Toxics Release Inventory and makes that available to the public. This information may also have to be made available to state and local officials, particularly those that deal with emergency planning.

Label Hazardous Substances. The Federal Hazardous Substances Act[58] requires hazardous substances and any packaging, to be labeled with consumer alerts about the hazards and precautions to avoid those hazards. Any product that is toxic, corrosive, flammable or combustible, an irritant, allergenic, asphyxiation, pathogenic, biohazardous or that generates pressure through decomposition, heat, or other means, or if it could cause injury particularly to children, must be labeled.

Transport, Store, Dispose. EPA also regulates the activities of "TSDs," which are facilities that transport, store, and dispose of hazardous and toxic substances. These regulations, created under RCRA, are largely based on the substance's persistence, degradability, corrosiveness, and flammability.

Underground Storage Tanks. There are also bodies of regulations dealing with underground storage tanks that are 10% underground and used for petroleum, hazardous substances, flammable liquids, among others.

MISCELLANEOUS TOXINS AND POLLUTANTS

Lead paint. Lead-based paint has been banned since 1978, but older buildings may still have it on walls, woodwork, siding, windows, and doors. Construction and demolition workers can be exposed to lead by cutting, scraping, sanding, heating, burning, or blasting buildings and bridges. Debris from lead paint also seeps into soil and water. Lead poisoning is dangerous for all people, but particularly kids. Most states regulate the handling and disposal of construction and demolition debris contaminated with lead paint. Most states operate training and certification programs for lead paint handling; EPA operates training programs in the 12 states that have no program (AL, AK, FL, ID, MT, NM, NY, NV, SC, SD, WA, and WY).

Mercury. Construction and demolition workers can be exposed to mercury, from things as common as thermostats, switches and relays, fluorescent lamps, and batteries. Mercury-contaminated stuff may be hazardous waste and federal rules may kick in. In some cases, these wastes may be managed as "universal wastes," which have less complicated rules for handling and recycling or disposal.

Asbestos. Asbestos in certain formulations and states – principally respirable, free-form asbestos - is banned. Respirable free-form asbestos is asbestos that is not bound, woven, or otherwise "locked in" by a glue or resin to a patching compound. If not locked in, asbestos fibers can get into the air and be inhaled if sanded or heated.

Batteries. Batteries are not hazardous waste if they are recycled. Since 1996, when Congress created the

Battery Act, the government has regulated the disposal of batteries.[59] The Battery Act served two purposes: to phase out the use of mercury in batteries, and to enable collection and recycling or proper disposal of used nickel cadmium (Ni-Cd) batteries and used small sealed lead-acid (SSLA) batteries, among others. Under the Battery Act:

- ✓ Batteries must be easily removable from consumer products to facilitate recycling
- ✓ Batteries must be labeled with their battery chemistry, the "three chasing arrows" symbol, and a directive to recycle or appropriately dispose of the battery
- ✓ Phase out some mercury containing batteries
- ✓ Create national standards for battery collection, storage, transport and disposal or recycling of batteries

Pesticides and Insecticides. The Federal Insecticide Fungicidal Rodenticide Act requires registration of pesticides before sale and distribution. Pesticides will only be registered if they will perform intended function without unreasonable adverse effects on the environment. In addition, you must become a Certified Applicator to use or supervise use of restricted use pesticides. Applicators must keep records, and, producers of pesticides must register as a producer. Further, pesticide regulation may have some bearing on food manufacturers or distributors.

Preserve Endangered Species. Endangered species are also protected from human activities and commerce by the Fish and Wildlife Service[60] and National Marine Fisheries Services.[61] Disappearing species of plants and animals can be listed "endangered" or "threatened." "Endangered" are species in danger of extinction. "Threatened" are species likely to become endangered in foreseeable future. To protect these animals, the law prohibits "taking" which is to harass, harm, hurt, shoot, wound, kill, trap, capture or collect, or causing significant habitual changes.[62] There is special protection for "critical habitat" for each listed species, which is a habitat where the species is or could be. Funding for the Endangered Species Act expired in 1992, but gets annual appropriations.[63]

Species can be nominated by Secretary or a person, group or state agency. The public may participate in the deliberations and the applicable cabinet secretary and staff makes the decision. The species is to be included on the list only on the basis of scientific data, not economic impact. Listed species gets reviewed every 5 years.

4. AIR EMISSIONS

The federal EPA, along with 50 state mini-EPAs, works to limit emissions to meet national air standards; and to limit emissions from particular sources.[64,65]

Air emissions are releases or discharges of a pollutant into the ambient air either 1) by a stack, or 2) as a fugitive dust, mist or vapor from manufacturing. Typical air emissions include: overspray and drying from painting or coating operations; evaporating solvents from parts cleaning/degreasing operations; perchloroethylene from dry cleaning operations; and aerosols containing ozone depleting compounds.

EMISSIONS STANDARDS

Air Quality Standards. The EPA sets air quality standards,[66] fixing the maximum tolerable concentration of substances identifiable as pollutants and enforcement measures to limit sources of emissions. Emissions standards, which form the basis for emissions compliance, are state or EPA limitations on quantity, rates or concentration of air pollutants and any schemes to get you there.[67] Emissions standards focus on the source – cars, industry, power plants and small machinery like lawn mowers.

Transportation. Transportation emissions are heavily regulated. Each year, states must submit studies on success of vehicle mileage, vehicle emissions, congestion implementation plan to achieve attainment with ozone standards. EPA puts out emissions standards for new cars and vehicles.[68] California got a waiver, because it had its own emissions standards in 1966. Each car sold in the US must have Certificate of Conformity from EPA. In addition, there are separate regulations for fuel additive and aircraft emissions.

OPERATING PERMITS FOR AIR EMISSIONS

Existing plants must obtain operating permits to emit pollutants into the air. These permits are often called Title V Permits (because they are provided under Title V of the Clean Air Act), and Part 70 Permits (because regulations prescribing the permit standards are at 40 CFR Part 70).

CONSTRUCTION PERMITS FOR NEW SOURCES OF EMISSIONS

Anyone doing new construction or major modifications to a factory or power house may need to get environmental permits before they start construction. This is called "new source review" or "NSR" construction permitting or preconstruction permitting.

CLEAN AIR ACT PRIVATE RIGHT OF ACTION.

People who live in a polluted area can sue for violations of the Clean Air Act, though not in a class action.[69] Those violations can include violations of an emission standard or an EPA order or state order. Civil penalties are put into a special U.S. fund. Private suits can also be brought against EPA for failing to carry out non-discretionary duties, like listing lead on an air pollutant list or to make a federal plan where a state failed.

5. WATER

Water gets polluted by farms, industry, and human organic waste, toxic chemicals, heated water and sediments. Pollution and organic waste in water sucks up all the oxygen. Lower levels of oxygen means indigenous fish get replaced with fish that don't need oxygen, like carp. Then CO^2 gets replaced with methane or hydrogen sulfide and the water turns brown. Or, water temperature increases, releasing oxygen and enabling the growth of algae.

To clean up the waters, EPA creates water quality standards under the federal Clean Water Act[70] to make waters safe for drinking, fishing, swimming, irrigation, and industrial use. Then, the states figure out how to bring their waters into compliance with those standards.

The states must set water quality standards every three years, and must identify waters that fail to meet standards and a total maximum daily load for pollutants. States conduct Total Maximum Daily Load ("TMDL") studies to figure out how much of a particular pollutant needs to get reduced to bring the water quality back into compliance. If your construction site runoff enters a water body that has a TMDL, then, in some states, you must consider the effects of your construction site runoff on water quality before you can receive coverage under the general storm water permit, although in some states you can get a waiver.

PERMITS FOR WATER POLLUTION

Under the Clean Water Act, the National Pollutant Discharge Elimination System ("NPDES") permit program controls water pollution created by point sources. Point sources are identifiable sources of water pollution, such as pipes or man-made ditches. Individual homes that are connected to a municipal system, use a septic system, and do not have a surface discharge do not need an NPDES permit.

Usually, permits are issued by the states. Permits can be general or individual. A general permit is for a region with similar businesses and common factors. An individual permit is for a single business. EPA can order a business to apply for an individual special permit. A state can also create its own program, and when it does, the Feds often step aside.

OCEAN DUMPING

Littering in navigable water is a crime. However, EPA grants permits to dump waste into the ocean[71] if material won't have an adverse effect on environment or in an emergency for science[72].

Oil Spills. It is against the law to discharge oil or hazardous substance into U.S. waters[73].

Protected Wetlands. Wetlands are areas of land where the water table is at, near, or above the land. Federal laws prohibit destruction of these areas, even if on privately owned land[74] or encroached without permission from the Army Corps of Engineers.

6. NOISE POLLUTION

There are a variety of laws that regulate the noise level of activities or areas. Anti-hawking ordinances and the Noise Control Act of 1972 are just a couple of examples. In fact, the EPA has a program in which it can certify products a Low Noise Emission Product.[75]

DO YOU DO BUSINESS OUTSIDE THE U.S.?

American citizens have special, and surprising, obligations when they do business overseas. For instance, (1) don't bribe foreign officials; (2) check the Prohibited Lists; and (3) comply with export laws.

1. DON'T BRIBE (OR REALLY EVEN PAY) FOREIGN OFFICIALS

The Foreign Corrupt Practices Act ("FCPA") is a big law that prohibits bribing your way to business success in a foreign country. FCPA outlaws giving money or value intended to improperly influence business decisions of a foreign official, a foreign political party, or candidates to get or keep business. Even if these are customary, they're illegal. Penalties include prison, fines, suspension of business, and cancelation of export licenses. There are two big areas of liability: (1) "intermediary" sales in which a representative, consultant or distributor bribes a foreign official; and (2) accidentally paying someone who turns out to be a foreign official. However, you can (a) reimburse or pay for legitimate expenses incurred by or for a foreign official to demonstrate your product or provide a service; or (b) make Facility Payments, which are payments to expedite or facilitate a routine government function, such as permits, licenses, visas, mail, police inspections, phones, and water.

Big companies get busted for this all the time, with multimillion and multibillion dollar fines, so this should be taken very seriously.

Here are some wise practices:

- ✓ Research the area to see how common corruption is – if high, you have to take extra precautions
- ✓ Get references for everyone you are going to pay and everyone you are going to do business with
- ✓ Get agreements in writing so you have a record of your deals
- ✓ Always pay by bank wire transfer so you have a record of your deals
- ✓ Be transparent in your dealings

2. CHECK THE AMERICAN PROHIBITED LISTS

The Federal Government keeps lists of people and countries around the world with whom you are not allowed to do business or with whom your dealings must be limited. These lists are called the "Prohibited Lists" and they must be searched before you do business with any person or entity outside the United States. Managed by The Office of Foreign Assets Control ("OFAC"), as well as the Departments of State, Commerce and Treasury, these lists include terrorists, criminals, non-military or law enforcement wanted lists, and foreign persons debarred from business with U.S. government.

The lists are at (and are briefly described in the box at right):

- ⇨ www.ustreas.gov/officials/enforcement/lists/
- ⇨ http://www.bis.doc.gov/complianceandenforcement/liststocheck.htm

LISTS TO CHECK	WHO'S ON THE PROHIBITED LIST
DENIED PERSONS LIST	People denied export privileges, usually because of some arms issue, by the Commerce Department. Any dealings with a party on this list that would violate the terms of its denial order are prohibited.
UNVERIFIED LIST	People the government has been unable to verify in past deals, their presence would be a "Red Flag" that should be resolved before proceeding with the transaction.
ENTITY LIST	People whose presence in a deal could trigger a license requirement under the Export Administration Regulations. The list specifies the license requirements that apply to each listed party.
SPECIALLY DESIGNATED NATIONALS LIST	A list compiled by the Treasury Department, Office of Foreign Assets Control (OFAC). OFAC's regulations may prohibit a transaction if a party on this list is involved. In addition, the Export Administration Regulations require a license for exports or re-exports to any party in any entry on this list that contains any of the suffixes "SDGT", "SDT", "FTO", "IRAQ2" or "NPWMD."
DEBARRED LIST	A list compiled by the State Department of parties who are barred from participating directly or indirectly in the export of defense articles or services.
NONPROLIFERATION SANCTIONS	Several lists compiled by the State Department of parties that have been sanctioned.

3. COMPLY WITH EXPORT LAWS

Anything sent from the United States to a foreign destination is an export. These things may be commodities, software or technology, clothing, building materials, circuit boards, automotive parts, blue prints, design plans, retail software packages and technical information. Its method of transport is irrelevant to its export regulations. Whether you send something prohibited by mail, fax, email or you deliver it in person, it is still subject to US export regulations. The main goals of laws limiting exports of U.S. products are: (a) to keep weapons and tools of war away from the bad guys; (b) to prohibit transactions with criminals and terrorists; and (c) to support sanctions and pressures on other countries imposed by the Federal government and other international groups like the U.N.

EMBARGOED COUNTRIES

These countries are under federal government restrictions regarding trade with U.S. citizens and U.S. full time residents. Cuba, Iran and Sudan are under full embargoes. West Balkans, Burma, Iraq, Liberia, North Korea and Syria are under partial embargoes.

GET AN EXPORT LICENSE WHEN REQUIRED

Some exports will either require a license or be completely prohibited. The penalties for blowing these laws are severe, so getting a lawyer specializing in International Trade or a consultant that specializes in exports is prudent.

DEFENSE RELATED ARTICLES

International Traffic in Arms Regulations ("ITAR") is a set of United States government regulations that control the export and import of defense-related items. The Department of State develops and enforces the Regulations, in performance of its authority under the Arms Export Control Act. Generally, the ITAR prohibit sharing of covered items to any non-U.S. persons, unless approved by the Department of State or excepted under a special exemption. Failure to follow the regulations may result in fines or imprisonment.

The twin benefits of ITAR, guarding military secrets and preventing access of information to potential economic competitors, are sometimes overshadowed by the difficulty of demonstrating that an article or service is exempt from the ITARs' scope.

EXPORT ADMINISTRATION REGULATIONS ("EAR")

Export Administration Regulations ("EAR") are developed and enforced by the Bureau of Industry and Security ("BIS"), within the U.S. Department of Commerce. Like ITAR, the EAR restricts exports of sensitive items to foreign countries. Unlike ITAR, which regulate items primarily intended for military use, EAR regulate the export of goods that have a legitimate commercial or personal function. These "dual-use" items include types of computer hardware and software, spare parts, and other seemingly innocuous products. The EAR place legal responsibility on persons who have information, authority or functions relevant to carrying out transactions subject to the EAR. Jurisdiction extends to persons in foreign countries who are involved in transactions subject to the EAR. Violations of EAR are subject to both criminal and administrative penalties. Administrative penalties can be as high as $250,000 or twice the value of the transaction, for each violation. Criminal penalties can include fines of up to $1,000,000 and up to 20 years of imprisonment. Additional penalties include denial of export privileges. Cases involving violations of the EAR are plentiful. The BIS publishes a guidebook, available on their website, entitled "Don't Let This Happen to You," with numerous examples of violations resulting in fines and imprisonment. The striking feature among many of these cases is the banality of the products.

ARE YOU BRINGING GOODS ACROSS A NATIONAL BORDER?[76]

If you bring goods from one country into the United States, you will have obligations just around the importation (not including all the other laws that pertain to things in the U.S.). You should be aware of

(1) marking obligations; (2) import duties; (3) quotas; and (4) products that you cannot bring into the U.S.

1. MARKING OBLIGATIONS

Goods made in one country and brought over to another form the basis of international trade and are called "imports" and "exports." "Export" means a thing that leaves your country bound specifically for another. "Import" means a thing that leaves one country and enters your country. Diversion to a domestic location doesn't make it an import.

Imports and exports are usually subject to a couple of restrictions. First, imports are often taxed when they cross a sovereign border – that tax is called a "customs duty" or a "tariff." Second, there are many rules against exporting and importing certain types of products to certain types of people for certain types of uses.

Imports into the U.S. must be conspicuously marked with the country of origin.[77] Failure to properly mark the goods in accordance with the law could result in a 10% duty.

2. IMPORT DUTIES INTO THE U.S

Tariffs in the U.S. are governed by the Harmonized Tariff Schedule of the United States ("HTSUS") and its accompanying General Rules of Interpretation. Under this schedule, the Customs Service, which lives in Treasury, (1) classifies goods; and (2) sets the rate of duty for those classifications. Under the Generalized System of Preferences,[78] the President can give duty free treatment to eligible stuff from eligible developing countries.

Tariffs are computed based on their classification and rate of duty. In picking which tariff classification applies, you have to identify the appropriate one based on the following rules, in this order: (a) the statutory assignment or classification that matches your product; (b) the heading in the interpretive rules that matches the product's commercial name; (c) the most specific classification applicable in the right class, or, if more than two could apply, pick the one that describes the good's "essential character; or (d) resort to a relevant catch-all.[79]

Merchandise should be classified based on its condition when imported. Merchandise can be fashioned to minimize duties. Like in tax, it is acceptable to avoid, but not evade duties. Merchandise can be classified by its entirety, by its components and by use.

In addition to custom duties, there are other expenses and taxes associated with importing products.

COUNTERVAILING AND ANTIDUMPING DUTIES

These are things governments use to balance out unfair trade actions. A "Countervailing Duty" is a duty imposed to balance out a foreign government's subsidy of an industry that hurts a U.S. industry. An "Anti-Dumping Duty" is a duty on a good that is sold at less than fair market value.

HARBOR MAINTENANCE TAX

This is a customs duty, and a tax, on commercial cargo at a port for use of a harbor.

IMPORT CHARGES

Import charges are expenses incurred in importing goods such as (a) freight; (b) brokerage fees; (c) customs duties; (d) incidentals.

DRAWBACK

This is a refund of duties paid for using the originally imported materials to make something new.

3. QUOTAS

An import quota puts a limit on the number of goods that can be imported into a country. Import quotas are used as a protectionist trade restriction to help local commerce. Quotas arise from Congressional authorization and Presidential decree. Quotas are listed in the Harmonized Tariff Schedule. There are two kinds of quotas: absolute and tariff-rate. Absolute quotas limit how many goods can enter the U.S. in a certain amount of time. Tariff-rate quotas limit how many goods can enter the U.S. at a particular rate – after a certain quantity are admitted, the rate increases.

A Foreign Trade Zone ("FTZ") is a port of entry that Congress designates to get preferential treatment under customs laws,[80] to stoke foreign commerce with the U.S. Goods in the FTZ are not subject to U.S. customs laws and exempt from customs duties, but not from the Harbor Maintenance Tax.

There are two types of FTZs: (1) general purpose; and (2) foreign trade subzones. A company can operate within a FTZ to store, break up, repack, assemble, sort, grade, clean and mix, but not manufacture or exhibit. The company can pick the duty on the raw material or finished good, depending on the rate of duty. Merchandise is exempt from antidumping orders while in the FTZ. But, once the goods are admitted into the U.S. customs, duties kick in.

4. PRODUCTS NOT ALLOWED INTO THE U.S.

Many things are prohibited from being imported into the U.S., including (a) commodities of Cuban origin; (b) African elephant ivory from non-ivory producing countries; (c) firearms; (d) lottery tickets (except from Canada if for U.S. lottery); (e) products from prohibited countries; and (f) obscene materials and sexually explicit photos. Goods made by slaves, forced labor, child labor or indentured labor are also prohibited.

FOOD, DRUGS AND DEVICES

The Federal Food, Drug and Cosmetic Act prohibits importation of (1) products that are manufactured, processed, or packed under unsanitary conditions or standards that fail to conform to our laws; (2) a product that is prohibited where it is made; or (3) adulterated, misbranded products. A product is "adulterated" if it is, or could be, injurious to health.

MERCHANDISE WITH AN AMERICAN TRADEMARK

If a foreign-made good bears a trademark owned by a U.S. person or entity, and the trademark is registered with the PTO and the Secretary of Treasury, it cannot be imported into the U.S. without written consent from the trademark's owner.

IN AT THE BORDER

When goods arrive at the border, they are stopped by the Customs Service. Often, the importer will have arranged for a CUSTOMS BROKER to facilitate importation. Customs brokers are agents licensed by the federal government (Treasury Department) to facilitate importation of stuff. When the goods are stopped at Customs, the importer of record or the Customs Broker files: (1) a form identifying the importer of record and the Customs Broker; (2) a "manifest," which is a sworn statement listing the goods; (3) the invoice(s) from the transactions when the goods were purchased; (4) the bill of lading, which is a detailed shipping receipt from the shipper; (5) potential government permits; and (6) the person or entity who is serving as the importer of record. If the list is accurate, the importer can post a bond to cover estimated custom duties and can take the goods. The importer then files another form with the duty owed and the payment. If a Customs Broker is used, the importer is the guy who is liable for discrepancies in the duty payment. All goods can be inspected by the Customs Service or by a 3rd party selected by the Customs Service. Goods can only be released once the duty is paid with currency or with a bond.

Sometimes, the Customs Service needs to value the goods. Usually, the value is the "transaction value" which is the price paid when sold for exportation, plus packing costs, commissions, royalties and other additions. However, where the transaction value seems like bullshit, the Customs Service may independently impose a value they determine more closely matches what would have been paid in an arms' length transaction. An importer can have the merchandise destroyed if he wants to avoid paying the duties. The government can and does sell merchandise that is unclaimed.

Bonded Warehouse. Sometimes, goods can be admitted to the U.S. and stuck in a Customs Bonded Warehouse, except for perishable goods or explosives. A Customs Bonded Warehouse is a storage space that is deputized by the Customs Service to serve as a safe house for goods until the customs issues are settled. Goods in the bonded warehouse are technically in federal government custody, even though run and secured by a private company. A customs officer supervises the warehouse. Fun fact: duty free stores are technically Customs Bonded Warehouses. Remember the scene from Beverly Hills Cop when Axel Foley breaks into the bonded warehouse where the bad guy has crates of art, and he threatens that "someone is going to lose their job over this?" That was a Customs Bonded Warehouse and the guys who worked there were Customs Officers.

HAP AND HAZ HAVE TO GO

Gravity paused. "Haz, do you have questions?"

"Yes. What are you talking about?"

BEST PRACTICES

"Sorry, this one may have been a little dense. Here is what you need to know:

- ✓ Stay current on the product laws and regulations that govern your activities, products and materials. Pay attention to changes.
- ✓ For manufacturing, don't just rely on a lawyer — make sure you also have a consultant with expertise in regulations applicable to your industry.
- ✓ Create processes and put compliance and safety first.
- ✓ Create a quality assurance program that includes testing raw materials, components and the finished product.
- ✓ Designate at least one person to work in compliance.

As for the regulations that govern your product, you will need to consider your product's materials and risks and designate actions to match those materials and risks to governing regulations. For instance:

RISK	ACTION
The MouseTrap could cause pain or injury in a few ways. First, there could be a material in the device, either in the substrate or the coating, that is toxic, restricted or banned. Second, since the solar receptors will feed into another device's electrical device, there is some risk of fire, overheating or explosion. Third, there could be some small parts that break off and carry danger of being swallowed by a toddler. It could produce unintentional radio waves under Part 15 of the FCC. It could also cause repetitive injuries.	Place warnings for risk on the packaging, on a special warning card, on the warranty and, if possible, on the product itself.
The greatest danger here is in what we are promising. The MouseTrap promises to provide 3 functions: (1) computer pointing and clicking; (2) solar energy capture and storage; and (3) delivery of solar energy to recharge a battery. Units may malfunction, but the design and manufacture of the device must meet all three functions. Further, the marketing cannot make promises broader than the device's performance. For instance, if the MouseTrap can power a computer for one hour, don't promise that it can provide 5 hours of power.	Test for performance. Ensure warranties and marketing materials match performance standards.
This is a consumer product.	Make sure materials comply with restrictions. Test and certify that the product complies with materials requirements. Make sure the certificate is included in shipments to distributors.
Manufacturing must comply with battery regulations. The battery may have materials that have to be properly dealt with on disposal. For instance, photovoltaic cells frequently include cadmium and lead. This may be an issue in the US and in Europe where the EU's 2003 directive on waste electrical and electronic equipment (WEEE) is being expanded.	Since you're farming out the manufacturing, get a promise from the manufacturer that it complies with all laws and that any hazardous substances are properly handled. Rechargeable consumer products containing regulated lead-acid batteries that are not easily removable must be labeled with the phrase "CONTAINS SEALED LEAD BATTERY. BATTERY MUST BE RECYCLED." The product's plastic components should also be included in a label about its level of recyclability. Finally, you must comply with the FTC and EPA rules on energy savings promises.

Now that we've covered regulations, the next step is for you to clarify your fulfillment strategy so that you can narrow your choices for a manufacturer."

Hap answered, "Gravity, we really need you to explain that to us. But, first, can you give us a bathroom break?"

"I CAN TRY."

FIGURE OUT FULFILLMENT

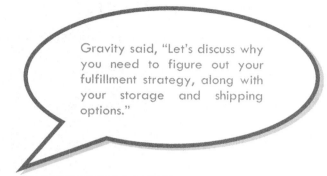

Gravity said, "Let's discuss why you need to figure out your fulfillment strategy, along with your storage and shipping options."

CHAPTER 17

WHY YOU NEED TO FIGURE OUT FULFILLMENT, MOVEMENT AND STORAGE

You need to decide the order of the manufacturing, storage and distribution steps in production of your product. This order will depend on your fulfillment strategy. "Fulfillment" is part of both getting it made and getting it sold and is a critical link in your supply chain. A "Supply Chain" is the system and physical work of sourcing, manufacturing, transporting and storing goods, and providing market research, credit programs and other marketing services.

Your fulfillment plans must fit hand in glove with your plans for making and selling your product. If you buy materials or make product before you have an identified path to using, storing and selling it, you could burn through too much cash. Once your product gets made, it needs to be secured from damage, theft and deterioration. The safety and sensibility of how you ship and where you store your products can make or break your company – accidents, fires and acts of God happen. Once your product gets sold, it may need to be pushed out to customers in a particular order. For instance, because of their limited shelf lives, food products must be shipped out in the order they were made. Failure to look ahead and plan your product's journey could wreak destruction on your business.

FULFILLMENT

"Fulfillment" is the strategy of deciding when in your supply chain you will manufacture, assemble or deliver your product. Fulfillment is a question of cash, capacity and timing: when do you make the product, what do you do with it once it's made and how much cash can you devote at any one time to the manufacture and storage of inventory.

Steps in Order Process. The product order process usually has a series of steps, from the buyer's expression of interest until the buyer and the product either live happily ever after or are separated by the product return. Here are some typical steps in the process:

> **Product Inquiry.** A website visit, inquiry about a product, a catalogue request.
> **Sales Quote.** Price quote.
> **Order Configuration.** Order options selected.
> **Order Booking.** Order placement, purchase order.
> **Order Acknowledgement.** Confirmation order received.
> **Invoice/Billing.** Bill presented.
> **Order Sourcing.** Source and location of materials.
> **Order Changes.** If necessary or permitted.
> **Order Process.** Distribution center or warehouse fills order, receives the inventory, picks, packs and ships the good.
> **Shipment.** Tender good to carrier.
> **Delivery.** Tender to recipient, end user or agent.
> **Settlement.** Payment.
> **Returns.** If necessary or permitted.

Your fulfillment process will shuffle these steps depending on the strategy you choose.

One good exercise to do when you start thinking about how to get a product made is to make a "value stream map." This is simply a diagram of every step involved in the material and information flow from the time a product is ordered to the time the product gets to a customer, including how raw materials get to you, and where the finished good is stored and eventually shipped to. By doing this early on, you can identify what steps are needed and what steps are perhaps unnecessary.

FULFILLMENT STRATEGIES

Below are 5 fulfillment strategies, commonly used, from the most cookie-cutter to the most customized. The key question for you to answer is:

> When, in your supply chain, will you have the product manufactured and what events will trigger the manufacture of your product?

FULFILLMENT STRATEGIES		
TITLE	DESCRIPTION	EXAMPLES
MADE TO STOCK (A/K/A BUILT TO FORECAST) ("MTS")	Products are made and sold based on sales forecast. These products are standardized, shipped, stored and sold from finished goods in stock. MTS requires an investment (bet) that people will buy the product with the included options. Investment is for manufacturing, transportation and storage costs. MTS is the most common model.	Most retail and consumer goods, grocery [81]
DIGITAL COPY ("DC")	The product is a digital master from which copies are ordered, made and delivered on demand.	Video On Demand[82]
ASSEMBLE TO ORDER ("ATO")	Product is made up of standard modular components built to customer specifications. The cornerstone of mass customization, this is based on modularity and option bundling.	Dell computers, shelving systems[83]
BUILT TO ORDER (A/K/A MADE TO ORDER) ("BTO")[84]	Product is based on standard design but only built upon customer's order and perhaps specifications.	High end motor vehicles, aircrafts, some houses[85]
ENGINEER TO ORDER ("ETO")	Product is designed according to customer's specifications and manufactured according to that design. Maximum customization, maximum wait time.	Big buildings, Formula 1 racing cars[86]

Picking a fulfillment strategy and picking a manufacturer will often go hand in hand. If you can find a manufacturer who can make products for you with a very short lead time in small quantities, it makes more sense to go with a strategy such as BTO or ATO. If the manufacturer requires long lead times, and piece price depends heavily on quantity, you might want to consider a MTS strategy. All things being equal, less inventory is better.

Part of your mission in crafting a fulfillment strategy will be to minimize inventory of both products and supplies. Gathering inventory takes cash flow in purchasing, manufacturing, shipping and storage. Greater inventory increases the stakes to keep inventory safe. Damaged inventory will hurt your operations – even with insurance. It will need to be replaced, and if you're storing large quantities then you probably can't readily get more inventory quickly. If you discover a defect in your parts or manufacturing process, the more inventory you've built up, the more inventory you'll have to scrap out.

WAREHOUSING & SHIPPING

Closely linked to your fulfillment strategy is what you do with your product once it's made. Do you ship it directly to a retailer, store it until you get orders, or ship it directly to the purchaser? If you need to store your products or raw materials, you may want to hire a warehouse.

Warehouses are usually big rooms or buildings owned by a company that stores someone else's stuff. Lots of things get warehoused – food, paper, plastic scrap, beer. Warehouses usually have loading docks for trucks, trains (the docks are often above the train tracks), or are close to airports and seaports.[87] Goods are moved inside using forklifts and pallet racks. Warehouses are increasingly automated, using conveyors and retrieval robots. Warehouses can be refrigerated (for food and other goods that have to stay cool) or hot as Hell (for things that don't have to stay cool, like paper).

Most warehouses use a warehousing and inventory management system that is a combination of logistics software and databases to coordinate storage and inventory rotation. Goods can be rotated using FIFO (First In First Out) and LIFO (Last In First Out) -- depending on the customer's direction. Inventory management can be done in a number of ways, from low tech (a card based "kanban" system), to more expensive and high tech (RFID chips that track the movement of goods into, throughout, and out of the warehouse). Regardless of how it is done, inventory management ought to tell you how much of which inventory you have in stock, which parts to order and which products to build if your business model is not a built to order.

In addition to storage, warehouses can also provide inspection and repackaging services. Many manufacturers or retailers pick locations that are central to their points of sale or shipping points. If you adopt a fulfillment strategy that manufactures right before or after purchase, your warehousing needs ought to be reduced substantially. You may also be able to arrange for warehousing through your manufacturer.

Let's focus on (1) selecting a warehouse; (2) the warehousing agreement; and (3) shipping.

1. SELECTING A WAREHOUSE

Picking a warehouse is like picking any other vendor; it may be helpful to use the 5 S-Steps for Staffing: Specify (what you need); Search (for candidates); Screen (for suitability); Solidify (for terms); Start (the work).

SPECIFY WHAT YOU NEED

List the characteristics of warehouses, which may involve their location, rates, temperature control, hours of operation, access to rail lines, highways, airports and seaports, experience with similar goods, security, quality control and additional packing, inventory management and inspection services.

SEARCH FOR WAREHOUSING CANDIDATES

To identify candidates for warehousing space, ask around to your network, including your accountant, lawyer and other business associates. Do a search online for warehouses and then scour their offerings to match your criteria. There are dozens of trade associations that work with warehousing and logistics companies.

You can find a list of those trade associations here:

⇨ http://www.idii.com/resource/
associations.htm

Some trade associations will also keep a mapped list of their member-companies, which may help narrow options. For instance, the International Warehouse Logistics Association maintains a list here:

⇨ http://www.logisticsservicelocator.com[88]

Your choices for storage and shipment will depend on the nature of your product, suppliers and customers. In some cases, you may need to order large quantities of something to be cost effective and warehousing makes sense – but beware of long lead times and make sure you've got a well-crafted raw goods testing strategy in place so you don't accept a large shipment of non-conforming goods. The other (most likely better) way is to partner with a local supplier that can give you more frequent smaller deliveries. This way, you have more flexibility in ordering the parts that you need, and if you get a bad set of parts, it can be quickly remedied. Also, smaller batches of parts moving quickly through your supply chain means less warehousing needed, less money tied up in inventory, and less risk (though this may lead to higher shipping costs).

Considering warehousing yourself as well. Obviously there are material handling, storage space, and inventory control issues that you'll need to think about. But if it makes sense, it can be good to have more control over your raw materials and finished goods – this also allows you to be more responsive to your customers. If you have raw materials and finished goods in house, you can respond immediately to an order (depending on whether you're shipping already manufactured goods, or building to order), rather than having another step in the process, i.e. contacting someone else to get your goods to you so you can manufacture your finished goods, or ship your goods to you.

Once you identify candidates for warehousing, you should contact them, preferably in writing (email is fine), explain your needs and request a quote.

Analyze the costs and operational logistics of storing in one warehouse over another. In picking a warehouse, you may want to tour the facility to get a sense of its cleanliness and quality. You may also want to get and check references, particularly if you can't visit the warehouse.

SOLIDIFY

Once you identify your favorite candidate, it is time to solidify the terms of storage and additional services. You will probably enter into a Warehousing Agreement with your warehouseman.

2. THE WAREHOUSING AGREEMENT

In the beginning, your warehouseman will probably provide a standard set of terms and conditions. You will want to have it read carefully, by a lawyer, and to negotiate fair terms.

The Facility. If there is a specific facility where your goods will be stored, that should be identified. If there is a specific location or amount of space inside the facility, that should be identified. There may be situations where the warehousing company may want to move some or all of your goods to another facility – you should talk about those. Alternatively, you can require your consent before any of your goods can be moved.

The Goods and the Process. The specific types of goods you will store, and how they will be stored and shipped, should be identified in detail. These details should prescribe how they will manage your inventory and how quickly they will respond to shipping and receiving requests.

Minimum Staffing and Handling. There may be times when you will have more product arriving or shipping out and you may need the warehouse to have sufficient staff to handle it. The minimum amount of product or staff necessary should be identified.

IP and Confidentiality. Your IP is valuable. Your warehousing company should agree to keep it confidential and not use it for any purpose other than storing it for your benefit under the warehousing agreement.

Fees. The fees will probably be some charge for each unit of product stored, plus charges for services provided in excess of the warehouse's standard services. Make sure the contract also includes rules about when the warehouse can raise prices and by how much.

Demurrage. Demurrage is a charge imposed by a rail or truck company for failure to comply with their timetables. Demurrage is controversial and inevitable. Who has to pay the demurrage must be worked out. As a result, you want to make sure that the warehouse has standards for staff for loading and unloading – at a minimum, any demurrage that results inside of those standards ought to be their responsibility.

Inspection and Damage. It is often prudent to obligate your warehousing company to perform extensive inspection and reporting services as a check against undiscovered damage. You may also want a right to inspect your stuff while stored.

Risk of Loss. Risk of loss ought to be the warehouseman's worry – after all, that's the whole point of giving a 3rd party your stuff and then working out a lengthy contract.

Insurance. Your warehousing company should not only have insurance, but you should see evidence of the insurance in the form of an insurance certificate. The amount of coverage will depend on what else is in the warehouse, but suffice it to say it ought to be well into the seven figures. (You also may want to keep your own property damage and inventory insurance as a backup.) Also, if you have enough goods with the warehousing company, you ought to be added to policies as an additional insured.

When you schedule the storage of your goods, you will probably need to synchronize storage dates with your fulfillment strategy and your manufacturing timetable.

3. SHIPPING

Your shipping options can also be analyzed and planned based on the 5 Steps for Staffing: Specify (what you need); Search (for candidates); Screen (for interest and interviews); Solidify (for terms); and Start (the work).

SPECIFY SHIPPING NEEDS

Your shipping options include rail, ship, truck, plane and the myriad services that deliver goods around the world. The shipping distance, season, fuel prices and speed of delivery will all drive your decisions.

SEARCH FOR SHIPPERS

You may want to work closely with your manufacturer or warehouseman in working out shipping arrangements. Of course, your business associates, contacts and searches may produce candidates.

SCREEN FOR RATES AND ABILITY

Request comprehensive rates from more than one shipper.

SOLIDIFY TERMS

Make sure you (a) pick a reputable company; (b) pick a company with insurance; and (c) keep your own insurance policy as backup.

START PICKUP AND DELIVERY

Your shipping schedule must be coordinated with your storage dates, fulfillment strategy and manufacturing timetable, as well as your distribution channel selections.

HAP AND HAZARD DISCUSS FULFILLMENT

Gravity and Haz and Hap talked about what they needed. They determined that without any orders and a limited amount of cash, they needed to conserve resources devoted to manufacturing and inventory until their sales strategy ginned up sales. But, they also needed to be able to cut production lead time quickly when they did get orders. As a result, they decided to start manufacturing based on a Built to Order strategy, which they hoped to spur with orders from web sales.

However, they believed that the marketplace would require them to adopt a MTS strategy in the near future. As a result, they agreed to create alternative budgets based on a BTO strategy with slightly higher shipping costs and an MTS strategy with lower unit shipping costs, but higher warehousing costs and upfront cash demands.

> Hazard said, "Gravity, I think we may be ready to hire a manufacturer. But, we don't know where to start. Can you help us?"

"I CAN TRY."

HIRE A MANUFACTURER

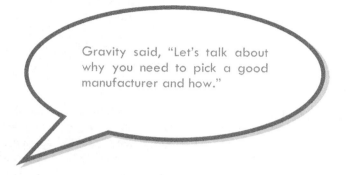

Gravity said, "Let's talk about why you need to pick a good manufacturer and how."

CHAPTER 18

WHY YOU NEED TO PICK A GOOD MANUFACTURER

The consequences for failure to deliver (1) on time; (2) at all; or (3) in compliance with the law or quality standards is make or break for your company. Your manufacturer's failure to deliver on time could kill your sales cycle, throw off your manufacturing schedule, and violate contracts with strategic partners. A problem with the manufacture of the product could also result in crippling defects. You may not be able to get compensated for the lost opportunities that flow from a failure at the plant. The key is to choose wisely, build in protections, and vigilantly monitor the progress of your manufacturer so that you can stay a couple of steps ahead of a looming catastrophe.

PICK THE COUNTRY OF MANUFACTURE

You can manufacture your product totally in the U.S., manufacture bits and pieces around the world and assemble in the U.S., or manufacture and assemble it in another country. In the olden days (before the 1980's), products sold in the U.S. were often manufactured in the U.S. But more and more, U.S. companies choose to manufacture stuff outside the U.S.

Labor is cheaper in other countries, which results in lower standards of living for factory workers. Some of those other countries lack employment protections, which is why some products are made by slaves and kids.[89] Further, some countries (like China) have governments that intervene in the economy by supplementing wages and benefits, controlling competition, imposing tariffs and manipulating the value of currency. Many countries lack environmental requirements, which means businesses have to spend less money on regulatory compliance and can use a wider array of cheaper raw materials. (Of course, since pollution has no borders, we are affected by the lack of environmental hygiene.) Many countries also create aggressive tax incentives for locating factories inside their borders, which may tip the balance towards manufacturing in one area over others.

The effects snowball. The increase in manufacturing in a concentrated area makes it easier and easier to hire a quick, skilled and efficient manufacturer in that area. Similarly, the decrease in manufacturing in the U.S. makes it harder and harder to find manufacturing options in the U.S.

There are added complexities - and added risks - to manufacturing your product abroad. First, you aren't there. Not only can't you personally inspect the plant, you also have a diminished ability to impact the manufacturer's reputation, so you may have less leverage. Second, language barriers can complicate communications and understanding. Third, it is probably more difficult and costly to enforce your rights in a court. It is extremely difficult to protect our intellectual property in a country like China and to enforce the contract once breached. Fourth, import costs can impose substantial costs and delays on the manufacturing process, so you have to factor in shipping times and costs. You should determine if the savings from manufacturing outside the US outweigh the increased costs and risks before you ship your manufacturing overseas.

Made In The U.S.A. For a product to be called "Made in USA," or of domestic origin without qualifications or limits on the claim, the product must be "all or virtually all" made in the U.S. "All or virtually all" means that all significant processing and parts that go into the product should be of U.S. origin. Any foreign content must be negligible. If a product is only partially made in the U.S.A., the manufacturer must provide a qualified claim. (e.g., "60% U.S. Content.")

PICK YOUR MANUFACTURER

You can use the Five S-Steps to Staffing to pick your manufacturer:

1. Specify (what you need)
2. Search (for candidates)
3. Screen (for interest and interviews)
4. Solidify (the terms)
5. Start (the work)

1. SPECIFY WHAT YOU WANT

Bundle the most current designs, the prototype, your prototype notes, delivery date, order amount and all other specifications into a request for proposal. Continue to have your engineer involved in the process, so that he can talk with the manufacturer, learn about what works and what may not, and then revise the designs and drawings if necessary. If any of the information in the bundle is confidential, require the candidate to sign a reasonable NDA before you disclose the information.

GENERAL CONTRACTOR VS. SUBCONTRACTOR

You can, and may expect yourself to, supervise every element of the manufacturing process – in that way, you would be acting as your own general contractor. However, you can also delegate the supervision to a company that acts as your general contractor. If you are sophisticated enough in the industry to deal directly with all your subcontractors and parts suppliers, then you could act as your own general contractor. If you are new to the business or lack a solid infrastructure, you may need a general contractor to take more responsibility off your shoulders (at a greater cost to you).

MANUFACTURING AND STORAGE

Some companies will store some amount of stock for you in their warehouse, which can reduce your warehousing costs. Some "lean" minded suppliers will set up a "pull" system with you where you can establish certain stock levels, and they will automatically replenish what you pull from stock each day. Try to get a manufacturer that understands what you're trying to do and will be flexible in trying to work with you and meet your changing needs.

2. SEARCH FOR CANDIDATES TO MANUFACTURE

Finding a good, reliable and professional manufacturer may require your resources. Many people find manufacturers by networking and getting referrals from friends, family and business contacts. Also, consider asking other companies with similar products to recommend manufacturers. There are also many resources on the web, including:

⇨ www.thomasregister.com
⇨ http://www.crowdspring.com/
⇨ http://www.ponoko.com/
⇨ http://www.coroflot.com/
⇨ http://hackerspaces.org/wiki/
⇨ http://www.emachineshop.com/
⇨ http://www.quickparts.com/home.aspx
⇨ http://redeyeondemand.com/Default.aspx
⇨ http://www.bigbluesaw.com/
⇨ http://www.becausewecan.org/

If you have the cash and access to expertise, you may want to consider manufacturing in house. Manufacturing your own product gives you full control over the production of the product, the quality testing, and scheduling. You may also adopt a hybrid strategy, by sourcing components and assembling and testing in house.

3. SCREEN QUOTES FROM MORE THAN ONE CANDIDATE

THE RFP

Make sure you are getting quotes on the same things so you can compare apples to apples. You need to compare and contrast the bids, and manufacturers need to fight for the business. When you ask for a quote, include the following:

1. Your prototype; detailed drawings that show dimensions and sizing for each component of the product; and a "spec sheet" with the specifications of materials used, seam allowances, etc.

2. A request for quotes on materials, labor, extra charges based on a couple of quantity of units on which you want them to base their bid and ask for a volume discount schedule

3. Ask them to provide their lead time, which is how long it will take from order to delivery

4. Ask them their standard shipping terms and charges

REFERENCES

Ask for at least three references. Here are some questions to ask when you call the former customers for their assessments:

1. Was the product made to specifications?

2. What percentage of the shipment was defective?

3. Did the manufacturer replace defective products?

4. Did the manufacturer meet his deadlines? If not, did he make amends?

5. Did he deliver on his promises?

6. Were the products up to your quality standards?

7. How long have you worked with this manufacturer?

8. How many orders have you placed?

9. Is your contact professional and easy to work with?

10. Does he return calls or emails quickly?

CONFIDENTIALITY AGREEMENT

Don't forget to get a confidentiality agreement if you are disclosing information that should stay secret.

If you have sufficient volume, you may want to negotiate and work with more than one manufacturer. You may find that one performs better than the other, and if one happens to have problems with quality or scheduling in your production, it won't shut down your operations. However, this may not be possible if you're using expensive tools to mold parts (and you can only afford to build one tool).

4. SOLIDIFY TERMS WITH YOUR MANUFACTURER

If you have narrowed your list down to one or two manufacturers, you may want begin negotiations on terms.

IDENTIFY PRECISELY WHAT IS BEING MADE

A detailed product specification is critical. You'd be surprised how often these tend to get either left to the last minute or never completed. That is another reason to have an engineer representing your interests involved in the deal.

MANUFACTURER'S PRICING

You can structure the pricing and rates in many different ways. Below are some examples:

Per unit. A "per unit" rate is usually a set price per unit delivered and accepted. The actual per unit rate usually goes down incrementally with greater volume.

Cost Plus. "Cost Plus" is payment of costs plus a fixed amount of profit for every unit. Cost Plus often has a cap per unit, per number of units or over a period of time so there is a built-in ceiling on the total price.

Shared Savings Under Budget. You can also split amounts saved under the project budget, which may encourage efficiency. If you are going to help subsidize increases in costs, you should share the benefits if costs go down.

Incentives for Early or Timely Delivery or For a Certain Quality Standard. You can also provide financial incentives that kick in if the manufacturer delivers on time or reaches a certain quality standard.

After you have some quotes, figure out your tariff code and how much it will add to your costs, including shipping, duties, customs and other fees. No matter what, ask for price reductions.

PAYMENT TERMS

The manufacturer may want payment up front or a letter of credit from a bank that gets paid on delivery of goods. It is never prudent to pay 100% in advance, because it kills your leverage. 30% is standard, but they may demand more, particularly if you are new.

If you get a letter of credit, try to negotiate the language that provides when the manufacturer gets paid.

QUALITY CONTROL REQUIREMENTS

Often, quality control standards, milestones and procedures are placed in the contract, in detail. Quality control is the process created to verify that the product meets the specifications and the minimal quality and functional standards. Quality control includes milestone deliverables, inspection, testing and peer reviews and early warning systems.

SCHEDULE OF DELIVERABLES

The contract may include a specific description of the number and delivery schedule of products. Consider:

- ✓ Your sales cycle
- ✓ The process of getting paid by buyers
- ✓ Storage costs and availability
- ✓ Inspection time and procedures
- ✓ Shipping costs and availability

SHIPPING TIME

Port to port deliveries often take between 3-4 weeks. Be aware also of local holidays that could disrupt business time. For instance, in January, Chinese industry can shut down for a couple of weeks.

TERM

The contract may include a specific duration. How long should the contract last? Maintaining flexibility with a shorter deal may be important, but a longer relationship gives you more assurances that, once you spend the initial capital needed to ramp up, you will have a contract for enough time to turn a profit. A longer contract could also enable you to negotiate a lower per unit price and to lock in prices as a hedge against inflation.

MANUFACTURER'S RISK MANAGEMENT

The manufacturing contract is a tool in recognizing, allocating and managing risk. Brainstorm potential problems to try to address contingencies during the contracting process, rather than leaving potential problems to be sorted out after they occur. Once you have identified risks, there are two key questions: (1) How can you structure the deal to minimize risks? (2) If certain risks can't be avoided, or should be taken in a calculated manner, which party will bear that risk? In addition, here are some ways to protect yourself.

Early Warning Systems. These can be created to help you learn things are going wrong while you still have time to fix them or to go elsewhere.

Level of Quality Necessary. Quality levels that determine which goods will be accepted should be listed (e.g. all-or-nothing vs. acceptance of substandard goods at a reduced price.)

"Plan B" Contingency Plans. A back-up plan for manufacture could kick in if certain quality or time thresholds aren't met.

Non-Disclosure Agreement. This should be put in place to protect your IP.

Performance Bonds. These may be an option to consider to hedge against manufacturer failure.

5. START YOUR MANUFACTURING

When you schedule your manufacturing will depend on your fulfillment strategy. If you pick MTS, then you schedule your manufacturing to meet your sales seasons and the stocking schedules and demands of your distributors and retailers. But, if you pick one of the fulfillment strategies that delays manufacturing until your get a sale, then you have to arrange manufacture or assembly to meet that strategy. It's a balancing act – you'd be surprised how many companies screw it up.

WAR STORIES

THE DELOREAN

THE WAR

After entertaining offers of capital assistance from several U.S. cities, John DeLorean decided to build the assembly plant for his new sports car in Northern Ireland. The Northern Ireland location had several advantages, most notably stronger backing by the government and cheaper labor. For instance, he raised $175 million to finance DeLorean Motors: $12 million in equity and $156 million in grants and loans from the British government. In exchange, DeLorean agreed to locate the DMC factory in Northern Ireland.

Production started two years late and with minimal training and oversight. Many DeLoreans, especially the first ones, had poor quality and sloppily produced interiors because there hadn't been time to train the plant's workers how to build cars. Doors leaked, and the car had electrical gremlins, among other problems. This forced the DeLorean operation to set up several U.S. "Quality Assurance Centers." They did major reworking of the autos before delivery to dealers and ate heavily into company profits. At one point, it took 140 hours to make the DeLorean suitable for sale--at a cost of up to $2,000 per auto.

The car hit the market in 1981 and was $26,000, $8,000 more than the Corvette. To break even, DeLorean needed to sell 12,000 cars per year. But, for the first 6 months, he had sold only 3,000. By 1982, the company was in receivership, and the British government shut it down.

THE WINNER

The Producers of *Back to the Future*.

MORAL OF THE STORY

Manufacturing in another country might save money in the short run, but the eventual cost depends on the quality of the workforce and management. And, wherever you manufacture, you need mechanisms in place that will detect quality problems at every step.

WAR STORIES

THE LIMITS OF A VEST

THE WAR

A police officer was shot and killed during a routine traffic stop while wearing the defendant's bulletproof vest. The bullet struck him just below the armpit in a spot the vest didn't cover (Linegar v. Armour of America 909 F.2d 1150 (8th Cir. 1990)). The officer's wife sued, alleging products liability.

THE WINNER

The vest's manufacturer (and not the victim's widow). The court thought that no consumer would expect the vest to protect an area it didn't cover. While the vest could be redesigned to completely cover the torso, that would make the vest more expensive and less maneuverable, needlessly restricting consumer choice.

MORAL OF THE STORY

The law will likely not seek to hold you as an insurer for every accident, though this should not alleviate your obligation to take safety measures.

THE PINTO

THE WAR

Ford's crash tests showed the Pinto's gas tank would rupture in rear-end collisions at relatively low speeds, often resulting in fires. In an infamous internal memo, Ford executives passed around a cost/benefit analysis showing it would be cheaper to settle lawsuits with burn victims than to fix the cars for $11 each.

THE WINNER

A victim won an award of $126 million. Ford was indicted for reckless homicide in an Indiana court after three teenage girls burned to death in a Pinto. Even though the punitive damage award was eventually reduced and the company was found "not guilty" in the criminal case, the publicity was a huge blow to Ford. They eventually did a voluntary recall.

MORAL OF THE STORY

If your product is defective, fix it.

HAP AND HAZ HIRE A MANUFACTURER

Hap and Haz talked at length about their manufacturing needs. They decided that:

✓ All things being equal or close to equal, they would rather manufacture completely in the U.S. because of the marketing benefits, reduced travel and storage costs as well as trade costs, and the availability of incentives from governments. In addition, Hap and Haz decided to trade the potential lower per piece price for better and easier oversight over suppliers and manufacturers, shorter lead times, better communication, easier quality checks, ability to quickly and cheaply inspect manufacturing facilities.

✓ They would need to follow the standard retail cycle, so they would need deliveries in May (for back to school) and by August (for Christmas).

Hap and Haz used the 5 S-teps to pick a manufacturer.

Specify. First, they gathered the information provided by the prototype manufacturer and the designs prepared by Seymour.

Search. Hap and Hazard next put out a broad request for manufacturers. They sent emails to dozens of people in their contacts. They posted a request for recommendations on their Facebook page. They called their prototype maker and asked for a recommendation. They asked Gravity. They asked Seymour. They searched the web. Eventually, they came up with ten candidates. They sent requests for proposals to each of the ten candidates along with NDAs. Out of the ten candidates, six returned the NDAs signed; in response, Hap sent back the package of designs and specifications. From the bids submitted by the six candidates, Hap and Hazard whittled the list down to three.

Screen. Hap and Hazard contacted the references provided by each of the three candidates. One of the candidates got 86'ed because a reference was the manager's brother; and the brother had nothing nice to say about the candidate. One of the two remaining candidates had scheduling limitations, which left just one: Bolla Manufacturing of Allegan, Michigan, which also offered distribution centers and trucking services.

Solidify. Now, it was time to negotiate terms. After the back and forth of 4 term sheets, Hap and Hazard agreed to the following terms:

ITEM	TERM
ENGAGEMENT	BOLLA will make the MouseTrap in accordance with MouseTrap LLC's orders
ORDER SPECS	1,000 bundles
PRICE	$7.00/unit for orders of 1,000-2,500 $5.50/unit for orders of 2,501-5,000 $4.00/unit for orders of 5,001+
DELIVERY	45 days following order date
IP OWNERSHIP	Hap and Haz own all IP
CONFIDENTIALITY/NONCIRCUMENTION	MFG may not disclose designs, plans, schemes or contract MFG may not make similar device
QUALITY CONTROL	Internally, MFG will implement quality control and inspections Externally, written notification (by email) when production begins, at the midway point, and at the end; overnight delivery of three product units for inspection Right to inspect plant during business hours
WARRANTY	Product will be free from defects for one year past the end user's initial purchase

Start. Once you have your contract, cash and a place to stick your product when it's done, you can start your manufacturer's engines.

With Gravity's help, Hap and Hazard entered into a manufacturing agreement with Bolla Manufacturing and promptly placed an order for 1,000 units.

With the product in development, Hap took over. Hap realized that he would need to put in place an entire sales infrastructure to move the MouseTrap into the market. So, they went to see Gravity.

"Gravity, I was hoping we could go over laws governing sales and marketing. Could you help me?"

"I CAN TRY."

END NOTES

1 The FCC was created under the Communications Act of 1934 (47 USC §151 and 47 §USC 154). The FCC regulates broadband, radio spectrum and broadcasting and interstate telecommunications including wire, satellite and cable.

2 47 CFR 15.

3 **Federal Statute**. There is no omnibus federal privacy law. Instead, there are a rag tag bunch of statutes. The big statutes include: Children's Online Privacy Protection Act of 1998; Fair Credit Reporting Act (consumer credit); Family Educational Rights and Privacy Act (student records); Health Insurance Portability and Accountability Act (health); Gramm-Leach-Bilely Act (banking).

FTC Act. Oddly, the biggest regulatory burden at the federal level comes from no statute at all, but from the FTC's interpretation of The FTC Act. The FTC Act prohibits practices that are unfair and deceptive. The FTC then says that failure to abide by security or privacy policies is deceptive; and, that it is unfair practice to not have reasonable data security practices. That means that if you take in consumer data, you have to have reasonable data security practices. And, if you have a privacy policy, you have to follow it.

State Law. There is also tons of state law that protects privacy.

4 All reasonable security policies should guard against internal threats and include administrative, physical and technical safeguards. These procedures follow the Health Insurance Portability and Accountability Act (which, with Gramm-Leach-Biliely Act, are the most well developed American laws on privacy). See Milewski, Anthony D. Jr., Compliance with California Privacy Laws, 2006.

5 *California Civil Code Section 1798.81.5*

6 In the Matter of Upromise, Inc., a corporation, File No. 102 3116 (April 3, 2012).

7 For instance, Gramm-Leach-Blilely requires financial institutions to create an Information Security Program. Massachusetts requires every company that maintains PII about a Massachusetts resident must implement and maintain appropriate security measures. Massachusetts Data Protection Law, MA 201 CMR 17.00.

8 CA Civil Code § 1798.83.

9 Massachusetts has a law (MGL Chapter 93H Section 3) which creates the obligation to report known security breaches and unauthorized use of personal information. Breaches and unauthorized use must be reported to the Massachusetts Attorney General, the Massachusetts Office of Consumer Affairs & Business Regulation ("OCABR"), and the owners of the personal information affected. Also, California Civil Code Section 1798.81.5.

10 The Fair and Accurate Credit Transactions Act of 2003 (15 USC §1681 et. seq) authorized the FTC's Disposal Rule (16 CFR 682), effective June 1, 2005. Go to: ftc.gov/os/2004/11/041118disposalfrn.pdf.

11 Go look at ftc.gov/privacy/privacyinitiatives/safeguards.html

12 Sections 604, 606, and 615 Fair Credit Reporting Act ("FCRA") 15 USC §1681 et. seq.

13 15 U.S.C. §§ 6501 et seq., 16 C.F.R. § 312.

14 The COPPA regulation defines the term "collects" to encompass providing a child with the ability to have an e-mail account or the ability to post to a chat room, bulletin board, or other online forum. COPPA also requires a covered Web site to disclose in a notice its online information collection and use practices with respect to children, and provide parents with the opportunity to review the personal information collected online from their children.

15 Called the "Single Operator Designee."

16 Law note: Section 15 of the Securities Exchange Act of 1934 is the big source of law for regulation of broker-dealers. People who sell stock for other people are usually required to be registered brokers with the Financial Industry Regulatory Authority ("FINRA"). Brokers do not (currently) owe fiduciary duties to their clients, but do have to limit recommendations to clients that are suitable for the particular client. Brokers typically get paid commissions on trades. Btw, dealers trade for themselves; brokers trade for others. There are also state laws governing broker dealers.

17 Law note: Investment Advisors Act of 1940 is the big source of law for regulation of investment advisors. 15 U.S.C. § 80b-1 through 15 U.S.C. § 80b-21.

18 Investment Company Act of 1940, 15 U.S.C. §§ 80a-1–80a-64.

19 The Conference Committee on Laws and Regulations works with the National Institute of Standards and Technology.

20 The Fair Packaging and Labeling Act 15 USC §1543(1967).

21 These labeling rules do not apply to industrial products such as insecticides, fungicides, and rodenticides which are under the jurisdiction of the Environmental Protection Agency (EPA). In addition rules for labeling cars, Christmas lights, greeting cards, hardware, ink, school supplies and sewing accessories, small arms ammunition, cigarette lighters, lawn and garden supplies, souvenirs, clothing and other textiles, magnetic recording tape, stationary and writing supplies, durable goods, paints and kindred products, threads, gift ties and tapes, pet care supplies, tools, gift wraps, safety flares, toys, safety pins, typewriter ribbons are handled elsewhere.

22 The Office of Weights and Measures of the National Institute of Standards and Technology, U.S. Department of Commerce, is authorized to promote to the greatest practicable extent uniformity in State and Federal regulation of the labeling of consumer commodities.

23 The Tariff Act, 19 USC 1304.

24 Restatement (Second), Torts, Section 402A. And See Restatement (Third), Torts: Products Liability, Editor's Note, Comment n.

25 Some states protect the parties down the chain, like distributors, wholesalers and retailers, from strict liability. Products liability is still developing in Europe and Australia and is nearly non-existent in the developing world.

26 Restatement (Third) Torts, Products Liability, Section 2(a).

27 Restatement (Third) Torts, Products Liability, Section 2(b).

28 Ford v. Matthews, 291 So.2d 169.

29 For instance, some states have a "cooling off" period which is an automatic return period for consumers.

30 The CPSC was created under the Consumer Product Safety Act of 1972, 15 USC 2051 et seq.

31 This list includes products excluded from CPSC jurisdiction.

32 To get acclimated to the site, try searching people in 2008 that were injured by "foreign bodies" trapped in their "lower trunks."

33 A "manufacturer" is anyone who makes, produces, or assembles a product, imports a product or donates a product.

34 Reporting obligation applies to all acts that the CPSC enforces (i.e. Federal Hazardous Substances act, Flammable Fabrics Act, Poison Prevention Packaging Act, Refrigerator Safety Act, in addition, of course, to the Consumer Products Safety Act).

35 Section 15(b) of the CPSA. Also applies to the other acts that the CPSC enforces (i.e. FHSA, FFA, PPPA, & RSA in addition to the CPSA)

36 Phthalates are a group of chemicals that are used to make vinyl and plastics soft and flexible.

37 Flammable Fabrics Act 15 USC §§1191-1204 (1953).

38 Consumer Product Safety Improvement Act of 2008, Public Law 110-314.

39 Some of the testing protocols may actually be created by industry groups. For instance, the Toy Industry Association sets testing standards for the toy industry.

40 Among the products that have to be currently tested are clothes, shoes, personal care items, accessories, jewelry, home furnishings, bedding, toys, electronics, video games, books, school supplies, educational materials and science kits. Failure to comply can result in fines of $100,000 per violation, $15 million for related violations, forfeiture and 5 years in prison.

41 Want an example of a statement about products intended for children that is the opposite of reasonable? Go watch:

   http://www.hulu.com/watch/115713/saturday-night-live-irwin-mainway.

42
http://www.toyassociation.org/AM/Template.cfm?Section=Toy_Safety&CONTENTID=1476&TEMPLATE=/CM/HTMLDisplay.cfm.

43 Consumer Product Safety Improvement act of 2008

44 Child Safety Protection Act of 1994 - http://www.cpsc.gov/cpscpub/pubs/282.html.

45 http://www.cpsc.gov/webcast/etsy.pdf

46 The Tariff Act of 1930.

47 Resource Conservation and Recovery Act ("RCRA") 42 USCA 690 et seq.

48 Some wastes are exempt from the regulations – the list of exemptions is in 40 CFR 261.4.

49 Resource Conservation and Recovery Act (RCRA) 42 USCA 6901-6992(k) regulates handling of hazardous waste and Comprehensive Environmental Response, Compensation & Liability Act (CERCLA 42 USCA 9601-9675 regulates emergency cleanup of hazardous waste

50 There are four lists of hazardous waste, called, essentially: F, K, P and U.

51 Comprehensive Environmental Response, Compensation, and Liability Act (CERCLA), 42 U.S.C.A. § 9622.

52 42 USCA 6903.

53 33 USCA 1362.

54 Toxic Substances Control Act ("TSCA") 42 USC §9604.

55 Id.

56 29 CFR 1910.1200

57 Emergency Planning and Community Right to Know Act ("EPCRA") 42 USC §11001 et. seq. (1986).

58 Federal Hazardous Substances Act ("FHSA") 15 USC 1261-1278 (1960).

59 Mercury-Containing and Rechargeable Battery Management Act, 42 USC § 137 (1996).

60 Endangered Species Act of 1973, 16 USCA 532.

61 Secretary of Interior/Administrators has jurisdiction for animals, but Secretary of Commerce watches over marine species.

62 Sweet Home Chapter, 515 US 687 (1995)

63 CRS Endangered Species: A Primer, updated 9/27/06

64 42 USCA § 7408 (a)

65 EPA has a list of nightmare pollutants and those that meet the criteria get named "hazardous air pollutants" under 42 USCA § 7412(r)(5)

66 Focused on six "criteria" pollutants: carbon monoxide, lead, sulfur dioxide, particulate matter, ozone and nitrogen oxides.

67 EPA has list of Class I and Class II substances that hurt the ozone layer. Class I are phased out. Class II are phasing out till 2030. There are regulations that affect the manufacture, sale and disposal or recycling of air conditioners, refrigerators, freezer and chillers.

67 42 USCA 7602(k)

68 42 USCA 7554

69 42 USCA 7604(a)

70 Clean Water Act, 33 USC §1251 et. seq (1972).

71 Marina Protection Research and Scat Act of 1972, 33 USCA 1412 and 1413

72 40 CFR 220.3(e).

73 33 USC 1321 (b)(3)

74 Section 404 of the Clean Water Act.

75 15USCA 2601 – et 4245CA 7401 et seq.

76 Federal government is authorized under the Import-Export Clause, US Constitution, Art I, S. 10, Cl. 2., to "regulate imports and levy customs duties." States cannot impose duties other than inspection without Congressional consent. The Treasury Department and its Customs Service creates the rules and run things. The Court of International Trade, an Article III court, has jurisdiction.

General Agreement on Tariff and Trade (GATT) of 1947 was the first post war trade agreement that (a) granted most favored nation status to signatories; (b) "national treatment for imported goods; (c) created anti-dumping frame; (d) created countervailing duties frame; and (e) customs valuation.

The Tariff Act of 1930 created the tariff regime. Under the act, "customs duties" are taxes on merchandise brought into a foreign country; "customs" are duties on commodities into a foreign countries; "export" means a thing that leaves your country bound specifically for another; and "import" means a thing that leaves one country and enters your country (a diversion to a domestic location make it not an import). Courts frequently interpret tariffs to protect American manufacturing particularly if highly manufactured are deemed to require a higher duty. Under North American Free Trade Agreement of 1994 (a/k/a NAFTA), US, Canada, Mexico created trilateral trade preferences.

77 Tariff Act of 1930 19 USCA 1304(a).

78 A trade program established by the Trade Act of 1974

79 The Rule of Relative Specificity.

80 Foreign trade Zone Act, 19 USCA 81(a) et seq.

81 Legal profession: never

82 Legal profession: Westlaw, Lexis

83 Legal profession: incorporation, real estate closings

84 Just in Time manufacturing ("JIT") is not included in this table. Often, people refer to JIT as the act of making or putting the product together only when you have an order and a customer. JIT is a method of manufacturing that triggers the next phase of production with some signal or trigger. Based on the philosophy that inventory is waste. JIT is more a process than a strategy, and can be used as part of any of these strategies.

85 Legal profession: most contracts, some motions

86 Legal profession: difficult, new contracts, most litigation

87 RIP, Frank Sabotka.

88 I can't vouch for this list or the members; I just point out that it's out there.

89 The Department of Labor's List of Goods Produced By Child Labor or Forced Labor: Report Required by the Trafficking Victims Protection Reauthorization Acts of 2005 and 2008, The United States Department of Labor, Bureau of International Labor Affairs, Office of Child Labor, Forced Labor and Human Trafficking (September 10, 2009): http://www.dol.gov/ilab/programs/ocft/PDF/2009TVPRA.pdf

GETTING IT SOLD

section five

CHAPTERS IN THIS SECTION:

PICK A SALES STRATEGY

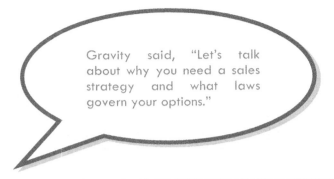

Gravity said, "Let's talk about why you need a sales strategy and what laws govern your options."

CHAPTER 19

WHY YOU NEED A SALES STRATEGY

Making your product is just the beginning – you also have to sell it. Your options for how to sell your product will bear on every aspect of your business. Your distribution channel selection will impact the execution of your fulfillment strategy. If you hire sales staff, you have to comply with employment laws. If you create an ad campaign, you're going to need a budget for advertising placement fees (a/k/a ad spend) and you'll need to clear the ads for compliance. If you adopt an Internet strategy, you're going to need to comply with the laws prohibiting spam.

Just like every other part of business, there are various laws that govern all of the options you have for selling your product. Some of the penalties for violating these laws are severe. Moreover, once you start selling, your actions and their effects make a wider arc across the world, exposing you to more risk. At stake is the successful roll-out of your product line and your continued freedom from prosecution.

PICK POTENTIAL CUSTOMERS

Knowing your customers help you make the plan to reach them. Who is the customer for your product? Who would use it? What features in your product appeal to particular people? For instance, the MouseTrap is a computer mouse that captures, stores and transmits solar power, for laptops. Potential customers include millions of users, companies who employ computer users, distributors

of office equipment, and computer bundlers like Dell. In addition, the renewable technology may appeal to consumers who value green technology, power cost reduction and extreme mobility. This technology, which has vexed thousands of businesses, may also be decoupled from its application in the MouseTrap and either sold or licensed. That means potential customers of the MouseTrap include:

- ✓ individual and corporate end users
- ✓ distributors
- ✓ computer bundlers
- ✓ retail stores
- ✓ licensees
- ✓ potential buyers of the business

PICK A DISTRIBUTION CHANNEL

Once you have an idea of who your customers will be, you need to plan how you will reach them. The DISTRIBUTION CHANNEL is the journey your product will take from manufacture to ultimate use. The Distribution Channel is part of the SUPPLY CHAIN, the system and physical work of manufacturing, transporting and storing goods, and providing market research, credit programs and other marketing support. Your sales (and your manufacturing) plans must be tightly coordinated with your supply chain. A link in the chain that comes undone or is not fastened to the next chain link in the right order can disrupt or kill your business.

In selecting a distribution channel, consider your future customers. You could reach them through retail stores, through representatives who then sell to retail stores, directly through your own store (with bricks and/or Internet routers), or as an addition to the bundled products they sell. You could also try and sell the entire product line to someone and get out of the business altogether. You can choose a dual channel strategy, which are two or more channels. Consider your sales cycle, the seasons of your manufacture and parties in the supply chain, world events, the needs of your customers to receive, inspect and distribute your product and a zillion other factors. The key is to plot every step along the way from raw material to delivery to your customer and make sure it all works together with plans for disruptions.

Channels include (1) direct, (2) retail, (3) middlemen, and (4) agents.

1. DIRECT CHANNEL

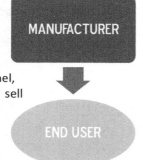

In a DIRECT CHANNEL, the manufacturer and seller are the same. Through a direct channel, you would seek to sell directly to any end user through your own retail store. Examples include Dell (though Dell also distributes from manufacturers), Apple, traditional mail order products and Hammacher Schlemmer.

For a direct channel, you may want the following direct channel contracts: (a) a purchase order that lists the good, price, quantity, specifications, delivery date, shipping arrangements and who bears the risk of loss; (b) a contract of sale, bill of sale or terms and conditions of sale that either confirms the terms in the purchase order or proposes a counter offer, which must be countersigned by the buyer to solidify the terms in the contract of sale; and (c) a warranty. If the contract of sale is in the form of Terms and Conditions on a website, then you want to make them applicable to the sale, point to the proof of order and payment and have the buyer acknowledge them.

Sales employees. You could hire a direct sales force in areas where you intend to concentrate sales efforts. Once you hire people, you become subject to employment laws. (See Section 1, Chapter "Getting Help") Further, many countries outside of the United States have laws that make it difficult to terminate employment or even independent contractor relationships, so make sure to consult a lawyer before proceeding.

2. RETAIL

In a RETAIL CHANNEL, the manufacturer sells either to or through a retailer on the way to the end user. This is the most widely known channel. Examples include every store in the universe that sells goods it did not make or have made itself.

The contract with a retailer is much different than the agreement with an individual user – particularly if your retail buyer is a chain of stores. First, you won't be able to write the contract – you'll get the buyer's standard form and you'll read it. Second, you probably won't be able to change much or any of the contract. Most, if not all, of it will be take-it-or-leave-it. Some of the terms may be onerous or surprising. For instance, you'll certainly need to prove you have a big insurance policy. You'll have to promise that you will protect the retailer if your product causes any trouble for the retailer. There may be substantial inventory obligations, which will require you to implement a Made-To-Stock fulfillment strategy. Some retailers will actually buy the product from you, often with a right to return unsold product units. But, some retailers will take the product "on consignment," which means they take possession, but not ownership and sell as your agent. If you sell product on consignment, you are best protected by retaining a security interest in the product and filing a UCC-1 to perfect your security interest (See Section 2, Debt). Also, your margin on products sold to big box stores will be very small.

INTERNET SALES

You can sell at retail through a brick and mortar store and through the Internet. You can also sell via the websites of brick and mortar stores. There are a number of platforms on the Internet where you can sell. Here is just a sample.

- ⇨ www.etsy.com
- ⇨ www.SupermarketHQ.com
- ⇨ http://en.dawanda.com
- ⇨ www.ponoko.com
- ⇨ www.ShopFlick.com
- ⇨ www.ebay.com
- ⇨ www.amazon.com
- ⇨ www.shapeways.com

3. SALE TO MIDDLEMEN

Middlemen take the product from the manufacturer and re-sell it. There are different varieties of middlemen.

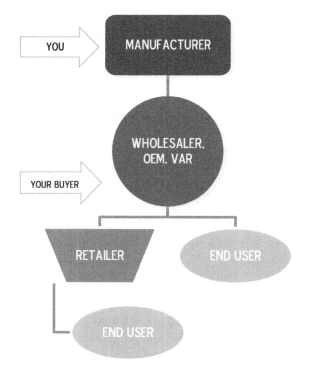

DISTRIBUTORS (A/K/A WHOLESALERS)

Distributors buy the product and keep it in inventory. As a result, they are treated as major customers of the manufacturer. Distributors may arrange for shipment and importation. Often to get access to certain markets, you really need to get a distributor to represent your products. For instance, food distributors can be critical to breaking food products into grocery stores.

IMPORT WHOLESALER

Import Wholesalers source product in other countries and bring it over for resale to retailers. Due to knowledge about laws and customs of the manufacturing home country, import wholesalers may also ease fulfillment.

ORIGINAL EQUIPMENT MANUFACTURERS ("OEM")

OEMs buy product from the original manufacturer, slap their brand on it and sell it as their own. This is a surprisingly widespread business practice. Many major brands have an OEM strategy that takes in product, subject to their strict contractual terms.

VALUE ADDED RESELLERS ("VAR")

VARs buy product, add some feature or modification to it and resell it, often as their own product.

4. SALES AGENTS
(A/K/A MANUFACTURER'S REPRESENTATIVE, BROKER)[1]

SALES AGENTS are people or companies who represent you and your products and try to sell your products on your behalf. Sales agents sell to both wholesalers and retailers, but often don't take ownership of product. Instead, they obtain samples and sell from the sample, leaving the party up the chain to supply. Agents often work only on commission.

RESIDENT SALES AGENT

Resident Sales Agents are manufacturer's representatives in a country who hold merchandise for others to come and view. These are good resources for smaller retailers with limited resources to find new products.

Buying Offices are businesses that match retailers to manufacturers and products, sort of like a product matchmaker.

AFFILIATE PROGRAMS

The Internet version of sales agents is the Affiliate Program, in which people are deputized to sell products for a website. If you create an affiliate program, you would provide a special, unique link for your affiliate's site to your product page. Each time a user clicks on the link and buys your product, your affiliate gets a cut.

SALES REP VS. MANUFACTURER REP

Sales representatives and manufacturer's representatives can have different definitions depending on the industry—sometimes one or both of them mean a member of the company's direct sales force or a wholesale distributor. A wholesale distributor takes title to the goods and resells them at her own price. A wholesale distributor taking title means less risk for you - you make the sale whether they are able to resell or not, unless the wholesale distributor extracts a promise from you to take back unsold product.

DIVVYING THE RETAILERS

Retailers can be broken up by their characteristics: (1) ownership; (2) pricing types; (3) product assortment; and (4) service level.

OWNERSHIP

Ownership means the kind of proprietor who operates the store. For instance:

- ✓ Large national chain store
- ✓ Smaller regional chain store
- ✓ Franchisee
- ✓ Independent retailer

PRODUCT ASSORTMENT

Product assortment is the number of products offered. Includes breadth or depth of products.

- ✓ **Breadth**. The number of brands for sale (Ann Taylor has lots of breadth).
- ✓ **Depth**. The number of product types (Kmart has lots of depth).

SERVICE LEVEL

Service level includes the package of services stores use to make you love them. Specialty shops have a higher service level, including store credit cards, alternatives, and a generous return policy.

RETAIL PRICING TYPES

Pricing trajectory includes discounter or full price stores. Types of discounters include:

- ✓ Factory outlet
- ✓ Consignment store
- ✓ Dollar stores
- ✓ Specialty discount stores
- ✓ Warehouse membership clubs

CONTRACT WITH MIDDLEMAN OR DISTRIBUTOR

Regardless of what you call her, there are common terms to work out with your middlemen and distributors.

Identify the Products. Specifically identify the products she will sell or represent.

Buy or Sell. State whether she will buy the products from you and then sell them to new customers or just sell them for you to new customers.

Credit Terms. She may need to buy products from you on credit. If you are extending credit, list the credit terms and get a security interest in unpaid for product and file a UCC-1 to perfect it.

Exclusive or Non-Exclusive. Exclusivity is usually pegged to a geographic region. Will there be others or will your rep have the market to herself?

Distribution Structures. Distribution arrangements can be (a) exclusive distribution; (b) selective distribution; and (c) intensive distribution. **Exclusive Distribution** is the sole right or obligation to sell in a particular geographic region. In exchange, the manufacturer may provide sales help, training and marketing materials. **Selective Distribution** means careful selection of distributor to highlight a feature of the product or appeal to a particular audience. For instance, some clothing designers will only sell in pricey boutiques to promote and preserve the rarity and luxury of their brand. **Intensive Distribution** means ubiquitous distribution, which requires a robust wholesale system. Not usually selected by the retailer, but picked by the manufacturer or market. (The perfect example: Crest Toothpaste.)

Territory. Even if it is not exclusive, frequently sales reps are given a specific geographic territory. The territory should be defined.

Quotas. Often, sales reps are required to sell a minimum amount of revenues or sales to stay in good standing, or even to earn incentive compensation. Is there purchase and sale quota? If so, how much and how often?

Minimum Support. With more complicated or novel products, often a sales rep has to make sure that her staff has enough knowledge in the product to be able to competently sell it. Sometimes, this knowledge requirement is met through training programs offered by the manufacturer. Does she have to provide a minimum level of staff and training? Will you provide training?

Your Marketing Obligations. Manufacturers often commit to minimum spending or marketing efforts in the sales rep's territory. What are your obligations on marketing materials or campaigns?

Pricing. Telling your distributors how to price your products is fraught with legal dangers. If you want to impose a pricing plan or policy, get a lawyer who knows antitrust law to guide you.

Commissions. What is the commission structure? Typically, commissions are somewhere between 5% and 25%. Payment is usually made monthly or quarterly with a true up at the end of the year.

Control Rights. You should keep the right to reject a sale, particularly if the sales rep is not taking ownership of the product.

Commission Earned. You should carefully define when your agent or rep has earned her commission. Specifically, you should stick in the contract (a) what events have to happen to equal a "sale"; (b) what events have to happen to give her credit for the sale; (c) what events could happen that would require her to pay the commission back; and (d) if different types of sales generate different commissions, define those clearly.

Noncompetition. List any prohibitions on her ability to sell competing products or any other products at all. This is often subject to negotiation. (See Section 1, Chapter 2, "Getting Help – Restrictive Covenants.")

Fights. Typically, the manufacturer would promise that the products don't violate third party intellectual property rights or applicable laws if used as intended. In return, the sales rep promises not to make any warranties about the product beyond what the manufacturer provides. Any breaches of these promises and any gross negligence or willful misconduct should trigger an obligation on the bad guy to indemnify the other person. Where and how you will litigate or fight disputes should be worked out, particularly if your sales agents or distributors are located far away.

Termination. Prescribe how you can end the relationship if things don't work out. Often, the parties require notice of a termination. Sometimes a sales rep will be able to sell through her existing inventory. Alternatively, you could demand the inventory back in exchange for payment.

Discounts. For sales to manufacturer's reps or bulk buyers, you may have to or want to give discounts to encourage big orders and early payment. Below are some typical wholesale discount programs.

WHOLESALE DISCOUNT PROGRAMS

"2/10, n/30" is a typical cash discount. Buyer gets a 2% discount (excluding shipping) if she pays in 10 days; otherwise, the entire amount is due in 30 days.

"2/10, 60 days extra" gives the buyer an extra 60 days before the usual terms of 2/10, n/30 take effect – so a June invoice is eligible for the 2% discount until September. Future dating is used to encourage retailers to buy in advance of the selling season.

"8/10 EOM" gives the buyer an 8% discount if the invoice is paid within 10 days after the **end of the month**.

As of a certain date is another type of discount, which allows a discount to begin in the future as of a certain date.

Price guaranty is a promise that if the wholesale price goes down, the vendor will refund the difference.

Off price merchandise is merchandise out of season, not selling well or returned, that may be provided at a discount based on a percent of the amount of regular merchandise that the retailer has purchased. Often, the retailer has no choice about the sizes and styles shipped and sales are final.

AVOID ANTI-COMPETITIVE TACTICS[2]

In your selling practices, you have to be careful that you don't stumble into anticompetitive practices. "Anticompetitive practices" are methods of doing business that unfairly squelch competition. Outlawed anticompetitive acts can be divided in two: the bad and the worse. The bad anticompetitive acts are the ones that could be ok if the market, motives, execution and the effects of the anticompetitive actions overall enhance competition to the benefit of the consumer. [3] The worse acts – ones that are so damaging to competition that no purpose or good intent can justify it – are just "per se illegal" – there is no defense.

Penalties[4] include prison, fines up to $10,000,000 or double your gain or your victim's loss caused by the violation. Worse, in private suits, treble damages – triple damages - are automatically awarded. The law against anti-competitive tactics is one of the bite-you-in-the-neck areas of law that you just don't see coming, particularly because some businesspeople use "standard" tactics as just a part of doing business that turn out to be unlawful.

Some things that can be "anti-competitive" include (1) agreements with competitors; (2) agreements with customers; (3) agreements with distributors; (4) relations with suppliers; (5) creating a monopoly; and (6) charging competitors different prices.

1. AGREEMENTS WITH COMPETITORS

Agreements with your competitors to shape the market are criminally illegal, including agreeing with a competitor on (a) pricing; (b) sales terms; (c) production limits or speed; (d) amounts of exports or imports; (e) division or allocation of customers, territories or products; and (f) design and quality standards. Agreeing with a competitor (g) to refuse to do business or limit business to a particular buyer or seller (an unlawful JOINT BOYCOTT); and (h) to rotate bids or disclose bids in advance (a/k/a Bid Rigging) are against the law. This type of "agreement" can even arise merely from comparing notes at a trade show.

2. AGREEMENTS WITH CUSTOMERS

Agreements with customers can be per se illegal, particularly if (a) you refuse to deal with someone based on your agreement with your customer; or (b) you make your customer buy one product in order to get a second. In addition, discriminatory pricing – giving customers at the same distribution level different prices – can be illegal, unless you can meet the technicalities of an exception. (Customer complaints about other customers' discounts is a huge source of antitrust liability.) It also may be illegal to pay a customer for services or placement of goods or ads unless the opportunity is available to all competing customers. Finally, exclusive dealing and requirements contracts may be anticompetition.

3. AGREEMENTS WITH DISTRIBUTORS AND MANUFACTURER'S REPRESENTATIVES

Requiring a distributor or a manufacturer's representative to sell your products at a minimal price may be against the law. I say "maybe" because the U.S. Supreme Court overturned a 96 year old rule that said requiring your distributor to sell at a minimum price was definitely illegal, unless you simply adopted a uniformly applied minimum price policy – so this state of the law is in flux.[5]

Now, agreements by distributors to sell at a certain, minimal price will be legal if the benefits to competition outweigh the dangers to competition. In the old days, a manufacturer could and had to create a resale pricing policy (a/k/a Colgate Policy) and impose a pricing obligation as a condition of distributing products. This was tortuously viewed not as an "agreement" on pricing, but just a term of sale. Now, manufacturers should still put in a place a Colgate policy, but make sure it states that it promotes one of the procompetitive benefits that the Court liked in the Supreme Court Case, Leegin v. PSKS, 551 US 877 (enhancement of interbrand competition, reduction of free riding, increasing service and fostering new entry). And, since state law has not changed, manufacturers should still do a Colgate plan.

4. RELATIONS WITH SUPPLIERS

Even contracts with suppliers can get you in trouble. For instance, you cannot knowingly get discriminatory pricing, promotional services or an allowance if not available to competitors. Quid pro quo arrangements in which you each agree to buy from each other as a condition can also be a problem.

5. CREATING A MONOPOLY

It is also, arguably, unlawful to create a monopoly through a deal that creates a dominant share of sales. Mergers with competitors that would unreasonably restrain trade may be illegal. However, in the last decade, it is rare for mergers or deals to be denied consummation on antitrust grounds.

6. CHARGING COMPETITORS DIFFERENT PRICES

Charging competing buyers of products for resale different prices for goods of like grade and quality, regardless of packaging, may be anticompetitive.

LIMITED EXCEPTIONS

However, here are some exceptions:

Functional Prices. You can charge different prices to customer based on their placement in the distribution chain.

Practical Availability. If a discount is available to all, you may not be liable if a customer skips it.

Cost Justification. A discount can reflect cost of manufacturing, delivery, sale, but the rule is very technical.

Geographic Price Differences & Meeting Competitor Prices. If made in good faith to meet (but not beat) a lower price.

Changing Market Conditions. Discounts can be unevenly given to avoid product obsolescence, deterioration or selling out a discontinued line.

Sales to Nonprofits & Government. Discounts can be given to not for profit entities if not buying for resale and to government.

HAP GETS HAUGHTY

"Wow," said Hazard. "I had no idea how many levels there were to getting a product into stores. I guess I just assumed all products get sold directly to the stores by the company listed on the label. This sounds very complicated. And intimidating."

"It is surprisingly complex," said Gravity. "But think of it this way. Since there are so many distribution models, there are many more opportunities than you anticipated to get your product onto the shelves."

"Enough of this naval gazing," interrupted Hap. "I already know this. Let's get to the fun stuff: advertising law."

Hazard chuckled and said, "Gravity, can you teach Hap what he needs to know about advertising law, so he doesn't put us in the pokey?"

"I CAN TRY."

PLAN YOUR PROMOS

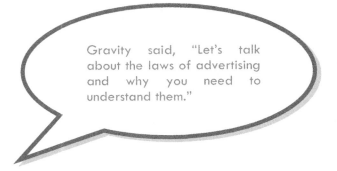

Gravity said, "Let's talk about the laws of advertising and why you need to understand them."

CHAPTER 20

THE LAWS OF ADVERTISING AND PROMOTING YOUR PRODUCT[6]

Advertising law is broad and robust. In the U.S., it begins with two prohibitions: First, you cannot use deceptive acts and practices. Second, cannot resort to "unfair competition," a broad set of strategies and tactics that are so egregious that they offend basic notions of commercial fairness. Examples of "unfair competition," include false advertising, price fixing and trade secret theft, among others.

Advertising is governed by the laws of the place where it is used. The U.S. has laws at the federal and state level. Internationally, each country has laws of its own. Violating these laws can be both expensive and embarrassing, particularly if you have to put out an ad retracting what you said before.

Regardless of your strategy, (1) your ads must be truthful, clear and fair; (2) your ads must be backed up with proof; (3) all the IP in the ads must be cleared; (4) you must comply with anti-spam laws; and (5) your communications with consumers must comply with all telemarketing laws.

1. ADS MUST BE TRUTHFUL, CLEAR AND FAIR

Anyone with a role in the promotion of a product has a risk of liability. Advertisers can be liable for deceptive ads, even if they don't know about the deception (strict liability). Individual officers could be held liable for deception. Ad agencies can be liable for deceptive ads if they knew or should have known about the deception. Endorsers, affiliate marketers

and ad networks all have a legal duty to avoid putting out deceptive claims.

TRUTHFUL, FAIR & NOT MISLEADING

It is illegal to use unfair methods of competition or unfair or deceptive acts or practices to sell stuff.[7] This is different, though intellectually similar, to the anticompetition rules we discussed in the previous chapter.

DECEPTIVE

A statement, promise or omission is DECEPTIVE if it is likely to mislead the average consumer in the target market and it is likely to affect the consumer's conduct or decision.

UNFAIR

A statement becomes UNFAIR if the ad is likely to harm the consumer without an offsetting benefit. UNFAIR METHODS OF COMPETITION include:

- ✓ Trying to force a business out of the market or to prevent them from entering the market, through predatory pricing and exclusivity
- ✓ Passing off someone else's goods as your own by associating your name, logo, or mark
- ✓ Defaming someone else's product's quality or characteristics
- ✓ Getting one to breach a contract with, or duty to, a competitor

2. ADS MUST BE BACKED UP WITH PROOF

All claims must be substantiated. Claims that cannot be substantiated must be disclaimed.

SUBSTANTIATION

A CLAIM is anything in an ad that is a fact that may be proven. Each claim must be a truthful statement: (a) on its own, without any other message; or (b) together in context with the other claims around it. Claims are SUBSTANTIATED by providing proof of the truthfulness of each claim.[8]

DISCLAIMERS

Any claims that cannot be substantiated should be disclaimed. A disclaimer is any statement that accompanies a claim in order to explain it. A disclaimer is used where the initial claim might be deemed unfair or deceptive in the absence of further explanation. A disclaimer qualifies a claim that might otherwise be deceptive if misconstrued. A disclaimer will not overcome an untruth. A disclaimer adds information to a claim, but should not be a way to backtrack on the claim. The disclaimer must be sufficiently conspicuous to have an effect on the consumer. The disclaimer must also have physical proximity to the claim. For instance, you can use a pointer or an asterisk near the claim to guide the reader to the disclaimer.

TESTIMONIALS

Testimonials must be substantiated on two levels. (1) If the speaker of the testimonial is saying the statement because it is scripted by the advertiser (whether or not for compensation) as if he means it, then the advertisement must make clear that the statement is not the actual thought or belief of the speaker; and (2) as usual, all claims must be substantiated.

COMPARISON TO COMPETITORS

Comparison to competitor advertising is allowed in the U.S., but the comparison must not be deceptive or unfair.

HEALTH AND DRUG ADS

Health and drug ads have special standards, including rules on disclaimers on possible side-effects.

GET RICH QUICK AND BUSINESS OPPORTUNITIES

Get rich business opportunities occupy a substantial amount of resources at the FTC and the FTC is wary of ads for them. Business and investment risks must be prominently disclosed in the ad.

KIDS

Ads for kids must be more circumspect since kids are a more gullible audience and less able to see an ad as mere puffery.

3. IP IN THE ADS MUST BE CLEARED

Ads are made from elements of intellectual property. Failure to get rights to ads could cost you money in legal fees or damages or your ability to use the ad. It is essential that all of the rights are obtained, including: (1) the rights to images, locations, music, graphics and animation; (2) all rights of publicity are obtained; and (3) all union payments and other talent payments are made.

4. RULES FOR SPAM

The CAN-SPAM Act of 2003[9] seeks to eradicate unsolicited ads sent by email and faxes. Only "commercial electronic mail messages" have to comply with CAN-SPAM, but not "transactional or relationship messages." Penalties for violation include fines and prison.

MESSAGES SUBJECT TO CAN-SPAM

A COMMERCIAL MESSAGE is one for which the primary purpose is to advertise or promote a commercial product or service. For instance, emails where there is a solicitation in the subject line, "above the fold" content" or the majority of the content is selling something are probably commercial messages.

MESSAGES NOT SUBJECT TO CAN-SPAM

TRANSACTIONAL OR RELATIONSHIP MESSAGES are emails to facilitate, complete or confirm a transaction, such as: warranty info; product information; product updates or upgrades; mostly invoicing information; sales receipt; account information; offers or ads in a transactional message if in a non-prominent position; emails to existing customers (even without permission); emails that are no more than roughly 20% commercial, 80% transactional; religious messages; political messages; content that complies with marketing requirements in law; and national security messages.

1. Give recipients a way to unsubscribe or opt out (a) that is clear and conspicuous; (b) that is either a reply to email or another "internet based mechanism;" (c) that is live (operational in the inbox) for 30 days after message is sent; and (d) that is fulfilled within 10 days. Have a process for handling unsubscribe emails within the 10-day window.

2. Make it apparent to a reasonable recipient that the email is an advertisement or solicitation (unless the recipient has given prior affirmative consent which is an opt in or double opt in). This may or may not require a specific disclosure, depending on whether the message is, on its face, clearly an advertising or solicitation.

3. Use accurate sender info.

4. Use relevant subject lines that relate to the offer in the body content and that are not deceptive.

5. Make the advertiser or publisher's address available.

6. Don't send sexually explicit content in the email unless you got an opt in from the recipient. Place a warning about access to sexually explicit content in the email's subject line. Limit the body of the email – or at least above the fold - to instructions on how to get to the sexually explicit content. Also, include your postal address, a notice the message is an advertisement or a solicitation, and a working unsubscribe mechanism. Precede adult content with the warning label "Sexually Explicit."

7. Don't send emails through an open relay (a SMTP server configuration used by spammers) to harvested email addresses or using a false header. Don't sell or give opt-out lists (suppression lists) to a third party.

8. To protect email addresses on your site from being harvested, add a notice that you don't "give, sell, or otherwise transfer" these addresses to "any other party for the purpose of initiating, or enabling others to initiate" email messages.

9. Offer recipients a way to receive some types of email from you while blocking others, along with a "global unsubscribe" option to stop all future email from your organization.

5. RULES FOR TELEMARKETERS

Telemarketing activities are sharply regulated by government at the federal and state level. For instance, under the Do Not Call law, people who want to limit sales calls to their homes can register their phone numbers with the Do Not Call Registry. Cell phones and fax numbers cannot be called by telemarketers.[10] Companies that engage in telemarketing must buy – for a surprisingly high price – the Do Not Call list in a certain geographic area and refrain from calling the people on the list. Do Not Call limits some calls, but there are many loopholes. Do Not Call does not bar: calls to businesses; calls from political organizations; calls from charities; calls from those conducting surveys; calls from companies with which there is or was purchases, payments or deliveries in the last 18 months, unless the person specifically asks the company not to call again; calls from a company up to 31 days after submitting an application or inquiry to that company, unless the company is specifically asked not to call; and calls from bill collectors (subject to laws regarding "reasonable hours" and bankruptcy). In addition to Do Not Call and similar state laws, the FTC prohibits deceptive acts and patterns of unsolicited telephone calls that a reasonable consumer would consider coercive or an invasion of privacy. The FTC also restricts calling hours and requires disclosure of the nature of the call. For the FTC's guide of current rules, go to: http://www.ftc.gov/bcp/edu/pubs/business/marketing/bus27.htm

CORTISLIM

THE WAR

CortiSlim ads promised that users would see fast and permanent weight loss after taking their weight loss pill. Unfortunately, the company had studies showing test subjects lost more weight taking a placebo pill than they did on CortiSlim. The ads featured celebrities in a mock talk show. The Federal Trade Commission sued the promoters of CortiSlim over the deceptive format of the ads and the inaccurate claims about weight loss.

THE WINNER

The FTC won, imposing $12 million in fines for deceptive advertising practices.

THE MORAL OF THE STORY

Substantiate. Only make claims that you can prove.

IF YOU SAY IT, IT MUST BE TRUE

THE WAR(S)

In September of 2008, the FTC announced eleven enforcement actions against various companies claiming their products cured or treated various forms of cancer. The following companies settled and are barred from representing that their products prevent, treat, or cure any type of cancer unless they can support such claims with "competent and reliable scientific evidence."

THE LOSERS (NO WINNERS HERE)

Nu-Gen Nutrition, Inc. Product: electrolyte liquid and apricot seeds. $830,434 settlement (paid $246,000 due to insolvency).

Westberry Enterprises, Inc. Product: herbal tea highlighting cat's claw, algae, burdock root, and slippery elm bark. $225,000 (paid $15,000).

Jim Clark's All Natural Cancer Therapy. Product: various metabolic therapy products. Each partner agreed to different settlements: 1) paid $25,000 out of $353,702; 2) paid $15,000 out of $207,676.

THE MORAL OF THE STORY

If you make any promises or give signs of hope that your product cures an incurable disease, you better have lots of peer-reviewed, credible studies to substantiate your claim.

A SOLUTION

THE WAR

POM Wonderful (makers of Pomegranate juice in those distinctive mod bottles) complained to NAD in October, 2008 about claims made by a competitor, Bossa Nova Beverage Group. The Better Business Bureau has an arm named the National Advertising Division (NAD). NAD's pronouncements, though non-governmental, have some influence in the industry. Other advertisers or watchdog organizations will register advertising complaints against companies and NAD will issue opinions which often lead to advertisers abiding by those opinions.

The Bossa Nova claims stated:

- ✓ "Bossa Nova sets the standard for antioxidant potency. The proof is in the numbers"
- ✓ "Bossa Nova is higher in antioxidants and lower in sugars."
- ✓ "more antioxidants"
- ✓ "higher antioxidant potency" and "highest antioxidant fruit"

THE WINNER

NAD's review (which appears to have included deferring to a University of Texas study on antioxidants and scientific documents) concluded certain claims of Bossa Nova be discontinued. Bossa Nova stated in a release that out of "deference to NAD's expertise" they would take into consideration the findings in future packaging.

THE MORAL OF THE STORY

Life really is like high school.

GEOCITIES

THE WAR

In the burgeoning Internet, Geocities was a popular source for unsophisticated users to create their own web pages. Among the personal web pages, Geocities maintained theme sites. One was called the "Enchanted Forest," which targeted young users. The Forest would, from time to time, host contests such as "Name the Princess" (a mascot for the site). Geocities represented that it collected and maintained the personal information required for the children to enter the contests. In fact, the contests were run by third-parties, and they (not Geocities) collected and maintained the personal information. In February 1999, the FTC began enforcement against Geocities.

THE WINNER

The FTC won. The FTC and Geocities entered a consent order by which Geocities was ordered to no longer misrepresent the identity of those collecting information, refrain from collecting information from children without knowledge of parental consent, abide by a number of notice requirements, hand over information to the FTC, and develop privacy training programs for its employees.

MORAL OF THE STORY

Your privacy policy must be absolutely accurate.

FIELD GUIDE FOR ADS AND PROMOS

Finally, here is some guidance about (1) ads; (2) clearing IP; and (3) affiliate programs.

1. ADS

You could place ads on television and movies through commercials, product placement and entertainment tie-ins; on radio through terrestrial, internet and satellite radio; in print through newspapers, magazines and other periodicals; using direct mail, billboards and public space ads; and on the Internet through banner and pop-up ads, pre-roll, mid-roll and post-roll ads, e-mail, blogs and online reviews. In all uses, your ads should comply with law.

YOUR AD MUST BE FAIR

Your ad should not contain anything misleading or untrue. Your ad can point out the reasons why someone should buy, but only if they are real. If your ad could lead to physical or financial injury, say so in a disclaimer. If you use a person talking, include a disclaimer saying that the person is just a paid actor. To discover and use a state of the art disclaimer, freeze the frame on a bunch of commercials of other, better-lawyered companies. If you compare your product to a competitor's, make sure it is absolutely accurate.

SUBSTANTIATE ALL CLAIMS

1. Dissect each ad to identify every claim — express or implied. Consider showing the ad to a focus group to identify what strangers believe you are claiming in the ad.

2. Support each claim with substantiation. Substantiation must be competent and reliable evidence of the claim you are making. For health, safety, performance and efficacy, your evidence must be competent and reliable scientific evidence.

3. Acceptable evidence includes tests, studies and scientific research built on credible methodologies, expertise of professionals in the field, conducted by qualified people that generate statistically sound results.

Acceptable evidence does not include money back guarantees, low return rates, anecdotal evidence, reporting and press coverage, and promotional materials.

4. Every claim should have a file filled with substantiation. Make your ad agencies and publishers get backup in the file to substantiate claims.

DISCLAIM APPROPRIATELY

Here are some suggestions for using disclaimers.

1. Each disclaimer should be clear and conspicuous in relation to the claim.

2. Ensure that an advertisement's text, graphics, hyperlinks or sounds do not distract consumers' attention from the disclaimer; display disclosures prior to purchase.

3. Place disclosures on the same Web page as the claim they apply to, and when necessary, provide adequate visual cues to indicate that a consumer must scroll down on the page to view the disclosure.

4. If you hyperlink to a disclosure, make the link obvious and noticeable, label the link accurately and place the link near relevant information.

5. Every disclaimer must be close to the claim, and may need to be verbal as well as written depending on the type of claim.

INTERNET ADS

If you pay for or post ads on a website, here are some ideas for disclaimers used in Internet ads.

1. Hyperlinks to disclosures must be obvious.

2. Label the hyperlink appropriately to convey the important nature and relevance of the information it leads to.

3. Use hyperlink styles consistently.

4. Place the hyperlink close to the claim.

5. Use frames and pop-ups to highlight the disclosure.

6. Display disclosures at the point of purchase, but remember that that posting may not be sufficient.

7. Incorporate disclosures in and around banners.

8. The size, color and location of disclosures should stand out from other elements on the page.

9. Use audio disclosures with audio claims.

10. Display rolling or motion disclaimers long enough for a reasonable person to read it. Even better, include a pause button to allow the user to stop the message for easier reading.

2. CLEAR IP

TRADEMARKS

Make sure you have rights to your trademarks (i.e. they don't infringe another's marks). Take care when using a competitor's trademark in advertising; if what results is likely to lead to confusion as to the origin or affiliation of the products, the advertisement violates the law governing trademarks (Lanham Act).

COPYRIGHT

Get ownership or a sufficient license to each element of the ad.

TALENT

Get rights to use all talent; make sure you comply with any union collective bargaining agreements and all residuals and other talent fees.

3. AFFILIATE PROGRAMS

Affiliate programs for websites have been around just long enough to start picking up a little law of their own. Here are suggestions for (a) Affiliates; and (b) Merchants who run affiliate programs.

TIPS FOR AFFILIATES

1. Affiliate ads must be is truthful, substantiated, and not deceptive or unfair.

2. Do not post "flogs" (fake blogs), a fake or unsubstantiated product claim, or offer incentives in return for response to an ad, unless the offer's terms and conditions of the offer are clearly and conspicuously disclosed.

3. Do not post fake news articles or titles, without clearly and conspicuously disclosing that the content is an advertisement.

4. Do not post a fake endorsement.

5. Disclose any material connections among the merchant, the network and the endorser.

6. Clear all IP rights you use, including personal rights, trademark, copyright, patent rights, service mark. If you can't clear the rights, don't use the content.

TIPS FOR MERCHANTS

1. Create a contract in writing for your affiliates. Make the contract require your affiliate to publish content only in compliance with all state and federal consumer protection laws and regulations including the FTC Act, the CAN-SPAM Act, and the FTC's revised Endorsement Guides.

2. Forbid your affiliates to infringe on the personal rights, trademark, copyright, patent rights, service mark, or any other intellectual property right of any third party.

3. Require your affiliates to clearly and conspicuously disclose the terms and conditions of any incentives, points, rewards, cash, or prizes promised to consumers in return for their response to any advertisement.

4. State specifically that violation of the contract will result in immediate termination.

5. Require all affiliates to sign the contract.

6. Terminate any affiliate who breaches the agreement and withhold their commissions.

HAP MAKES A MARKETING PLAN

Hap shut himself away for a few weeks to create a plan to sell the MouseTrap. He did lots and lots of research on his market, competitors and some recent surveys. He spent a little time with his gut, doing some naval gazing. And, he wrote and wrote and wrote.

BENEFITS OF PRODUCT

- ✓ Nearly constant access to power
- ✓ Portable
- ✓ Source of renewable energy
- ✓ Multi-functional
- ✓ Energy cost savings
- ✓ Improved productivity

COMMONALITIES AMONG CUSTOMERS

- ✓ They always want to be able to power their computer
- ✓ Even if they forgot to plug it in
- ✓ Even if they aren't near a power source
- ✓ Even its not for work
- ✓ They want to save money
- ✓ They want to maximize productivity
- ✓ They want the financial and/or marketing benefits of adopting green technology

THREE MARKETS (IN ORDER OF PRIORITY)

- ✓ Computer hardware OEMs (to purchase and package the MouseTrap)
- ✓ Large purchasing departments for corporations, governments and universities (with "renewable energy," "green," and "sustainable" in the text of their website)
- ✓ Consumers and families

STRATEGIES FOR MARKET PENETRATION

As a new company with a small staff, Hap knew that MouseTrap LLC would not have the sales force to blanket the market, so he would have to use other means.

AFFILIATE STRATEGY

Hap planned to set up an affiliate program that would get lots of other people to sell the MouseTrap for a commission of 5% gross sales. Hap suspected that no more than 5,000 units would sell through affiliates, but he also knew that the sum total of marketing from deputized sales people would substitute for paid advertising.

PR STRATEGY

Hap planned to launch a public relations strategy featuring the nutty, lab locked inventor: Seymour. Hap was betting that Seymour's web celebrity and back story, coupled with the functionality of the MouseTrap could get them coverage in some of the more influential magazines and sites, like *Tech Crunch* and *Wired*.

ADVERTISING STRATEGY

Content. Hap planned to create advertisements that focused on the novelty of the product. Each of the advertisements would be targeted at a specific audience.

For computer hardware OEMs, the ad would take advantage of the inherent competitiveness and paranoia of the computer hardware makers around the tagline: "ALWAYS IN POWER."

For large purchasing departments, often riddled with inferiority complexes, the ad would feature the tagline: "TAKE CHARGE!"

For families, the advertisements would take advantage of green guilt and a love of gadgetry materialism around the tagline: "WE DO OUR PART."

Rollout and Placement. The rollout would include placement of ads in magazines which target the particular market, plus a mix of guerilla marketing strategies, like blog posts, blog commenting, and contests. Hap also planned an aggressive search engine optimization campaign to put the MouseTrap at the top of the search results for "computer accessory" and "portable power."

With Hazard's consent, and Seymour's reluctant assent, Hap began to execute the plan months before the MouseTrap was ready. Hap planted images of the prototype in blogs and press releases. He got Seymour to do some podcasts on the MouseTrap. He had a website set up, showing an image of Queen Elizabeth and the MouseTrap with the caption:

> "What do the Queen and the MouseTrap have in common? They are always in power."

The web and the press ate it up. They also started receiving milestone reports about product in process from the manufacturer. They knew they were just six weeks away. Gravity called them in.

> "Boys, I know that you plan to let the MouseTrap loose on the market in less than two months."

> "That's right, Gravity. Maybe sooner."

> "Good. There are a couple of things we need to deal with now, before you get any further. How are you going to protect yourself?"

> "Gosh, Gravity, we haven't thought of any of that. Can you give us some guidance?"

> "I CAN TRY."

END NOTES

1 A wide range of common law, statutes, regulations, treaties, and union laws and collective bargaining agreements govern sales efforts. Under state laws, there are laws dealing with contracts, torts, labor and employment. Under federal law, there are laws dealing with antidiscrimination, antitrust, labor, advertising and commerce. Under laws of other countries, there is the EU Commercial Agents Directive, anti-corruption laws; competition law, including the Treaty of Rome, and privacy laws

2 The Sherman Act of 1890 15 USC 1-7 prohibits deals that restrain trade and that result in monopolies. A "monopoly" is at least 58% of a market (based on Standard Oil v. US, 221 US 1 (1901) and progeny). Robinson-Patman Act of 1936 15 USC 13(a) and (b) prohibits price discrimination among buyers and buyer induced price discrimination. There is also a prohibition against predatory pricing under state statues and Section 3 of Robinson-Patman Predatory pricing is cutting prices below cost to drive out competitors and then to profit from a cleared field. Clayton Act of 1914 15 USC 12-27 prohibits (a) exclusive dealing and tie-ins vertical integration by contract which center monopoly in a line of common (Section 3); (b) mergers or transactions that lessen competition or create a monopoly (Section 7); and (c) identical membership of boards of competitors worth $1 million or more (Section 8/15 USC 15a). Federal Trade Commission Act of 1914 15 USC 41-57 prohibits unfair methods of competition and unfair or deceptive acts or practices. 5 USC §45(a). Each state has its own mini antitrust statute as well

3 A/K/A the rule of reason.

4 Mechanisms for getting sued or busted for antitrust are in the Clayton Act. Under Section 5(a), the FTC can go after violators of Sherman Act Clayton and Robinson-Patman Act. However, the FTC cannot get money damages, but can get injunctive relief and divestiture. Section 4(2) lets private parties sue for antitrust violations. The remedy is treble damages and attorneys' fees 15 USC 15. Section 4(c) empowers each state's attorney general to sue for treble damages on behalf of the state's citizens 15 USC 15(c). The federal government can sue for damages (but not treble) and injunctive relief which includes divestiture. There is a 4 year statute of limitations for suits for money, but not for FTC actions for injunctive relief 15 USC 15(b).

5 Leegin v. PSKS, 551 US 877 (2007).

6 Lanham Trademark Act 15 USC 1051 et seq prohibits passing off, false advertising and false claims about competing products. The Federal Trade Commission Act of 1914 15 USC 41-57 prohibits unfair methods of competition and unfair or deceptive acts or practices. 5 USC §45(a). State deceptive practice statute and state common laws govern ad laws at the state level. Most ad law applies to commercial speech and not political speech.

7 Unfair, Deceptive and Prohibited: "Unfair methods of competition in or affecting commerce, and unfair or deceptive acts or practices in or affecting commerce, are hereby declared unlawful." 15 USC 45(a)(1).

8 FTC Policy Statement Regarding Advertising Substantiation Appended to Thompson Medical, 104 FTC 648 (1984), aff'd 791 F2d 189 (DC Cir 1986), cert. denied 479 U.S. 1086 (1987).

9 Controlling the Assault of Non-Solicited Pornography and Marketing Act of 2003. FTC has rulemaking and enforcement jurisdiction.

10 Telephone Consumer Protection Act, 47 USC 227 (1991); Do Not Call Implementation Act of 2003 15 USC 6101 et. seq.; Do Not Call Improvement Act of 2007.

GETTING PROTECTION

section six

RISK MANAGEMENT STRATEGY

Gravity said, "Let's discuss why you need a risk management strategy."

CHAPTER 21

WHY YOU NEED A RISK MANAGEMENT STRATEGY

Doing business in the world is risky. Risks of injury to people or property, loss of money, loss of life, prosecution, litigation, and loss of the most elusive commodity – time – abound. For every turn you take, it's possible to identify five bad things that could happen that will keep you up at night.

Here is a sample of bad, but very common, stuff that could happen to you.

- ✓ You could sell stock to someone who later sues you, because the promises you made or he heard weren't fulfilled
- ✓ You could sell stock to someone who then pushes you out of your business or steals your secrets
- ✓ You could hire someone who makes a huge mistake or leads the company to commit a crime; you could hire someone who steals from you
- ✓ Your manufacturer could make a defective product that injures users; or your manufacturer could go out of business, steal your secrets, make you a crappy product or fail to make your products at all
- ✓ One tiny ball bearing you buy from a Vietnamese supplier could be filled with lead, poisoning your users; or, that ball bearing could simply be hollow, forcing you to recall all products, find a new ball bearing supplier and fix every product
- ✓ Your product could simply break after first use

- ✓ You could be prosecuted over a conversation with a competitor in which you commiserated over pricing pressures
- ✓ Russian hackers could invade your website and steal your customer payment information

And on and on.

THE 3 RISKS

There are really three big risks we always have to care about:

- ✓ The risk that you'll get sued, pursued or screwed.
- ✓ The risk that you'll have to fight.
- ✓ The risk that you'll lose.

You can never, ever eliminate risk. But, with risk management strategies, perhaps you can narrow that window of risk to a porthole.

RISK MANAGEMENT FUNDAMENTALS

Every risk management strategy ought to be a sturdy 3-legged stool built on:

1. Contracts
2. Insurance
3. Vigilant Due Diligence

Let's go.

CONTRACTS

Gravity said, "Let's discuss what goes into a contract, and why they are a critical part of your risk management strategy."

CHAPTER

22

WHY CONTRACTS ARE A CRITICAL PART OF RISK MANAGEMENT

Contracts are a critical part of a liability limitation program because they define your obligations and rights as well as the liability of each party to each other and the world.

MAKING A CONTRACT

A "contract" is a promise by two or more people to trade something for something else. Contracts can be made in writing or during a conversation. However, contracts made during a conversation are no good if they create a deal for purchase of products over $500, securities, real estate, marriage, or anything else that cannot get done in a year.

It can be easier to make a contract than to comply with it. Technically, a contract requires (1) an offer; (2) an acceptance; and (3) consideration (that's the mutual trade).

1. AN OFFER

A contract must begin with a proposal to do or pay something for something else. The proposal becomes an "offer" if, objectively, it can be reasonably interpreted as an invitation to accept the proposal, converting it to a promise. What you intended and what the other guy heard are less important than what can reasonably be concluded from what you said and how you acted about your intention to make an offer and a contract.

That means you can make a contract without meaning to make a contract. So, when making proposals or probing opportunities, be careful and be clear about the steps left to create a promise.

2. AN ACCEPTANCE

"Acceptance" is agreement to the terms in the offer. Agreement to the offer with revisions is not really acceptance – it's a counteroffer. To form a contract, any new terms must be accepted by the original offeror. However, if the original offeror does not accept the new terms, but instead starts doing business as if they have a deal, then the actual terms of the deal will be defined by their conduct or guessed later by a judge or both.

3. CONSIDERATION

"Consideration" is what a recipient gives for what she gets. Consideration is not just cash. Consideration can be a return promise, property, cash, an action or an obligatory inaction. Every contract must be supported by consideration. When thinking about consideration, think of all the promises of one side in a contract as a bundle of promises – that bundle must be traded for something bargained for. And, later, if the parties amend the contract and add more promises to the mix, those new promises become a new bundle of promises, requiring new consideration. A contract without consideration is not a contract - it's a gift and probably not enforceable.

CLARITY

A contract creates the record of promises made between two people. Contracts are made up of equal parts: exchange, incentives and roadmap.

Contracts should be clear. Every word should either matter or be discarded. Any word that doesn't belong just creates confusion. The contract should follow rules of good writing. Paragraphs should start with a topic sentence. Most verbs should be active, because they need to identify precisely who is obligated to act and the obligatory action.

Resist, as much as possible, the instinct to inject a lawyerly tone. Avoid words like "hereof," "herein" and "thereof" unless the writer lacks space, time or energy. And, under no circumstances, should any contract writer draft "the party of the first part..."

PARTS OF A CONTRACT

There are parts of a contract that play a special role. Let's discuss the parts of a contract with an example, including: (1) the banner; (2) recitals; (3) defined terms; (4) the body; (5) boilerplate; (6) disclaimers and limitations of liability; (7) indemnities and disputes; and (8) creative compensation.

1. BANNER

"The Banner" is the strip of content at the top of the contract that identifies the contract title, the date the contract gets signed and the parties.

CONTRACT TITLE

The contract title ought to describe its reason for being. For example, a contract that exists to pass a license to software should be called a "License Agreement."

DATE

The date can be the day the contract is signed or the date the contract becomes effective. However, if you sign a contract later than it was actually effective, don't backdate it to change history. Instead, date the contract as follows:

Dated April 1, 2011, but effective as of February 1, 2011.

PARTIES

The parties to the contract are the people or companies who have to do things under the contract and who get stuff under the contract as an exchange. You can make a contract for yourself; you can also make a contract for your company ("actual authority"). And, someone else can make a contract for your company, if the other party has some decent reason to think that the guy has authority to make deals for your company ("apparent authority"). There are also "third party beneficiaries" – people who specifically benefit from the contract and can sue to enforce those benefits, even though they are not parties to it.

2. RECITALS

"The Recitals" (a/k/a the Whereas Clauses) give the context and the story of the contract. Recitals can tell a story about who the parties are, why they are coming together and what they want from each other through this contract. Years, or even months, later, the parties may need the memory refresher that the Recitals provide. In many states, the Recitals are not contractually binding. If you want the Recitals to be part of the contract, you should incorporate them into the contract, by adding this sentence to the body:

> The Recitals to this Agreement are hereby incorporated herein and made a part hereof.[1]

3. DEFINED TERMS

"Defined Terms" are nicknames created for people, obligations, rights and things in the contract. Defined Terms are little nuggets of wonder – they create their own language for the contract, making the whole document shorter and more consistent. Defined Terms consist of the term itself, which is usually put in quotes the first time it's created, and the definition itself.

The Defined Terms get used again and again in the contract, so define them surgically. Give each

Defined Term a name that is descriptive of its meaning or function to ease the review of the contract.

(And, please, don't create a bunch of Defined Terms containing nothing but initials).

Defined Terms can be defined within the body of the contract, in a special section called "Defined Terms" or both. Here is an example of each type:

> You hereby grant to me a limited, non-transferable, non-exclusive license ("License") to make one (1) digital copy of your recording of "Sinnerman."

* * *

> "License" means the limited, non-transferable, non-exclusive license to make one (1) digital copy of your recording of "Sinnerman."

4. THE BODY

TOPIC SENTENCE

Section One should be used to kick off the contract terms with the topic sentence of the whole shebang. So, for a License Agreement:

> **License Grant**. You hereby grant to Me a worldwide, fully paid right and license to use Your Stuff.

EACH PARTY'S BIG RESPONSIBILITIES

The business terms should be dealt with upfront and first. Often, agreements may provide general terms in the actual body and put the specific details in exhibits, schedules and statements of work attached at the end.

CONSIDERATION, PAYMENT AND PAYMENT TERMS

Not only should you write down what consideration is being exchanged, you should also record how and at what rate it will be exchanged.

TERM, TERMINATION AND EFFECT OF TERMINATION

You need to list how long the contract will last, who, how and why it can be terminated and what happens after the contract gets terminated.

RISK MANAGEMENT

Every contract includes risks, so every contract should include strategies to manage that risk.

INSPECTION, QUALITY CONTROL AND ACCEPTANCE

Everything you buy or provide has to hit a certain set of standards. The one getting the product or service ought to have a reasonable opportunity to reject a deliverable that does not comply with the bargain. And, every contract ought to give the giver a chance to breathe easy, knowing that the receiver has either accepted the product or service or has missed the chance to reject it.

REPRESENTATIONS AND WARRANTIES

Representations and warranties are the promises about the quality or condition of parties, products or services. Representations and warranties are the promises about the quality or condition of parties, products or services. Reps and warranties take a huge role in some contracts, though usually not in service contracts like this. But, in contracts where the parties are selling a business, the reps and warranties are the places where the seller makes all the valuable promises and disclosures. Also, for some reason, reps and warranties are different than the warranty. They don't mean different things, but they are used in different ways. Warranty is usually a specific promise about a product.

RISK OF LOSS AND TITLE

Risk of Loss. If the contract deals with transferring stuff, then the contract should list who has the risk of loss and when. "Risk of Loss" is the obligation to pay for the goods if they get damaged, destroyed or lost and usually also includes an obligation to buy insurance to cover the loss. Risk of loss is usually worked out in negotiations and often follows Incoterms (see below).

Passage of Title. There must be a moment in time when whatever product is being sold becomes the property of the buyer. This moment is called the passage of title and it should be specifically prescribed in the contract.

TRADE TERMS

"Incoterms." These are the universal code words for when risk of loss passes between the parties and who has to pay for insurance, shipping and customs at points in the distribution channel. The Incoterms were revised in 2000 and 2010 – the new 2010 Incoterms are effective as of January 1, 2011.

FOB Factory. When used, this typically means that risk of loss passes to the buyer at the manufacturer's loading dock and the buyer is thus responsible for insurance.[2]

FOB Warehouse. This typically means that the seller pays shipping and insurance from the manufacturer's dock to the warehouse, but that risk of loss passes at the warehouse door. That risk of loss could pass to the buyer or the warehouseman, but in any event the manufacturer is off the hook for damage to goods after that point.

Landed Cost. This means the total cost from manufacture to importation, including duties, transportation, insurance, raw materials and services.

5.   BOILERPLATE

Boilerplate clauses are the parts of the contract that deal with interpretation of the contract and dispute procedures. Below are explanations of different boilerplate clauses and an example.

ASSIGNMENTS

Contracts can be transferred (also called "assigned") by any party unless the contract prohibits or limits it. The "Assignment" clause makes rules about when, who and why a party can assign the contract.

> No Change of Control or Assignment. Neither party may, without the other party's prior written consent, assign, sublicense or transfer to any third party all or any part of this Agreement.

PARAGRAPH HEADINGS

If you don't want the paragraph headings to be used to interpret the contract, stick in a sentence that the headings are for convenience only.

FURTHER ASSURANCES

Further assurances clauses are used to obligate the other parties to take actions in the future to confirm the rights of the parties in the contract, particularly where those future acts may involve the signing of various documents.

> **Further Assurances**. Each of the parties agrees to take such further action to execute and deliver such additional documents as may be required to them to effectuate the purpose and intent of this Agreement.

SEVERABILITY

This clause is used to protect the rest of a contract from being stricken when one part of it is found unenforceable (such as a covenant not to compete).

> **Severability**. In the event that any of the terms, conditions, covenants or agreements contained in this Agreement, or the application of any thereof, shall be held by a court of competent jurisdiction to be invalid, illegal or unenforceable, such term, condition, covenant or agreement shall be deemed void and shall be deemed severed from this Agreement. In such event, and except if such determination by a court of competent jurisdiction materially changes the rights, benefits and obligations of the parties under this Agreement, the remaining provisions of this Agreement shall remain unchanged, unaffected and unimpaired thereby and, to the extent possible, such remaining provisions shall be construed such that the purpose of this Agreement and the intent of the parties can be achieved in a lawful manner.

COUNTERPARTS

This clause allows the parties to sign on different signature pages that get attached to the contract.

> **Counterparts**. This Agreement may be executed in multiple counterparts, each of which shall be deemed an original, but all of which together shall be considered one and

the same instrument. Signature pages transmitted by facsimile or portable document format (PDF) shall be as valid as original ink signatures.

NON-WAIVER OF REMEDIES

Non-waiver provisions allow you to give someone a mulligan without them later claiming they're breach is excused forever.

> **No Waiver**. The waiver by any Party hereto of the breach of any term, covenant, agreement or condition herein contained shall not be deemed a waiver of any subsequent breach of the same or any other term, covenant, agreement or condition herein, nor shall any custom, practice or course of dealings arising among the Parties hereto in the administration hereof be construed as a waiver or diminution of the right of any Party hereto to insist upon the strict performance by any other Party of the terms, covenants, agreement and conditions herein contained.

NOTICES

The Notice provision prescribes how you have to communicate with a party officially under the contract. It is important, particularly where there are deadlines and the triggering of clocks.[3]

> **Notices**. All notices, requests, consents and other communications under this Agreement will be in writing, addressed to the receiving party's address appearing on the signature page to this Agreement or to another address as that party may designate in a written notice, and will be deemed to have been given (a) if by hand, at the time of the delivery thereof to the receiving party; (b) if made by email or facsimile, at the time that receipt thereof has been personally acknowledged in writing by the receiving party; (c) if sent by overnight courier, on the next business day following the day such notice is delivered to the courier service; or (d) if sent by

registered mail, on the fifth (5th) business day following the day such mailing is made.

TIME

Time Clauses transform a seemingly nonmaterial breach into a material breach.

> **Time Is of the Essence**. Time is of the essence with respect to the performance of each of the covenants and agreements herein set forth.

ENTIRE AGREEMENT

This provision allows you to define what gets included in the contract, including all exhibits, schedules, and recitals, and to exclude any prior term sheets, contracts or other proposals. However, make sure any related contracts among the same parties get referenced in the clause.

> **Entire Agreement**. This instrument, including the body of the Agreement and the Recitals and Schedules hereto, contains the entire Agreement between the parties hereto with respect to the transaction contemplated herein, and may not be amended or modified except in writing signed by each of the parties.

AMENDMENT AND/OR MODIFICATION

To prevent mistakenly changing the contract, make sure changes to the contract have to be done in writing and signed by both parties. See the example above.

GOVERNING LAW, VENUE AND CONSENT TO JURISDICTION

Governing law sections are selected for a number of reasons. First, they enable the contract to be governed under well-developed laws of a particular state. For instance, New York has excellent commercial law; California has extensive computer and software use law. Second, if the parties come from different states, it is efficient to avoid heavy conflicts of laws questions by just picking the state law in advance.

If you want to specify where you will litigate disputes, you can prescribe the court's location.

However, you should also include a consent to jurisdiction so the court where you want to litigate the dispute will be able to compel the appearance of both parties.

> **Governing Law**. Submission to Jurisdiction. This Agreement and any claim or dispute arising out of or related to this Agreement or the transactions contemplated hereby, whether in contract, tort or otherwise, shall be governed by and construed in accordance with the laws of the State of <<GOVERNING LAW STATE>>, without giving effect to its conflicts of law principles. Any legal actions, suits or proceedings arising out of this Agreement (whether for breach of contract, tortuous conduct or otherwise) shall be brought exclusively in the state or federal courts located in <<VENUE CITY AND STATE>>, and the parties to this Agreement hereby accept and submit to the personal jurisdiction of these <<VENUE CITY AND STATE>> courts with respect to any legal actions, suits or proceedings arising out of this Agreement.

LIMITATION OF ACTIONS

Many statutes of limitations (the time period when you can sue by law) run for 6 years on contracts. If you want to shorten the amount of time when you can sue each other, then you can add a limitation of action clause.

> **Limitation of Actions**. No action whether in contract or tort, including negligence, arising out of the performance of either party under this Agreement may be brought by the other party more than two (2) years after the cause of the action has arisen.

6. DISCLAIMERS & LIMITATIONS OF LIABILITY

"Disclaimers" are written statements that attempt to emphatically reject the possibility of being responsible for someone's loss, even if it's your fault. "Limitations of Liability" are caps on the amount of total liability. Disclaimers and Limitations of Liability are valid only if (a) the other guy had a chance to review them before he did the deal; (b) they relate to a knowable risk; and (c) they are conspicuous.

Consumer Protection Laws. A disclaimer's scope of protection isn't always easy to figure out. Many states have consumer protection statutes that emphatically reject disclaiming liability for a consumer.

Your suppliers/manufacturers. You may want to negotiate the limitations of liability with your suppliers and manufacturers to appropriately place the risk of their failure with them.

Chance to Review and Accept. If a party did not have a meaningful opportunity to review and understand the agreement (and in some states, negotiate), then the contract could be thrown out. For instance, if the limitation of liability is buried in the fine print or if buyer has no meaningful remedy against the seller if the goods are defective. Generally, limitations of liability against consumers are harder to enforce than against commercial parties, because the commercial parties are viewed as having the opportunity and the skill to review and negotiate the contract before signing.

Conspicuous. A section of a contract is conspicuous if it clearly stands out from the rest of the contract and draws the eye of the reader. Disclaimers that are hidden or in really small type are also often disregarded. Common ways to make disclaimer clauses conspicuous is to put them in bold type, different colored type, larger type, or in all capitals.

Disclaimer Against Future, Unknown Liability Often Not Valid. Disclaimers that try to get someone to relinquish losses from future, unknowable events are often disregarded by a judge. Limitations of liability for personal injury of your consumer customers will likely not be enforced.

Consequential Damages Can Usually Be Disclaimed. Disclaimers of liability and consequential damages are typically upheld, particularly among commercial parties. Limitations of liability for economic injury may be enforced against consumers and has a better chance of being enforced against merchants.

Limitation of Liability. NEITHER PARTY SHALL BE LIABLE TO THE OTHER PARTY FOR ANY INDIRECT, INCIDENTAL, CONSEQUENTIAL, SPECIAL, EXEMPLARY OR PUNITIVE DAMAGES (INCLUDING WITHOUT LIMITATION DAMAGES FOR HARM TO BUSINESS, LOST REVENUES, LOST SALES, LOST SAVINGS, LOST PROFITS (ANTICIPATED OR ACTUAL), LOSS OF USE, DOWNTIME AND CLAIMS OF THIRD PARTIES), REGARDLESS OF THE FORM OF ACTION, WHETHER IN CONTRACT, WARRANTY, STRICT LIABILITY, TORT OR BREACH OF STATUTORY DUTY (INCLUDING WITHOUT LIMITATION NEGLIGENCE OF ANY KIND, WHETHER ACTIVE OR PASSIVE), OR ANY OTHER LEGAL OR EQUITABLE THEORY, WHETHER OR NOT SUCH PARTY HAS BEEN APPRISED OR NOTIFIED THAT ANY SUCH DAMAGES OR LOSSES ARE POSSIBLE OR LIKELY, AND WHETHER OR NOT ANY PERMITTED REMEDY HAS FAILED ITS ESSENTIAL PURPOSE.

7. INDEMNITY

An "Indemnity" is another contract provision that forms a part of the limitation of liability program. An indemnity is a promise to reimburse, protect and defend someone because of something you did or are responsible for. It is reasonable to ask your business partners to promise to indemnify you for damages, claims and attorney's fees you suffer because your business partner screwed up in some way. Some big companies have a policy against agreeing to indemnify you for anything, though they will insist you promise to indemnify them. Also, although indemnities are critical, they are generally only worth the resources or insurance of the party on the hook.

Indemnity. OWNER shall defend, indemnify and hold CONTRACTOR and its directors, officers, employees, agents and contractors harmless from any and all losses arising from OWNER's negligence, misconduct, or any breach of OWNER's representations,

warranties or covenants contained in this Agreement.

FEE SHIFTING PROVISIONS

A "Fee Shifting Provision" is a couple of sentences in a contract that makes one of the parties pay the legal fees of the other. This is important, because by default, American courts will only make someone pay your legal fees if there is a statute or a contract that supports the obligation and says they should. For instance, the Copyright Act, the federal law that governs copyright, specifically tells the judge she can make the infringer pay the winning copyright owner's legal fees.[4]

Fee Shifting Provisions can be used to minimize the risk of a frivolous suit or incentivize good behavior by increasing the costs of bad behavior. However, these can also be used to dissuade people from suing a bad guy, particularly if they say that either party who loses has to pay the other guy's fees. Fee Shifting Provisions can be a double edged sword, making it easier for you to get justice from a bad guy, but they can also worsen your own pain if you lose a meritorious lawsuit. Even if you have a fee shifting provision in a contract and you win, you still have to collect the money from the guy you sued, which can be hard or impossible.

Attorney's Fees. In any action brought in connection with this Agreement, the prevailing party will, from trial through all subsequent appeals, be entitled to reimbursement from the non-prevailing party of its related, reasonable attorney's fees, legal costs and expenses.

ALTERNATIVE DISPUTE RESOLUTION PROVISIONS

Litigation in a court of law is expensive, public and unpredictable. In the last few decades, the legal profession has tried to come up with more efficient ways to resolve disputes. The main choice is arbitration. "Arbitration" is a sort of mini trial where the two parties and their lawyers square off in front of 1-3 people who are not sitting as government judges, but as respected, impartial experts.

Arbitration arguably keeps things out of the public eye and may be faster. Arbitration is mildly controversial among attorneys as to whether it is really a better option than just going to court. If you pick arbitration as the dispute resolution mechanism, make sure to reserve fights over confidentiality and intellectual property, as well as collection of any awards, for the courts.

The arbitration decision is enforceable[5] under state, federal and international law and the requirement to arbitrate and contractually mandated procedures are also enforced. Because of gaps in international treaties, arbitration may be the best practical choice to resolve disputes under cross-border contracts. Contracts that provide for arbitration of all disputes under it must be submitted to arbitration at every phase.[6]

> **Arbitration**. All disputes or controversies that may arise between the parties with respect to the performance, obligations or rights of the parties under this Agreement, shall be settled by arbitration to be held in Chicago, Illinois in accordance with the then current Rules of Commercial Arbitration of the American Arbitration Association. The dispute shall be referred to a panel of three arbitrators, one to be selected by each party and the third to be selected by the first two. If an agreement on the third arbitrator cannot be reached within thirty (30) days after the appointment of the second arbitrator, such arbitrator shall be appointed by the American Arbitration Association. The decision and award of the arbitrators, or that of any two of them, shall be final and binding on the parties, and judgment may be entered upon it in any court having jurisdiction thereof.

FORCE MAJEURE

Force majeure clause lets a party off the hook in the event of an act of God or act of war. Be careful to limit the amount of time obligations are tolled under the agreement as a result of force majeure. Don't let the definition of "force majeure" start to include all kinds of things that could excuse failure of performance.

> **Force Majeure**. No Party shall be in default of this Agreement to the extent that any delay or failure in the performance of its obligations results from any cause beyond its reasonable control and without its fault or negligence, such as acts of God, acts of civil or military authority, embargoes, epidemics, war, riots, insurrections, fires, explosions, earthquakes, floods or strikes ("Force Majeure"). If any Force Majeure condition affects any Party's ability to perform for a period of five (5) consecutive days, such affected Party shall give immediate notice to the other Parties not affected by such Force Majeure. Any non-affected Party may elect to either: (a) terminate the Agreement or any affected portions thereof without any liability to the other Parties; (b) suspend the Agreement or any part thereof for the duration of the Force Majeure condition, with the option to seek performance from another party notwithstanding anything to the contrary in this Agreement; or (c) resume performance under this Agreement once the Force Majeure condition ceases, with an option to extend any affected performance date up to the length of time that the Force Majeure condition existed.

8. CREATIVE COMPENSATION

The contract and terms of your deal can be structured to incentivize the behavior you want through performance bonuses, automatic rate deductions and other contractual consequences for results. Below is an example of a provision designed to incentivize a manufacturer to deliver on time by paying more for on-time delivery and less for late delivery.

> **Compensation Schedule**. If Manufacturer fails to deliver Product in accordance with the Delivery Date, Buyer shall be entitled to the corresponding liquidated damages:

DAYS LATE	DISCOUNT
Delivered 7 – 13 days late	$25.00
Delivered 14 – 20 days late	$50.00 (purchase price reduced to $0.00)
Delivered 21 – 27 days late	$100.00 per unit in cash

One way of looking at creative compensation is to embed a set amount of money to be paid by the breacher to the victim – this amount of money is called "liquidated damages." The compensation schedule listed above is a form of liquidated damages. If you embed liquidated damages into your contract, the liquidated damages cannot be a penalty – they must be a reasonable estimate of the actual damages to be suffered by the victim from a breach.

WARRANTY[7]

A warranty is a promise about the quality, performance or characteristics of a product. Warranties spring up from everywhere – from promises, from ads, from retailers, and automatically by law.

Crafting a warranty is a risk management strategy, because it allows you to define the threshold of acceptable performance. For instance, if you buy a car, it is reasonable to expect it to start every time and drive up to 80 miles per hour on a road. However, it is not reasonable to expect it to fly or pop wheelies. Your warranty ought to clarify what is the acceptable level of performance, or, alternatively, what is not an acceptable level of performance.

Let's discuss (1) types of warranties; (2) the consumer warranty; and (3) how to craft your warranty.

1. TYPES OF WARRANTIES

Warranties can be express or implied.

EXPRESS WARRANTY

An "express warranty" is a warranty that is promised either orally or in writing, and can be created by a certificate or even an ad.

IMPLIED WARRANTY

An "implied warranty" is an unspoken, unwritten warranty created by state law that automatically tags along with the product for 4 years after purchase, unless specifically disclaimed. There are two types of implied warranties: (a) Merchantability; and (b) Fitness for a particular purpose.

Implied warranty of merchantability[8] is a merchant's basic promise that the goods sold will do what they are supposed to do and that there is nothing significantly wrong with them. Merchants make this promise whenever they sell something they are in the business of selling.

Implied warranty of fitness for a particular purpose is a promise made by a merchant when the customer relies on her advice that a product can be used for a specific purpose. The warranty must be specifically disclaimed, but some states prohibit disclaiming implied warranties.

2. THE CONSUMER WARRANTY

There are special and tricky rules for consumer warranties. A "consumer warranty" is a warranty for products normally used for personal, family or household purposes that cost more than $15.

You are not required to issue any written warranty to a consumer; but once you do issue one, you must comply with federal and some state laws.[9] The consequences for failing to comply with federal law (particularly Magnusson-Moss) is liability for breach of contract, FTC enforcement, class actions and massive liability under warranties.

3. CRAFT YOUR WARRANTY

In crafting your warranty, there are a bunch of practical things to ask yourself. In addition to being prepared to list all of the information required by law (which is listed below), consider these questions:

WHAT WILL "BREAK" MEAN?

At its core, a warranty is a promise that a product will do what it's supposed to, for a defined period of time, and nothing more. So, you have to decide:

1. What has to go wrong with your product before you will fix it.

2. How persistent must the problem be before you give warranty service - not operational or just occasionally on the fritz?

3. Who determines if it is broken?

WHAT HAPPENS IF YOUR PRODUCT BREAKS?

Before you solidify your warranty terms, you should figure out what you are going to do when broken products get returned.

1. What can you afford to do in the event of a "break?"

2. Operationally, how will you handle warranty claims?

3. Who will pay for shipping to and back?

4. Will you use refurbished parts?

5. Can you work out a market or process to recycle parts or products that you keep to fix when you issue a new one to the customer?

6. Can you get warranty insurance? Affordably?

7. What is the standard in your industry? Often, consumers expect your warranty to match your competitors. Are there standard warranties in your industry that you have to meet or beat?

WRITE THE CONSUMER WARRANTY

Magnusson-Moss, the federal consumer warranty statute, and the nice people at the Federal Trade Commission, have very particular rules for what has to be in a consumer warranty.

Full Warranty. A warranty must be named either "full" or "limited." A warranty is "full" only if it has all of the following:

1. There is no limit to duration of implied warranties

2. Product owners, not just initial purchasers, can get warranty service

3. Warranty service and shipping is free

4. The consumer can choose replacement or refund for any product that cannot be fixed after a reasonable number of attempts

5. There is no requirement that consumers do anything as a condition to getting warranty service, except for reasonable acts

Name your written warranty "Limited Warranty" unless you meet all of the Full Warranty criteria above.

Headings and Clarity. The warranty should contain all of the information below in a single, clear, and easy-to-read document, using these headings:

1. What the warranty covers and does not cover

2. Who can claim warranty service

3. How long the warranty lasts

4. What will and won't be done to fix problems

5. A step by step guide on how to get warranty service

Mandatory Disclaimers. There are some disclaimers mandated by the FTC.

For state law impact on rights under the warranty:

> This warranty gives you specific legal rights, and you may also have other rights which vary from state to state.

If you limit the duration of implied warranties, post this FTC disclaimer:

> Some states do not allow limitations on how long an implied warranty lasts, so the above limitation may not apply to you.

If you limit consequential damages and special damages, post this FTC disclaimer:

> Some states do not allow the exclusion or limitation of incidental or consequential damages, so the above limitation or exclusion may not apply to you.

If you want to include a dispute resolution mechanism, talk to a lawyer first.

Point of Sale. Ensure that your warranties are available where your consumer products are sold so that consumers can read them before buying.

Don'ts. Do Not:

✓ Disclaim or modify implied warranties (although you can limit the duration of them)

✓ Condition warranty coverage on buying some other product (a/k/a "Tie-in Sales")

✓ Include deceptive or misleading warranty terms

HAZ IS SHOCKED (AND SO IS GRAVITY)

Haz couldn't believe what he was hearing.

"You're saying that you take the warranty card from your iPod and read it? You actually read it?"

"Sure. I love a well written warranty. And, I like to see who had lawyers who hadn't heard of Magnusson-Moss."

Haz asked Hap, "Do you think we could give a lifetime warranty? It may be a selling feature, but it is possible that the MouseTrap may not last forever."

Hap said, "I don't know, Haz. We should talk to Seymour about it. But, I'm not sure it matters. If the MouseTrap retails for $19.00, do people care if that is a one-time $19.00 investment? And, are the marketing benefits more valuable than the cost to replace or repair units forever? I don't think so."

Haz and Gravity looked surprised. "Hap, that was so cogent and smart."

Hap replied, "You're not the only one listening. Now, can you keep going, Gravity? I want to learn about insurance policies."

Again, there was a shocked look on Gravity's face. But, she managed to choke out her reply.

"I CAN TRY."

HYUNDAI'S 10-YEAR WARRANTY

THE WAR

When Hyundai introduced its cars into the U.S. market in 1986, they were riddled with problems. They eventually improved in quality, but perception lagged behind reality. In 2000, Hyundai rolled out the most comprehensive new-car warranty in the business. It included: 10-year/100k miles coverage on engine and transmission, 5-year/60k miles coverage on parts and labor and 5-year unlimited roadside assistance with a 24-hour, toll-free number.

THE WINNER

Hyundai sales soared but the warranty costs might have brought Hyundai down if they hadn't been so quick to fix problems with their cars—as evidenced by a 50-percent drop in warranty costs since 1998.

MORAL OF THE STORY

Your warranty may be a symbol of your confidence in the product. But a comprehensive warranty can also turn into a financial quagmire if the product doesn't turn out to be reliable.

APPLE: iDON'T

THE WAR

Apple frequently battles litigation and class action suits over its warranties. For instance, in August, 2008, Jessica Alena Smith filed a class action suit in the Northern District of Alabama for breach of "express warranties" from Apple advertisements which stated its 3G network was "twice as fast at half the price" as its predecessor. She claims she could connect to the 3G network only 25% of the time. She also claims breach of implied warranty of merchantability. A similar suit was filed in the Eastern District of New York on September 22, 2008 by Jai Sen, adding breaches of warranty based on the iPhone's defective casing.

Most recently, as soon as problems with the iPhone 4 hit, consumers brought class action suits. (Goodglick v. Apple is filed by Kershaw, Cutter & Ratinoff LLP in the Northern District of California; Ngyuen v. Apple is filed in the Southern District of Texas; McCaffrey v. Apple, Case 1:10-cv-01776-RDB, US Dist. Ct Maryland, Filed July 30, 2010.)

THE WINNER

Plaintiff's lawyers (who find opportunities to file class action suits against deep pockets).

THE MORAL OF THE STORY

Litigation is often a cost of doing business.

INSURANCE & BONDS

> Gravity said, "Let's discuss why you need insurance coverage, and the types of insurance available."

CHAPTER 23

INSURANCE

"Insurance" is a promise by an insurer to pay money to someone if something bad happens. The possible amount of payment (the "coverage amount"), the person who gets paid (the "insured") and the bad thing that has to happen (the "occurrence" or "loss") is part of the contract you negotiate and pay for. The final amount actually paid for an insurance claim is determined based on the insurance policy, the insurance company, your negotiation posture and, if necessary, a court of law.

Let's discuss (1) parts of insurance coverage; and (2) types of insurance.

1.   PARTS OF INSURANCE COVERAGE

Insurance can be claims-made or occurrence. Claims-made insurance covers lawsuits filed during the life of your policy. Occurrence-based insurance covers events that happen during the life of the policy, regardless of when you get sued.

YOUR POLICY

Insurance policies are legal contracts. Like all contracts, there is fine print buried there that can mess you up. Insurance coverage comes with a certificate of insurance, also called the **Declarations**, which lists the amount and type of coverage. But, the actual insurance policy with the **Insuring Agreement** comes in the mail later is the real set of rules - most people don't read them. The insuring agreement is going to say which risks it will cover and how you get coverage. It is in the insuring agreement where the traps are set. The insuring

agreement includes the coverage promises, plus endorsements and exclusions. An **"endorsement"** is a coverage addition. An **"exclusion"** is a coverage taken away. Endorsements can be negotiated and purchased, most of the time. But, frequently a policy endorsement gives with one hand and an exclusion takes away with the other.

It will also contain the notice requirements. These obligate you to tell your insurance company about claims before the insurance company will start paying. In addition, there will probably be **conditions** that are rules you have to follow to get the policy to work for you. In addition to the notice requirements, typically these conditions include an obligation to try to limit the loss, cooperating in adjusting and requirements for settling the loss. They also may discuss what happens if another policy covers the same loss.

AMOUNT OF COVERAGE

Insurance policies have ceilings on their amount of coverage. These are called policy **"limits."** How much coverage you take depends on how much liability exposure you have and how much you can afford. Sometimes the amount of the coverage may be driven by your contracting partners. To estimate how much liability coverage to get, you may want to find a recent lawsuit settlement in your industry.

Insurance policies also have internal ceilings called **sublimits**. Sublimits are limits for specific coverage, like bodily injury. Sublimits can be flat amounts or percentages of the total. Sometimes, a holder gets the right to allocate recovery to various coverages.

How much coverage you take depends on how much liability exposure you have and how much you can afford. Sometimes the amount of the coverage may be driven by your contracting partners.

DEDUCTIBLE V. SELF-INSURED RETENTION

Most policies have deductibles. A deductible is the amount you have to pay before the insurance company starts paying. The deductible is actually subtracted from the policy limit. So, if you have a $100 policy limit with a $5 deductible, you actually only have $95 in coverage. There may also be a different type of deductible called a Self-Insured Retention, which still obligates you to pay upfront, but that amount doesn't get subtracted from the policy limit.

All insurance decisions are gambles on risk. The less risk, the less control; the more risk, the more control. If you are more risk averse, then a policy with a lower deductible (or self-insured retention) may be for you. Since the insurance company will more quickly be on the hook, they'll have more power to hire their own defense counsel, who will likely consider the insurance company to be their primary client. The higher your deductible is, the more control you will have over the defense of lawsuits against your company and the lower your premium. Consider whether you want to buy coverage starting at the first dollar of loss or coverage that starts after your deductible, and everything in between. And make sure you factor in enough coverage to pick up defense costs.

2. TYPES OF INSURANCE

There are different types and bundles of insurance.

LIABILITY INSURANCE

"Liability Insurance" covers you when you get into trouble — it ought to pick up your legal fees or provide a lawyer, reimburse you for any damages you suffer and pay any damages you are obligated to pay. Commercial General Liability is a standard bundle for business liability. There are also errors and omissions insurance, which covers you for your foibles and mistakes.

PROPERTY INSURANCE

"Property Insurance" protects against damage or loss to property — yours or others — caused by all kinds of hazards.

PRODUCTS LIABILITY AND RECALL INSURANCE

"Products Liability and Recall Insurance" is a form of liability insurance, in that it covers you if your product injures someone.

DIRECTORS AND OFFICERS LIABILITY INSURANCE

"Directors And Officers Liability Insurance" (often sold with Employers' Liability Insurance) is purchased to cover legal fees and liability of directors and officers in suits by owners. This insurance also covers economic loss to the company flowing from having to reimburse D's and O's under these suits.

EMPLOYMENT PRACTICES LIABILITY INSURANCE

"Employment Practices Liability Insurance" covers legal fees and liabilities of companies in suits for wrongful termination, sexual harassment and discrimination.

SURETY BONDS

After straight up insurance coverage, there is a whole universe of hedges you can get against problems. "Surety Bonds" (a/k/a guarantees) are smaller insurance policies issued by an insurance company, surety company[10] or bank to guaranty satisfactory completion of a project.[11] Surety bonds often serve as an inducement to get the beneficiary to hire the performer.[12]

1. PARTS OF SURETY BONDS

PARTIES

There are 3 parties to a bond:

1. The principal (performer)
2. The beneficiary or obligee (usually the boss)
3. The surety (insurance company and issuer, such as JW Surety Bonds)

The amount of the coverage is the **penal sum** or **penalty amount**. The premium is the fee for the bond itself, which is often paid by the performer.

If the performer fails to perform, the performer and the surety are joint and severally liable to the beneficiary. That means that the performer and the surety can each be forced to pay the whole obligation; the one who pays can then go collect from the other.

2. THE 4 TYPES OF SURETY BONDS

There are 4 types of surety bonds:

1. Contract
2. Commercial
3. Fidelity
4. License and Permit

Contract bonds protect a contracting party from default or breach of the other guy.

Completion Bond. Completion Bonds guarantee to a project owner that a general contractor will comply with the contract.

Bid Bonds. Bid Bonds guarantee the contractor will enter into the contract honoring his bid if he wins the contract. The surety penal amount is the beneficiary's cost of cover and is usually calculated as 10-20% of the bid amount.

Performance Bond. A Performance Bonds guarantees that the contractor will perform the work as specified in the contract, particularly price and time. Performance Bonds are frequently issued as part of a "Performance and Payment Bond" which ensures that the contractor will pay labor and materials costs. These are typically obtained in building construction. The builder buys a performance bond that kicks in to compensate the client if the builder fails to comply with specifications in the contract (or fails to finish at all). These are also used to protect against bad or no work by project managers and sub-contractors. Surety bonds often give the surety three options: (1) completing the contract itself by hiring a completion contractor; (2) selecting a new contractor to contract with the beneficiary directly; or (3) pay the costs for the owner's completion of the work. The penal amount is the construction contract price, but it could be higher if the surety has the work finished.

Letter Of Credit. A Letter of Credit is a bank's promise to pay upon performance.

Payment Bonds. A Payment Bond guarantees that the contractor will pay for services and materials. Both the owner and the subcontractor can sue on the bond, since the owner is the obligee and the beneficiaries are the subcontractors and suppliers. These induce the subcontractors to stay engaged and can substitute for mechanics liens.

Maintenance Bond. A Maintenance Bond guarantees that the contractor will provide warranty and maintenance services for a particular period of time.

Completion Guarantee a/k/a Completion Bond. A Completion Bond, often used in film production, guarantees that the producer will complete and deliver the film based on the scrip, cast and budget. The beneficiary is the distributor or investor who financed the production. Upon delivery of the bond, the producer gets a "minimum distribution guarantee" which is usually paid to the investor, but if no delivery, the bond kicks in and pays it. The parties to the bond are the producer, the investors, the bond company and the distributors. The bond is often 3-5% depending on risks. If the players are higher risk (not bondable because of bad health or drugs), the rate is higher.

Commercial, license or permit bonds guarantee to a government that a performer will comply with laws, regulations and codes.

Import Entry Bond. An Import Entry Bond must be posted by every importer to guarantee payment of import duties and taxes and to guarantee compliance with laws, regulations, and directives.

These can be one off or continuous and self-renewing. A continuous bond is 10% x $10,000 of duties, taxes and fees per year; the minimum price is $50,000.

Bail Bonds. A Bail Bond secures release from custody of a person charged with a criminal offense. The performer is the defendant, the beneficiary is the government and the insurer is the bail bondsman. Often, if the defendant fails to appear, a fugitive recovery agent is the surety. (See *Midnight Run* (1988) with Charles Grodin and Robert DeNiro.)

Government Contracting Bonds. The Federal Government under the U.S. Miller Act[13] obligates general contractors on federal construction projects in excess of $100,000 to get a payment and performance bond unless the contracting officer determines that a lesser amount is adequate for the protection of the government. A performance bond is 100% of the original contract price.

For any construction contract between $25,000 and $100,000, the government contracting officer will require two or more of the following payment protections from the successful bidder:

- ✓ Payment bond from an approved corporate surety, the list of which is maintained at www.ustreas.gov
- ✓ An irrevocable letter of credit, which is a written commitment by a federally insured bank to pay a stated amount until the expiration date of the letter
- ✓ Tripartite escrow agreement, in which the government makes payments to the contractor's escrow account, and the escrow agent distributes the payments to the contractor's suppliers of labor and material
- ✓ Certificate of deposit from a federally insured financial institution, executable by the contracting officer
- ✓ Deposit of the amount of the bond in U.S. bonds or notes, certified or cashier's checks, bank drafts, postal money orders or currency

Sometimes, master bid bonds and performance bonds might be used instead of separate bonds for each project.[14]

FIDELITY BONDS

Fidelity Bonds are insurance policies that protect employers from bad acts of its employees if their acts have a greater capacity to injure. Examples include employee benefits[15], public officials, manufacturers, small businesses, non-profit organizations, real estate managers, title agents, financial institutions, precious metal exposures, and armored cars.

LICENSE AND PERMIT BONDS

A License and Permit Bond guarantees a person will get the licenses and permits necessary. For instance, requirements for a licensed driver to be present in the vehicle may be protected with a bond. This type of bond may be required, along with taxes, fees and consumer protections, as a condition to granting licenses related to selling real estate or motor vehicles and contracting services.

HAP AND HAZ THINK ABOUT RISK

"Gravity, how do we know how much insurance we should take?"

"That's an excellent question, Hazard. The amount of insurance will depend on a bunch of factors. You want to estimate your potential liability from things that could go wrong. You want to estimate legal fees and costs. You want to price insurance policies and see how much insurance you can afford. You need to find a really good business insurance broker who is honest and smart. You should then buy as much as you can afford. Finally, you should protect the parts of your life that you cannot insure through vigilant due diligence."

"I don't know what that is. Can you explain?"

"I CAN TRY."

WAR STORIES

WORLD TRADE CENTER PROPERTIES V. HARTFORD
THE $3.5 BILLON QUESTION

THE WAR

Real estate developer Larry Silverstein leased the Twin Towers mere weeks before their collapse. He took out a $3.5 billion "per occurrence" insurance policy spread amongst insurers across the globe. However, none of the many insurers had issued a final insurance policy. Instead, they had issues temporary "binders" or "slips," which provide interim coverage until a final policy is issued. The insurers involved included Swiss Reinsurance Co., Allianz Global Risks U.S. Insurance Co., the former Royal Indemnity Co., Zurich American Insurance Co., Travelers Companies Inc. and Employers Insurance of Wausau.

There were two problems. First, no one was certain which documents represented the actual policy terms. Second, depending on which policies governed, the destruction of the Twin Towers was either two occurrences (because two planes crashed into it), or just one.

Each side argued that it was their opponent's binder, not their own, which was accepted by the parties Silverstein's binder was written to favor the insured by interpreting a series of similar events as a single occurrence. Normally, the insured wants to keep occurrences down to limit the number of deductibles that need to be paid. The insurance companies binder's did the opposite, incorporating language that classified events as multiple occurrences. However, the sides are juxtaposed when the destructive event exceeds the monetary limit of the policy. In that case, the insurance companies want to pay out for one occurrence only, while the insured wants to collect the policy limit per occurrence multiple times.

THE WINNER

The court ruled that over half the insurers involved had not accepted the Silverstein binder; thus, their own binders were controlling and the attack on the WTC was considered two separate occurrences. The court awarded Silverstein $4.6 billion.

MORAL OF THE STORY

Gap-Fillers. If necessary, the court will look outside the four corners of the contract to determine intent.

Get a lawyer. It pays to get a good insurance policy and an even better lawyer to review and compile it.

VIGILANT DUE DILIGENCE

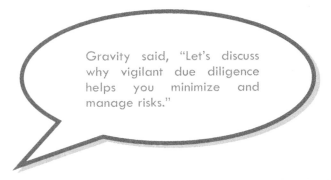

Gravity said, "Let's discuss why vigilant due diligence helps you minimize and manage risks."

CHAPTER 24

VIGILENT DUE DILIGENCE

Vigilant due diligence is good, smart, proactive, calibrated examination, preparation and operations to manage and minimize risks.

The risks can be boiled down to 4 types:

1. You could hurt someone
2. Someone could hurt you
3. You'll have to fight
4. You'll lose

1. YOU HURT SOMEONE

Your product, your conduct or your promises could hurt someone. The pain could be financial, emotional or physical. Businesses ought to embrace, with care and sobriety, the responsibility to do no harm. But, if you cannot be persuaded by the moral case, then be persuaded by the financial case: hurting people is bad for business. Your business depends on your brand – your brand gets hurt or destroyed if people associate it with injury. Dealing with the fallout of injury costs money, time and attention.

Put your product through stress tests to make sure it works and it won't hurt anyone. Establish solid operations and processes to keep things running smoothly, and seek constant improvement and refinement.

2. SOMEONE HURTS YOU

Of course, the bigger risk is that someone will hurt you – financially, emotionally or physically.

Research the reputation of your investors, manufacturers, and sales representatives, including internet comments, litigation history, any UCC filings through the Secretary of State's office of their home states. Ask for and call references. Resort to insurance and reserves when necessary.

3. YOU HAVE TO FIGHT

There are many kinds of fights. You can sue someone; you can be sued by someone. You can be sued by a lot of people all at once. You could get in a fight with the government – maybe the government claims you didn't comply with a law or regulation; maybe it claims you committed a crime, didn't pay your taxes or dumped sludge in the creek next to your parking lot.

Fights are draining in every way. First, you have to get a good picture of the fight and your chances. Then, you have to hire a lawyer. Hopefully that lawyer will return your phone calls quickly, won't bill you out of house and home and will be just enough of a fighter, and enough of an adult, to lead the charge. Then, the bills will roll in. Maybe insurance will cover some of it – if not, you may feel like someone is stabbing you each time you open the envelope. Along the way, whoever you are fighting, and their lawyers, will say mean things about you. At some point, your lawyers will need a lot of information, documents and time from you.

During your deposition, the other side's lawyers will grill you. Try not to say something stupid. By the time you start with settlement talks, your nerves will be so tight, you'll need exercise and body work just to stand straight. Then, if the case doesn't settle, there's a trial, which may last and last; if you thought the bills were big during discovery, wait until you have a couple of lawyers, a paralegal and messengers running around for you 24-7.

In the meantime, the time, money and energy you are giving to your fight, you are not giving to your business, your health or your family. And in the end, even if you should win, you could lose. Many, if not most, fights should be avoided.

IF YOU HAVE TO FIGHT

But, there are the exceptions. When you have to fight, there are things you can do to make it easier:

Notify Your Insurance Carrier. If you have any hope that your insurance carrier will pick up litigation fees and damages, notify your carrier as soon as you learn of the suit.

Pick a lawyer with enough brains and bravery to put up a good fight. There are, in fact, crazy, cranky and crappy lawyers out there. Get recommendations, interview candidates and pick the one you want.

Get a budget from your lawyer. If you ask your lawyer for a budget, you train her attention on cost containment.

Make it a project, not a job. Try, try, try to limit the amount of energy and brain space you devote to your fight. Schedule appointments with yourself and your lawyer to deal with your fight and try and ignore it other than those times. And, don't talk about it at cocktail parties.

Create Process. You may have to treat claims and litigation as a recurring bucket of expenses and activities. If that is the case, then you may want to create a policy to handle the litigation as if it were another business unit. The policy can include: (a) keeping track of each case; (b) assigning personnel to handle it; (c) evaluating the strength of the claim and opposing counsel; (d) estimating the value of the claim; (e) standard defenses or offensive strategies; and (f) decision trees to facilitate whether to fight or settle. The key is to minimize the amount of resources devoted to litigation that is unavoidable.

4. YOU LOSE

In the end, all the money you spent and lost fighting the war may be just the beginning – you could lose. If you sue a guy who did you wrong, he could win – if you sued over a contract with an attorney fees provision, you could owe your lawyer and his lawyer. If you get sued, you could lose – on top of lawyer fees, you could owe money for damages. If you lose a suit against the government, you could owe a penalty, you could be stopped from doing whatever you are doing and you could be put in jail. Or, you could sue someone, win, but get awarded damages of $1.00.

HAZARD MAKES A PLAN TO LIMIT LIABILITY

To Hazard, if a little insurance is good, then a lot is much, much better. So, he loaded up on insurance:

TYPE OF POLICY	AMOUNT
Workers Compensation	Statutory
Employers Liability	$500,000
Commercial General Liability (Including Contractual Liability) Bodily Injury and Property Damage	Each occurrence $1,000,000 Aggregate limit $2,000,000
Automobile Liability, Bodily Injury and Property Damage Combined Single Limit	$1,000,000
Warehouseman's insurance	$2,000,000

HAP AND HAZARD MAKE THE WARRANTY

Hap and Hazard worked together on the warranty. After talking about both their values and the costs of measures to fulfill their values, they came up with this warranty:

Full Warranty. For 1 year, the MouseTrap will provide 1 hour of power for every 3 hours exposed to light, if operated properly. If the MouseTrap fails to provide 1 hour of power for every 3 hours exposed to light, if operated properly, then MouseTrap LLC will repair or replace the MouseTrap. If the MouseTrap cannot be fixed after two attempts, MouseTrap LLC will give a full refund. The customer must email or call customer support and will be given a return authorization code. The shipping via UPS will be free with that code.

Hap and Hazard then hired a third party call center located in Iowa to act as their customer support line.

HAP AND HAZARD CREATE POLICIES FOR QUALITY

After a lengthy conversation, Hap and Hazard decided that the fundamental values of their business would be quality, sustainability and service. Hap and Haz pledged through resolutions of the Managers to pursue these values.

Over the years that followed, Hap and Haz's strategies were mostly successful. The affiliate program sold less than 1,000 units, but generated an enormous amount of publicity and goodwill. Hap's advertising campaigns won web and print awards. They signed deals to supply product to two of the big box chains, only to discover that the terms made those deals unprofitable. They sold the MouseTrap through mass purchasing departments of big corporations, including the soap maker. Most profitably, they sold the MouseTrap as a bundled product with two different computer bundlers (so big, the odds are you are using their hardware as we speak). They took in a yearly average of $12,000,000 – not bad for a little accessories maker. But, they didn't sleep or see their own beds for more than three days each week.

And, then one day, they got a call from Gravity.

"Boys, I have some interesting news."

"What's that, Gravity?"

"I've just received an offer for your company."

"What kind of offer?"

"A purchase offer. Zemkin, the giant computer accessories maker, wants to buy your company."

"Seriously?"

"Seriously. I should have the term sheet very soon. Can you both pay a visit sometime this week?"

"Of course. But, Gravity, we don't know what goes into selling a company. Can you help us?"

"I CAN TRY."

END NOTES

1 I have used herein and hereof, because space, time and energy are at a premium.

2 Technically, under Incoterms, "FOB" is only intended to be used for ships, but common usage has broadened its application.

3 The notice provision also contracts around the Mailbox Rule. The Mailbox Rule says that if you accept a contract in writing, the acceptance is effective as soon as you stick it in the mail and it gets postmarked. (That is sort of why you can mail your taxes on April 15th, the day they are due.) The Mailbox Rule does not apply to rejections – rejections are effective on receipt.

4 Section 505 US Copyright Act. Additional statutory sources of attorney fee awards include class actions, civil rights violations, freedom of information act violations, patent cases, lemon law violations and some suits against the government.

5 Both federal and state law governs the practice of arbitration under the Federal Arbitration Act and state laws (49 states have adopted the Uniform Arbitration Act (1956.

6 Rent-A-Center, West v. Jackson, 581 F. 3d 912 (2010).

7 Law Note. Warranties are governed by (a) at the federal level, Magnusson-Moss Warranty Act, which governs consumer warranties, and the FTC Act, which deals with unfair competition; (b) at the state level, the UCC governs sales of goods; state consumer protection statutes protect consumers and contract and commercial laws govern transactions. Consumer warranties may also be governed by parts of the Service Contract Model Act created by the Service Contract Industry Council, a lobbying group, which has been adopted in most of the states. **Consumer Product** are products normally used for personal, family or household purposes

8 Section 2-314 of the UCC covers implied warranties and is law in every state but Louisiana.

9 These rules do not apply to oral warranties or warranties on services.

10 It is critical to verify the creditworthiness of the insurer. Sureties often reinsure to spread the risk.

11 In Europe, these are issued by banks and called "Bank Guarantees" and "Caution" in France.

12 These are regulated by state Insurance Commissioners and brokers or agents must be licensed.

13 States have "little Miller Acts."

14 FAR Subchapter E, Part 28 Bonds and Insurance

15 Employee Retirement Income Security Act ("ERISA"), Pub L 93-406, 1974.

GETTING RICH

section seven

VALUATION BASICS

Gravity said, "Before you sell your company, we should discuss how to value a business."

CHAPTER 25

VALUING A BUSINESS

Valuing a business is usually subject to a bit of debate. Different methods may produce different valuations, so choosing one that is both appropriate and reasonable is critical. Valuation goes from math to craft when appraising a new business. Without products, cash flow, assets or history, it is difficult to find a variable to plug into a formula; often, valuation becomes a creature of a lot of guessing. Your projections and valuation should be reasonable and important assumptions explained.

There are three parts to valuing a business:

1. Measure
2. Method
3. Process

MEASURE

The measure in valuing a business is the unit of value[1] the buyer seeks to pay and the seller seeks to accept. Every measure seeks to find a price for something. Measures are really goals. When the goal is to come up with a reasonable price for a business, then companies look at Fair Market Value, Fair Value and Liquidation Value, which are three common measures.

1. FAIR MARKET VALUE V. FAIR VALUE

Let's say you need to come up with a value for something – a company, a hard asset, intellectual property, shares of stock. The measure is often FAIR MARKET VALUE or FAIR VALUE – two terms that get

treated as if they are identical. Except FAIR MARKET VALUE and FAIR VALUE are not identical and their differences matter.

So, what is the difference between FAIR MARKET VALUE and FAIR VALUE? Let's start with the definitions.

FAIR MARKET VALUE is the search for the price at which the property would change hands between a willing buyer and a willing seller under no compulsion to buy.

FAIR VALUE is the search for the price to sell an asset or paid to transfer a liability in an orderly transaction between market participants.

To my eye, these definitions look identical. But, they are different. And the reason they are different is because of where they come from and how they get used. FAIR MARKET VALUE is the Internal Revenue Service's ("IRS") measure. The IRS has actually defined FAIR MARKET VALUE in an IRS Revenue Ruling (59-60). Since FAIR MARKET VALUE is the tax man's measure, there is an enormous amount of case law analyzing and defining FAIR MARKET VALUE. Case law and history beget comfort, so appraisers and accountants rely on FAIR MARKET VALUE as a standard measure for assets and enterprises and real estate.

In contrast, FAIR VALUE is the standard of valuation under Generally Accepted Accounting Principles, which is the sort of official set of accounting rules put out by the Financial Accounting Standards Board ("FASB") FASB gets its authority from the Securities Exchange Commission, the regulator of stocks and bonds. FASB's job is to set standards for financial reporting under US GAAP. So, FAIR VALUE is the sort of the publicly-traded stock valuation measure. Fair Value is used in Black Scholes, Lattice Model and other valuation strategies for options. Sometimes, Fair Market Value valuations conducted for tax purposes don't comply with Fair Value and have to be revalued.

The difference goes beyond source – it also includes inputs. Fair Market Value is an objective estimate of what fictional, fungible, fully-informed reasonable and willing buyers and sellers would pay and accept for something. Fair Value is what "two specific parties taking into account the respective advantages or disadvantages that each will gain from the transaction.[2]" Fair Value tries to pull in the idiosyncrasies of the parties while Fair Market Value approaches valuation from a slightly more theoretical position.

There is actually a horse race between Fair Market Value and Fair Value. Though Fair Market Value started in the lead, Fair Value is coming up on the outside, propelled by globalization. If Fair Market Value represents the old economy, market oriented approach, Fair Value has developed into a set of three tiers that starts off by using lofty variables from the market and drills down to take into account hard-to-get information as well as grass roots facts.

Fair Value is picking up steam. In 2009, FASB got its arms around GAAP and reorganized it into a single collection of rules called the FASB Accounting Standards Codification (ASC). FASB claims it didn't kill GAAP, but it did seem to start to sedate it. GAAP were American rules for accounting – now that America's financial statements get shared increasingly around the world, our methods of accounting are out of step, sometimes requiring restatement to match International Financial Reporting Standards ("IFRS"). The IFRS are established and maintained by the International Accounting Standards Board ("IASB"). IASB and FASB are right now working together to converge the international and US accounting standards – their report is due during the second half of 2012.

2. LIQUIDATION VALUE

Liquidation Value is the price you'd get if you had to sell the business, in whole or in its parts, in a fire sale.

In any event, you should arrive at a measure – do you want a lowball offer – if so, liquidation value is ready. Do you want a traditional, objective measure? Then Fair Market value may be appropriate. Or if you want something a little more worldly and subjective, you can pick fair value. Once you pick your measure, you have to pick your method.

METHODS

The Methods are the strategies used to determine the value based on the measure you chose. Below are some common methods, including (1) comparables, (2) income method, and (3) asset methods.

1. COMPARABLES

The most common and often most justifiable method is to take a look at what other companies of similar size or industry have sold for. Comparables are businesses in the same industry segment, with the same capital structure, same profit growth potential and similar company transactions. The problem is that often this information is not public. However, there are resources that list selling prices and transaction terms. For instance, Practical Law, a law subscription service, maintains a database of prices and terms. A little research may also produce the "real value," which is the actual price that a buyer actually paid.

2. INCOME METHODS

The Income Methods try to get the present value of future income. In the Income Method, you count the benefit streams and then discount them by a percentage chosen to approximate the risk of the investment. There are many income methods, some of which are summarized below.

DISCOUNTED CASH FLOW ("DCF")

DCF is based on the idea that a dollar received today is worth more than one received in the future. The DCF method adds up estimated future cash flows and then discounts it by an interest rate that approximates its lifetime average interest rate. Projected future cash flow is reduced by an interest rate selected to calculate the risk of failing to achieve the cash flow projections. The present value of the discounted cash flows should equal zero. DCF is widely used in investment finance, real estate development, and corporate financial management. DCF is useful for companies with actual cash flow, but not really for startups with no operating history. This method is also used to test the prudence of the purchase price by seasoned buyers and finance professionals.

VC METHOD

A variant on the DCF method, the VC Method of valuation attempts to appraise a company that lacks operating history. The VC Method estimates the company's net income at a point in the future based on the projections in the business plan and multiplies the net income by the Price/Earnings ratio from similar companies (see below). That creates the "terminal value." The terminal value is discounted to get the present value of the investment. Often, VC's use discount rates of 35% to 80% to accommodate entrepreneurial optimism.

Picking a discount rate is more art than science. Here are some approximate discount rate guidelines, based on the stage of the company:

DISCOUNT RATE GUIDELINES FOR VC METHOD	
Seed stage (business is just an idea)	80%+
Startup (business plan & prototype development)	50-70%
First-Stage (commercialize product)	40-60%
Second-Stage (expand beyond initial market)	30-50%
Bridge/Mezzanine (expand exponentially and prepare for investor exit)	20-35%
Public (exit and/or IPO)	15-25%

Price Earnings Multiple (a/k/a price to earnings multiple, a/k/a the multiple of a company, a/k/a P/E) shows the price an investor in the stock is paying for the company's income growth. P/E is a company's share price divided by its earnings per share. Multiply P/E by net income to get a value for the business. P/E is not helpful if there is no income or the stock is not publicly traded.

In P/E, the company's "Earnings" (a/k/a income) means revenues minus costs of sales, operating expenses and taxes over a particular period. One of the most important metrics, it enables you to compare two companies' P/E to see which is the better value.

SALES & EARNINGS MULTIPLE

Many valuations (including pre-money valuations) are really just a multiple of earnings.. In this method, the cash flow of the business is calculated and then multiplied by a negotiated amount. Specifically, after the business's earnings are calculated, the number gets multiplied by a number between 1.5 and 8 to get the negotiated business value and purchase price. The multiple is a cross between what is standard in the industry and what the buyer says he will pay.

Valuing the earnings of the business is usually done in one of three ways: (a) Net Income, (b) EBITDA and (c) S.D.E.

(a) **Net Income**. Net Income is the bottom line profit appearing on the tax return and income statement. This is the least valuable.

(b) **EBITDA**. This is Earnings Before Interest, Taxes, Depreciation and Amortization ("EBITDA"). People often use "EBITDA" as the measure of a business's cash flow.

"EBITDA" means gross receipts less expenses but including interest, taxes, depreciation expense and amortization charges. There can also be an Adjusted EBITDA that provides for changes in working capital, extraordinary items or costs which should be normalized.

By the way, EBITDA stands for Earnings Before Interest, Taxes, Depreciation and Amortization.

(c) **Seller Discretionary Earnings (S.D.E.")**. SDE is sometimes called Cash Flow to Owner, SDE is calculated to show what the company's cash flow would have been if the owners were paid salaries at market rates. It is regarded as a more realistic view of a closely held business' cash flow (though it is a little cynical).

To calculate, you adjust (called "recast") the income statement. Depreciation, Amortization, interest, officer compensation, family salaries and benefits, officer insurance, officer auto, officer fringe benefits and rent.

Business Pretax earnings

+	Non-operating expenses
-	Non-operating income
+	Unusual or one-time expenses
-	Non-recurring income
+	Depreciation and amortization expense
+	Interest expense
-	Interest income
+	One owner's total compensation
+/-	Adjust other owners' comp to MV
	Seller's Discretionary Earnings

Getting to Pre-Money Valuation has 3 possibilities: (i) Income Method; (ii) Market Method; and (iii) Asset Method.

3. ASSET METHODS

Asset methods count the value of the business's assets. Asset-based methods often produce a lower value than fair market value.

Replacement Value. Replacement value is how much it would cost to replace the assets and the business. In this method, you add up all of the assets – real estate, selling channels, goodwill, IP, contracts - to get to the replacement cost. Replacement value is what you would have to pay if you misplaced the whole business and you rebuilt it after repaying all the liabilities. This is usually higher than book value.

Book Value. Book value is the value of the company's assets as they are listed on the company's balance sheet. Book value is often used for retail and manufacturing because of the physical assets and inventory, as well as to test other valuations. Book value may produce an inaccurate value. It may overstate manufacturing or other asset-heavy companies and it may understate service businesses (since they lack assets). Book value also does not include goodwill. Book value deprives the seller of his share of the business goodwill and any appreciation in the company's balance sheet assets. To solve the disadvantages in this method, you can value the business at the book value times a multiple.

Tangible Book Value. Tangible book value deducts from book value the intangible assets, like IP and goodwill. This is often used for insolvent businesses.

Economic Book Value. Economic book value adjusts assets to their market value, including goodwill, real estate, inventories and other assets.

Liquidation Value. Liquidation value is the total amount of cash you would raise if you sold everything in the business for parts and paid off all liabilities. This is the lowest common denominator.

Debt Assumption Method. Debt assumption method shows how much debt a business could take on and still operate using cash flow to pay the debt. This often generates a comparatively high price.

PROCESS

The process is the way the parties apply the measure to the method to get to the value. There are basically three ways to arrive at a value for a company: (1) you and your buyer can just agree on a price; (2) you can have the business appraised; or (3) you can apply a formula. You can also have a combination of any of them.

1. AGREE ON A PRICE

You and your buyer can try and agree on a price that he would pay and you would accept. This gets dicey, particularly as the world turns during drafting and due diligence and things change. Still, this can be quick, efficient and satisfying.

2. APPRAISALS

People often hire appraisers to value the company. An appraiser is a person who calculates the value of a business. Appraisers offer an independent third party expert opinion on fair price. But, they may generate a price that one side thinks is too low or high.

There are many ways to hire an appraiser. For instance:

- ✓ The company could select an expert
- ✓ The appraiser could be named in the text of the governing contract
- ✓ Each side could hire an appraiser and these appraisers select third
- ✓ Each side hires an appraiser and the company's accountant or an arbitrator selects the winner
- ✓ Each side hires an expert, who jointly manage process and perform the appraisal

---

APPRAISAL PROCESS CRITICAL QUESTIONS

If the valuation process is an appraisal method:

- ✓ Who is entitled to require an appraisal?
- ✓ Can there be multiple appraisals?
- ✓ Who pays for each appraisal?
- ✓ If multiple appraisals are permitted, how are different appraisal values resolved?
- ✓ Who pays for a third-party appraisal?

---

3. MECHANICALLY APPLY A FORMULA METHOD

You can also try and make the calculation totally objective by calculating or prescribing a formula into which you plug numbers from the company's financial statement. Realistically, there is always wiggle room in the application of a formula. Selecting an independent third party to apply the formula or resolve disputes may be prudent.

VALUING (LESS THAN ALL OF THE) STOCK

Often, the sale involves buying some of the stock of the company, rather than the company itself. Valuing the stock, as opposed to the enterprise, may be complicated by additional issues. Below are some additional methods and measures that may be factors in valuing some, but not all, the stock of a company.

In addition to all the measures we discussed earlier, there are also some special measures chosen to value stock.

1. DISCOUNTS AND PREMIUMS. RE: CONTROL

Sometimes, discounts are applied to stock when its sale would not provide majority control over the company. Similarly, sales of majority control of stock may generate a premium. Discounts are sometimes applied to stock that is restricted from resale. However, for tax purposes, you can only factor in discounts if the resale restrictions are permanent and hardwired into the stock.

Fair market value - what a willing buyer would pay a willing seller in the open market with plenty of time to negotiate - may be an appropriate measure for valuing stock. However, if the stock is less than all shares in the company, fair market value may include potentially minority discounts. A minority discount reduces the total value of the purchase price to reflect the lack of voting control.

2. CAPITAL ACCOUNT BALANCE

Capital account balance of the departing owner may be an appropriate measure when the partner leaves soon after inception. A capital account is the accounting of a partner's or member's investment less any economic benefits taken plus any other benefits given. This is a pretty low price for someone's interests.

3. INVESTMENT BACK

Another low ball measure is simply to give the guy his investment back. This simply means return of the money he put in the company for his equity less money he took out in dividends or distributions. Alternatively, you can give him "Investment Back plus Interest." This is a more lucrative price – it means he would also get some rate of return over the years the company had his investment.

4. LOOK BACK

Sometimes, in owner buyouts, the selling owner gets the right to get paid his pro rata share of a sale of the company for 1-3 years after he sells. This is usually only granted when the selling owner left because of retirement, disability, death or election to the Vice-Presidency.

5. DEPARTURE PENALTIES

How you add up the value of your departing partner's share will probably depend on why he left. If he left because he decided to retire after 10 glorious years, maybe you pay him the fair market value. If he left because he called your biggest client a "m*****r f****r", maybe you want to short him a little. One way to deal with this is to value the company or shares and then apply a discount for bad conduct.

For instance, on the following page is a set of discounts based on reason for departure.

DISCOUNTS OFF VALUATION BASED ON REASON FOR DEPARTURE	
REASON FOR DEPARTURE	PURCHASE PRICE
Quit before 65	75% of Valuation
Retire at or after 65	100% of Valuation
Disability	100% of Valuation
Termination for Cause	50% of Valuation
Termination without Cause	100% of Valuation
Death	100% of Valuation

HAP AND HAZARD START TO DO THE MATH

"Gosh, Gravity, there are so many factors in valuing a business," said Hap.

"It's okay, Hap," said Hazard. "Like everything, valuing a business can be complicated or simple. Hopefully, we'll be able to "keep it simple, stupid.""

Turning back to Gravity, Hazard said,

"Gravity, can you tell us a little bit about the process of selling a business?"

"I CAN TRY."

STRUCTURE YOUR DEAL

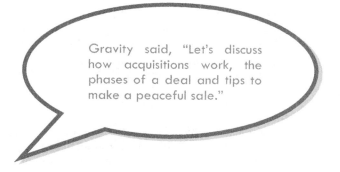

Gravity said, "Let's discuss how acquisitions work, the phases of a deal and tips to make a peaceful sale."

CHAPTER 26

HOW ACQUISITIONS WORK

There are infinite ways to craft a sale. Four variables to work through are: (1) structure of the deal - stock or asset; (2) form of payment and the amount of the purchase price; (3) disclosures, reps and duration; (4) taxes; and (5) the role company owners or employees will have after the deal.

1. STRUCTURE STOCK SALE, ASSET SALE OR MERGER

The buyer can buy the stock of the whole company that owns the business or just the assets from the company that owns the business. If you structure the deal as a stock sale, then you have to comply with the securities laws, including making sure the sale is exempt from registration. You can also merge your company with or into another company.

2. PAYMENT - FORM AND AMOUNT

AMOUNT OF PAYMENT

The amount of the purchase price could be determined in many different ways. See Chapter 25, "Valuing a Business."

FORM OF PAYMENT

The buyer can pay with cash, stock, a promissory note, assumption of the seller's liabilities, other property or any combination of the above.

DEAL PAYMENT CAN BE FIXED OR ADJUSTABLE

The purchase price in a transaction can be fixed or adjustable. A fixed purchase price is a static price

that does not grow or shrink due to the company's financial results. An adjustable purchase price is often called an earn out.

Earn Outs. Often, a purchase price for a business is calculated after closing based on the eventual results of the company. This type of compensation, called an "earn out," can stretch on for a couple of years after the transaction. The earn out should be based on financial results that are hard to fudge. For instance, you could base your earn out on revenues or gross profit. However, if you tie it to EBITDA or net profit, it is relatively easy to either manipulate the amount of expenses included or to argue that expenses increased for various reasons. Make sure you have a well written mechanism for disputing the calculation and the means to do your own calculations. A good rule: trust your friends but cut the cards.

3. DISCLOSURES, REPS AND DURATION

The purchase agreement is going to have a giant section called Representations and Warranties. There, the seller will make a minimum of fifteen pages of promises about the conditions of its assets, ownership, liabilities, structure and condition. These reps and warranties were written in about 1803, and they haven't changed much. They take some getting used to, but basically, each statement is your promise that something is good — like you have no litigation — except for the stuff listed on another piece of paper. That piece of paper is called a Disclosure Schedule. These reps and warranties, coupled with the disclosure schedules, are the vehicles for disclosing all of the facts about your company to your buyer. Then, later in the contract, there is language saying that you promise the reps and disclosures are accurate and that you will protect them if you're wrong. How long you have to protect them is part of the negotiations. Often, sellers keep a part of the purchase price aside in escrow for a few years to fund any problems in the disclosures. These are huge issues. You will spend 300% more time negotiating reps, disclosures and survival then you spend on purchase price. If you discover a problem during due diligence that you didn't know about it, you'll deal with it in the reps, the schedules and the survival section of the contract. (See Representations and Warranties below)

4. TAXES

The tax consequences of a transaction drive the overall structure and much of the nitty gritty of the terms. The taxes you have to pay following sale will vary depending on the tax treatment of your business entity and the structure of your transaction.

Smart, qualified tax lawyers (or at the very least, a qualified accountant) should be engaged early, early, early to supervise and create the structure of the deal. Anything other than a plain vanilla sale of assets should be shaped based on the advice of tax professionals.

5. PERSONNEL POST CLOSING

There are two major issues for personnel after the sale: (a) their role after closing and (b) restrictive covenants (if any).

ROLE AFTER CLOSING

Sellers often agree to a period of employment in order to provide continuity and institutional memory for the buyers. Because successful entrepreneurs are often regarded as critical to the business, their continued involvement with the company may be a condition of the sale.

RESTRICTIVE COVENANTS

Frequently, shareholders or members of management who cash-out agree to refrain from competing with the company for the first couple of years after closing. In a noncompete, there are four things that need to be defined: (a) What activities constitute "competition?" (b) What geographic region(s) are included in the competitive market? (c) How long will the noncompete period last? (d) What triggers the noncompete?

Although noncompetes are often difficult to enforce, they are more easily enforced when given in a sale of a business. Allocation of purchase price to noncompetes can have tax consequences, so you need to include that in the mix of issues for your tax lawyer.

Frequently, a selling owner will agree to refrain from asking employees to leave the buyer's business for new opportunities with the seller and asking customers to leave the buyer's business. This is all subject to negotiation.

DEAL PHASES

Each successful deal has these phases: (1) negotiation; (2) due diligence; (3) drafting; (4) closing; and (5) post closing.

1. NEGOTIATION & LETTER OF INTENT/TERM SHEET

IN THE BEGINNING

Negotiations of a sale of a business are often initiated by the business's officers or by investment bankers brought in to find a deal. At the very least, representatives from the buyer and seller express an interest in doing a deal. At the most, these representatives work out structure, price, terms, closing date and transition matters. When these representatives either reach agreement or boredom, they bring in their lawyers and financial advisors to help. The lawyers often take the lead in negotiations and keep track of the terms that are on the table and that have been resolved.

CONFIDENTIALITY AGREEMENT

It is important to put in place a nondisclosure agreement to coax confidentiality out of each side about the terms being discussed, the existence of discussions and confidential information that gets passed back and forth.

A letter of intent (LOI) or term sheet is a document that lays out in fairly simple detail the terms of the deal. Term sheets or Letters of Intent can be handy - if you cannot get past the term sheet or letter of intent phase, you will never get to the more arduous phase in which you draft and negotiate agreements.

Difference between Term Sheet and Letter Of Intent. A term sheet is usually not signed by the parties and is not usually intended to guide drafting of the agreements, although it can. Instead, it is usually used to guide negotiations towards a letter of intent. A letter of intent is a letter agreement that contains the final business terms agreed to and is signed by the parties. Letters of intent usually say that the terms are not actually a legal agreement, just in case things break up in drafting (which they often do).

Sometimes, a buyer does a little due diligence before it sends a term sheet or letter of intent in draft form. The term sheet/LOI at an early phase allows the opening negotiations over price.

Here are the things that usually get covered:

- ✓ **The structure.** The structure of the deal – whether there will be a purchase of stock, a purchase of assets or a merger – must be listed.

- ✓ **Price and price range.** The proposed purchase price and purchase price variables should be listed, although this is sometimes maddeningly left out.

- ✓ **Not binding.** Usually, term sheets and letters of intent include a couple of sentences making it clear that the terms or not contractually binding on the parties. However, courts have held people liable if they don't try and close the deal in good faith after the LOI is signed.[3]

- ✓ **Assets and liabilities**. What happens to certain assets (like cash) and whether the buyer will take liabilities (debts) may be defined.

- ✓ **Representations, warranties, indemnities**. Usually, there is just a mention that reps and warranties will be included in the transaction documents.

- ✓ **Survival and Caps**. The duration of the reps and warranties should be listed. For instance, some

may last 1 year more; some may last forever. If there is any kind of limit on how much the sellers could be liable for under the reps and warranties, they should be in here too.

- ✓ **Payment terms**. How the purchase price will be paid should be included. For instance, part of the purchase price could be paid under a promissory note. Some or all of the purchase price could be paid in stock of the buyer.

- ✓ **Confidentiality**. The LOI should say that the terms of the deal and any information about the seller is confidential. The obligation to keep these items confidential should be legally binding, even if the rest of the LOI is not.

- ✓ **Related Contracts**. If there are any employment, noncompete or other agreements that have to be delivered at the closing, these should be listed.

- ✓ **Exclusivity/ standstill**. Sometimes, an LOI prohibits the seller from negotiating with anyone else for a certain period of time to give the buyer a chance to close the deal.

- ✓ **Closing**. The action steps that must get completed before closing should be listed.

2. DUE DILIGENCE

Due diligence is a thorough examination into a possible deal. Due diligence includes business due diligence and legal due diligence. Business due diligence starts with an examination of financial statements and products and proceeds to an examination of a business's nitty gritty. Legal due diligence is an examination of all of a company's contracts and obligations.

In due diligence, the buyer is looking for 3 things:

1. Problems, including phony accounting or sales, pending litigation, labor and employment strife, weaknesses in the products or services, warranty issues, cancellations by suppliers or customers, environmental dangers, ownership issues, weakness in intellectual property protections and security holes, among others

2. Integration and synergy

3. Information necessary to raise the financing for the deal

Due diligence is just horrible. Find a good, dependable, honest person to provide the information and disclose everything. The consequences of disclosure can be a dead deal, but the consequences for failing to disclose can be a lawsuit that rages and drains you for years.

3. DRAFTING PHASE

After the parties sign the LOI, lawyers start to draft the definitive documents and to ramp up due diligence. During this phase, if the lawyers had not previously taken the lead, they usually do during drafting. Guided by the LOI, everyone tries to clarify what was not solidified earlier and memorialize the terms of the deal. This phase can take anywhere from a few weeks to many months. It will be very expensive.

REPRESENTATIONS AND WARRANTIES

Representations and warranties (Reps and Warranties or just Reps) are the promises you make about the condition of your business and assets as of the day of the sale. The Reps are a cause for battle, because they are so integral to the deal – that's why we talked about them as a critical part of the deal and a part of the contract. A breach of the reps usually triggers the buyer's right to indemnification in which you may have to essentially refund all or some of the purchase price or even to unwind the deal. The reps also play another critical role: they provide the vehicle for memorializing every item that is being acquired and every facet of the business being acquired.

Following is a list of promises and information the seller often provides to the buyer:

1. Seller owns the businesses and assets completely

2. Seller has no more than the debt listed on a schedule given with the reps

3. Seller's business does not infringe any other third party intellectual property (though you may want to carve out promises about 3rd party patents)

4. A description of the identity of employees and contractors and the terms of their employment or work

5. The intellectual property and the ways in which it is protected

6. That there are no environmental problems

7. That there is no litigation on the horizon other than what is listed on a schedule given with the reps

8. A description of the company's employee benefit plans and insurance policies, and that all are in good standing

9. A description of the company's real estate and leases

10. A description of any deals that have transpired among people in the business or the business and family members of people in the business

INDEMNIFICATION

Indemnification – the promise to stand behind someone and pick up their legal fees and damages – is the most common remedy for a breach of the Reps. A savvy seller will get (or try to get) some limitations on his indemnification obligations and the buyer will resist these limitations. These limitations include the following:

✓ Expiration date for claims under the Reps

✓ Minimum amount of damages to Buyer before Seller has to pay (called a "basket")

✓ Maximum amount of money Seller has to pay (called a "cap")

✓ A requirement that the buyer has to sue all sellers, not just the richest ones; when a buyer has to sue all sellers for their share of damages, the liability is JOINT BUT NOT SEVERAL; when a buyer can sue just one seller and make that seller go after others for their share of damages, the liability is called JOINT AND SEVERAL

ANTITRUST & HART-SCOTT-RODINO

Part of the law against creating monopolies requires big deals to get federal approval before they can close. Specifically, you have to get the approval of the Federal Trade Commission if the deal is worth

$283.6 million or $70.9 million plus one party has $141.8 million and the other party has $14.2 million in annual net sales or assets[4]. There are exemptions to the filing requirements – they are convoluted. The filing fees are $45,000, $125,000 and $280,000 depending on the size of the deal. This approval is loosely called HART-SCOTT-RODINO approval.

4.   CLOSING THE DEAL

CLOSING – HOT OR COLD

Closings can be "hot" or "cold." A hot closing is when you sign the contracts and exchange the purchase price for whatever is being purchased on the same day. A "cold" closing is when you sign the contracts, but do not exchange the purchase price and property until a date in the future.

Generally, you have to close cold when:

- ✓ You have to get FTC– Hart-Scott-Rodino approval
- ✓ You have to get approval of public shareholders
- ✓ You have to get SEC approval
- ✓ Odd or alarming facts crop up during the negotiation phase – failure to pay some taxes, delays in getting permission to transfer licenses or leases – and the parties need time to look into it

In a cold closing, the documents will include some limited escape clauses. Buyers always want the right to quit the deal if there is a "material adverse change" in the business. Often, "material adverse change" is subjective and therefore controversial. Sometimes, a mathematical standard is attached. For instance, it could be a decline of trailing cash flow or revenues. The buyer may have the right to back out if during due diligence, the buyer discovers something really bad about the seller's business. Also, any of the facts which made the parties close cold could be used by a buyer to back out, if the problems were sufficiently severe.   At the final closing where the seller sells and the buyer pays, the seller usually delivers a written promise to the buyer that all of the reps and warranties in the documents are true and correct as of that day.

OPERATING THE BUSINESS BETWEEN SIGN AND CLOSE

The seller should be obligated to operate the business just like it always has (assuming those were good practices).

5.   POST CLOSING

CLOSING BOOK

After the closing, all of the final documents that were signed and exchanged as part of the closing should be bound in a book and copies should be delivered to the parties and the lawyers. For really big, multibillion dollar deals, these books are leather bound, but for most deals these books do not have to be fancy. They should, however, be well organized and comprehensive so that all of the parties have one reference for what happened. Sometimes, it may be helpful to include an objectively written memo summarizing the transaction to make reviewing the documents easier in the future.

EARNOUT

If you have an earn-out, calendar the key dates when the cash gets counted and the earn-out paid; follow those dates and don't rely on the buyer to count the money for you.

TAXES & CREDITOR NOTICES

Sale of your business will probably trigger some tax obligations and tax filing obligations. There also may be some obligations to file taxing reports related to your employees. Some of these tax filings will be at the state level. For instance, some states will require you to notify the state of the sale and make a deposit to cover all potential state tax liability. In addition, Article 6 of the Uniform Commercial Code in many states obligates sellers of inventory to notify their creditors of the sale. These filings and notices may be called **BULK SALE NOTICES** or **BULK SALE FILINGS.** Work with your tax and legal advisors to make sure all notices and filings are made immediately after you wake up from the closing.

TIPS TO MAKE FOR A PEACEFUL SALE

Lawyer Up. Get a lawyer who understands your business and knows how to work a deal. Trust your lawyer and don't undercut your lawyer unless it is part of a negotiating tactic.

Be Realistic About the Deadline. If it's a rush, it's a rush. But, if it's not really a rush, give the lawyers a chance to get it done carefully. Your bill will be cheaper and the quality better.

Disclose, disclose, disclose. If there is a fact about your business that makes you nervous and makes you want to hide it – disclose it. (Though, your deal may die.)

Read the contract. Then read it with your lawyer. Every inch, even the boring parts (and it's all boring).

Make sure you understand the agreement. This is critical – if you cannot understand the agreement, then maybe no one else can either. If no one understands it, maybe it doesn't actually contain the terms you think you agreed to.

Read the disclosure schedules. The disclosure schedules list things very specific about the business you are selling. You and your employees are the only ones who can judge the accuracy and completeness of those disclosures. Make sure they are accurate and comprehensive.

Get the third party consents and bulk sales filings drafted and out the door as soon as you sign. Part of due diligence and preparation for closing is alerting your customers and creditors of the pending sale and getting consents from some of them. This can take a while. If you have a major customer whose contract requires you get its consent to a sale of your company, and you can't because of its bureaucracy, your deal could die while you wait. If you have to get Hart Scott Rodino approval, that can take a while also. So, get someone organized and on top of the consent and notice process as soon as possible.

Calculate the earn-out computations yourself. It's your money.

Get limits and caps on your liability. At some point, you just want to be done with these people already.

Most deals die. Don't count your chickens or let your business go to pot during negotiations. Wait to buy the boat until after you close.

HAP AND HAZ MEET THE FUTURE

Once Gravity finished talking, her assistant walked in with a fax.

"Ah, this must be the term sheet."

Gravity took a look and said, "Boys, how much money did you make last year?"

Haz answered, "We grossed $12,000,000 with a profit of $4,500,000. Why? What's the offer?"

"$20,000,000."

"Fuck me," whistled Hap. "Oh, sorry, Gravity."

Gravity waved away his apology.

"Boys, is the company for sale?"

"It is for that price."

"Would you like to respond to this offer?"

"Yes, Ma'am," said Hap.

Gravity took them through the offer.

"They seem to have estimated that you had EBIDTA of $4 million and they applied a simple multiple of 5."

"What is the standard multiple in accessory companies?"

"Accessories? 5 is appropriate. But, you're more than an accessory company – you're also a green tech company. And, you have a track record and revenues. A reasonable multiple could be 6 or even 7."

"Let's go back with 7 and with our actual EBIDTA number."

"Ok. Oh, wait," Gravity said. "There's an odd condition here. Post closing, they want you out."

"Out?" Hazard asked.

"Out of the business. They want you to resign, to sign a noncompete and to go away."

"What about our deal with Seymour?"

"They want the license."

"They just don't want us," Hazard explained to Hap.

"Huh," said Hap. "I don't know how I feel about that. This is our baby. Our company. Our life's work."

"What would we do without the MouseTrap?"

The three of them sat for a few minutes in silence until Hap answered.

"Take a nap."

"Get married," said Hazard.

"See some theater," offered Hap.

"Make a mix tape," Hazard said.

"They don't make mix tapes anymore."

"Make a playlist," corrected Hazard.

"For the person you married," Hap added.

"Gravity, can you get us this deal?" Hazard asked.

"I CAN TRY."

END NOTES

1 The gold standards come from the International Valuation Standards Council, an international group of valuation standards makers. http://www.ivsc.org/index.html

2 International Valuation Standards 2007.

3 Texaco, Inc. v. Pennzoil Co, 729 S.W.2d 768 (Tex. App. 1987).

4 As of February 27, 2012.

EPILOGUE

It's February. Hap and Hazard are lying on deck chairs, side by side, under a palm tree. It's 82, but there is a tender, cool breeze coming off the ocean. A band behind them is playing soft rock classics. Right now, it's "On and On," sweeter than Stephen Bishop.

A waitress in a short black skirt and a crisp white polo shirt drops off two margaritas, their third of the day. Hazard is watching his wife swim in the surf. Hap drifts off to sleep, a little drunk, a little dreamy. Until Hazard interrupts.

"Hap."

"Yes, Haz?"

"I'm bored."

"Me too."

"What should we do?"

"I don't know. We're retired."

"We could unretire."

"And do what?"

"I don't know."

"Should we call Gravity?"

"Maybe." Hap takes a drink and hesitates. "How much do you think she'd bill us for the call?"

"Too much?"

INDEX

Limited Liability Company, 44-47, 52-53, 55-60, 68, 76, 100, 156, 159, 208, 231, 256
Limited Partnership, 45, 47, 53, 59-60, 76
liquidation preference, 55, 65
liquidation value, 65, 111, 260-261, 264
LLC, 44-47, 52-53, 55-60, 68, 76, 100, 156, 159, 208, 231, 256
loan, 91, 96, 106, 108-112, 114
loan amount, 111
loan covenants, 91, 111-112

M

management, 5, 12, 14-15, 26, 32, 45-47, 57-63, 65, 69-71, 79, 87, 93, 97, 100, 104, 110-111, 142, 155, 158-159, 171, 173, 182, 197, 204-205, 211, 235-237, 239, 245, 262, 268
manufacturer, 123, 141, 150, 153, 163-166, 177-181, 184, 194, 197, 199-208, 210, 217-222, 232, 236, 240, 245
manufacturing defect, 178
market value, 56, 68, 70, 110, 116, 190, 260-261, 263-265
marketing defect, 178
marking obligations, 190
marks that can be registered, 124
marks that cannot be registered, 124
maturity, 14, 109, 113-114
merger, 24-25, 58, 267, 269
minimum wage, 31-32
minute book, 49-50, 52
MSDS, 35, 184

N

noise pollution, 187
noncompete, 26-27, 268-269, 273

O

office lease, 82
officer titles, 59
old employers, 24
operating agreement, 49-50, 53
overtime, 31-32, 34
owner's contract, 53
owner's equity, 74

P

parody, 127-128
partnership, 19, 22, 45-47, 49-50, 53, 55-56, 59-60, 76
parts of a contract, 238
parts of a loan, 106, 109

U

V

W

Made in the USA
Columbia, SC
02 September 2021